Bureaucracy, the Marshall Plan,
and the National Interest

Bureaucracy, the Marshall Plan, and the National Interest

By HADLEY ARKES

PRINCETON UNIVERSITY PRESS
PRINCETON, NEW JERSEY

For my wife Judy,
and for my father and mother,
Morris and Pauline Arkes

PREFACE

IN THE WAKE of the Pentagon Papers, no one can feel entirely comfortable in relying on the public record, or even the files of administration, as a source of explanation for the things leaders do. Clearly there are recesses of confidentiality that lie beyond even the classified documents, and the most important motives of statesmen may be the ones that, for reasons of their own, they prefer not to express in writing. In this respect, what the record is silent about may be far more decisive than what is printed. Yet it is also clear from the Pentagon Papers that leaders who are forced to justify their policies in public are not likely to hold back the most convincing arguments they think they could make. And thus, while it has been common to indict the protagonists in the Pentagon Papers for deceiving themselves, it would be hard to argue that the justifications that were offered to the public differed in any significant way from the justifications that were advanced within the Administration.

I would not expect, then, that there is something hidden away beyond the classified material that would throw off the main points I have drawn in reconstructing the character of the Marshall Plan. The confidential material I have seen has usually added a bit of juice to the story, and I use it where I can, but I have not encountered anything that would affect the principal strands of interpretation. If I were writing this book again, I might give more attention than I did to the role of organized labor in the program, and particularly to its activities in Europe. Perhaps when that account is written it will provide a muted counterpoint to the patterns I have described. But my hunch, again, is that it will still bear out the main lines of analysis in the book; for the character of the Marshall Plan, as I have suggested, was built into the structure of the agency that administered the program, and the meaning of its features was established on the public record by men who sought to understand what they were building.

Preface

Most of the research on this project was carried out in Washington in 1965-66, when I was a Johnson Fellow at the Brookings Institution. I would like to thank the Institution for its support, and for the services that were made available to me. Among the members of the Brookings staff at the time, I am particularly indebted to James L. Sundquist, D. A. FitzGerald, Robert W. Hartley, and Edna Birkel for helpful advice—and recollections.

The Bureau of the Budget proved to be the source of the most useful information that was not on the public record. I am grateful to Hope Grace, the former archivist of the bureau, for the generous help she provided in tracking down the files I had to see and suggesting other sources that I had not known about. She and her staff went out of their way to make my extended "residence" at the Budget Bureau as profitable as it could be.

In the area of secondary sources, nothing stands out as importantly for a study of the Marshall Plan as Harry Price's early book, *The Marshall Plan and Its Meaning.* I mention it here for the sake of recording my debt in a place more visible than the footnotes.

Several people have been kind enough to read the entire manuscript and give me the benefit of their comments and criticism. Among them I would like to thank Morton Kaplan, Earl Latham, N. Gordon Levin, Jr., C. Herman Pritchett, and Herbert Storing. I would reserve a special word of appreciation for Richard Ullman of Princeton University and Sanford Thatcher of Princeton University Press for their very close reading of the manuscript, and for criticisms that I know helped to improve it measurably.

The Brookings Institution has kindly permitted me to quote from documents in its private files, and on a more modest scale, *The Economist* of London has allowed me to reprint some of its own copyrighted material. In preparing the manuscript, the secretarial services were provided with funds from the Brookings Institution and, later, from Amherst College. Anne Filippone typed the whole of the original manuscript with a rare judgment and good humor; and for their timely help in typing large portions of the manuscript later, I want to express my thanks to Diane Souci and Barbara Bond. In addition, Dale Swartz gave me the benefit of his steady competence as he helped me work over the galleys and prepare the index for the book, and it made these tasks considerably lighter.

Finally, my deepest gratitude goes to my wife Judy, who has lived with this project as long as I have. She has been an enduring source of encouragement and sensible advice, and at those moments when it became impossible to review a passage once again and see with any freshness, I found it invaluable to have her judgment at hand as a check upon my own. She has shared with me some of the strains in the work, and she has shared the satisfaction of bringing this project to completion.

H.A.
Amherst, Mass.
November 1971

CONTENTS

TABLES

FIGURES

xiv

Bureaucracy, the Marshall Plan,
and the National Interest

1. INTRODUCTION

THE MARSHALL PLAN had its brief but celebrated moment, and in a rather anomalous way it passed into history with the warm regard of liberals and conservatives alike. Everyone may have reservations about the current foreign aid program, but no one finds anything objectionable in the Marshall Plan, and with good reason. For liberals, the Marshall Plan avoided the tone of strident anti-Communism. The telling phrase was in Marshall's commencement address at Harvard in 1947, when the Secretary of State declared that "our policy is directed not against any country or doctrine but against hunger, poverty, desperation and chaos." The program was addressed to Europe as a whole, and in principle it was perfectly capable of accommodating the Soviet Union. The only conditions called for closer cooperation in aligning national economic policies, improving the international monetary system, and breaking down the barriers to trade. On their face they seemed to be reasonable conditions, clearly related to the ends of the program. They could present a formidable threat, though, to countries that were too fearful of opening their economies to the influence of outside forces. But whether the dangers of integration were serious enough to offset the advantages of Marshall aid was something that the Soviet leaders would have to decide for themselves. For liberal opinion in the United States it was important that the Marshall Plan did nothing to aggravate the inchoate division in Europe. Its everlasting credit was that it held the door open.

Despite the heavy emphasis in grant aid, the program had its attractions for conservatives as well. It was a temporary measure that was directed, for the most part, to countries that were already in an advanced state of industrialization. It was not a development program, but a restorative action. The interlocking wheels in a complicated economy had come unmeshed. The task was to connect them again, and that could be accomplished mainly by supplying large quantities of food, fuel, and raw materials. It did not re-

3

quire a sophisticated theory for redistributing wealth, and it did not demand American intervention for the sake of engineering social change. One could be satisfied instead with a very minimal amount of American interference. Aid could be allotted on the basis of the relatively simple measures contained in the balance of payments analysis. A deficit with the dollar area meant a lower foreign exchange reserve in dollars, and dwindling reserves made it that much more difficult to finance the imports that were required in feeding the production process at home. Larger and smaller deficits could provide a rough but helpful indication of the magnitude of outside assistance that might be needed. Thus, the accent was placed on raising production and achieving some overall balance in the international accounts. There was very little here to disturb the good conservative. There was nothing unorthodox in the methods of the program, and certainly nothing revolutionary in its aims.

On the strength of a remarkably wide consensus, then, the Marshall Plan stands out to us today as a significant program, a successful policy, and a wise construction of the "national interest." It did not over-promise; the scale of expenditure was large, but the goals were modest, and the means were realistically measured. Altruism was tempered with a sober regard for self-interest, but the selfish ingredients were never so unreasonable as to obscure the enlightened and generous nature of what was done. Few policies, therefore, would seem to offer as many advantages for an inquiry into the theory of national interest in foreign policy, a problem that has become even more urgent for us recently as a result of our involvement in Vietnam. Since the Marshall Plan was bound to affect a host of substantial interests, both at home and abroad, it promised to reveal the fuller range of considerations that could enter the scheme of a national interest in foreign policy.

I would not pretend to have found some formula we could use to define the national interest in Vietnam and thus dissolve all our problems. But I do think we could use a study of the Marshall Plan to clear away some of the most important confusions that have plagued the issue of national interest in the past. My own dissatisfaction would center on two areas of distortion. First, there is the practice of employing "the national interest" as a wholly descriptive term. In this view, the national interest refers to a set of hard empirical conditions that remains, in the words of one author, "relatively permanent" through time and space. The fallacy lies in the failure to recognize the quality of "the national interest" as a moral

4

or prescriptive term. That is, like other moral terms, "the national interest" acquires an empirical content as it is used to describe or articulate the standards of what is "good." But it is in the nature of moral terms, also, that their meaning can never be exhausted by the terms that fill out their descriptive content from time to time. For in addition to their descriptive function, moral terms have a prescriptive or commendatory function: They can be used to commend *new* practices or policies, including things that have not been accepted yet as good or desirable. In short, it is part of the meaning of moral terms that they can be detached from current conventions —including the current standards of "the national interest"—and they can be used to generate a change in values.

Secondly, the analysis of national interest has been warped by the fashion of conceiving the problem as a tension between "ideals" and "self-interest." This second muddle, though, is largely an outgrowth of the first. Both are affected by the same positivist outlook, and they both suffer from the same reliance on the fact-value distinction: "Ideals" are equated with values—subjective, imprecise, unverifiable—while on the other hand, "interests" are supposed to refer to the more concrete and factual measures of physical "security." It is assumed that the imperatives of security are, indeed, unambiguous and empirical, and that anything beyond these very circumscribed requirements are beyond the hard core of the national interest. It is admitted, of course, that interests can be misconceived, but the interests themselves are regarded as objective. The misconceptions are thought to arise from the faults of individuals, and not because there may be anything problematic about the nature of the national interest.

Apparently there is no room for the understanding that began with the classics, that the discipline of politics involves the application of general rules to individual cases, and that individual cases may call the rules themselves into question. Rather than ignoring the difference between a world of abstract ideals and a world of empirical reality, this older view was founded on the distinction between theory and practice. But at the same time, it was no part of this understanding that ideals were less real or more nebulous than what have come to be called "interests."

The aim of this study, then, is to use the signal case of the Marshall Plan in making another approach to the theory of national interest—to examine the kinds of interests that may be considered in the design of a major foreign policy program; to estimate the significance of "power" interests against interests that are supposedly less concrete and definable; and to determine whether ideals can enter the definition of national interest in any more meaningful role than that of ideology or rationalization.

The question of national interest will remain as the central concern of this book. But we shall view that question in a somewhat different way, as it was seen through the problem of administration: in the efforts to design an agency that could accomplish the ends of the program, and through the operations of that agency over the course of the Marshall Plan. Facing the problem of administration lent a certain concreteness to the question of national interest that was otherwise lacking when the matter was viewed entirely in the abstract; and whether the arguments over administration took place in the Executive, in the legislative drafting and the sparring of the agencies, or whether they occurred in the Congressional hearings and floor debates, the process seemed to move in the same direction: The question of *how* to accomplish the ends of the program led back to the question of *what* those ends were. The question of what powers were appropriate for a Marshall Plan agency gave way to the question of what ends were appropriate for the Marshall Plan itself.

As Congress tried to reconcile the jurisdiction and procedures of the Economic Cooperation Administration (ECA) with the authority of other agencies, it was forced to confront the reasons behind the established procedures and the interests that supported the previous assignment of jurisdictions. For one could not simply declare the existence of a new agency; it had to be connected to an elaborate Executive structure, and its purposes had to be meshed with an existing body of law. Establishing an agency for the Marshall Plan was quite the same thing, in effect, as attaching a new cluster of ends to the total complex of "the laws." And the commitments of the standing law were so thoroughly bound up with the relations and interests of our basic political institutions, that the task of giving proportion to the Marshall Plan became, at its highest level, a task of assimilating the Marshall Plan to the American regime.

Accordingly, I would go on to argue in that vein that the definition of the national interest cannot take its prime reference to the "territorial integrity" of the state, or to any of the other metaphors of physical security. It must start instead from some essential core of values that defines the nature of the thing one would try to pre-

6

serve. In the case of a society, that would mean the character of the community or its "way of life." In classical theory, the character of the community was known most importantly through the values it held up as authoritative, i.e., the values that were embodied in its laws and political institutions. In a word, the society was known through its political regime.

If we follow David Easton and identify politics in general with the "authoritative allocation of values" or the process of making binding decisions for a society,[1] the "regime" would be one step lower in the scale of generality. Instead of referring to the general features that all political systems have in common, the regime would refer to the *character* of particular systems—the *particular* structure of authority and the *peculiar* pattern of values that distinguish one political system from another. In this respect, the understanding of a regime dates from Aristotle's *Politics* and the classic discussion of "constitutions": The famous schema of constitutions was organized along the same two axes we have followed here, i.e., the distribution of power in the polis (whether concentrated or dispersed), and the substantive ends to which power was directed (to the private interests of the rulers or to the good of the whole).[2] That is, the initial focus was on the "organization of a polis, in respect of its offices," and very clearly, the formal structure of government was basic to the definition of "constitution." But very patently, also, it was insufficient. After the legal institutions were set in place, the critical distinction in the schema turned on the difference between decent and "perverted" government, and that went beyond the question of forms to the question of practice. The difference between aristocracy and oligarchy was not, in that case, a difference in the distribution of power. It was a difference, rather, in the way power was used and the ends it was made to serve. It involved the judging or evaluation of public policy, and according to the classic understanding, policy could be judged only by testing the substance of what was done in particular cases.

Thus, the meaning of constitution in the *Politics* could not be confined to the arrangement of legal offices, and for that reason, as

[1] David Easton, *The Political System* (New York: Alfred A. Knopf, 1953), pp. 129-34.

[2] *The Politics of Aristotle*, ed. and trans. Ernest Barker (New York: Oxford University Press, 1958), pp. 110-15, 117-20 (1278b-1279b, 1280a-1281a).

well as others, a serious question has been raised on the appropriateness of rendering Aristotle's *politeia* as "constitution." Leo Strauss has argued on this point that the classics used *politeia* in *contradistinction* to "laws":

> The *politeia* is more fundamental than any laws; it is the source of all laws. The *politeia* is rather the factual distribution of power within the community than what constitutional law stipulates in regard to political power. . . . No law, and hence no constitution, can be the fundamental political fact, because all laws depend on human beings. . . . *Politeia* means the way of life of a society rather than its constitution. . . . When speaking of the *politeia*, the classics thought of the way of life of a community as essentially determined by its "form of government."[3]

Strauss preferred, then, to translate *politeia* as "regime," "taking regime in the broad sense in which we sometimes take it when speaking, e.g., of the Ancien Regime of France."[4] The regime marks some connection between the ethos of the community and its authoritative institutions, either because the institutions reflect the values of the community, or because they act upon the character of the community through the force of public law. Either way, the question of the regime is tied in to the corporate personality of the community and the questions we still tend to regard as the most important in political life: What are the ends of the community? What human qualities does it promote or discourage through the

[3] Leo Strauss, *Natural Right and History* (Chicago: University of Chicago Press, 1953), p. 136. Cf., however, Carl Friedrich, *Transcendent Justice* (Durham: Duke University Press, 1964), pp. 6-7.

[4] Strauss, *op.cit.*, pp. 136-37. It is interesting, from this standpoint, that Easton broadens his own definition of regime to include "values (goals and principles)" and "norms," as well as the structure of authority. Explaining the components in his definition, Easton has written: "Even if members of a group displayed the strongest feelings of mutual identification . . . they would still be left with the task of establishing some regularized method for ordering their political relationships. Ultimately, for the outputs to be accepted as binding, the members would need to accept some basic procedures and rules relating to the means through which controversy over demands was to be regulated and work out some ends that would at least broadly and generally guide the search for such settlements." Easton, *A Systems Analysis of Political Life* (New York: John Wiley and Sons, 1965), pp. 190-93, at 191 and 193.

8

teaching of its public policies? What understanding of justice does it convey through the way in which it orders its internal life?

But the fact remains, there have been two views traditionally on the meaning of "regime," one that is restricted to "fundamental institutions," and another that moves beyond things like the separation of powers to take in the content of the laws and the way of life of the community. On the surface the difference may not seem that important, but there are times when it does raise some fundamental questions of political understanding. Two examples may illustrate. The case for the more restricted, legal definition of the regime could profitably be drawn from the problem of democracies in wartime. We know that under the conditions of war, democracies may resort to forms of compulsion that can be fully as effective as anything one is likely to encounter in authoritarian systems. The experience of the United States during the Second World War stands as a rather good example: dissenters were vigorously repressed under the sedition laws; members of an alien minority were moved to centers of detention; and the economy was subjected to a thoroughgoing system of controls that not only covered wages, prices, and rationing, but the freedom in certain instances to move from one job to another.

By a strict empirical standard one might have been tempted to argue that there was little difference any more between the United States and some of its adversaries. And yet, we know, there was a difference. But aside from what we know about the differences that were still visible in wartime, the more telling question is this: Was there anything in the nature of the system itself that made it that much more probable that a country like the United States would begin to withdraw controls and return the system to what it was once the war had ended? Did one have to go much beyond the fact that a population grown restive under rationing and other controls would be able to make ready use of elections to force the hand of the Administration? Certainly, we could have picked out many other things, though regardless of the line of reasoning we took, we would have to concede that our sense of the matter would not be based on anything we could see at the moment, but on the plainest things we understand about the Constitution and the nature of our legal institutions.

On the other side, the more expansive view of the "regime" can find some reflections on the current scene. One frequently hears it said, for example, that it will require some basic "institutional change" to set this country right. Yet it soon becomes apparent that the people who make this argument are not really about to change things like the independence of the judiciary or the restraints of the First Amendment; and it is even rare that they find the solution to our problems in a program of socialist ownership and state control. In most instances, the argument does not cut to the level of our legal institutions, but to the patterns of public spending or, as the saying goes, to the "priorities" of our public policy. One is inclined to say that the aim, more accurately, is not to change the system but the results. And yet, that would not be entirely fair, because the kind of change that is sought may really be more basic than that, and in some sense it may even be "institutional." It would not be institutional, of course, in the sense of describing legal bodies, but in something closer to the understanding of a recurring and fundamental practice. The drive to change the priorities of our public policy may be nothing less than a move to change the habits of our wanting: Commitments can be firmed up very quickly with new agencies and budgets and the creation of new clientele groups that can lend the weight of self-interest to a new order of things.

As we surely recognize by now, a dramatic change in the pattern of policy can alter the balance among institutions. One has to think only of the expansion of our commitments in welfare and defense, and the effect they have had in enlarging the federal government and tilting the advantage even more decisively to the side of the Executive. This concern, then, for the pattern or character of policy may seldom challenge the structure of the legal order, but to say that it is absorbed into the very nature of the regime is an argument I find it hard in principle to reject. For to reject it would be to deny that it is possible to experience a profound and principled change within the framework of a constitutional order. It would deny the significance of those great crises that have occurred in our own past where political alignments were shattered and the regime itself was in some way redefined. At the turn of the century, it would have been hard to believe that the federal government would one day be involved in building housing in the central cities and sponsoring birth control; and if it would have been hard to believe before Roosevelt and the New Deal, it would have been even harder to conceive before the great nationalist revolution of the Civil War. In short, the more expansive view of the regime would be very hard to deny unless, for one reason or another, one was determined to deny that politics in a democracy can ever be about the things that really matter—that within the limits set by a constitutional order the issues that divide the parties may ever in fact be disagreements over first things.

It is the broader understanding, then, that I would have to follow here: The regime would have to encompass more than the bodies named in the Constitution, but it should be kept as close as possible to the level of basic "institutions" in the sense I suggested earlier of a recurring and fundamental practice that affects the ordering of power and policy in the society. It would take in things like the seniority system in Congress or a system of private ownership in the economy, but it would probably leave out such familiar "institutions" as coffee breaks, baseball, and Mother's Day.

The concern here, once again, is with the regime and the interests of a nation in foreign policy. There is nothing brashly new about my main thesis, but the understanding may seem unfamiliar as it comes filtered through the texture of events and the rich play of detail in any concrete case: The definition of the national interest in foreign policy must begin with the political regime, and to put it even more sternly, it must be tested against the understanding of the good regime.

In respect to the Marshall Plan, I would extend the argument just another step further. I would suggest that the link between substance and process was so firm in this case that one could not account for the character of the program without treating matters of process, and one could not explain the process without being drawn back in turn to the nature of the American regime. In the same way that the decision-makers were led from questions of administration to issues reaching the character of the regime, any study of the Marshall Plan would have to lead outward to touch the system itself. For example, any analysis of the Marshall Plan would have to give a central place to the performance of the Economic Cooperation Administration (ECA) in its management of the program. Even with all its shortcomings, and perhaps at times in spite of itself, the ECA turned in a performance that has to be judged on the record as a strikingly principled effort. It is often tempting to credit this record to the nature of bureaucracy itself as an engine of rational management. And yet, in explaining the episodes that make up the pattern, one is repeatedly drawn outside the bureaucracy to features of the larger "system," and particularly to the role of Congress.

11

Introduction

It could be shown, I think, that the success of the ECA was due in no small measure to the constant "intrusions" of Congress into questions of administration. In the first place, it was because of the involvement of Congress in designing the agency that the program was stamped with an operational code of policy values. This working code became evident after a while to anyone who simply worked within the structure created by Congress; it would become indispensable later as one strategy or another proved unworkable in practice and policy guidelines began to vanish. Secondly, the frequent intervention of Congress in administrative decisions not only clarified the grounds of policy, but as we can document quite readily now, it exerted a profoundly "rationalizing" force within the agency itself. For all of that, however, the outcome might have been far different if the principals had been left to their own theories of administration, or if they had been governed by the reigning myths about Congress and its place in administration. It is altogether likely that they would have missed the insights that came from facing the issues of administration were it not for certain inducements that grew out of the system itself and compelled them to deal with these questions. In other words, the ECA depended for the completion of its bureaucratic character on sources outside the bureaucracy that were bound up with the character of the American regime.

Following out that line of thought, we return very briefly in the last chapter to the classic analysis of bureaucracy in the writings of Max Weber, and to the foundation of bureaucracy in "rational-legality." My intention there is to recall the place where bureaucracy stood in Weber's sociology, and to emphasize what Weber left understated: the connection between bureaucracy and a particular kind of political regime. In Weber's understanding, bureaucracy was a form of administration, but not all forms of administration were bureaucratic. Bureaucracy was the peculiar form of administration that arose in a rational-legal polity, or what we might call a constitutional order. The biases could often be hidden in the machinery, but bureaucracy came to us laden with political commitments. It carried the premises of a constitutional system, and what might appear on the surface to resemble all the outward forms of bureaucracy could actually become a perversion of bureaucratic rule when it was attached to a different political order.

There is a vital connection, then, between the interests of a nation in foreign policy and the character of the political regime.

12

There is a fundamental relation, also, between the political regime and the character of the bureaucracy. All three came together in the Marshall Plan in a remarkably direct way, and the aim of this study is to show how those connections were made.

A separate word ought to be said on the methods and organization of the book. The main approach was foreshadowed to some extent in a study done by Herbert Simon in the early fifties.[5] Writing with the aid of personal experience, Simon recalled the first several months in the life of the ECA. Apart from the sections on management and staff services, he found that the various subunits in the agency reflected the different approaches that prevailed on the problem of European recovery. These were not merely differences in method, but different perspectives on the nature of the problem and different judgments on the ranking of policy ends. The constellation of units in the agency mirrored the pattern of policy values that defined the character of the Marshall Plan. In this initial period, the relative standing of the subunits could alter rather quickly as one approach or another failed to work out, and as some units proved more successful than others in the search for allies in Congress. The shifting balance in the agency, the advance and recession of the subunits, signalled the changes that were taking place in the character of the program.

Thus, if one were interested in finding the full ensemble of values that was present in the program—and which was therefore incorporated in the definition of national interest—it was possible to apply Simon's findings in a rather novel approach: One could arrive at the meaning of the program by uncovering the meaning contained in the administrative structure. To that end, Part I is given over to the background of the Marshall Plan and the efforts to shape the new agency. It begins with the setting of postwar foreign policy and the relation of the Marshall Plan to the beginning of the Cold War. It moves on from there through the legislative history of the ECA, including the discussions in the Executive, the bureaucratic infighting, and the deliberations that occurred in the Congressional hearings and floor debates. The object throughout these chapters is to clarify the issues of power and principle that

[5] See Herbert A. Simon, "Birth of an Organization: The Economic Cooperation Administration," *Public Administration Review*, Vol. XIII, No. 4 (Autumn 1953), pp. 227-36.

lay behind the conflict over forms of administration. In this area, one is forced to pay close attention to matters of detail and nuance, and it may be necessary at times to linger with legalistic things. At those moments, I hope the reader will understand that it is done for the sake of tapping those basic issues of principle that the problem of administration was uniquely capable of reaching.

But even if one managed to identify all the major issues of principle, there would still remain the question of how those issues fit together to form a theory of the Marshall Plan. How are the separate sets of preferences joined to one another? On what basis can we claim that one value was primary and another secondary, or that both were subordinate to a third? Are we forced to rely on impressionistic or arbitrary judgments, or do we have some reliable means of arranging the various policy values in a coherent order? I propose that we do have the means available to us through the ordinary language concept of "presumptions." The success of the Congressional leaders in giving structure to the Marshall Plan was in large part a function of their success in impressing the program with a clear set of operating presumptions—a set of stable biases or policy inclinations that could express an ordering among preferences. These operating presumptions furnished a practical guide to action, and they could offer some principled direction, also, when lines of policy came into conflict. Operating presumptions could establish the relation between two or more policy commitments, and when they were extended in a larger network, they could reproduce the peculiar ordering of values that defined the Marshall Plan.

Through the device of presumptions we can fashion a working model of the Marshall Plan, and in terms that were understood by the administrators themselves. Making use of the presumptions then in our analysis, we can follow the decisions of the administrators over the three-year history of the ECA and test the validity of our model in practice. Changes were naturally bound to occur, but we can still determine whether the administration of the program remained faithful *in principle* to the original design: Were the different values given the same precedence; did they bear the same relation to one another in practice that they did in the legislation? Strangely enough, these are questions that remain foreign to the positivism that still dominates the science of administration. But we are assuming in this approach that it is indeed possible to com-

14

bine deliberation with commitment; that the existence of discretion does not imply the absence of principle, and still less does it prove the hopeless vacuity of all value questions.

From a close reading of the legislation it was possible to anticipate the main lines of policy development. But it was very hard to foresee how the different features in the program would act upon one another; and the results were often paradoxical. The liberal preference for non-intervention made it even less likely that the Marshall Plan would be used as an instrument for social change. On the other hand, the strongest supports for a more permissive and pluralistic approach came from those parts of the program that reflected the concerns of domestic conservatives. All things taken together, the results describe a rather suggestive portrait of American policy in this period, and one that was not so easily predicted. After a brief summary of these issues, there is a chance to collect the strands of analysis on the problem of the "national interest" and its relation to the political regime. And as we follow the argument through to its final level, we move in the last chapter to the institutional setting and the connection between bureaucracy and the character of the regime.

This is a study, then, of several parts, but if there is one theme to which it can be said that all others point, it is the centrality of the regime in political life. If there had been room within the boundaries of this project, I might have gone on to suggest the possibilities of a political science that made the study of regimes the basis of its science. In a sense, there would have been something faintly archaic about a proposal of that sort, because it would have looked forward to a time when all of political science becomes, once again, a branch of constitutional law. But one could argue quite persuasively, I think, that the most important empirical statements about politics—the things we most want to know—are propositions drawn from the nature of regimes rather than systems in general. They are statements about the conditions that sustain certain forms of political life and make others untenable; the distinctive patterns of political behavior that mark the change from one regime to another; and the principled differences between polities that generally make political life better or worse.

But that, again, is a separate agenda, and it rightly deserves a separate undertaking. My own claims here are far more limited. I

15

hope I will have said enough at least to recall the import of Leo Strauss's words when he restated the understanding of the classics, that "the paramount social phenomenon, or that social phenomenon than which only the natural phenomena are more fundamental, is the regime."[6]

[6] Strauss, *op.cit.*, p. 137.

16

Part I

2. BACKGROUND TO THE MARSHALL PLAN: GERMANY AND THE DIVISION OF EUROPE

I

CONSERVATIVES as well as liberals have come to celebrate the Marshall Plan; and conservatives as well as liberals have come to regret the effects of thc Cold War on our domestic life.[1] And yet, one could argue that the Marshall Plan did more than any single measure to dissolve the ambiguity in East-West tensions and consummate the Cold War. An interesting test of this proposition is to consider the very elusive question of "turning points." In the judgment of one of the most thorough students of Soviet-American relations, the antagonism between Russia and the United States became sharply defined by the end of 1946, and the change could be marked in two key events: (1) the American loan to Britain (approved by Congress in July), which seemed to put the finishing touches on a new Anglo-American alliance; and (2) General Clay's announcement in May that he would curtail deliveries to Russia from the American zone in Germany until the Russians gave an account of their reparations removals and agreed to treat Germany as an economic unit.[2]

On closer examination, the circumstances surrounding the British loan hardly justified the images used by Churchill in his Fulton speech, when he spokc of a "special relationship" and a fraternal alliance among the English-speaking peoples. During the war the British had drawn heavily on their overseas assets to finance im-

[1] Arthur Burns has made a thoughtful statement for the conservative position in "The Defense Sector: An Evaluation of Its Economic and Social Impact," in his Moskowitz Lecture at New York University, November, 1967, reprinted in the *Congressional Record*, March 10, 1969 (Daily edition), S2523-27.

[2] William H. MacNeill, *America, Britain, and Russia: Their Cooperation and Conflict, 1941-46*; Royal Institute of International Affairs (London: Oxford University Press, 1953), p. 652, and see also p. 653 n. 1.

ports from their main source of supply in the dollar area. As a result, Britain's traditional status as a creditor nation had evaporated with the war. Faced with a difficult balance of payments situation, the British were still forced to rely on the dollar area as the source of the food and raw materials that were needed in reconstruction. With the end of the war, then, the British stood in critical need of dollar aid. For that reason they were affected even more seriously than the Russians by the abrupt termination of Lend-Lease. The British had received 69 percent or nearly $32 billion in goods and services under the Lend-Lease program, but they were confronted now with a President who shared the opposition of the Senate to grant aid unconnected with the war effort. It was a position from which Truman would later lead a bizarre retreat in the Marshall Plan. But for the present he reflected the aversion in Congress to grant aid, and he was attended by a chief of staff who stormed out of an interdepartmental meeting once when an attempt was made to revive Lend-Lease aid.[3]

With the prospect of further Lend-Lease removed, the British sought a line of credit from the United States in the amount of $5–6 billion, at a reduced rate of interest, and with payments staggered over a period of 50 years. Nothing is harder to reconcile with the notion of the British loan as the symbol of Anglo-American solidarity than the tone of the discussions in Washington.[4] The State Department was quite willing to use these meetings as a lever for its free trade enthusiasms, and it began to squeeze hard for concessions on tariffs, cartels, and quotas.[5] It is one of the ironies of Cold War history that this fixation on free trade would be interpreted as a clear sign of hostility when it was applied to the Russians. But somehow it would fail to shake the image of an Anglo-American entente when it was pressed against the British, who had special responsibilities in the sterling area, and who were even less free to bargain over these issues.

In his memoirs, Truman recounts with a sly pleasure the way he stood up to the British and forced them to accept his compromise

[3] Harry S. Truman, *Memoirs: Year of Decisions, 1945*, Vol. I (New York: Doubleday and Company, 1955), p. 46. Cited hereafter as Truman, *Memoirs*. William D. Leahy, *I Was There* (New York: McGraw-Hill, 1950), pp. 376-77.

[4] See, for example, Hugh Dalton, *High Tide and After* (London: Frederick Muller Limited, 1962), pp. 73-77.

[5] Truman, *Memoirs*, I, pp. 478-79.

figure of $3.75 billion—a rather strange satisfaction in view of the fact that the loan quickly proved inadequate, and that it virtually melted away in the next several months. In the end, the United States had to come to the rescue anyway, but Truman's obvious relish over mastering the British must stand as a mordant commentary on the state of American-British relations in 1946, and what it meant at the time to be the chief ally of the United States.[6]

General Clay's decision to halt reparations deliveries to the Russians had undeniable significance as a public gesture and a pointed tactical move. But under the circumstances, one has to regard it as little more than that. The move was carried out under the sanction of the Potsdam accord, and rather than being designed to hasten a split, it is probably more accurate to say that its purpose was to preserve the structure of Allied cooperation. The object was to induce the Russians to maintain the Potsdam agreement, and as the Americans now seemed to conceive them, the primary terms of the agreement called for the administration of Germany as an integrated unit. Clay himself emphasized the limited aims of the maneuver when he announced that plants would continue to be earmarked for reparations. Deliveries could be resumed fairly easily then if the disagreement were resolved.[7]

Thus, the decision was put forward as revocable, and it need not have implied anything in the way of an enduring division of interests. That is to say, important as the Clay decision was, it hardly compared in significance to the decision reached two months later to proceed with the merger of the British and American zones. And that later decision must recede in comparison to the decision taken at the end of 1947 to build openly political institutions in the Western zones. Bizonal merger gave hardness to the rift between Russia and the West by marking it with organizational forms. Every subsequent decision elaborated the administrative apparatus, giving

---

[6] What is all the more remarkable is that the British encountered much the same kind of attitude in Washington three years later, when the Marshall Plan was well under way, and when they were facing a crisis over devaluation. Recalling the situation in his memoirs, George Kennan wrote: "The episode depressed and disillusioned me as a revelation of the difficulty that would obviously be involved in trying to find understanding among Washington political circles for anything resembling a close and collaborative association with the British. . . ." *Memoirs, 1925-50* (Boston: Little, Brown and Company, 1967), pp. 458-62, at 461-62.

[7] Lucius B. Clay, *Decision in Germany* (New York: Doubleday and Company, 1950), pp. 131-32.

21

it further articulation and compactness. With each administrative step, the differences among the former allies were given new public emphasis and, what is more important, a greater promise of finality. When at last the Western powers moved to the creation of a central government in the Western zone, and General Clay could feel free to acknowledge the political character of the institutions he was building—when, in short, the split was not merely administrative, but explicitly political—the fissure had reached its final stage.

Strictly speaking, none of the earlier decisions entailed a later one; and while each step made a settlement more difficult, the break could never be regarded as entirely beyond recall until the very last step had been taken. In making his case for the bizonal merger, Clay assured Secretary of State Byrnes that the arrangement would not undermine the Allied Control Council. The invitation to enter the merger was extended to all the occupying powers, including the Soviet Union; and when Byrnes made the announcement, he was careful to note, as Clay recalled, "that the administration of these zones would be limited to economic matters and would not function as a government, and that the merger would last only until agreement was reached for the treatment of Germany as an economic unit."[8] A separate currency was not introduced until the beginning of 1949, and even then, as the subsequent discussions with the Russians made evident, the issue was highly negotiable.[9] Two years later, in the midst of the Berlin crisis, Stalin would go so far as to say that he could understand the case for bizonal merger and, if necessary, he could accept it. It was the need to create *political* institutions in the Western zone that he could not understand, and found impossible to accept.[10] Yet even here, perhaps because he had no illusions, perhaps because he simply could not afford to be precipitate, he would not despair of negotiating. The Western powers were threatening to create a new government in western Germany, and the Soviets were turning off the electricity in Berlin, but Stalin could remark to the American ambassador that "After all, we are still allies."[11]

---

[8] *Ibid.*, p. 165. "For these reasons," Clay added, "German organizations established in the bizonal area were never made responsible to the German people through the election process."

[9] Walter Bedell Smith, *My Three Years in Moscow* (Philadelphia: J. P. Lippincott Company, 1950), p. 245.

[10] Clay, *op.cit.*, p. 369.   [11] Smith, *op.cit.*, p. 244.

The onset of the Cold War has to be measured then in the elaboration of organizational commitments that gave firmness, stability, and finally, political recognition to the differences that separated Russia and the United States. It is primarily for this reason that Germany became the clearest barometer for the emerging Cold War. The management of the occupation lent itself to a wide range of organizational responses that could mark the progress of Soviet-American relations. As the conflict over Germany sharpened, the changes in organization were charged with even greater import, and each successive step enlarged the meaning of the dispute. One could argue, therefore, that the Cold War did not really begin until the problem of Germany was linked explicitly to the problem of Europe and registered in organizational forms. The escalation of American moves in Germany followed the drift of Secretary Marshall's thought in identifying the unity and recovery of Germany with the unity and recovery of Europe as a whole. It is significant, in this respect, that when the Marshall Plan was proposed, the United States still felt constrained to hold the program open to Soviet entry, but when the offer was refused, it would be refused for the last time. Henceforth, the nations of Europe would be labeled and grouped by the simple fact of their membership or nonmembership in the European Recovery Program (ERP). The division would be drawn between those countries that were integrated in the Marshall Plan and its ancillary organizations, and those nations that were compelled to join the Cominform and Comecon, as the Russians responded with their own organizational defenses.

At that point, the idea of rival blocs acquired organizational substance. Where the situation had previously been far more fluid, and Czechoslovakia could assume that it was permissible to join the Marshall Plan, alignments were clearly fixed now, and mistakes of that kind could no longer occur. Once the consciousness of rival blocs was given the firmness of organizational supports, it was a much shorter step to the accretion of military counterparts in the form of NATO and the Warsaw pact.

Thus, in setting the context for the Marshall Plan, it would be useful to review the trend of events that saw the various irritants in Soviet-American relations concentrate themselves in the problem of Germany, and the problem of Germany dissolve into the problem of Europe. Against this background, the Marshall Plan stands out as the device that gave organizational expression to these doctrinal connections. It extended the zone of organized confrontation across the continent of Europe, and in doing that alone it made the Cold War into something more than a metaphor.

II

About a month after he succeeded to the Presidency, Truman held a meeting with Secretary of War Stimson, in which he expanded on his views of a postwar settlement in Europe. His thoughts ran back at the time to the conversations he used to have with Sen. Elbert Thomas of Utah. Taking a map of Europe, Truman would point out the "breadbasket" of the continent in the east, "with Hungary a cattle country and Rumania and the Ukraine as the wheat area," while up in the northwest lay the heavily industrialized countries.

> The problem, as Senator Thomas and I talked about it, was to help unify Europe by linking up the breadbasket with the industrial centers through a free flow of trade. To facilitate this flow, the Rhine and the Danube could be linked with a vast network of canals which would provide a passage all the way from the North Sea to the Black Sea and the Mediterranean. This would constitute free waterways for trade, while each country bordering on the waterways would have the riparian rights it should have. . . .[12]

Accordingly, the first proposal made by Truman at Potsdam was to place the Danube under international control. It was a measure aimed at unifying a natural economic community, and in Truman's thinking, it was the first critical step toward the stability and peace of Europe.[13] The stability of Europe, he believed, would assure world peace, and world peace in turn would preserve the security of the United States. Thus Truman could maintain that "the reconstruction of Europe was a matter that directly concerned us, and we could not turn our back on it without jeopardizing our own national interest."[14]

[12] Truman, *Memoirs*, I, p. 236.

[13] So closely, in fact, did this measure become identified in Truman's mind with the restoration of peace that those who opposed it were immediately suspect. When Stalin finally rejected his plan, it only proved to Truman "how his mind worked and what he was after. . . . The Russians [he concluded] were planning world conquest." *Ibid.*, p. 412.

[14] *Ibid.*, pp. 46, 262.

In Secretary Stimson, Truman had an adviser who shared his basic views on Europe. Writing to the President in July, Stimson observed that the United States had "immediate interests in a return to stable conditions" in Europe. In the short run, the elimination of distress conditions was necessary "to ease our problems of administration and the speed and success of our redeployment." But there were also long-run, strategic interests involved. "I take it," he wrote, "that all our objectives are included in one fundamental purpose—the achievement of security and peace under conditions which preserve to us our concepts of liberty."[15] Viewing the destruction in Europe, Stimson reported to the President that he was taken with "the great loss in economic values . . . but even more with the loss in widespread moral values which destruction and war conditions have caused in Europe." Stimson ordinarily looked at foreign countries with the conservative's sense of limitations and with a certain skepticism about the potential of democratic government as a universal experience. Looking now at a devastated Europe after the collapse of two major dictatorships, he seemed more than ever impressed with the fragility of constitutional government. Therefore, he was convinced that the restoration of a stable economy in Europe was absolutely necessary for the maintenance of a constitutional order.[16]

Echoing and, at the same time, sharpening the President's thoughts, Stimson argued in a memorandum that the recovery of Germany was central to the recovery of Europe. Before the war, he noted, the commerce of Europe was "very largely predicated" on German industry:

> There was a period, substantially before the war, when Germany became the largest source of supply to ten European countries— viz. Russia, Norway, Sweden, Denmark, Holland, Switzerland, Italy, Austria-Hungary, Rumania and Bulgaria, and the second largest supplier of Great Britain, Belgium and France. At the same time she became the best customer of Russia, Norway, Holland, Belgium, Switzerland, Italy and Austria-Hungary, and the second best of Great Britain, Sweden and Denmark.[17]

[15] U.S. Department of State, *Foreign Relations: Conference of Berlin (Potsdam)*, Vol. I (Washington: Government Printing Office, 1960), p. 755. Cited hereafter as *Conference of Berlin*.
[16] *Ibid.*, p. 808.   [17] *Ibid.*, p. 756.

25

But it was also true that the recovery of production in Germany would require something more than a liberal policy on reparations removals. As Stimson warned, the mere retention of plants would not be sufficient "unless there is a flow of commerce, establishment of transportation systems and stable currency." Recovery would depend on the restoration of this flow of commerce, both in Germany and in Europe as a whole. To that end, Stimson recommended two lines of policy: (1) the treatment of Germany as an economic unit, including uniform policies on transportation, communications, rationing, and price control; and (2) a coordinated plan for the "economic rehabilitation of Europe as a whole," involving credits from the Export-Import Bank or whatever other resources the United States could bring to bear.[18]

As it was conceived by Truman and Stimson, then, American policy on Germany was locked in a syllogism: Economic reconstruction in Europe was essential to political stability and world peace; the recovery of Germany was central to the recovery of Europe; and the recovery of Germany depended on the treatment of Germany as an economic unit. Hence, the key to stability in Europe was the integrated administration of the German economy. Unfortunately, the Russians would not admit to the same understanding, but the matter could never simply rest there because the syllogism forced the disagreement into its own cast: If the Russians refused to carry out this one part of the Potsdam agreement, it was assumed that they were rejecting the essentials of the agreement itself.[19] That meant they were refusing, in effect, to treat Germany as an economic unit; which meant that they did not care to see the rapid recovery of Germany; which meant, in turn, that they did not wish to see the restoration of economic and political stability in Europe.

The estrangement of Russia and the United States could be measured in a series of discrete steps taken by the United States, but all the basic confusions were present in the first public break on German policy. In May 1946, General Clay ordered a halt to the removal of plants from the American zone. The principal American complaint was that the Soviets had refused to provide

---

[18] *Ibid.*, pp. 757, 809.

[19] Thus, General Clay: ". . . [R]eparations was only one of the bricks that built the house. If you pull out any of the bricks the house collapses. . . . [To] live up to Potsdam you live up to it in whole and not in its individual parts." Clay, *op.cit.*, pp. 121-22.

an inventory of the reparations they were taking from the eastern zone. And while the Western powers continued to dismantle plants for delivery to the Soviet Union, General Zhukov had declared as early as July 1945, that there was not enough food available in the Soviet zone to permit shipments to the West. Thus, industrial resources were being drained off from both the Eastern and the Western zones, while the Western zones were not even receiving compensation in the form of food. As Clay put it, "we were being placed in the position not only of financing reparations to the Soviet Union but also of agreeing to strip our own zone . . . without getting the benefits which would come from the amalgamation of all zones."[20] All this, in addition to the high-handed tactics of the Russians seemed to violate the agreement to treat Germany as an economic unit.

But did it? The United States never contested the claim of the Russians that they were not in a position to supply food to the Western zones. Nor did anyone suggest that the Soviets should maintain their population at the level of subsistence rations for the sake of diverting food to the rest of Germany. In other words, it was likely that the United States would have had to import food for Germany in any event, and if the Soviets had been forced to reduce rations in their own area, it might have been necessary to bring in food for the Eastern zone as well.

As far as the removal of plants was concerned, Clay did not say that the removals themselves blocked the recovery of the economy. The real bars to production were in the lack of raw materials and the disarray in transport and communications. Retaining more plants in Germany would have contributed very little to recovery. It was even arguable, in fact, that recovery could be accelerated if the plants were transferred to other countries, where the infrastructures in the economy had not been so thoroughly shattered. Curiously enough, this was the argument used by Secretary Marshall almost two years later when he made a complete turnabout on the issue. By that time, however, he was trying to *justify* the policy of plant removals—when it was a matter now of delivering the plants to Western Europe.[21] Using much the same kind of analysis, J. P. Nettl has also refuted the argument, made by Clay at the time, that

[20] *Ibid.*, p. 121.
[21] See Marshall's memorandum to Senator Vandenberg, reprinted in U.S. Department of State, *State Department Bulletin*, Vol. 18, No. 451 (February 22, 1948), pp. 239-44.

the zonal divisions in Germany were acting as barriers to the flow of trade.[22] On any of these counts, then, it was difficult to charge that the Soviet Union was out to violate the Potsdam agreement, either by retarding German recovery or by blocking the management of Germany as an economic unit. Furthermore, Clay himself never raised these charges. His argument moved instead to another level.

Clay insisted that the Soviet refusal to give an account of their reparations removals made the overall industry plan meaningless. And even if it was true, as the Soviets claimed, that the level of industry plan was too problematic to be followed, Clay replied that the reparations program was based on the industry plan. If the level of industry plan were abandoned, then the reparations program would also have to be discarded.

On the first point, the Soviet position was quite tenable. Under the conditions then existing in Germany, it was virtually impossible to get a realistic overall plan, and considering the methods by which the plan was finally put together, even its architects were rather modest in their claims.[23] The Russians argued that the balance between imports and exports would have to be handled by the separate zones until there was a favorable trade balance for Germany as a whole and reparations had been paid. The issue turned then on two questions: (1) In the event of disagreement on the level of industry plan, might the regulation of imports and exports be left to the separate zones? (2) If the answer to the first question was yes, what was the priority of reparations? Was it legitimate to consider reparations as a first charge on exports, as the Russians were now suggesting? General Clay to the contrary,[24] both of these points were sanctioned in the Potsdam agreement, and by a provision that was enacted at the initiative of the United States.

On July 29, 1945, rather late in the Potsdam conference, Secretary Byrnes told Soviet Foreign Minister Molotov that there were two major issues outstanding: the western boundary of Poland and German reparations. What Byrnes proposed was to link the two questions in a package deal. The United States would agree to the

[22] J. P. Nettl, *The Eastern Zone and Soviet Policy in Germany* (London: Oxford University Press, 1951), pp. 270 ff.

[23] See B. U. Ratchford and William D. Ross, *Berlin Reparations Assignment* (Chapel Hill: University of North Carolina Press, 1947), especially chs. 8, 13, and 14.

[24] See Clay, *op.cit.*, pp. 121-22.

line of the Oder and Western Neisse rivers for the western boundary of Poland. In return, Byrnes would offer a new arrangement on reparations that would "do away with almost certain points of friction in the future."[25] It was agreed that the Soviet Union should have 50 percent of all the reparations exacted from Germany, but a good part of that share would have to come from the more industrialized western zones, which contained the Ruhr and the Saar. Rather than fixing dollar amounts or percentages for each zone, Byrnes suggested that each power should satisfy itself first from its own area. Assuming that the yield to the Russians would be less than the 50 percent they were allowed, the Western powers would deliver a certain percentage of the industrial capital equipment in their own zones that was considered to be in excess of peacetime needs. Some of the equipment would be transferred free, while a larger amount of capital goods would be delivered in return for essential products in the Soviet zone (e.g., food, coal, potash, zinc).

The Western Neisse was an important concession for the United States to make, and presumably Byrnes would not have traded it away for something unimportant.[26] It has been suggested that Byrnes was determined to get reciprocal deliveries of food from the Soviet zone.[27] That might have been a prominent consideration, yet there was no significant discussion on the point, and it seems very unlikely that Byrnes would have exchanged the Western Neisse for something as uncertain as the availability of food stocks. Certainly he would not have done it without a more detailed agreement on the criteria for allocating food. But that was exactly the kind of situation he was trying to avoid—the necessity of maintaining surveillance over the major powers and applying very complicated formu-

[25] *Conference of Berlin*, II, p. 474.

[26] Churchill had apparently regarded the Western Neisse as nonnegotiable. He later declared that he would never have retreated from the Eastern Neisse had he been able to continue at the Potsdam conference. See Winston S. Churchill, *Triumph and Tragedy* (Boston: Houghton Mifflin, 1953), p. 672. The United States military thought it "impracticable to offer serious objections to this transfer of territory from Germany if the USSR insists upon it." On the other hand, it was thought that "the bargaining possibilities of this issue . . . should be observed." *Conference of Berlin*, II, p. 755. American thinking here might have been affected by a British memorandum in July, which warned that an indefinite delay on a settlement of the boundary would only work in favor of the Poles and Russians by allowing them to consolidate their control of the territory. *Conference of Berlin*, II, pp. 778-79.

[27] MacNeill, *op.cit.*, p. 623.

las. Byrnes's primary motive was very probably, as he said, to find an arrangement that would "do away with almost certain points of friction"; and precisely how much that covered was revealed in the subsequent discussions at the conference.

As the Byrnes proposal was understood by Molotov and Ernest Bevin, the British Foreign Secretary, it would have undermined the authority of the Allied Control Council, particularly in the regulation of the economy. Molotov asked whether Byrnes's plan did not in fact mean that "each country would have a free hand in their [*sic*] own zones and would act entirely independently of the others?" According to the notes of the meeting, Byrnes replied that "that was true in substance but he had in mind working out arrangements for the exchange of needed products between the zones."[28] In that case, the next logical question for Molotov, which he raised somewhat later, was, Who would determine the amount of equipment that was in excess of peacetime needs? On that determination rested the deliveries to the Soviet Union and the "exchange of needed products." Since the discussion of the moment centered on the Ruhr, Byrnes answered that it would be the British who had the decision, since the Ruhr was in their zone. Molotov replied quickly in protest that reparations had to remain as a central responsibility of the Allied Control Council or the Reparations Commission. That was the principle they had been working with from the beginning, and it was the only one that assured the Russians of participation. Byrnes suggested that the Control Council might still determine the general norms or living standards, but under the terms of the proposal, "the final authority would probably remain in the commander-in-chief of the given zone since he was responsible for that zone."[29] Thus, the basic premise in the scheme was clearly that of zonal authority: As applied in the first instance, it meant a free hand for the occupying power in determining the standard of living and the availability of reparations. And by establishing individual responsibility for economic conditions in each zone, the plan also implied some basic national authority over what would go into and out of the separate zones.

Where, then, did the Byrnes plan leave the priority of reparations? The powers accepted the proposition that enough resources had to be left in Germany to allow the Germans to subsist without the need for extraordinary outside assistance. But after that their

[28] *Conference of Berlin*, II, pp. 450, 474.   [29] *Ibid.*, pp. 481, 513.

30

positions diverged. The United States and Britain argued that the payment for imports should constitute the first charge on the proceeds from export sales. The Soviets, on the other hand, sought to amend the agreement by stipulating that "after payment of reparations," enough resources would be left in Germany to allow the Germans to subsist without external assistance.[30] The Russians came to soften their position later when they allowed that reparations might be reduced along with internal consumption if exports declined.[31] But at no point did they accept a secondary status for reparations; and thus the major powers came to an impasse. It was at this point that Byrnes had presented his package deal. When Molotov subsequently raised the question of first charges again, Byrnes reminded him that they had taken care of the whole matter through the agreement on zonal authority. The sticky question of principle had been pushed aside in favor of local option.

But Ernest Bevin also found it hard to believe that such an important question could have been avoided so easily. And so he, too, raised the question of first charges, but this time it was Stalin who made the rejoinder. Stalin pointed out to him that when they accepted the Byrnes proposal, they deleted the entire section in the protocol (section 19) dealing with the issue of first charges. When Bevin could still not agree, Byrnes asked why the British "did not handle this in their own way since they were in control in their zone."[32] Bevin retorted that he could not accept that either, because it broke with their previous agreement to treat Germany as a whole. This new plan, he maintained, would divide Germany into three zones. At this moment of rare explicitness, Stalin intervened once again. Indirectly conceding the truth of Bevin's remarks, he observed that the unified control of Germany required central administrative machinery, and that was the *next thing* to be discussed.[33] That is, the allies were not entirely rejecting central administration, but that would be a secondary feature. They would come to it *after* the basic pattern of zonal authority was established.[34]

---

[30] *Ibid.*, p. 810. [31] *Ibid.*

[32] *Ibid.*, p. 521. [33] *Ibid.*

[34] The divisive paragraph 19 was later revived in a diluted form by Bevin, but it was accepted by the United States only after the addition of the following language: "if the Control Council failed to agree [on an import-export plan], each zone commander would still be free to import into his own zone such supplies as his government considered essential, for the pay-

Part I

When General Clay asserted, "I could not accept the principle of zonal import-export programs, nor did I see how an over-all program could be administered without a central agency,"[35] that might have been a pertinent opinion, but it was a deficient reading of the Potsdam agreement. The Soviet leaders were clearly given to understand that they had a free hand in their own zone as far as reparations were concerned. If they could not accept an overall level of industry plan, they now had the authority to follow a different program in their own zone and apply their own priority on reparations.

Technically, therefore, the later actions of the Soviet Union were defensible. And on the cold pragmatic grounds of either raising productivity or forcing the Russians to back down, Clay's decision to stop deliveries could have been shown to be useless. One may wonder, then, what the real issue was that was serious enough to warrant a public face-down with the Russians. There was, of course, the brutal thoroughness of the Russians as they went about stripping their zone, and the complete lack of pretense over their intentions. But the only objection open to the United States that resembled a point of principle was the complaint voiced by General Clay that "we were being placed in the position . . . of financing reparations to the Soviet Union."[36] Lest this reason be slighted, it should be remembered that it was a view emphatically held by Truman, and indeed, it was one of the cardinal points in his personal program to avoid the mistakes of the First World War: No more would the United States come in through the back door to finance the reparations of victor states.[37] Still, what seemed to be an elementary point of fairness could have serious shortcomings when it was taken as a principle. It was particularly questionable as it was applied here, where the larger task of statesmanship was to reach an equitable—and prudential—settlement with the Soviet Union.

At the Paris Peace Conference in July 1946, Byrnes was closeted for a while with Molotov, and he took advantage of the opportunity

---

ment of which he might assess a first charge on exports from his own zone." Byrnes insisted that this language was necessary "because of the agreement on reparations" reached earlier. See *ibid.*, pp. 522, 572, 827-28.

[35] Clay, *op.cit.*, p. 122.

[36] *Ibid.*, p. 121. This was the conclusion also of Michael Balfour, *Four-Power Control in Germany, 1945-46*; Royal Institute of International Affairs (London: Oxford University Press, 1956), pp. 135-37, at 135.

[37] See, for example, Truman, *Memoirs*, I, pp. 323, 365, 367.

32

to hold a candid discussion on Germany. Byrnes asked Molotov directly what the basic Soviet objectives were in Germany. Molotov replied that the Russians had two principal demands: the $10 billion in reparations that were promised to them at Yalta, and four-power control of the Ruhr industries. "Since that time," Byrnes wrote in 1947, "there has been much speculation on the ambitions of the Soviet Union in Germany. . . . but I am sure the statement made by Molotov that night represents the real desires of the Soviet High Command."[38]

Moreover, all the evidence seems to point in this direction. Reparations were, in fact, the overriding end of Russian policy in Germany. They were so primary, as J. P. Nettl has shown, that they forced the Russians to undercut the German Communists and weaken the integration of Eastern Germany in the Soviet bloc. That is to say, the frenzied dismantling operation that so alarmed the United States and cast shadows of ill purpose was actually nothing more than it appeared. It did not reflect a Soviet desire to jettison the Potsdam accords, divide Germany, or integrate the Eastern zone in a satellite bloc. Rather, it implied just the reverse of these things. It was in the Soviet interest to maintain the Potsdam agreement and continue to receive capital goods from the Western zones. But at the same time, as the Russians persisted in a policy of exploitation, they made it far more difficult for Germany to participate in the economy of the Eastern bloc. In addition to removing plants, the Soviets failed to supply raw materials to the factories remaining in Germany, and beyond that, there was a lingering bitterness in Eastern Europe that continued to restrain trade with the Germans. The result was that the Eastern zone became even more dependent on the West and the non-Communist countries.[39]

The Russians were resolved to enforce their reparations policy at almost any cost, and under the circumstances of the occupation, part of those costs would have had to be shifted to the Western powers. It would have been possible to avoid a conflict, then, if the United States had been willing to accept these indirect costs. Al-

[38] James F. Byrnes, *Speaking Frankly* (New York: Harper and Brothers, 1947), p. 194.

[39] See Nettl, *op.cit.*, pp. 292, 303-304. As Nettl also notes, the further consequence of Russian policy was to damage the legitimacy of the German Communists. Either the Russians could allow the German Communists to cultivate their own internal sources of support, or they could force them to act as apologists for the "regime of reparations." But they could not do both.

ternatively, the Soviets might have been deflected from their pro-
vocative reparations policy if the United States had been willing to
offer grant aid or a large postwar loan.

At first glance, the Soviet desire for $10 billion worth of recon-
struction aid would seem to be staggering. Yet the United States
had contributed over $9 billion in Lend-Lease aid to Russia during
the war. If the gift was well worth the cost then, it might have been
an equally good investment in the postwar period. Admittedly the
notion of "protection" or ransom money was offensive, but the
question did not have to be posed in that way. Postwar aid to Russia had been considered earlier as a measure of compassion and
enlightened self-interest; and the money did not have to be given
as an outright grant, which could bear all the earmarks of a "pay-
off." Instead, it might have been possible to offer subsidies in one
form or another for commodities purchased in the United States
(e.g., by picking up the dollar costs and accepting a reduced figure
in Russian currency that would not be convertible). Or better yet,
the subsidies could have been built into a multilateral scheme, and
the incentives could have been arranged in such a way as to draw
the Soviet Union into a tighter web of relations with Western Europe. While the Soviets might have increased their leverage in
Western Europe, they would have enlarged their vulnerability as
well. The incentives could have been attractive enough to make the
price of obstruction higher than the Russians were willing to pay.

But even putting these things aside, the United States had already established a precedent for subsidies in lieu of reparations.
The scheme had arisen when Germany encountered heavy demands
for reparations in shipping. If the demands had been honored, they
would have revived the shipbuilding industry and restored an important part of the German war capacity. At the same moment, the
shipbuilding industries in the United States and Canada were ex-
pecting postwar layoffs. The American plan then was to urge the
Europeans to fill their shipping needs from American stocks, and
as an incentive, the government would offer liberal terms of purchase.[40] Thus, the principle was already accepted; the only question was whether it was reasonable to apply it to the Soviet Union.

For the United States, however, grant aid was entirely out of the
question in the postwar period, and where the Soviet Union was
involved, the government was scarcely more pliable on loans. In

---

[40] See *Conference of Berlin*, I, pp. 567, 571.

January 1945, Stalin requested a postwar loan of approximately $6 billion, but the request was refused—ostensibly because of the large sum, but in reality because there was opposition in the Administration to any line of credit for the Soviet Union that did not carry some quid pro quo.[41] A second application in August actually appeared to get lost in the American government in the process of liquidating the Foreign Economic Administration. When the application was finally acted upon, the United States attached such demands in the form of trade concessions that the Soviets found the terms unacceptable.[42]

One can raise a serious question, then, as to whether the Russian and American objectives in Germany were really as irreconcilable as they appeared. What stands out as particularly tragic to one who reviews the documents of the period is the way in which these basic confusions in interpretation became cumulative. Not only did one incident set the stage for another, but the interpretations of one event hung on to misinform the next, until understanding itself became a mixture of caricatured estimates and half-articulated suspicions. With each American move in Germany, the United States and the Soviet Union were driven farther apart. Despite the fact that some of these moves were clothed in economic rationales, they were taken for reasons that were largely political, and which were therefore affected by all the previous misjudgments. This was most notably the case in the merger of the British and American zones.

As early as April 1946, General Clay had recommended a merger of the British and American zones to Secretary Byrnes. There was something intrinsically appealing about a union of the industrialized British sector with the pastoral American zone. But it was hard to see precisely what the justification for such a merger might be. General Clay made the unexceptionable point that neither zone was self-sufficient by itself, but that together they might be.[43] It was not clear, though, as to why that should have been a relevant consideration. Self-sufficiency for the zones was certainly not a valid concern under the Potsdam agreement, nor was it particularly relevant to the problem of recovery. The only economic advantage in the merger was that it would save the British from the necessity of drawing on their dollar reserves to pay for the import of food from

[41] See Walter Millis (ed.), *The Forrestal Diaries* (New York: The Viking Press, 1951), p. 41.
[42] See Balfour, *op.cit.*, p. 137n.   [43] Clay, *op.cit.*, p. 199.

35

the United States. Of course, that could have been achieved more simply by giving the food to the British as a form of grant aid. But that solution promised no gain for the United States, while bizonal merger brought a distinct political advantage: It moved the United States into joint control of the Ruhr. American representatives would be able to participate now in decisions governing export levels, foreign exchange, and the allocation of coal. Secretary Byrnes understood that control of the Ruhr was important to European recovery, and as General Clay recalled, he believed "we were entitled to at least a share in this control. With fusion, this resulted and gave us a much more influential voice in German affairs."[44]

For the United States bizonal merger was a political decision, and when it was eventually approved, it was not in response to the economic indicators but in reaction to what was seen as a Russian political move. Although Clay's initial recommendation was in April, Byrnes had been reluctant to take such a serious step except as a last resort. When the decision finally came in July, it was made in a rather precipitate way, in response to Molotov's speech on Germany at the Paris Peace Conference. Byrnes interpreted the speech as the beginning of a new competition for the favor of Germany and a break in the Allied front. Molotov attacked the policy of "annihilating Germany as a state, or of agrarianizing her with the destruction of her main industrial centers." Where the Soviets had previously held to an annual steel production level of 4.5 million tons, Molotov announced support for a new level of 10 million tons. He criticized the view that Germany should be dismembered or federalized or separated from the Ruhr, a position he identified with the "Allied authorities in the Western zones of occupation." In publicly cracking the united front on Germany, it was clear that Molotov was appealing to a public beyond the Allied governments. "We Soviet people," he declared, "hold it incorrect to impose any particular solution of this question on the German people."[45] Byrnes was convinced that the meaning of the speech was unmistakable, and on the very next day he ordered Clay to proceed with the bizonal merger.[46]

[44] *Ibid.*, p. 172; cf. p. 336.

[45] The Molotov speech is reprinted in Alvin Z. Rubinstein (ed.), *The Foreign Policy of the Soviet Union* (New York: Random House, 1960), pp. 223-26.

[46] As Clay remembered the decision, "Byrnes believed that Soviet intent was [now] clear and further delay in consolidating the western areas of

It is interesting that Byrnes remembered only one speech by Molotov, which he read as a new pitch to the Germans and, to that extent, a fresh Soviet power play. In contrast, Clay remembered two speeches, one on July 9 and another on the tenth. What stuck in his mind was the first speech, which was about disarmament, demilitarization, and reparations. If Molotov's speech on July 10 contained a new tone of liberality, the speech on the ninth had an altogether different emphasis. In a firm and candid manner, Molotov reminded the Germans of their implication in the Nazi regime. While disclaiming any spirit of revenge, he nevertheless defended the policy of reparations and the need for Allied controls over German industry. His main point of assurance to the Germans was that Allied controls did not preclude a unified German state with an industrial economy. The two policies, he said, were really compatible, for in the long run they were both "in the interests of world economy and tranquility in Europe."

Rather than being a new policy break, the Molotov speech was more nearly a restatement of existing Soviet policy. The rejection of dismemberment for Germany had been agreed upon by the major powers by the opening of the Potsdam conference. As for the statement on Allied controls, it was made in reply to Byrnes's proposal for a Soviet-American treaty of security. Molotov rejected the American plan as inadequate, and he went on to restate the Soviet demand for demilitarization and four-power control of the Ruhr. Byrnes had seen his proposal as a generous measure that should have satisfied any legitimate Soviet fear concerning Germany. Its rejection seemed to confirm his suspicion of Soviet motives, and it colored his understanding of the Molotov speech.

In the original proposal by Byrnes, the four major powers would have maintained an inspection force in Germany to detect the conversion of plants to war production. This arrangement was meant to obviate the need for large numbers of ground troops, but with the vote of a majority, it would have been possible to apply sanctions in the form of air strikes.[47] According to Byrnes, the treaty would have offered both security against Germany and assurance "that the United States would not return to a policy of isolation."[48] Stalin showed some definite interest in the treaty at first, but Molo-

---

Germany would increase economic distress and make political reconstruction impossible." Clay, *op.cit.*, p. 165.

[47] Byrnes, *op.cit.*, p. 172. [48] *Ibid.*, p. 171.

tov insisted on a longer time period and a more effective provision on disarmament. As Byrnes lengthened the coverage of the treaty to twenty-five, and later, forty years, Molotov still seemed evasive. When Molotov finally rejected the proposal in his Paris speech, Byrnes concluded that "the Soviet High Command . . . did not want the United States involved in the maintenance of European security" and stationed in a permanent role in the Continent.[49]

That explanation, however, was far from convincing. For at the same time they were rejecting the Byrnes proposal, the Soviets were advocating four-power control of the Ruhr, an arrangement that would have made the American role in Europe far more regular and decisive. Conversely, the Byrnes plan was objectionable to the Soviet Union because it was advanced as a substitute for control of the Ruhr. It withheld from the Soviet Union what Molotov said was the second of their two main objectives: some share of control over the most important single center of German production.[50] What the Byrnes plan concealed was that the Administration had already made its decision, and the Russians would be granted no such participation in the control of the Ruhr. In June 1945, a State Department paper cast doubt on the prospect of creating organizing principles for the Ruhr when "the several trustees brought . . . divergent conceptions of economic organization and equally different views of the uses to be made of the trusteeship."[51] Apart from reservations on economic and administrative grounds,[52] it was felt that "the extension of Soviet power and influence into the heart of Western Europe through the device of trusteeship would manifestly be open to grave doubt."[53] The international control of the Ruhr was also opposed by the military, who argued that the loss of Silesia and the Saar would be enough to eliminate Germany as a military threat. Detaching the Ruhr might only serve to damage economic stability or, as the State Department feared, it might reactivate the extreme nationalist groups.[54] Finally, a committee of the Joint Chiefs of Staff warned that placing the Ruhr under international control "could not but inject Russia into the affairs of

---

[49] *Ibid.*, p. 176.

[50] In 1937 the steel production of the Ruhr alone exceeded that of any country except the United States and the Soviet Union. Its production of coal, iron, and crude steel comprised about 70 percent of total German production. See *Conference of Berlin*, I, pp. 590-91.

[51] *Ibid.*, p. 588. [52] See *ibid.*, p. 589.

[53] *Ibid.*, p. 587. [54] *Ibid.*, pp. 587, 596.

Western Europe to an undesirable degree, which might well require larger United States commitments in the areas internationalized and for longer periods of time."[55]

Although he professed a willingness to find some acceptable arrangement with the Russians, it is a matter of record that Byrnes was never willing to yield on this one form of control that the Russians regarded as the most meaningful of all. In his Stuttgart speech in September 1947, Byrnes again proclaimed that the United States would consider controls "over the whole of Germany, including the Ruhr and the Rhineland, as may be necessary for security purposes." But at the same time, he hedged, the United States could not accept any arrangement that would "subject the Ruhr and Rhineland to [the] political domination or manipulation of outside powers."[56]

Whether American officials were responding to Soviet actions in Eastern Europe, or whether their decision was based simply on an estimate of Soviet character, it was nevertheless clear that the issue of the Ruhr had already been prejudged by the time of the Potsdam conference. In fairness to the men who had to make this decision, a reasonable argument might have been made for their position along the following lines: Even if it were true that the Soviet Union had no revisionist aims in Europe, it was also true that intentions are rarely static in politics. Experience has taught that there is a dynamic relation between power and ends. Ends may

[55] *Ibid.*, pp. 595-96.

[56] U.S. Department of State, *Germany, 1947-1949: The Story in Documents* (Washington: Government Printing Office, 1950), p. 8. In his memoirs, Byrnes dismissed four-power control of the Ruhr as "impractical" in the light of the experience in Germany with the Allied Control Council. If space permitted, one could question whether the overall performance of the Control Council was really as conclusive on this point as Byrnes suggested—and beyond that, whether the arrangement of zonal division was really analogous to a functional sharing of control. There were incentives for reaching agreement in a functional scheme that were not present in the system of geographic divisions. A functional arrangement probably would have strengthened the Soviet interest in the recovery of production in the Ruhr, and through that, the recovery of Western Europe. At any rate, even if we discount all these arguments, the case against the Control Council had much less force in 1946, when the control of the Ruhr was at issue. As Clay himself admitted, the Control Council "appeared to be functioning with some effectiveness during the remainder of the year 1946," even though it worked in a climate of political tension. See Clay, *op.cit.*, p. 131; Byrnes, *op.cit.*, p. 194.

grow in proportion to means; intentions may change as new possibilities are opened. Bringing the Russians into joint control of the
Ruhr might well have given them a stake in the stability of Europe.
But if conditions happened to worsen, if the lag in recovery
brought a decline in political stability, could anyone say with assurance that the Russians would not have been tempted to exploit
the situation? If the Communist parties in Western Europe seemed
to be on the verge of a political breakthrough, could one have expected that the Russians would always turn a deaf ear, or that they
would refuse to make use of their new leverage in Western Europe
to aid a fraternal party?

Like any exercise in political conjecture, the judgment was highly problematic, and it may be appalling to believe that something
so grave should have been risked on the basis of something so rid-
den with guesses. But one would have to concede that the case for
the other side was no less problematic. And when the issue hung
in this way on a balance of intuitions, one could not simply wipe
away history. In the end, the Soviets could not evade the consequences of their own revolutionary past. Given the character of the
Soviet regime, given the peculiar quality of its ties to foreign parties
and subversive movements, the burden of proof by 1946 had to rest
with the Soviet Union. If the evidence were no more than evenly
balanced, one could not expect responsible men to put history out
of mind, or forget the few reliable things they knew.

There was no convenient solution to the diplomatic impasse, but
if only one had the detachment to view the dilemma in its true
dimensions, without the overlay of slander, there might have been
some chance to break the careless cycle of reactions. When the
United States placed the matter of the Ruhr beyond consideration,
the Russians were made to look intransigent and demanding when
they refused to do the same. That in turn seemed to verify the
American fears; it finally pushed the United States into bizonal
merger, and from there to a series of administrative measures that
confirmed the split with Russia.

After the bizonal merger, the next major step for the United
States involved the tightening of administration in the Western
zones of Germany. Under the guise of economic agencies, the
United States created a system of institutions that was really political in nature. An elected Economic Council (or legislature) was
established in the center, along with an Executive Committee to

40

organize the business of the council and direct the administration. These arrangements were adopted in May 1947, and they were described by General Clay as "the second step in the transfer of responsibility to German hands."[57]

But the circumstances of their adoption are again worth noting. The decision was approved by Secretary of State Marshall on his way back from the Moscow conference in April 1947. In spite of the progress that was made in Moscow on other questions, Marshall saw no indication that the Soviets would relent on their reparations policy. From that he concluded that there was no hope of reaching an agreement on a unified program for Germany. Thus, on the return flight from Moscow, Marshall stopped in Germany for a hurried meeting with General Clay at the Tempelhof airport. Clay was given his authorization on the spot "to proceed vigorously with the strengthening of the bizonal organization"; for both Marshall and Bevin were resolved that any "further delay would serve no purpose."[58] Clay was instructed to hasten the upward revision in the level of industry plan and take further steps to assure the self-sufficiency of the area. On balance it was a gratuitous move, since the Soviets had already accepted a higher level of industry plan. Any additional move toward self-sufficiency could only support the impression of the Soviet Union that the Americans were violating the Potsdam agreement.[59]

The Council of Foreign Ministers met again at London in November, and this time Marshall was clearly in no mood for compromise. He demanded nothing less of the Soviets now than a surrender of their basic policy on reparations. More precisely, he insisted that the Russians stop their removals from current production, except in return for payment, until the German economy became "self-sustaining." Molotov replied forcefully, but Marshall continued to press his attack, and in one final exchange, Marshall retorted with a sharpness that caused Molotov to wince.[60] For the first time, a meeting of the Council of Foreign Ministers was allowed to adjourn without designating a time or place for another meeting.

[57] Clay, *op.cit.*, p. 174.   [58] *Ibid.*

[59] When confronted with the American plan in August, the Russian representative on the Control Commission remarked that "the very appearance of this document is witness to the fact that U.S. and British administrations have taken the road of a complete breaking away from the decisions of the Potsdam conference." *Ibid.*, p. 157.

[60] *Ibid.*, p. 347.

Once again, a failure in diplomacy led to administrative action in Germany. The disruption of the London conference paved the way for what Clay called "the final step"—the establishment of a separate currency and the creation of explicitly political institutions in the Western zones.

If Marshall no longer seemed to be taking the meetings of the foreign ministers seriously, it was because many things had happened between the Moscow and London conferences that combined at last to settle his thinking. Europe suffered a series of calamities during the winter of 1946-47 that set back the progress of recovery and threatened a breakdown in civil order. The continued impasse with the Soviet Union promised to prolong the division of Germany and, in Marshall's view, obstruct the recovery of production. To that extent, it seemed to underscore the political dangers in the crisis.

In June 1947, Marshall delivered the famous commencement address at Harvard in which he announced the program of economic aid that came to be associated with his name. By July the definitive Russian reaction was in, and as Russia prevented Poland, Rumania, and Czechoslovakia from participating in the program, the formation of blocs acquired a new explicitness. Thereafter, Marshall was convinced that a settlement in Europe would depend on the progress of consolidation within the separate blocs. A solution in Germany, if it came, would be the reflection of a battle fought elsewhere, and by other than military means. When the Council of Foreign Ministers broke off its meeting in London, General Clay understood that it marked the beginning of a new engagement, "a competitive struggle, not with arms but with economic resources, with ideas and with ideals."[61]

[61] *Ibid.*, p. 348.

3. COMMENCEMENT 1947: TOWARD A NEW CONCEPT OF AID

IF GREAT POWER unity could have been carried through into the postwar period, the international system might have coincided with the United Nations system. There would have been little need for diplomacy as it was traditionally understood, for there would have been much less need to tailor national power to an understanding of ends, or to measure both against the claims of morality and the interests of the international community. The tensions that gave diplomacy its moral ambiguity were scheduled for extinction in the world of the United Nations Charter. Instead of separate nations seeking their own interests through the cultivation of power, there would be a centralized agency for the enforcement of law. Responsibility would rest with the Security Council of the United Nations under the aegis of "collective security." The armed forces would be composed of national contingents, except in those places where a Great Power was acting within its own sphere of influence. Yet even there, according to the theory, the Great Power was not engaged in the old game of power politics. It was acting instead as a policeman or deputy, and its mission was to enforce the peace on behalf of the Security Council and the community of nations.

Apart from these regional embroilments, diplomacy would be an intramural affair within the United Nations. National interests would still exist, and perhaps in some refined sense it would still be meaningful to talk of foreign policies and commitments. But where policies were previously devised in contemplation of action and sobered with an awareness of risk, the policies in this new world were not like that. They were closer to the strategies of administrative infighting and bargaining; for the promise of the new world was to insulate the international order from the "quivering, precarious balance of power" that Churchill described, and which seemed to be endemic to a system of sovereign nations wielding military power. Involvement in world politics would be emptied of its usual cost in men, material, and even the intellectual effort required in defining the national interest. That was all to be replaced by an international administration of things; the traditional and varied costs would be supplanted by the simple subscription fee for organizational membership.

If the planners of the postwar world did not expect to banish national interests, they could still hope to make the United Nations the principal arena of their confrontation. If nations were forced to work out their interests in this rational and universal framework, there was some reason to believe that the interests themselves might be modified. The thrust of selfishness could be softened, the commands of "self-preservation" could begin to lose their urgency. After a while, the interests of the separate states might be brought into closer harmony with the interests of world order.

But as the division among the former allies came to penetrate every area of international relations, the peculiar claims of the United Nations were also affected. The impartial and "universalistic" criteria of the United Nations—the criteria that made no distinction between friends and enemies, between the decent and the corrupt—were no longer seen as neutral in their political effects. Nor was it so evident any more that they were serving the interests of world order.

An especially seminal experience in this regard came with the American participation in the United Nations Relief and Rehabilitation Administration (UNRRA). The UNRRA presented a good case in point of an international agency using impartial, "nonpolitical" criteria. Relief aid was dispensed to nations on the basis of need and without reference to the character of their political regimes. Despite the fact that the United States contributed a disproportionate share to the support of the UNRRA, it was not in a position to control the policy of the agency; and as one of the founders of the program it did not really expect to exert such influence. But even so, it could be rather galling when a sizable amount of aid went to countries that were actively hostile to the United States, or which were threatening the use of force to alter the postwar balance.

In this respect, the case of Yugoslavia proved particularly vexing. The ruling Communist party in Yugoslavia was at this time the most militant in Europe. In the closing days of the war Tito skirmished with Britain over the control of Trieste; he continued to support the insurgents in Greece; and there were rumors throughout 1946 that he would seize Venezia Giulia. In August, an American transport plane operating on the run between Rome and Vienna was shot down when it lost its way and wandered over Yugoslav territory. Within ten days a similar incident occurred, this time resulting in five American deaths. The survivors were kept prisoners in Belgrade, where they were refused permission to see the American ambassador. One of the passengers, who was an official of the UNRRA, tried to communicate with the representatives of the UNRRA in Belgrade, but his request, too, was denied. Reporting on his conversation with the survivors, Secretary Byrnes later wrote:

> Within an hour after this request was rejected, they looked out the window and saw an American-made locomotive over at the railroad depot with the letters UNRRA printed on it. They knew that 70 per cent of the cost of that locomotive had been furnished by the American taxpayers and the thought contributed little to the comfort of their internment.
>
> The incident [of the shootings] was ended, but it was not obliterated from the minds of the American people. And this, together with the experience with Czechoslovakia [whose government had loaned Rumania $10 million out of a $50 million credit received from the United States], led me to believe that when UNRRA expired, any new appropriations by Congress for foreign relief should be allocated by the United States and should go to those countries who would not denounce us for granting them the relief they asked for.[1]

In September, a State-War-Navy meeting in Washington was discussing possible assistance to Turkey in light of the renewed Soviet demands in August. Still smarting from the Yugoslav affair, Byrnes wired from Paris that the United States might consider helping countries like Greece and Turkey, rather than those nations "who either from helplessness or otherwise are opposed to our principles."[2]

What was building in the Administration, then, was a willingness to break away from the idiom of the United Nations Charter, though not, it was felt, from the ends of the United Nations. There

---

[1] James F. Byrnes, *Speaking Frankly* (New York: Harper and Brothers, 1947), p. 146.

[2] Walter Millis (ed.), *The Forrestal Diaries* (New York: The Viking Press, 1951), p. 210.

was a willingness to take public responsibility for the use of selective political criteria that were geared more directly to the interests of the United States and the American view of the postwar world. And there the matter lay in February 1947, when the British government informed the United States that it would not be able to maintain its forces in Greece. The more immediate result was a program of emergency aid to Greece and Turkey. Beyond that, however, the crisis brought the first official statement of the containment thesis as part of the Truman Doctrine. It was also the first time in public that the American government would justify a course of unilateral action outside the United Nations. In his speech to Congress on March 12, the President restated his support for the United Nations and the universal goal of "peaceful development of nations, free from coercion." But those objectives could not be realized, he said, "unless we [were] willing to help free people to maintain their free institutions and their national integrity against aggressive movements that seek to impose upon them totalitarian regimes."

Within a month, the new course was given a sharper accent with the creation of an American foreign aid program to succeed the UNRRA. While even countries in the Soviet bloc would be eligible for aid, the program would be administered under the control of the United States. The obligations of each country would be set forth in a bilateral agreement with the United States, which would also provide the legal basis for enforcement. There would be direct American supervision over the procurement and distribution of materials to insure that the funds were being used for their intended purpose. In addition, the United States would require reports from the member nations on the production, import, and use of any supplies that might affect their overall needs in relief aid.[3]

A further provision was made at the time for the use of counterpart funds, a device that came into being under the UNRRA and that would have considerable importance later when it was carried over into the Marshall Plan. Under the counterpart procedure, the local funds that accrued from the sale of relief goods were deposited in a special account. The account could be used for further expenditures at the local level, but it could be used only with the consent of the host government and the UNRRA. As they were

[3] See U.S. Department of State, *Bulletin*, XVI, No. 408 (April 27, 1947), pp. 756-57.

originally conceived, the counterpart funds signified a sharing of authority between the local government and the member nations of the UNRRA. But when they were used now in a bilateral framework, the wedge of authority they opened would be filled only by the United States.

Thus the American outlook had altered, and an active, unilateral bias seemed to be taking hold. Once the Greek-Turkish aid program was undertaken, once it was justified in doctrine and reinforced with the scheme of post-UNRRA aid, it was a much shorter step to the Marshall Plan. If internal disorder justified an American assistance program in Greece and Turkey, where the United States previously had no direct responsibilities, was there any less of an interest in Europe, where American forces had fought a major war, and indeed, where American troops were presently stationed?

Concern for the state of Europe mounted with the severe winter of 1946–47. After two successive years of drought, Western Europe suffered an extraordinary wave of storms, floods, and cold that inflicted even heavier damage on the production of food and fuel. The economies of Europe had not yet recovered from the disruptions of the war, and industrial production was still below its prewar level. Governments had been forced, as a result, to depend on the dollar area for the import of materials, such as coal, steel, and machinery, which were desperately needed in reconstruction. And now, with this recent series of disasters, they would have to draw on their dollar reserves to cover such elementary needs as food and fuel.

Before the war, Germany supplied almost 42 percent of the engineering goods, metals, and chemicals in intra-European trade; but now Germany lay weakened and divided. Before the war, the countries of Western Europe could enjoy a surplus of trade with Britain, while the British played the role of balancer and linked European trade to the outside world. At the same time, the British managed to earn enough through trade, investment, and shipping to overcome their own deficit with the Continent. However, the British could no longer play the role of the balancer, at least not in the same way. For they, too, were more dependent on the dollar area for raw materials; and after more than a half-century of neglect, their industrial plant was not geared to competition in the dollar markets.

47

The balance of payments had become a serious problem for the British as early as 1931, but until the war they were able to rely on their "invisible" earnings in shipping and overseas investments to pull them through. Throughout the war, however, the British were forced to draw on their overseas assets in order to cover their debts in the dollar area. The full seriousness of the problem became evident with the termination of Lend-Lease, which only served to bring on the British loan of 1946. The credit of $3.75 billion was to cover a five-year transition period, by the end of which it was expected that the British would overcome their deficit in trade. The five-year period was the time that was usually allowed in the Bretton Woods Agreement for making currency freely convertible in current trade (as distinguished from capital transactions). It was the inspiration of the State Department, though, that the British did not really need the five-year period. With the cushion of the American loan, it was thought that the British could reach convertibility sooner; and so, as part of the loan agreement, they were required to make sterling convertible within a year. When the British tried it, in July 1947, their reserves became dangerously vulnerable. With the dollar depreciating by about 30 percent in the United States, the multi-billion dollar credit seemed to be melting away. At the early rate of withdrawals, the credit figured to be exhausted by September 1949.[4]

The loan turned out, then, to be insufficient, and to some it seemed too isolated a measure for a crisis that was becoming European in scope. The disparity was especially noticeable to George Marshall, who succeeded Byrnes as Secretary of State in January 1947. Whether Marshall was simply dissatisfied with a partial effort, or whether he guessed that partial efforts were likely also to be futile, he was convinced that any useful program would have to deal with Europe as an economic whole. Consequently he ordered a policy review in which the problem was conceived in the broader terms of *European* needs.

Rather than taking the country by surprise, it was decided to test the climate of opinion for a major policy initiative. The task fell to Dean Acheson, who was then Undersecretary of State, to point out the gravity of the situation in Europe and the responsibility that was emerging for the United States. The occasion was a policy speech in Cleveland, Mississippi, on May 7, 1947. With highly

[4] Hugh Dalton, *High Tide and After* (London: Frederick Muller Limited, 1962), pp. 82, 84, 220-21.

48

vivid language Acheson reviewed the consequences of the "planned scientific destruction of the enemy's resources" that had been carried out on both sides during the war: Factories were demolished, "transportation systems wrecked, populations scattered and on the borderline of starvation, and long-established business and trading connections disrupted." In agriculture, the fields were laid bare, and there was a lack of the machinery and fertilizer that were needed to revive them. The dislocations gave rise to a vicious cycle. The European economies were not producing the necessary quantities of farm machinery and fertilizer; nor, on the other hand, were they generating the stock of consumer goods that could elicit production from the farms. As exchange reserves were spent on mere subsistence needs, smaller and smaller proportions were available for the import of basic reconstruction materials from the dollar area.

Contrasted with this picture of spreading crisis was the state of the American economy. Untouched by the destruction of the war, the American industrial plant was left intact and enlarged. Agriculture was flourishing to yield problems of surpluses, while American production was operating at an annual rate of $210 billion. There was no doubt, then, as to where the principal source of supply lay in the materials Europe needed for reconstruction. Nor was there very much doubt on where the principal source of liquidity was in reviving European trade.

We estimate [said Acheson] that we will receive commodities and services from abroad to the value of about eight billion dollars. This is just about half as much as we are exporting. This volume of imports is equal to about two weeks' work of all the factories, farms, mines, and laborers of the United States, and consists largely of things which are not produced in this country in sufficient quantity. We wish that the imports were larger, but the war-devastated world is just not able to supply more.

The difference between the value of the goods and services which foreign countries must buy from the United States this year and the value of the goods and services they are able to supply to us this year will therefore amount to the huge sum of about eight billion dollars.

How are foreigners going to get the U. S. dollars necessary to cover this huge difference? And how are they going to get the U. S. dollars to cover a likely difference of nearly the same amount next year? . . .

The facts of international life . . . mean that the United States is going to have to undertake further emergency financing of foreign purchases if foreign countries are to continue to buy in 1948 and 1949 the commodities which they need to sustain life and at the same time rebuild their economies.[5]

Acheson reviewed the various programs in which the United States was already participating, but he suggested that the present crisis was beyond the means of existing programs and agencies. Quite apparently, the United States was prepared to entertain something vastly more ambitious:

Requests for further United States aid may reach us through the International Bank, or through the Export-Import Bank, *or they may be of a type which existing national and international institutions are not equipped to handle* and therefore may be made directly through diplomatic channels. But we know now that further financing, beyond existing authorizations, is going to be needed. No other country is able to bridge the gap in commodities or dollars.[6]

While Acheson defended the concept of foreign aid in terms of "our duty and our privilege as human beings," he was even more emphatic in pointing out that the government was pursuing the policy "chiefly as a matter of national self-interest." And thus, apart from the humanitarian value of the program, the United States would have its own ends in view, and it would tend to be more selective in its approach:

Since world demand exceeds our ability to supply, we are going to have to concentrate our emergency assistance in areas where it will be most effective in building world political and economic stability, in promoting human freedom and democratic institutions, in fostering liberal trading policies, and in strengthening the authority of the United Nations.

In a revealing passage, Acheson noted that this selective approach was "in keeping with the policy announced by President Truman in his special message . . . on aid to Greece and Turkey."

[5] McGeorge Bundy, *The Pattern of Responsibility* (Boston: Houghton Mifflin, 1952), pp. 48-49. The speech is reprinted also in U.S. Department of State, *Bulletin*, XVI, No. 411 (May 18, 1947), pp. 991-95.

[6] Bundy, *op.cit.*, p. 49. Emphasis added.

50

Free peoples who are seeking to preserve their independence and democratic institutions and human freedoms against totalitarian pressures, either internal or external, will receive top priority for American reconstruction aid.[7]

Less than a month later, on June 5, Marshall made the official offer of aid in his commencement address at Harvard. He was able to build then on Acheson's description of the situation and argue with even greater vigor that the only practical policy was a comprehensive one. "Assistance," said Marshall, "must not be on a piecemeal basis as various crises develop. Any assistance that this Government may render in the future should provide a cure rather than a mere palliative." The need was for an integrated program rather than a collection of random or isolated measures. If the problem of recovery was European in its dimensions, then it stood to reason that any effective program would depend upon a thorough coordination of resources in Europe.[8] Here Marshall found some added wisdom in the propriety of nonintervention. Not only was it presumptuous for the United States to define a program for the Europeans, but there were serious limits on what the United States could accomplish on its own without the efforts of the Europeans themselves. Thus, before the United States would intrude itself in Europe, there would have to be "some agreement among the countries of Europe as to the requirements of the situation and the part those countries themselves will take":

It would be neither fitting nor efficacious for this Government to undertake to draw up unilaterally a program designed to place Europe on its feet economically. This is the business of the Europeans. The initiative, I think, must come from Europe.[9]

[7] *Ibid.*

[8] As George Kennan remembered, "We had serious doubts about the success of any movement toward European recovery that rested merely on a series of uncoordinated national programs; we considered that one of the long-term deficiencies of the European economy as a whole was its excessive fragmentation. . . . By insisting on a joint approach, we hoped to force the Europeans to begin to think like Europeans, and not like nationalists, in their approach to the economic problems of the continent." George Kennan, *Memoirs, 1925-50* (Boston: Little, Brown, and Company, 1967), p. 337.

[9] U.S. Department of State, *Bulletin*, XVI, No. 415 (June 15, 1947), p. 1160. It is now confirmed that the language in this passage came from George Kennan. Indeed, despite the many claims of paternity for the Marshall Plan—and despite Kennan's own demurrer—it is now clear that it

As far as anyone could tell, Marshall's invitation was open to Communist countries as well, since there was no attempt in the speech to limit the definition of Europe. In this respect Marshall made a significant revision in the ground rules set down by Acheson a month earlier. There was no retreat from the view that distinctions had to be made between countries that were friendly or hostile to the ends of the program. The difference was in the mode of selection, or in the way in which entrance into the program would be regulated. Acheson talked of *concentrating* scarce resources and setting priorities among nations. It was the United States that would define the standards of the program and determine who was more or less qualified for American aid. But now Marshall left the question open. What he proposed instead was to posit the conditions of collaboration and leave it to the separate nations to define themselves in or out of the program. "Our policy," said Marshall "is directed not against any country or doctrine but against hunger, poverty, desperation and chaos. . . . Any government that is willing to assist in the task of recovery will find full cooperation, I am sure, on the part of the United States Government. Any government which maneuvers to block the recovery of other countries cannot expect help from us."[10]

This change in emphasis came about at the end of May, when George Kennan and his staff pleaded for a less divisive policy. In the opinion of the Policy Planning staff, the Communist activities in

---

was Kennan who was responsible for the principal ideas that gave the program its character. See, generally, Kennan, *op.cit.*, ch. 14, and particularly pp. 335-45.

[10] *Ibid.* Admittedly, something of Marshall's ecumenical spirit was present in Acheson's Cleveland speech: "When Secretary of State Marshall returned from the recent meeting of the Council of Foreign Ministers in Moscow he did not talk to us about ideologies or armies. He talked about food and fuel and their relation to industrial production, and the relation of industrial production to the organization of Europe, and the relation of the organization of Europe to the peace of the world."

The difference, however, was in the explicit connection Acheson made to the Greek-Turkish program, which set the United States in opposition to all totalitarian movements. Marshall maintained the same practical sense of a distinction between regimes, but he clearly backed away from ideology as the prime test for inclusion in the program. It should be said, though, that Acheson was one of the most important men in the Administration who urged the shift to a more open and less ideological stance. See Joseph H. Jones, *The Fifteen Weeks* (New York: The Viking Press, 1955), pp. 252-53.

Europe were threatening, but they were not at the root of the problem.

> The Communists [said the staff] are exploiting the European crisis and . . . further Communist successes would create serious danger to American security. [But the] American effort in aid to Europe should be directed not to the combatting of communism as such but to the restoration of the economic health and vigor of European society. It should aim, in other words, not to combat communism but the economic maladjustment which makes European society vulnerable to exploitation by any and all totalitarian movements. . . .[11]

However, the most important reason for the change was that American policymakers were still reluctant to accept the responsibility for dividing the world into blocs. Marshall himself was originally skeptical of a program that was open to the whole of Europe. But according to Joseph Jones, Acheson argued that "it would be a colossal error for the United States to put itself in the position where it could be blamed for the division of Europe."[12] That advice was substantially echoed by Kennan, who insisted, as he put it later, "that if anyone was to divide the European continent, it should be the Russians, with their response, not we with our offer."[13] A short time later, as Jones reported, the Secretary was firmly in agreement with his advisers that "a proposal to aid European reconstruction would have to be addressed to all Europe— that he would have to take a calculated risk both as regards the Russians and Congress."[14]

As for the risks of Soviet participation, they were probably never as real as they were made out to be. The conditions laid down by Marshall might have seemed reasonable enough, but they were not entirely neutral in their consequences for the Soviet Union. In disclaiming political considerations, Marshall put himself squarely on the side of economic recovery. The urgency of recovery justified whatever efficiency demanded, and what efficiency demanded, said Marshall, was a high level of coordination among the Europeans themselves. At the very least, coordination would involve a vast exchange of information. The substance of planning throughout the program would require comprehensive data on national develop-

[11] Quoted in Kennan, *op.cit.*, p. 336.
[12] Jones, *loc.cit.*   [13] Kennan, *op.cit.*, p. 343.
[14] Jones, *loc.cit.*

ment plans and the state of capital and consumer needs. To reveal information of this kind to other nations was to lay bare the strengths and weaknesses of a national economy. Further, by linking internal decisions to an outside program of aid, by opening investment plans to the scrutiny of a supranational group, and finally, by merging one's economy in a multilateral trading bloc, one was admitting outsiders to an unusual degree of influence in determining the course of the national economy. It is hard to see, in fact, how the Soviet leaders could have entered such an intimate relation with the West without accepting some basic change in their regime.

It might have been, of course, that as long as the United States held its monopoly on the atomic bomb, the Russians would have always felt too vulnerable to participate. Even so, one would have had to believe that the Soviet leaders were willing to give up their monopoly in the control of information and the direction of their economy. But on the other hand, if the atomic bomb was not the most decisive consideration, and if Marshall's conditions were in fact reasonable and necessary to the ends of European recovery, one would have to acknowledge that the ultimate barrier to reconciliation lay in the Soviet regime itself.

Moreover, all of this was well understood in the State Department at the time the decision was being formed.[15] That did not mean, however, that the invitation was deceptive. The Soviet Union and its satellites were important producers of the food and raw materials that Western Europe needed. A revival of East-West trade could have reduced the burden on the United States and relieved some of the pressure on the Europeans for exports to the dollar area. Therefore, Russian participation offered some immediate economic benefits, and there was the added possibility of subjecting the Soviet regime to pressures that could have been even more beneficial in the long run. Thus Kennan urged Marshall to "play it straight"—to make the offer an open one and then, if necessary, see how the Soviet Union could fit in.[16]

In no sense was a trap laid for the Russians, for the implications of membership were as clear to them as to anyone else. The initial Soviet response was a denunciation of Marshall's conditions, which were clearly seen as making inroads into national sovereignty.[17] But

[15] See Jones, *op.cit.*, p. 253.   [16] *Ibid.*

[17] See the Soviet statement of June 29, 1947, reprinted in Alvin Z. Rubin-

the Russians were also willing to discuss the matter on the possibility, perhaps, that the terms might have been negotiable. On June 27, Molotov led a high-level delegation to the Big Three conference in Paris, where they met with representatives from Britain and France to discuss the American proposal. The Russians walked out of the conference three days later, when they found that the Americans would not yield to their demand for collaboration and the exchange of information on investment decisions.[18] After that, the understanding of the Soviet leaders was registered in the line of their public attack on the Marshall Plan. The program was vilified as an effort of American capitalism to destroy socialism abroad by intervening in the economic decisions of sovereign nations. It was also denounced as a device for heading off a depression in the United States by dumping goods in Europe and capturing new markets for American products.[19]

After the deadlock of the Big Three, it was decided to call a general European conference for all potential members. The Russians announced regrets for Poland, Yugoslavia, and Rumania. The Czechs were in a delicate position, but they decided to send a delegation, until Premier Gottwald was called suddenly to Moscow. From Russia Gottwald telephoned instructions for his government to refuse the call to Paris, explaining that "acceptance of the invitation might be construed as an action against the Soviet Union."

Sixteen nations, however, did accept the invitation to Paris, where they formed the Committee for European Economic Cooperation (CEEC).[20] The committee met in Paris from July 12 to September 22, preparing estimates and determining goals. At the

---

stein (ed.), *The Foreign Policy of the Soviet Union* (New York: Random House, 1960), pp. 232-33.

[18] The Russians had proposed that the United States announce the exact amount of aid it was willing to grant, and each nation would then work out its own surveys and estimates.

[19] A more scholarly Marxist statement on the Marshall Plan (though still rather polemical) can be found in J. J. Joseph, "European Recovery and United States Aid," *Science and Society*, XII, No. 3 (Summer 1948), pp. 293-383. See also Andrei Vyshinsky's interpretation of the Marshall Plan before the United Nations General Assembly in Rubinstein, *op.cit.*, pp. 234-35.

[20] The sixteen member nations were Britain, France, Italy, Austria, Belgium, Denmark, Greece, Iceland, Ireland, Luxembourg, the Netherlands, Norway, Portugal, Sweden, Switzerland, and Turkey.

end, a report was issued in which the members pledged themselves to mutual cooperation in three classes of activities: the increase of production, the stabilization of currencies, and the enlargement of cooperation. More specifically, cooperation would involve measures to promote the free movement of goods and persons across national borders; the establishment of a multilateral trading system; and the pooling of resources where it was immediately feasible (e.g., in the production of steel and electrical energy). In addition, the committee set production targets in agriculture, coal, steel, and electricity.[21]

Simultaneously, the Administration was moving to build support at home for the new program. In June, the President appointed a committee under Edwin Nourse, the chairman of the Council of Economic Advisors, which was to consider the domestic supply situation and the general capacity of the economy. A committee was appointed under Secretary of the Interior Krug to gauge the impact of the program on natural resources, and particularly on oil and coal. With prodding from Senator Vandenberg, the President also named a committee under Secretary of Commerce Harriman that was composed of representatives from business, labor, and other nonofficial groups. Still, there was some dissatisfaction in Congress on confining the fact-finding process to the Administration; and so the House created a Select Committee on Foreign Aid under the leadership of Christian Herter that would go abroad and make an independent study.

The estimates of the CEEC and the Administration put the total cost of the program at approximately $22 billion over four years. The Administration decided to yield to the conservatism of the Harriman committee—and the anticipated reaction of Congress— and reduce the overall estimate to $17 billion. If the reduction of a speculative figure could soften some of the opposition to the program, then it seemed to be a worthwhile compromise, if indeed it was a compromise at all. For as Vandenberg argued, the overall figure had to be tentative; and it could always be enlarged later if the venture proved successful and the program managed to attract more support in Congress.

Besides, whatever promised to complicate the issue and delay the passage of the bill threatened to injure the substantive interests at stake in Europe. For the Administration the crisis was here and

[21] See the statement by the Rapporteur General of the CEEC in U.S. Department of State, *Bulletin*, XVII, No. 431 (October 5, 1947), pp. 681-83.

now, and events were moving quickly. At the end of August, Secretary of Defense Forrestal was informed by Robert Lovett, the Undersecretary of State, that a policy paper had been prepared dealing with American alternatives in the event of a Communist victory in Greece. In September, Forrestal and Lovett were considering similar questions, this time on the possible formation of a Communist regime in the north of Italy.[22] As for Marshall, he was becoming exasperated with the Soviet Union over Germany— the dispute on the Potsdam agreement, the continued extraction of reparations from current production, the constant stalling on the treaty of peace. Before he embarked in November for the London conference of Foreign Ministers, the Secretary of State told an audience in Chicago that these differences stemmed from a "direct clash between the national interests" of the United States and the Soviet Union. He was certain that the tensions would not abate as long as instability in Europe continued to offer a temptation to adventure. In that case, the European Recovery Program would hold the key to the diplomatic conflict and to the future course of relations with the Soviet Union. "If Europe is restored as a solvent and vigorous community," said Marshall, "this issue will have been decided and the disturbing conflict between ourselves and the Soviets, insofar as Europe is concerned, will lessen."[23]

After meeting frustration again in London, his belief was confirmed that any future settlement would await the outcome of the current crisis. Explaining the impasse in December, Marshall declared that:

> ... in the war struggle Europe was in a large measure shattered. As a result a political vacuum was created, and until this vacuum has been filled by the restoration of a healthy European community, it does not appear possible that paper agreements can assure a lasting peace. Agreements between sovereign states are generally the reflection and not the cause of genuine settlements.[24]

The diplomatic situation was deteriorating, and the burden of response was being loaded, of all places, on an economic assistance program; for the United States was still operating in the framework

[22] Millis, *op.cit.*, pp. 307, 318.
[23] U.S. Department of State, *Bulletin*, XVII, No. 439 (November 30, 1947), p. 1025.
[24] *Ibid.*, No. 433 (December 28, 1947), p. 1247.

57

of demobilization. Marshall complained that he was being "pressed constantly, particularly when in Moscow, by radio message after radio message to give the Russians hell."

> At that time [he observed], my facilities for giving them hell—and I am a soldier and know something about the ability to give hell—was 1 1/3 divisions over the entire United States. That is quite a proposition when you deal with somebody with over 260 and you have 1 1/3. . . .[25]

Yet, despite the added urgency of the economic program, it was too late in the year to get Congressional action on the Marshall Plan. A program as ambitious as this could not be bulled through Congress. The various study committees would have to make their reports, and there would have to be extensive hearings before the foreign relations committees of both houses, followed by the floor debates and the appropriations hearings. A great many questions remained to be answered; a good number, indeed, were still to be conceived. The Administration's only choice was to seek an emergency appropriation for interim aid, which Congress granted fairly quickly. After that, the main task was to plan the program itself and prepare for the Congressional hearings.

[25] Quoted in John C. Sparrow, *History of Personnel Demobilization in the United States Army* (Washington: Office of the Chief of Military History, Department of the Army, 1951), p. 380.

4. CALCULATIONS

I

IN THE AFTERMATH of Marshall's speech at Harvard, the structure of Executive planning reflected the current Administration view of how the program itself would be administered—a vast complex of consultation between agencies, with a leadership nucleus in the State Department. To some extent, the planning of specific programs was held in abeyance until the Select Committee of the House, the Committee of European Economic Cooperation (CEEC), and the assorted Presidential committees could bring in their reports. These reports, however, were not expected until the late summer or early fall of 1947. In the meantime, the various Executive departments could estimate their own participation in the program and lay the groundwork for their future claims.

The President indicated his own position on the control of the program rather early when he delegated responsibility to Secretary Marshall in organizing the preparations in the Executive. Marshall divided his own responsibilities in turn among three committees, the chief of which was an Advisory Steering Committee headed by Robert Lovett. In addition to the State Department, the committee ranged widely to represent the President's staff, War, Navy, Commerce, Agriculture, Interior, and the Budget Bureau. When the estimates of the CEEC were made available in September, this was the group that would activate the Executive machinery in substantive program planning; and in some measure, therefore, its composition reflected the existing consensus at the time as to who had a legitimate interest in the program.

The earliest planning, however, started informally in June under the direction of Willard Thorp, who was then the Assistant Secretary of State for Economic Affairs. But by July, the planning process had extended far beyond the State Department, and it was becoming increasingly more specialized and regular.[1] The Execu-

[1] For an account of the evolution in planning and the growing articulation of the administrative machinery, see Carrol S. Hinman to S. S. Sheppard,

tive Committee on Economic Foreign Policy divided into subgroups to consider, for example, the relation of ERP to the United Nations and other international organizations, the requirement in domestic economic controls, and the problems of obtaining strategic materials. The National Advisory Council considered questions that bore on international financing—the revision of the European exchange rates, the possibilities for a multilateral payments system, and the feasibility of using loans as well as grant aid. In addition, there were various specialized committees on food, coal, shipping, and petroleum; and all the while the State-War-Navy coordinating committee was still available to deal with larger problems of a political and military nature.

In short, interdepartmental planning seemed to be working quite well. As a potential pattern of operation it seemed so acceptable that it promised to continue into the future. What made this pattern seem natural was the fact that the relevant skills were widely dispersed within the government. In Commerce, the Office of International Trade could contribute figures on production and the flow of industrial commodities. Agriculture could estimate farm production while its Office of Foreign Agricultural Relations could project some comparable figures on the situation in Europe. The Labor Department could present statistics on worker productivity, the Maritime Commission could argue its view of postwar shipping conditions, and Treasury could offer some counsel on the methods of finance and procurement.

But if the interdependence of skills made cooperation feasible, it was the very strong interest of the agencies in the program itself that made the discussion productive. Almost every consulting agency could find a vital interest here, either because it possessed some relevant expertise, or because its own programs were very likely to be affected.

At the end of the war, for example, Congress authorized the President to delegate export controls to the Secretary of Commerce for the sake of achieving a fuller coordination. While the preparations for the Marshall Plan were getting under way in July 1947, Congress reaffirmed the earlier decision by extending all the con-

---

July 16, 1947; Sheppard to The Director (Webb), September 19, 1947; Staff memorandum, "Outline of Memorandum on Marshall Plan" (n.d.); Bureau of the Budget, Series 39.18.

trols, except those relating to rubber, and reemphasizing the focal position of the Commerce Department. This subject of export controls proved to be a critical one in the structuring of the European Recovery Program, and considerably more will be said about it later. For the present it is sufficient to note that there were three principal controls: the assignment of export priorities in order to facilitate the export of certain materials; the allocation of scarce commodities among competing domestic uses; and the licensing of goods slated for export. The vigor and effectiveness of enforcement was far from uniform, and despite the commitment to integration the authority over controls was still more widely diffused than the statutes would have suggested. The enforcement machinery for export priorities and domestic allocations at this time was practically nonexistent—for domestic allocations, two or three attorneys and a few hearing examiners. Both of these controls over private business were troublesome, and their executors in Commerce had already lost whatever enthusiasm they might have had for enforcing the regulations. There was a perceptible division in the department over the desirability of maintaining controls, but the export control function was still vital, and what was more important, it had the continuing support of Secretary Harriman. In contrast to the other control programs, export licensing had the advantage of a large staff—approximately 130 people in July, and scheduled to rise to 180 or 190. The expectation at this time was that the Marshall Plan would take a sizable chunk out of a domestic economy characterized by scarcities. Thus, the diversion of goods for export to Marshall Plan countries would have added to the inflationary pressures of an economy that was already rather tight, and in that event the management of export controls would have become even more important politically.

The reign of the Commerce Department over export controls was qualified with the addition of an Advisory Committee that included other agencies with interests in the field, principally State, Agriculture, and Interior, along with the Office of Defense Transportation. The earlier division of authority between Commerce and Agriculture raised questions of consistency in policy and enforcement, and it was largely on that account that Commerce interpreted the renewal of its authority as a mandate for closer surveillance over exports in general. But at the same time it saw no reason to depart from its current practice, in which the substantive work on food exports was delegated to the Department of Agriculture.[2] Agriculture would still determine the quotas for foods under allocation, and Commerce would simply issue the export licenses. Further, Agriculture would continue to fix quotas and handle the actual licensing on import controls, most notably in the case of fats and oils. Altogether, then, it was a comfortable working relation, and one that neither party had an interest in disturbing. After a conference at the Department of Agriculture in October, a member of the Budget Bureau staff reported that:

> Agriculture is reasonably well satisfied with the arrangement but recognizes that it exists only because of the tacit agreement of the Secretary of Commerce. Under the Second Decontrol Act the Secretary of Commerce, they concede, could take over these functions and operate them himself or could issue regulations governing the Secretary of Agriculture. . . . It is their hope that the present arrangement will not be altered, since they feel it is working satisfactorily.[3]

It was evident then to the people in Agriculture that the problem of reorganizing for the Marshall Plan threatened some rather serious dislocations. Along with everyone else they began to recognize the very real stake they had in the present distribution of functions in the Executive. Therefore, when Secretary Anderson put in his bid for a role in export controls and procurement, he was not thinking in terms of efficiency, or even of the possible interests of his department abroad. Rather, he emphasized the significance of these controls as instruments for modulating the impact of the foreign aid on the domestic farm situation. As the Secretary wrote to the Director of the Budget Bureau:

> The emphasis on agricultural commodities and foods of many kinds for the purposes of the European Recovery Program makes it desirable that control over agricultural commodities and food be with the Department of Agriculture, as during the war period. The centralization in this Department of authority in this respect is necessary *in order that we may be enabled to coordinate activities under the European Recovery Program*

[2] R. L. Hirshberg, Memorandum, October 6, 1947, Bureau of the Budget, Series 39.18.

[3] Memorandum on Conference at the Department of Agriculture, October 16, 1947, Bureau of the Budget, Series 39.18.

with our domestic program. These domestic programs involve the acquisition and disposition of large quantities of agricultural commodities.[4]

The Treasury had already been assured that the National Advisory Council would be formally involved in the approval of loans. The Commerce Department, for its part, knew that its own participation was guaranteed because of export controls. Thomas Blaisdell, the head of the Office of International Trade, insisted in fact that the program would be almost entirely one of regulating exports, so that little more than a staff of 200 professionals would probably be necessary in the United States.[5] Even if procurement under the program was performed, as State assumed for a while, by government rather than private agencies, the function could be handled by ongoing units like the Commodity Credit Corporation or the Bureau of Federal Supply. If procurement was confined to private channels of trade—as the Treasury preferred—then it was expected that export controls would be even more decisive.[6] But either way, the argument ran, the Marshall Plan would not require much more than an enlarged staff effort. The separate agencies were willing to contribute their facilities, and as long as their prime responsibilities in their own spheres of operation were recognized, they were more than willing to accept State Department leadership on the questions of foreign policy. The existing arrangements seemed perfectly workable, then, and for a while it looked as though the program might well go forward as an interdepartmental effort. After all, this same coalition of agencies had been able to respond to the worsening conditions in France, Italy, and Austria with the program of Interim aid, and it had managed to keep the pipeline of relief aid going without so much as an interruption in the planning for the major program.

Thus, at an early stage in the preparations for the Marshall Plan, it was not flatly assumed that a new administrative agency would be needed. And as late as December 1947, there were many participants who regarded the movement toward a new organizational unit as a serious mistake, both administratively and politically. By

[4] Anderson to Webb, November 7, 1947, Bureau of the Budget, Series 39.18. Emphasis added.
[5] Memorandum on interdepartmental conference, December 1, 1947, Bureau of the Budget, Series 39.18.
[6] S. S. Sheppard to Webb, September 23, 1947, Bureau of the Budget, Series 39.18.

the middle of December, though, the organizational issue was no longer in the hands of the Executive. The organizational idea had evolved from interagency cooperation under State Department leadership in foreign policy, to a new administrative unit under State Department direction, and finally, to an autonomous agency, vested with Cabinet status and divorced from the State Department. In a matter of months, a highly integrated and apparently congenial system of interagency collaboration had been disrupted. From any standpoint it was a remarkable development, not simply because of the sharp organizational changes in themselves, but also because the partners, so confident and efficient before, had completely lost control of the organizational issue and, indeed, lost the ability even to communicate with one another in anything but the most veiled gestures.

What proved to be the unstable factor in the situation was the leadership of the State Department. Unfortunately, in the passing of twenty years, the bureaucratic maneuvers have become caricatures in the minds of most people who were on the scene at the time. In retrospect the events grow in drama and intensity. Almost uniformly the picture emerges of a truculent and vengeful Congress determined to take the Marshall Plan away from the State Department—and of a State Department resisting vigorously to the end for the integrity of American foreign policy. The documents, however, present a version that is far less dramatic, but considerably more ironic and human; and the truth of the matter goes a great deal deeper than our standing images of bureaucratic power-seeking.

II

As early as August 1947, proposals for a corporate form of organization were acquiring sufficient currency in Washington that the State Department was beginning to take them seriously. The response of the department at this time was interesting for what it revealed in the way of a determination to maintain control of the program, but also for what it readily acknowledged about the condition of State's relations with Congress. In assessing the corporate plan, one analyst in the department was frank to concede that "Congress would be more willing to appropriate money if 'operations' were separated from the State Department." Still, as long as the main alternative to the State Department was a government corporation, State was inclined to dismiss the threat of separation as a practical matter. "In view of Congressional antipathy to new corporations," the same writer went on, "or appropriations over which they do not have close control," the corporation would not look as inviting.[7]

The most decisive point for the department however, was the danger of cutting operations off from effective policy control:

> Separation of agencies means division in policy making. Theoretically the State Department could decide the policy and the operating agency carry it out. Actually policy is made by operation to a great extent. Our experience in occupied areas and in war-time agencies illustrates this. There are already too many agencies crowding the foreign field.[8]

Whatever their other mistakes in political judgment, at least it could be said for the men at State that they harbored no illusions on what the consequences would be in separating the Marshall Plan from the State Department. But for that very reason it was prudent to plan for contingencies, just in case the program *were* taken out of State. The question was raised, then, as to what organizational arrangements would be most suitable to the ends of program if the department had to settle for something worse than its first choice. What emerged as a primary goal was flexibility—the capacity to adjust resources quickly in response to a fluid political situation. This theme was to carry through the preparations and bargaining as the focus of the State Department's maneuvers. The immediate legislative strategy was to avoid rigid limitations and seek a substantial contingency fund. Thus, if the calculations of the department proved wrong, and a corporation was in fact established, there were still better and worse positions in retreat:

—It would have been better, for example, if the corporation were attached to a regular department—that is, if it were brought

[7] R. P. Bramble to Phillips, "Use of Separate Agency or Corporation to Administer Operation[s] in ERP" (August 1947), p. 1, copy in Bureau of the Budget, Series 39.18. The department was willing to admit the advantages of using a corporation as a specialized instrument in the foreign field, as for example in preclusive buying or in the dumping of surpluses. But as Bramble very aptly observed, the issue did not hinge on the existence or absence of profits. More critically, it was a matter of whether the "prices charged for commodities and services determine their allocation among recipients rather than some social criteria coupled with nominal charges."

[8] *Ibid.*, p. 1.

within the existing network of relations among the agencies, where it could be controlled more easily.

—If it were brought into a regular department, it would have been better to place the new unit under Treasury. Since the interests of the Treasury in the foreign field were almost exclusively financial rather than political, it could be expected to acquiesce more readily to the leadership of the State Department. Furthermore, Treasury had no close relation to any of the "special commodity interests" that might have been tempted to exploit the program.

—The services of other agencies were to be used as much as possible. The operations could be contained then along lines very close to the existing pattern of collaboration. Consistent with this purpose, also, there might be restrictions on the life of the agency— provisions, incidentally, which could make the program more palatable to Congress and private industry.[9]

If State tended to doubt that Congress would be a source of wholesale obstruction, other people in the government were less confident. Roger Nelson of the Fiscal Division of the Budget Bureau despaired of getting any program out of the Congress that involved an annual expenditure as high as $5 billion, regardless of who administered it. In September he began to circulate a proposal to finance the program entirely with federally guaranteed bonds.[10] Averell Harriman warned in November that the insistence on keeping the Marshall Plan in the State Department might lead to some form of mixed Executive-Legislative board to direct the program.[11] By this time, though, Marshall had seen the writing on the wall, and he decided himself in favor of a new organization, or more precise-

[9] *Ibid.*, pp. 4-5.

[10] Roger Nelson to Arthur Smithies via Everett Hagen, "Federally Guaranteed Obligations and the Marshall Plan," September 10, 1947, Bureau of the Budget, Series 39.18. Under Nelson's plan, the program would have been administered by a new corporation or the Export-Import Bank. The corporation could charge insurance fees to the foreign borrowers and in this way build up a reserve that could be used in covering defaults. Budgetary expenditure could then be withheld as a last resort, in the event that the reserves were exhausted. Nelson's scheme ran into the opposition against doing any more large-scale loan financing. However, his idea on the insurance reserve and his method for avoiding budgetary expenditures were carried forward into the legislation.

[11] James Webb to Truman, November 10, 1947, Bureau of the Budget, Series 39.18.

ly, a distinct administrative entity within the State Department, rather than an independent agency.

Marshall's public commitment to a new administrative unit came in his November testimony on the Interim Aid bill. Three aspects of that statement warrant particular notice for the purpose of fixing his meaning. First, the term "independent agency" was never used; he referred only to a "new organization." Second, the acceptance of a new unit was stated as a tightly drawn counterpoint, and it was placed, quite consciously, at the end of a very carefully constructed text in which Marshall challenged the appropriateness of a large agency. He started from the view of sixteen European nations that were highly conscious of their sovereignty, and that displayed a great diversity in their cultures and economies. Most of them had already accumulated the skills needed for running modern economies without outside aid. In Marshall's estimate they were quite capable of diagnosing their own problems and carrying out their own measures of correction. They did not need skills and advice so much as dollars and commodities. "Consequently there is no necessity of our becoming deeply involved in their own economic operations," and therefore, he argued, "seasoned judgment must constantly guide us against improper intrusion and against unfriendly distortions of our activities."

There was no need, then, for an organization geared to extensive operations within Europe. Similarly, the Marshall Plan provided no justification for a giant governmental procurement program working outside the normal channels of trade. A program of that kind said Marshall, would "constitute a threat to private enterprise in this country and to sovereign governments in Europe." Nor was there a need to supersede the established Executive agencies. Although the operations were complex, they were, in most cases, extensions of "activities now being performed by a number of government agencies in cooperation with business, agricultural, and labor groups." All these considerations, along with the requirements of working in a vast interdepartmental program, counseled simplicity in administration. It was at this point, after making the case for a taut administration, that Marshall added: "The scope and importance of this program, however, warrant the creation of a new organization to provide central direction and leadership."

Thus, the idea of a new organization was introduced very circumspectly. Marshall was nothing if not a precise man, and his language left no doubt about the exact status of the new agency.

The key point was in Marshall's denial that the agency would have any autonomous purposes of its own beyond the perimeter of foreign policy. The fact that the agency would deal with an economic program was of no consequence on this issue. Marshall insisted that the political and economic aspects of the program were "inseparably woven," and for that reason political supervision would have to be continuous.

> This program is not merely a commercial operation. It represents a major segment of our foreign policy. Day in and day out its operations will affect and be affected by foreign policy judgments. . . . This program will affect our relationships with the ERP countries in matters far beyond the outline of the program itself. Its administration must therefore be fully responsive to our foreign policy. The Administrator must be subject to the direction and control of the Secretary of State on decisions and actions affecting our foreign policy.

The new agency, said Marshall, would have to work closely with the State Department in the "determination of country programs, the assessment of individual projects, and many other matters"— in short, in its most essential substantive activities.[12]

Yet Marshall was taking a chance in accepting the principle of a new administrative agency. When he advanced the claim to govern the new unit because its activities "affected" foreign policy, the same formula could apply to Commerce and Agriculture in their foreign operations. And once he opened the issue to argument in this way, he opened himself also to the objection that not everything this agency did was "foreign policy" in the traditional sense. It was arguable then that the agency might bring something distinctive to the problem of foreign assistance that was not strictly part of diplomacy, and which deserved some greater insulation from the pressures of foreign policy.

As it turned out, these nuances in the language and meaning of legislation were at the center of the debates going on in the State Department. The first draft to appear was on November 2, and it contained no mention of a separate agency. Instead, responsibility was assigned to the President, with the authority to determine the

[12] U.S. Senate Committee on Foreign Relations and House Committee on Foreign Affairs, *Hearings, Interim Aid for Europe*, 80th Cong., 1st Sess., 1947, pp. 2-10, at p. 5. Cited hereafter as *Interim Aid Hearings*.

administrative organizations of the program by using any agency of the government. A draft of November 6 brought the first mention of a separate agency, the Economic Cooperation Administration (ECA). Section 4 of that draft provided that all those functions of the ECA which "involve the foreign policy of the United States shall be performed subject to the direction and control of the Secretary of State." Thus, it seemed to adopt the view of weaker State Department control by describing an agency with some functions apart from foreign policy. However, a draft of the next day, November 7, altered that language again, this time emphasizing the subordination of the ECA Administrator to the Secretary of State: The Administrator "shall be subject to the direction and control of the Secretary of State and . . . shall perform such other functions as the Secretary of State may designate." It was emphasized that the ECA was subject to the direction and control of the Secretary of State "except as otherwise specified."

Now, against the backdrop of these alterations, Marshall made his recommendation of a new agency on November 10. The context suggested that the preference was again for the stronger version, yet the additions of November 7, which would have made this meaning unmistakable, were left out. It would seem, then, that Marshall was leaning toward the concept of fuller State Department control, but that he was reluctant to spell out his intentions too fully. It was conceivable also that Marshall was trying to deflect responsibility from his own department through the creation of a new agency, while at the same time retaining an important measure of policy direction. Either way, Marshall was engaged in a very subtle game, played with fine shades of meaning. It was a game, too, that could be very tricky to control. All this tinkering with language carried grave risks, and while the State Department might have been content to keep turning over phrases, the people in the Budget Bureau began to grow uneasy. As everyone understood, the language in the law distributed power; but before that language was settled, there were dangers in being too casual in throwing phrases about in public. To speak of State Department control over "aspects," or over activities "affecting" foreign policy, was to convey a much different view of authority than that contained in the expression of State Department "direction and control." As Donald Stone of the Budget Bureau wrote to Robert Lovett:

While the language does not sound very different the end result administratively is vastly different. In one case the Secretary of State would be forced to use remote control methods and be put in a negative position. . . . In the other, the vague relationships and the duality of responsibility would be eliminated and the Secretary could by direct action secure the working arrangements and processes that he felt were desirable.[13]

The Budget Bureau staff in the International Activities Branch shared Marshall's view that the program was fundamentally political. What it feared now was that the "unity of command" doctrine would be invoked by a separate agency, and State would be reduced to the role of consultant or "concurrer" rather than leader.[14]

In the light of these risks, then, which Marshall surely must have appreciated, what brought him to the decision for a new agency? On November 10, when Marshall was testifying on Interim Aid, the subject was raised by James Webb, the Director of the Budget Bureau, in a memorandum to the President. Webb reported to Truman that Marshall "appears to believe that the administrative arrangements proposed by the Bureau of the Budget would be, in general, the most suitable for effective operation of the program." On the other hand, Webb noted, the Secretary felt "that he could secure from the Congress greater flexibility in the terms attached to U. S. aid if he can advocate the establishment of an independent agency. . . . He feels that an independent agency has a stronger sales value. . . ."[15]

In the opinion of the bureau staff, however, Marshall and the State Department were making a serious tactical mistake, and in the weeks to come this disagreement on strategy would deepen to the point of bitterness. The Budget Bureau would come to identify the authority of the State Department with the larger interest of sound administration in the Marshall Plan. At the same time, State would become more uncertain and divided over the question of

[13] Stone to Lovett, November 12, 1947, Bureau of the Budget, Series 39.18.

[14] See "Administrative Arrangements for the European Recovery Plan," *loc.cit.*, and "Staff Memorandum Concerning Administration of the Program for European Recovery," November 4, 1947, especially pp. 9 and 16, Bureau of the Budget, Series 39.18.

[15] Webb to Truman, November 10, 1947, Bureau of the Budget, Series 39.18.

70

what its interests in the program really were. As the officials at State began to shrink from an active assertion of their claims, the bureau staff took it upon itself to save the program—and the State Department—from State's own timidity. The result was a strange turnabout of affairs: The Budget Bureau staff grew ever more emphatic in promoting the leadership of the State Department, while the State Department, in an odd combination of embarrassment and defense, slipped into the role of resistance. For the members of the Budget Bureau staff, however, the issue was more important than the immediate desires of the State Department, so they persisted in playing their part, almost to the very end. At that point, no one was prepared to deny them their rightful exasperation. They could claim, with full justice, to have been the only ones who had seen the situation clearly. But one wonders, in retrospect, whether they were as sensitive as they might have been to the concerns that were complicating the situation for the State Department at this time.

As late as January 5, only three days before the hearings on the Marshall Plan, one might have been surprised to find the State Department hobbled with doubts on a question of constitutionality. E. A. Gross, the General Counsel at the State Department, wrote Lewis Douglas that the department was still studying "legislation and Supreme Court decisions which justify the broad language in Section 4(a) whereby it is provided that 'all those functions of the Administrator which affect the conduct of the foreign policy of the United States shall be performed subject to the direction and control of the Secretary of State.' "[16]

It seems remarkable that as late as 1948 anyone would have been sufficiently concerned about the problem of delegation that he would have interrupted the momentum of doing what he wanted to do. At least since the Curtiss–Wright case in the mid-thirties it seemed clear that the restraints that bore on the delegation of authority in domestic affairs did not apply with the same force in the foreign arena, where the President was seen as having special responsibilities, and where his prerogatives were conceded to be broader.[17] Besides, in the experience of carrying on relief operations abroad since the war, there was already ample precedent for the kind of delegation involved here, which would have extended

[16] Gross to Douglas, January 5, 1948, Bureau of the Budget, Series 39.18.
[17] See 294 U.S. 304 (1936), especially 315-19.

from the President through the Secretary of State to the agency in the field.[18] But State had reason now to be especially meticulous in documenting its claims. Only two days before his memo to Douglas, Gross had met with the staff of the Senate Foreign Relations Committee in the hope of getting some advice on dealing with the committee. The staff members seemed vaguely sympathetic to the State Department, but they warned that the relation of the department to the ECA would be one of the most difficult features to justify.

> They considered it important for the witnesses to spell out the reasons and need for this relationship and to present strongly the case for this recommendation. They expect considerable detailed questioning on the meaning of the word "affect" on the working mechanics of relationship (cables, programming, etc.). They unofficially expressed the view that State should not retreat from its position.[19]

[18] In the program of aid to Greece and Turkey, the Congressional authorization went directly to the President, who was given the discretion to arrange the responsibilities for administration as he saw fit. The President delegated his authority to the Secretary of State through an executive order [No. 9857], and it had since been accepted that the Secretary had sufficient authority under that order to secure the services of other agencies—e.g., the procurement services of the Bureau of Federal Supply. When the same pattern was followed in the program of post-UNRRA assistance, the precedent was re-enforced.

Relief assistance in the occupied territories had been carried out by the Army. A transfer of responsibility to the State Department seemed to rest on two bases. First, the President had authority under the First War Powers Act to shift functions and funds, but the termination of these powers was already overdue. However, since the current organization of the War and Navy Departments depended on that Act, Congress was not likely to repeal the law until the merger of the armed services was settled. Second, one could claim the President's constitutional authority as Commander-in-Chief. But if the first condition rested on prediction, the Budget Bureau found the second source of authority much too ambiguous to justify anything but further legal research. "The President's powers are broad," they allowed, "but also vague." Fox to Lawson, "Legal Authority to Organize the Government for Administration of Foreign Economic Assistance Programs," July 1, 1947, Bureau of the Budget, Series 39.18. (Lawrence Fox was in the Administrative Management Division of the Budget Bureau, and George Lawson was head of the International Activities Branch.)

[19] *Ibid.*

Thus even if State had not been bothered by doubts on the issue of constitutionality, there would have been a severe strain on its confidence now. As early as August, when the department was considering retreat positions, it was already contemplating a provision that would have gone as far as to share authority with Congress in the management of a contingency fund.[20] As the hearings drew nearer, that initial willingness to compromise became exaggerated, until finally it began to dominate the character of State's maneuvers and inject a rather unseemly element into its relations with other agencies. State appeared to become almost slavish in its anxiety to anticipate the whims of Congress. It seemed determined to satisfy and, indeed, overfulfill those Congressional demands even before they were explicitly raised. The behavior that followed seemed almost inexplicable, and perhaps because it was so contrary to expectations, the passing of the years has tended to blot it out in the memories of most people. What most observers failed to see at the time, however, was that once the prospect of a new agency was accepted, there was a convergence of interests between Congress and the State Department. If State had to control the agency from afar, that task would become more manageable if the agency were tightly penned in. At least it would have been more difficult for a new agency to go off into the foreign field on its own and develop its own base of support. As its primary objective the department would insist on its own ultimate authority in the program, and it would urge that critical aspects of the operations be left open and flexible. For the sake of those guarantees it was now ready to accept almost any other restrictions. In fact, as the other agencies were soon to discover, State was prepared to be quite illiberal with the interests of the new agency.

The participating agencies had already agreed that the Administration would seek the greatest amount of flexibility in personnel regulations. The purpose was to attract talented men from private industry who might have been reluctant to leave their high-paying jobs for the normal civil service rates. Therefore, one can understand the protest raised in the Legislative Drafting Office in January when State held its own conversations with the Civil Service Commission and produced a far more restrictive measure. The

[20] Bramble to Phillips, "Use of Separate Agency or Corporation to Administer Operation[s] in ERP," August 1947, p. 3; copy in Bureau of the Budget, Series 39.18.

Drafting Office argued that exemptions from the standing regulations should be granted in general terms. Instead, State's plan provided for a special administrative waiver by the Civil Service on a case-by-case basis.[21]

In another inscrutable decision, State provided for the *mandatory* use of the Export-Import bank in financing all ERP loans. Since the Administrator would have the option of using the Export-Import bank, just as he would have the freedom to employ any agency of the government, the Budget Bureau people were rather incredulous when they learned that State was now favoring a more rigid arrangement.[22]

Soon, State was encountering opposition at every point. The erratic behavior of the department was beginning to annoy the other agencies, and so, too, was the casualness with which the department seemed to be treating the interests of the new agency. In desperation, someone at State began to leak information to the press, and at the end of January, Joseph Alsop came out with a blistering attack on the Budget Bureau that happened to recite the State Department line. In tell-tale fashion, it also contained some surprisingly detailed information. Alsop accused the Budget Bureau of promoting a form of administration that placed the program under the domination of the State Department. He scored the bureau staff for insisting on the inclusion of an overall figure in the authorization (which State had consistently opposed). It was the bureau, he noted, that cut back on State's estimate for the first 15 months from $7.5 billion to $6.8 billion, and yet, having done that, it still allowed only $4.5 billion for Fiscal 1949. Aside from this last charge, it appeared that the general fault of the bureau was in forcing too many provisions into the bill that were certain to be disliked in Congress.

The attack was particularly galling to Alvin Roseman, who had probably given more concentrated attention to the Marshall Plan than anyone else in the Budget Bureau. Roseman blamed the "leaks" on members of the policy staff at State, "who worked them-

[21] Alvin Roseman to Donald Stone, "ERP Legislation—Administrative Questions Raised by Senate Committee Staff," Bureau of the Budget, Series 39.18. Alvin Roseman was in the International Activities Branch of the Budget Bureau.

[22] S. S. Sheppard to Webb, "Issues Remaining after [the Director's Review] Committee Review Consideration of European Recovery Plan (ERP) Legislation," December 12, 1947, Bureau of the Budget, Series 39.18.

selves almost to the death in the preparation of the program and now find that their brain child is being kicked around by Congress." More pointedly, Roseman got to the basic dispute between State and the Budget Bureau:

> One of our major criticisms of the State Department's activities in connection with the preparation of the bill, was the fact that the State Department staff was attempting to tailor the administration of the program on the basis of assumptions as to Congressional acceptability, without consideration of administrative feasibility. The attitude of many of the State officials was that almost any sacrifice on the administrative side could be made in advance to avoid anticipating Congressional attempts to limit the discretion and flexibility which State believed was essential for determining the amount of aid to be provided to each country and the terms and conditions of such aid.[23]

About two weeks later the bureau staff sharpened its response, and while the argument was still couched in the terms of administration, the reasoning this time was more explicitly political. In a memorandum, the staff addressed itself to the question of strategy in dealing with Congress. Once again, the staff members urged the President to come out strongly for the administrative plan having the greatest coherence (the Budget Bureau plan). Replying to the State Department, they warned that the Congressional reluctance to grant flexibility was not an isolated issue, but part of a developing desire in Congress for more power over foreign affairs in general. It was a misjudgment then to suppose that Congress could be bought off with an independent agency. The Administration was throwing away its most important bargaining counters in advance, and with no assurance that Congress would grant the flexibility sought by the State Department. They had no guarantee that Con-

[23] Roseman to Stone and McCandless, "Bureau's Role in Development of ERP Legislation (Alsop Column of Feb. 1)," February 3, 1948. The dispute about the reduction in aid figures is also worth mentioning, because it sheds some light on the divisions within the State Department at this time. Roseman reported that the opposition to the $4.5 billion figure came from the policy staff rather than the people who had worked on the Interim aid program and who already had experience in procurement operations. The latter group not only did not oppose the reduction to $4.5 billion, but "concluded that the figure was high in the light of their experience with similar programs." *Ibid.*, p. 3.

gress would not simply take the concessions with a polite thank-you and go on to do a more thorough job of weakening the agency. "The real question here," the bureau staff pointed out, "is a political one. Should the President compromise administrative soundness or should he place upon Congress responsibility for deviating from a sound administrative plan?"[24]

The Bureau raised a convincing rejoinder here, and if we expanded on the argument, it might be restated in this way:

—Congress has made no commitment in return for the concessions that the State Department has virtually given away. If the State Department is engaged in tacit bargaining, there is no evidence that Congress is responding. In the meantime, these concessions are weakening the bill and eroding the Administration's bargaining position.

—Worse yet, the concessions are not responding to any explicit or concrete demands in Congress. They are merely anticipations, which may or may not be correct. At least it could be said of the original administrative plan that it had some coherence and rationality. It could be defended in terms of administrative soundness, the lessons of wartime experience, and the preeminent interests of the State Department in foreign operations. Once we retreat from that firmer plan, we would also lose a vastly more defensible position. But more than that, we would be making changes without reason, or equally bad from a practical standpoint, with reasons that could not be expressed in public.

—If the administration of this program is going to be crippled, the Administration has no obligation either to engineer or to sanction that result. It is better for us to advocate a plan that we can defend, and that gives us something to bargain with. If Congress wants changes, let Congress make a conscious and explicit decision as to what it wants changed. Let the Congressional leaders share in the responsibility for finding an alternative administrative formula. And then, let *them* carry the burden of justifying their own changes.

As events were to prove, the bureau's estimate of the Congressional reaction was far superior in accuracy. However, by February 1948, Roseman and the Budget Bureau were honing their arguments much too late. The matter was already in the hands of Congress,

[24] Bureau of the Budget, Staff Memorandum (mimeographed), February 18, 1948, Series 39.18.

so the question of tactics was now beyond the exclusive control of the Administration. But even if it were still a live issue, there is evidence that the situation had already become entangled in other considerations, and that the State Department was being plagued by further doubts. Some of these doubts were detectable as early as November, when James Webb wrote to the President and reported on Secretary Marshall's position. Buried in Webb's account, and skipped over rather quickly, was this additional comment: that despite his own preference for the Budget Bureau plan, the Secretary "[did] not seem inclined to advocate these arrangements in view of his disinclination to bring more functions into the State Department."[25]

But what were the precise grounds of this disinclination, and how long had it really been present? If we did not know more about Webb, we might almost suspect that he skipped over this comment because he did not take it very seriously. It is clear enough, though, that he did not give it much weight. One reason was that the question had been raised before, and it seemed to be universally accepted that the administrative strain on State would be greater if the Marshall Plan was *not* placed in the department. State was already directing the Interim Aid program, and its assistance would be necessary to any new agency in the foreign field. Along with the diplomatic missions, State had staff experienced in overseas work. The department could lend its cables and translation skills, and it was equipped, in addition, to provide a large variety of personal services, from training to transportation. More directly to the point, even if one conceded nothing more to the State Department than an interest in being informed, there would still have been a need for liaison or coordination work.[26]

---

[25] Webb to Truman, November 10, 1947, Bureau of the Budget, Series 39.18.

[26] For an acknowledgment of this view on the part of the State Department, see, for example the memorandum from R. P. Bramble to Phillips, *loc.cit.* Cf. Webb's comments to Truman on the problems created by an independent agency in terms of "many complex arrangements for review and checking on the foreign policy implications of the operations . . . ," *loc.cit.* See also Donald Stone's remarks to Webb two days later: "As a matter of fact, it will no doubt require greater adjustment and addition of new facilities if the Administration is not placed within the [State] Department." Stone to Webb, November 12, 1947, Bureau of the Budget, Series 39.18.

It seems unlikely then that Marshall was principally concerned with avoiding a larger volume of administration. He was going to get that increased volume in any event. Still, liaison and supporting work were not the same as governing. To control this agency would bring a wholly different set of obligations and strains. Even the bureau staff admitted that the program would present a serious administrative challenge to the department, perhaps the severest test of its cohesion.[27] Simply putting the agency in the State Department did not insure foreign policy control. It would present a continuing need for State to administer in the highest sense—to pull the department together and show a will to govern. If this was "administrative control," then it was administration as a continuing test of character; the potential consequences of running this program were no less.

The difference was that Webb and the Budget Bureau staff were not at all deterred by the prospect of some minor convulsions in the State Department. In fact, they found the idea rather appealing. Apparently they had seen Marshall's tenure at State as the most promising moment for making some overdue changes in that tradition-bound department. The Marshall Plan itself seemed to provide an excellent vehicle for those purposes, and in Marshall's initial response to the question of organization they found some cause to believe that there was room for "further encouragement to him [Marshall] in the internal improvement of the State Department." Thus, on November 7 hopes were raised in the Budget Bureau when Marshall, according to reports, was "prepared to create the necessary facilities, *including appropriate reorganization*" [emphasis added] if it were decided finally to give the program to State.[28] Yet only three days later he seemed to have lost his surety. As Webb told the President, Marshall was now disinclined to add functions to the department.

A few weeks later, at an interdepartmental conference, some of the anxieties in the department came closer to the surface. Colonel Charles Bonesteel was the representative of the State Department at this meeting, as he had been in previous meetings of this sort.

[27] Bureau of the Budget, "Staff Memorandum Concerning Administration of the Program for European Recovery," November 4, 1947, *loc.cit.*, pp. 25-26.

[28] Donald Stone to Webb, November 12, 1947, Bureau of the Budget, Series 39.18.

But now he seemed much less concrete to his colleagues. He spoke of "intangible" advantages for the department in receding from control of the program. There now seemed to be a growing sentiment in Congress for a "business-like" approach, as opposed to the diplomatic–political characteristics associated with the State Department. That would require the kind of hard business sense that would be found mainly (it was believed) among businessmen. Bonesteel was now inclined to give this subject more importance than it previously attracted. In this vein he confessed to some fear for the morale in the department as a result of bringing new personnel in from the business world, who would be paid also at a higher rate. Southard (from Treasury) recalled similar experiences in the Treasury with the Division of Monetary Research, and the strains that occurred there from having a separate staff with different standards of pay and recruitment. His tendency then was to second Bonesteel, especially "in view of the Congressional reaction." They were joined by Blaisdell from Commerce, who thought the Budget Bureau plan was superior logically, but not psychologically, again considering the mood in Congress. The others were generally willing to go along with the idea of an independent agency, but Orr (from Agriculture) and Colonel Cheseldine (Army) saw more inconveniences for their own departments. They would now have to establish contacts with the ECA in addition to their regular links to the State Department.

But no one was responsive to the argument that State was preeminently a policy, as opposed to an "operating," agency. That is, no one believed that there was something intrinsic to the character of the work that made ERP unsuitable for the State Department. That vision was simply inconsistent with the understanding that arose after several months of work on the project. As Blaisdell had remarked, the whole program would require little more than an enlarged staff effort. Thus no one was quite able to understand what Bonesteel was now worrying about. As one observer wrote, "It was clear from the discussion that no one outside State expected that the new agency would become involved in any large scale operations."

Nor was anyone able to penetrate that cloud of "intangible" advantages. There was a strange new idiom here, a new way of speaking that was not at all in harmony with the easy-going frankness that characterized the earlier meetings. One gets the sense here of a certain uneasiness on the part of the discussants, and a certain reluctance to make their thoughts explicit. And thus the record of the conference ends rather cryptically:

> Col. Chesseldine [sic] summarized by asking whether the issue was one of wanting to give an agency a job that it didn't want.[29]

III

On several counts the actions of the State Department people during this period were misguided, and at times indefensible. It could be said, on the other side, that they had motives that few of their colleagues seemed able to understand, and which they could never begin to understand, perhaps, without a personal commitment to the department. So the people at State decided to keep their own counsel and arrange this matter by themselves. But the image of the practical men of affairs proved false, for instead of political judgment they showed only a vulgar notion of "realism" and a tendency to identify wisdom with a passionless concocting of "deals." They found themselves, to be sure, in a delicate political situation, which would have tested the prudence of the practical statesman. In response they tried only to be clever. Thus, they rejected any formal responsibility in the program, but by no means had they surrendered their ambitions to control. Instead they went craftily about, searching for some convenient arrangement by which they would be able to control the new agency through the back door.

What informed their thinking in this instance were the lessons of wartime experience. They had learned then that formal integration was important, but that it was not necessarily the most critical factor in establishing the structure of authority. The Office of the Coordinator of Inter-American Affairs had not been formally attached to the State Department; nevertheless, coordination became highly effective by virtue of a simple Presidential order that required the agency to submit its projects to the State Department for clearance.[30] On the other hand, there was an egregious failure to coordinate with the Office of War Information, even though the

---

[29] Memorandum on Conference, December 1, 1947, Bureau of the Budget, Series 39.18.

[30] See U.S. Bureau of the Budget, Committee on Records of War Administration, *The United States at War* (Washington: Government Printing Office, 1946), pp. 218 ff., especially pp. 231-33.

OWI was nominally subject to the directives of an Overseas Planning Board that included the State Department. The case of the OWI was particularly relevant for the Marshall Plan, because it illustrated the problem of maintaining lines of control with overseas units. As the war progressed and the armed forces extended their communications networks abroad, the OWI became less dependent on the facilities of the State Department. The existence of a field veto in the hands of the theater commander served to decentralize the organization even further. The local OWI men began to see themselves as more nearly a part of the theater operations, and with the protection of the commander they were able to avoid directives from the center.[31]

To a remarkable extent, the men at State fell back now on the lessons of those wartime operations. Rather than seeking formal authority, their hopes were concentrated on getting a clear directive from the President. They knew that the organizational structure would not really be completed until the arrangements for coordination were settled and the President determined his procedure in appeals. In the meantime they put special emphasis on the language in the bill. The ECA Administrator was to work under "the direction and control of the Secretary of State." As Marshall told the Senate Foreign Relations Committee, the language was specifically designed to avoid the problems that existed during the war with the Office of War Mobilization. In that case, the language in the Executive order had provided for coordination with the foreign policy of the United States as "defined by the Secretary of State." But in practice, the phrase was interpreted to mean that the Secretary was allowed merely to submit his views. Thus, "direction and control," would now mean exactly that. If the Administrator was not willing to obey the directives, it was he who had to go to the President in order to get them rescinded.[32]

[31] The study of the OWI experience was contained in a series of memoranda entitled "Lessons," which was prepared in the State Department as part of the planning for the Marshall Plan. The papers reviewed the organization of all American programs in the foreign economic field both during and after the Second World War. As a source of insight into the assumptions and analogies that were guiding the planners at this time, this collection is unparalleled. Copies of these papers can be found in Bureau of the Budget, Series 39.18, dated October 1947.

[32] U.S. Congress, Senate Committee on Foreign Relations, *Hearings, European Recovery Program*, 80th Congress, 2nd Session, 1948, pp. 17, 19. Cited hereafter as Senate Committee on Foreign Relations, *ERP Hearings*, 1948.

Next, steps would be taken to prevent a recurrence of that field autonomy that had disrupted coordination between the State Department and the Office of War Information. The legislation provided that the ECA staff in each recipient country would work under the supervision and control of the American ambassador. Marshall laid particular stress on this unity of foreign service operations abroad, both in the Congressional hearings and in his previous discussions with the Budget Bureau.[33] Again it was clear that the overseas operations would simply be a projection of the relations that existed in Washington between the Secretary of State and the ECA Administrator.

Thus, while the State Department did seem to forego a significant part of formal authority, there was some belief, based on previous experience, that the department could still succeed in guiding the new agency. Further, in surveying the post-UNRRA assistance program, even the Budget Bureau admitted that State had shown itself able to provide policy direction while using other agencies for procurement and shipping—i.e., even when the department was not involved itself in the operations.[34] Moreover, State found this strategy especially appealing at this particular time, when it made good sense to cut its liabilities. With Congressional hostility apparently reaching a peak, one could hardly blame the department for trying to reduce its formal responsibilities in the recovery program. If the supply situation at home remained tight, then the Administration might have to get serious about controls. If the supply situation eased and surpluses started to appear, or if the United States reduced its unusually large export surplus in an effort to import more goods from Europe, then the department would become the target for every domestic group with a commodity interest. One did not have to go outside the Administration to see the signs. One could see the way the Department of Agriculture and the Treasury Department were behaving, or the way in which everyone from the Labor Department to the FTC was jockeying for a place in the program.

Again, one could not dismiss the concerns of the people at State, but one could raise serious questions about their judgment. If Congress did not appreciate their string of unsolicited gestures, all their clever maneuvers might have served only to prejudice their own

[33] *Ibid.*, pp. 47-48; Webb to Truman, Bureau of the Budget, *loc.cit.*
[34] See the paper on the post-UNRRA program in the series on "Lessons," October 1947, Bureau of the Budget, Series 39.18.

case; for it might then have appeared that they were seeking covert controls over an independent agency. But by this time, unfortunately, they could no longer afford to believe that Congressional politics might be anything other than that simple-minded gamesmanship they had all the while supposed it to be. In mid-December the legislation was finally sent to the Senate Foreign Relations Committee. All that was left now was the hope that Congress would understand and be decent.

5. VANDENBERG, CONGRESS, AND THE NEW DIPLOMACY

I

STATE had made its concessions; it accepted a new organization, the Economic Cooperation Administration, headed by a single administrator and open in its key positions to businessmen. Now it fell back on the hope that Congress would accept the other parts of the legislation that allowed the department to interfere where it had to and maintain its traditional authority in foreign affairs. But with the Republicans in control of Congress, the chairman of the Senate Foreign Relations Committee was Arthur Vandenberg, and Vandenberg was not conditioned to respond to such unverbalized bargaining. Even if he had recognized a tacit appeal here he had no reason to feel bound to any arrangement that had not been discussed with him. He had agreed to nothing, signed nothing; and despite the alterations in the bill, there was still too much of the State Department in the legislation to suit him.

On the advice of his committee staff, Vandenberg decided to seek an independent study from the Brookings Institution. As an independent research organization, Brookings seemed to meet the requirement of a disinterested outside agency, and before the end of December 1947, Vandenberg wrote to Harold Moulton, the President of Brookings, to request a special study. He referred immediately to the question of administration and described it as the "one overriding problem in connection with [the Senate committee's] consideration of ERP." The problem, he told Moulton, was to find an administrative form that recognized the "appropriate jurisdiction of the State Department over foreign policy," but at the same time, one that preserved the autonomy of the ECA Administrator as "the business head of a business operation."

> There is a strong feeling in Congress that the actual day-to-day management of ERP [European Recovery Program] is a business proposition which should be effectively separated from the

84

State Department which is neither equipped nor intended to deal with economic administration. . . .

However, he also acknowledged that there was another body of opinion:

There is an equally strong feeling that ERP actually becomes our foreign policy in essence and effect; and that the proper jurisdiction of the two agencies must be carefully defined and delimited lest we find ourselves at the mercy of rival foreign policies. The obvious problem is to resolve these two concepts on a workable basis.[1]

In this way Vandenberg ordered the independent study whose "objective" character provided him with such a strong talking point later. But in the same breath he succeeded in defining the issue and recasting the role that Brookings could play. Patently the Brookings staff was not asked to enter the situation to deal with issues in the abstract, as though it had no knowledge of the interests at work. It was asked instead to produce an organizational plan, given a certain state of opinion in Congress that made some alternatives less acceptable than others. As Robert Hartley of the Brookings Institution recalled, it was simply a matter of common sense that Vandenberg would never have requested the Brookings study if he had been satisfied with the draft legislation.[2] Thus the Brookings staff knew from the outset that it was futile to bring in a recommendation for the complete integration of ECA in the State Department; and it was this knowledge that made its position more nearly that of an active participant. This was still scholarly work, but the writing had to be done consciously within an area marked off by established policy preferences.

Work at Brookings started almost immediately. Vandenberg wanted a report in ten days to two weeks, but Moulton put him off and won an extension to three weeks. As soon as the study was announced to the public, though, the Brookings staff began to receive "feelers" from agencies, journalists, and other interested parties. Again, it is hard to conceive how anything as apparently bloodless as the question of administration could arouse so much excitement.

[1] Vandenberg to Moulton, December 30, 1947, Brookings Institution (Files of the Institution). I am grateful to the Brookings Institution for permission to quote from this correspondence.

[2] Robert Hartley, Interview, March 15, 1966.

But as the later incident with Alsop revealed, the question of administration was invested with symbolic meaning, as well as being tied to the principal issues of substance. It may be, then, that Vandenberg was not indulging in his usual overstatement when he remarked to Harold Moulton that the question of administration was the "one overriding problem in connection with [the] consideration of ERP" that the Senate committee had to confront.

Along with Moulton, the direction of the work at Brookings was shared by Robert Hartley and the redoubtable Leo Pasvolsky. For Pasvolsky in particular this was a task that touched the center of his life's work. His specialty was in international economics, and before joining the State Department under Cordell Hull, he wrote several estimable books in the field for Brookings. In October 1939, one month after the beginning of the war in Europe, Hull called him back to his old position as Special Assistant to the Secretary. His assignment then was to work on long-range problems for postwar planning as Hull's principal adviser on foreign economic affairs. Through Hull, Pasvolsky would become involved in the problems of all the major international conferences, and with topics as varied as disarmament and trusteeship. When Hull established a drafting group for the United Nations Charter in July 1943, Pasvolsky was appointed to direct the effort, and he stayed on at the center of the negotiations through Dumbarton Oaks and the founding sessions at San Francisco.[3]

Thus, in going to Brookings for advice, Vandenberg was tapping a unique source of knowledge and experience. In Pasvolsky he was also approaching someone with a deep commitment to the program at hand and perhaps, also, to one of the interested departments. But if Pasvolsky had any inclination to favor the State Department, he apparently did not press it on his colleagues. And if he tended to agree with the assumptions of the State Department—that ERP was basically a political program, rather than a problem of business investment—it was a perspective he shared with the other members of the Brookings staff.

Vandenberg received the Brookings statement on January 22. It was a fairly brief document; he read it in twenty minutes and

[3] One can find references to Pasvolsky scattered through both volumes of Cordell Hull's memoirs. But the references that give a fuller understanding of his involvement are concentrated in the chapters on postwar planning. See Cordell Hull, *The Memoirs of Cordell Hull* (New York: The Macmillan Company, 1948), chs. 116-119, 120.

86

liked what he read or found what he wanted to find, for he released it to the press almost immediately.

The statement itself was a strange amalgam in which segments of thoughtful analysis mingled with crude assertions of administrative dogma. No doubt it reflected all the peculiar weaknesses of a staff product. But in large measure it bore the traces of a studied vagueness and the delicate task of writing in a political context.

The staff demurred from Vandenberg's premise that the Marshall Plan was essentially a "business operation." The report declared that the program was "neither a purely business job nor a purely governmental operation, but a mixture of both." On the other hand, the staff could follow Vandenberg in arguing that everything in the program was not foreign policy. The program would touch the interests of many different agencies, including Agriculture, Commerce, and even the Army (as, for example, in its administration of occupied territories). The mere fact that operations occurred abroad could not be enough in itself to give State the sole or preeminent claim to control. At the same time, the foreign policy content was strong enough to establish some claim for the State Department and discredit the proposals for an independent corporation. In the opinion of the Brookings staff, the corporate device threatened to insulate the Marshall Plan from the constitutional authority of the President in foreign affairs. As Vandenberg had suggested, the problem was indeed one of finding a form of administration that could reconcile the rival claimants and give each sphere of policy its "appropriate" place.

Rather than facing that question directly, the Brookings staff decided to approach the issue through the relation of the ECA to the President. Its method of disposing of the question, however, left something to be desired. Given the interests of the other agencies in the program, it seemed obvious to the members of the staff that conflict would be inevitable. Some procedures would be necessary for resolving conflicts, and "no system . . . has yet been devised," they warned, "that can escape the necessity of final appeals to the President as the superior authority in the event of unreconciled differences between the heads of the agencies involved."[4] From this proposition they leaped over the argument they had to make about the relative weight of the interests in the Marshall Plan. Instead of

[4] Brookings report, p. 30. The conclusions of the report were reprinted in Senate Foreign Relations Committee, *ERP Hearings*, 1948, pp. 855-59. The quotation appears on p. 856.

resolving the various claims and deciding who would get what jurisdiction, they merely concluded that the Administrator of the ECA
deserved direct access to the President—"as direct an access . . .
as the heads of the other agencies with which he will need to coordinate his activities." For that access to be effective the Administrator would require the prestige of an "equal" in interagency conflicts, and that could be accomplished most decisively by creating
an independent agency with Cabinet status.

Apart from these formal issues, the requirements of administration were fairly simple: The central need was for speed and flexibility, and in the estimate of the Brookings staff a single administrator was preferable to a governing board. An advisory board might
be added later, but only as a device for building "public confidence." The ECA could be given the power to sue, make contracts,
and hire consultants; and without too much trouble it was possible
to relax the controls of the General Accounting Office. In short, the
agency could enjoy a wide range of choice with very few
inhibitions.

For Vandenberg this was all quite sufficient to tell him what he
wanted to hear: that the ECA should not be subordinated to the
State Department, that it deserved a separate and equal status, because it brought something distinctive to its tasks. But the paradox
in the report was that the members of the Brookings staff never
really answered the question that was put to them. They established
appeal rights, but they did not indicate who it was who would have
to raise the objections and carry the burden of appeal. Equally important, they said nothing about what was to happen while the appeal was pending. For example, it was perfectly consistent with
their proposal for the Secretary of State to object to a policy decision and order a suspension of activity, and conceivably that suspension could hold until the *Administrator of the ECA* managed
to convince the President to countermand the order.[5] Vandenberg
read the Brookings report and reached the opposite conclusion,
and the difference would later prove significant.

It is hardly likely that the Brookings staff failed to recognize the
ambiguity in the report. In fact, there is some evidence that the am-

---

[5] It may well be that the experts at Brookings were never really clear on
this matter themselves. As Robert Hartley recalled, they sought to assure
a "suspensive veto" for the Secretary of State, but they did not go very
much farther, apparently, in weighing the precise meaning of that term.
Robert Hartley, Interview, March 15, 1966.

biguity was a matter of design. At separate press conferences, both Truman and Marshall professed to see no essential difference between the Administration plan and the Brookings Report.[6] Reportedly, Marshall went so far as to claim that the Brookings plan was the one he had favored all along, but that for some reason he had been induced to abandon it.[7] A short time later, Donald Stone of the Budget Bureau had lunch with Robert Hartley and Leo Pasvolsky. Hartley and Pasvolsky were generally critical of the way the Administration had managed the legislation, but they thought the handling of the Brookings Report was particularly inept. Recounting the conversation to James Webb, Stone wrote:

> Pasvolsky thought neither Marshall nor the President had taken proper advantage of the Brookings Report when they both pointed out that it was almost the same thing as the State proposal. I felt this same way, for the greater the identification of the Brookings proposal with the State plan, the more would be the inclination to make undesirable changes in the legislation. If the Brookings Report could be viewed as something different but yet something which the Administration could accept, negotiations would be on a better basis.

In the judgment of Hartley and Pasvolsky, it would have been better to have said nothing in the legislation on the connection between ECA and the State Department. The administrative responsibility should have been given simply to the President, where it fundamentally belonged, and Truman would have been free then to delegate his authority in any way he chose.[8]

[6] See the transcript of the President's news conference on January 29, 1948, in Harry S. Truman, *Public Papers* (Washington: Government Printing Office, 1964), p. 115.

[7] A transcript of Marshall's "off-the-record" comments appears in the Brookings files. The language in the transcript suggests that there had been no editing or alteration. This, as well as the appearance of secondary accounts, leads one to believe that the report was valid.

[8] Stone to Webb, February 4, 1948, Bureau of the Budget, Series 39.18. The potential weakness here was the assumption that Congress would not make any distinction between the Greek-Turkish and post-UNRRA programs on the one hand, and the Marshall Plan on the other. It did not necessarily follow that what Congress was willing to do in an emergency relief program (or one with urgent military overtones) it would be willing to do for a four-year program involving $17 to $20 billion. But the criticism still had some point, especially to Stone, who had urged the same approach in

What they were suggesting, in so many words, was that Brookings left enough room for Truman and Marshall to arrange the program to suit themselves. According to Hartley, the staff had been guided by two primary considerations: (1) that the program was one of supplying dollars and goods rather than basic investment, and therefore there was no real need for a large administrative organization; and (2) that the program had to be launched quickly, since the problem was basically one of short-term dislocations. Along with its other objections the staff thought a corporate administration would take too long to work out in Congress. Thus, from its own point of view, and without even considering the interests of the State Department, it preferred an arrangement that would be simple, acceptable, and open to easy alteration. Did the plan conceal some expectation that the State Department would eventually control the program? Possibly, but there was no necessary commitment to that end, as shown clearly in the fact that Vandenberg could read the report and find "objective" support for his own, quite opposite views.

At any rate, even the modest aims of the Brookings staff seemed to be prejudiced by the performance of the Administration. In the opinion of Hartley and Pasvolsky, the State Department in particular had done an incredible job of mismanaging the bill. In their judgment, also, the Administration made a grievous error in failing to consult Vandenberg and Charles Eaton, the chairman of the House Foreign Affairs Committee. In fact, as Donald Stone reported "they suggested that both Vandenberg and Eaton might have sponsored a bill if it had been drafted in consultation with them beginning with some proposed plans suggested by the Executive branch."[9] As it was, State allowed its Congressional relations to deteriorate badly, and at a time when the department could least afford it. Pasvolsky had the Alsop column in his hand when he met Stone for lunch, and he thought it was but another indication of the way the whole issue had been mishandled when articles of that kind began to appear. His own sympathies moved him to pass along some words of warning for his old department. As Stone relayed to Webb,

---

mid-January. See Stone memorandum to Roseman and Levi, January 14, 1948, Bureau of the Budget, Series 39.18.

[9] Stone to Webb, February 4, 1948, Bureau of the Budget, *loc.cit.*

[Pasvolsky] suggested that I have you mention the old Russian proverb to General Marshall: "One shouldn't spit in the well out of which he expects to drink."

II

It would be a serious distortion of history to pretend that the State Department was the helpless victim of Congressional hostility in 1948. Such a view would overlook the very important contributions State made to its own misfortunes, including the failure to press its own interests coherently. Still, once we have acknowledged the shortcomings of the department, there is no denying that it was working under the pall of a very real antagonism in Congress. State's domestic troubles were bound up with those international changes that were now imparting urgency to the Marshall Plan, and with Roosevelt gone the department could be identified with all the wartime decisions that were allegedly responsible for the postwar problems.

Precisely what those mistakes were was hard to tell. No alternatives were immediately forthcoming as to what the United States might have done for Poland at Yalta. It was never entirely clear as to how FDR "sold Chiang Kai-shek down the river" at Yalta, as Vandenberg declared, especially when Chiang seemed well satisfied at the time with the settlement he worked out with Stalin.[10]

Instead of a policy critique, one finds a vague feeling of unease and some suspicion, after all, that the problem was really one of attitude—that the State Department was too "soft." It was too reluctant to find fault with the Soviet Union; it was too solicitous of foreigners, and simply too timid in general to mount a vigorous defense of American interests. Yet once again the creation of a myth tended to cloud over the historical record. When the question of occupying Germany had arisen during the war, it was the State Department that wanted to press the Russians for an agreement on

[10] See *The Private Papers of Senator Vandenberg*, ed. Arthur H. Vandenberg, Jr. (Boston: Houghton Mifflin Company, 1952), p. 535. For his conviction that the State Department had allowed the situation in China to deteriorate, see pp. 527 and 530. On Chiang's general satisfaction with the Sino-Soviet treaty, see Tang Tsou, *America's Failure in China, 1941-50* (Chicago: University of Chicago Press, 1963), pp. 284-85; and for a more extended treatment of the Yalta agreement in relation to China, see pp. 237 ff.

zones. In that case, it was the War Department, with its fear of interrupting military operations, that proved to be rather skittish about raising political questions.[11]

Doubtless the department opened itself to the charge of being "one-worldish" during the period of the UNRRA; and it shared all the embarrassments of that episode with Yugoslavia, in which the United States found itself in the position of supplying aid to Yugoslavia, while at the same time bringing its own complaint against that country to the United Nations. But the critics conveniently ignored the deft performance of the department in its handling of the foreign assistance program in French North Africa, an operation that also happened to provide some useful intelligence for the North African landings.[12]

Whatever the source of this oppositionist sentiment, it was nevertheless clear that the State Department had now become its focal point. The fact that the Republicans were now in control of Congress only made things worse as far as the immediate interests of the department were concerned. Thus, it was no surprise when the question of administration arose very early in the floor discussions of the Marshall Plan in March. Some key members of the Republican majority in the Senate had already served notice that nothing important was going to be decided on the Marshall Plan until the matter of administration had been settled. Senator Wherry, the Republican majority leader, struck at this nerve almost immediately on the first day of debate. His warning to Vandenberg indicated the depth of feeling in the Congress, and for that reason it is worth quoting at length:

> I want to point out to the Senator from Michigan that during the past two years, and even since V-J day, the administration has appointed in the Department of State administrators of legislation who, to my mind, have demonstrated total inability to administer our foreign policy. The distinguished Senator mentioned in support of the program that such distinguished men as Dean Acheson have testified in its behalf. . . . The same Dean Acheson testified in support of the International Bank, he testified regarding Bretton Woods. He testified to the Morgenthau plan, and he

[11] Philip E. Mosely, "The Occupation of Germany: New Light on How the Zones Were Drawn," *Foreign Affairs*, Vol. 28, No. 4 (July 1950), pp. 580-604, at pp. 584-85.

[12] See Cordell Hull, *op.cit.*, pp. 951-52.

is the man whom the administration selected to carry it out. He also signed the International Aviation Agreements in Chicago, which agreements had to be repudiated by the Senate. In fact, if there is one man in the United States whose judgment I should not want to follow, it is Dean Acheson. . . . If he should be the Administrator of the act, some of us would feel that its administration would be similar to the administration of another plan during the past two years, in connection with which more than $20,000,000,000 have been expended, and conditions are worse today than they were originally. The Morgenthau plan is out of the window and Mr. Acheson is out of the Government, and I think that is a good thing.[13]

In the House Foreign Affairs Committee hearings in February, an explicit connection was made between the opposition to the State Department and the potential for increased Congressional authority in foreign relations. J. T. Sanders of the National Grange urged that the ECA be ruled by a board, cut off from the President and the State Department because, "very frankly, we believe too many secret agreements have been entered into during the conduct of the war and since, without the knowledge of or acquiescence of the Congress, and we want to see the administrators of this program *responsible to the Congress.*"[14]

Now, with the debate moved to the floor of Congress, the theme was picked up in the House by Karl Mundt. Mundt suggested that the perversity was not confined to the State Department, but that it was a characteristic more generally of Executive behavior in foreign policy. He pointed out, for example, that the Commerce Department was still permitting the shipment of machine tools and industrial equipment to the Soviet Union. This particular complaint could be handled by removing the subject from Executive discretion, but for more general assurance he thought it would be better if the authority were taken away from the President and vested in the ECA. "It is our hope and our expectation," Mundt told his colleagues, "that the Economic Administrator will succeed where the President and his Department of Commerce have so conspicuously failed."[15]

---

[13] U.S. *Congressional Record*, 80th Congress, 2d Sess., 1948, XCIV, Part 2, 1963.

[14] House Foreign Affairs Committee, *ERP Hearings, 1948*, p. 1387. Emphasis added.

[15] *Congressional Record*, XCIV (1948), 3756.

Part I

One of the best insights into this trend toward Congressional assertiveness could be found in the experiences of Arthur Vandenberg. Vandenberg's metamorphosis might stand as the prototype for the changes that were occurring in many others at this time: traditionally isolationist, shaken by Pearl Harbor into a form of utopian internationalism, and sobered by the postwar years into support for a bipartisan foreign policy. But if he was moved by the force of events to accept an internationalist foreign policy, it was still important for him to separate that support from the kind of Executive power that usually came along with a strong foreign policy. On partisan as well as personal grounds, he grew to resent the expansion of the Presidency under Roosevelt, and in the course of the war his suspicion of Executive power was extended to the State Department.

The signal incident in Vandenberg's relations with the Department of State came in the summer of 1943. Preparations were under way for the invasion of Sicily, the war in the Pacific was turning, and the Senate Foreign Relations Committee was moving toward a consideration of postwar objectives. The advance of the military overseas brought the question of relief for war-torn areas coming under Allied control. A United Nations Relief and Rehabilitation Administration was proposed, and a draft agreement was subsequently submitted to the Allied governments. But when the State Department published the text of the agreement, Vandenberg recoiled from what he saw as a blank check that "pledged our total resources to whatever illimitable scheme for relief and rehabilitation all around the world our New Deal crystal gazers might desire to pursue."[16] As if to compound his indignation, there was no mention of submitting the measure for Congressional approval. He took the matter to Hull, who told him that the decision to use an Executive agreement had been made after consultation with the majority and minority leaders in both houses of Congress. The Republican minority leaders, Senator McNary and Congressman Martin, were away from Washington at the time, but Vandenberg was not content to await their return. In an exchange of letters, both McNary and Martin denied that they had consented to the use of an Executive agreement.

As the news began to circulate on Capitol Hill, the resentment spread across party lines. Vandenberg chaired a special subcom-

[16] Vandenberg, *op.cit.*, pp. 67, 70.

94

mittee to investigate the affair, and a tense session developed when Hull and Acheson arrived to testify. Hull fell into a heated exchange with Sen. Tom Connally, while Vandenberg and Acheson determined to work out a settlement. A compromise was finally reached in which the agreement would be approved by a majority vote in both houses of Congress. In this way the Congress would not be by-passed, and the Executive could avoid the requirement of a two-thirds vote in the Senate. However, the convenience of circumventing the two-thirds rule in the Senate brought its price. The Executive implicitly accepted the principle that authority in foreign relations could be shared more widely with Congress as a whole. In lieu of the lopsided Senate majority, a new competence was vested in slighter majorities, but in *both* houses of Congress. For Vandenberg the outcome implied nothing less than a new structure of decision-making that included a "direct system of consultation between the State Department and the Senate Foreign Relations Committee which should be able to avoid many of the stalemates of which we are historically aware."[17]

The notion of a larger role for Congress in foreign policy now began to take hold. The following year brought proposals to recognize a formal position for the House in the treaty process. Sol Bloom, the Democratic chairman of the House Foreign Affairs Committee, laid out an elaborate brief in favor of sharing the treaty power with the House.[18] A constitutional amendment was introduced, and after hearings covering most of the year, it was reported out with a favorable recommendation.[19] By the time the hearings on the Marshall Plan opened in 1948, Christian Herter could tell his colleagues in the House that the advent of foreign economic programs, with their huge demands in appropriations, was creating a larger role for the Congress in foreign policy. Thus the two issues had become fused—the claims of the House for consultation on

[17] *Ibid.*, pp. 71-73.

[18] Sol Bloom, *The Treaty-Making Power* (Washington: 1944). Around the same time, Lindsay Rogers was attacking the machinery for advising and consenting to treaties as obsolete and undemocratic. See his *Constitutional Aspects of Foreign Affairs*; Cutler Lectures, William and Mary College (Williamsburg, Va.; 1944).

[19] See U.S. Congress, House Committee on the Judiciary, *Amendment to the Constitution on the Making of Treaties*, Hearings before subcommittee no. 3, 78th Congress, 2d Sess., 1944, on H. J. Res. 31, H. J. Res. 238, H. J. Res. 246, H. J. Res. 264, and H. J. Res. 320 (Washington: Government Printing Office, 1944).

95

treaties, and the general Congressional claim for an increased share of power with the Executive in foreign affairs. It is difficult to appreciate the depth of Congressional feeling on the issues of administration, or the subsequent behavior of the ECA, without a sense of this movement, which had built up considerable force already by 1948.

There was a bridge between Vandenberg's oppositionist bent and the rationale he eventually conceived for separating the ECA from the State Department. The transition seemed to begin with the serious intellectual problems he encountered in coping with the issues of foreign policy. Vandenberg's efforts to treat with the substance of what was being done in diplomacy proved unproductive (and, one might add, uninstructive). At some point he came around to the view that the problems were too intractable once they had emerged in a real situation; the only sensible corrective lay in striking at the source. Somehow there had to be a change in the process or the way things were done, perhaps through a change in the character of the performers.

This development in Vandenberg could be traced in his reactions to the Soviet Union and China. He complained during the war when Stalin's absorption of the Baltic States began to appear as something more than a temporary wartime measure. He grew alarmed at the situation in Eastern Europe, and the thrust of Russian demands in the Mediterranean and the Middle East. He knew that the Kuomintang regime in China was imperiled; he knew the record of its ineptitude and corruption, and he was aware as much as anyone else of its dwindling capacity to evoke popular support. And yet, while he was quite blithe in thrusting responsibility on the Democratic Administration, he had not been willing himself to break with Russia during the war, and if anything, he was even more emphatic than the Administration in rejecting the use of ground troops in China.

In place of workable alternatives, Vandenberg succumbed to the appeal of good sentiment unreservedly joined. In December 1947, he commented in respect to China that "if we now give the Chinese Nationalist Government . . . the moral support it deserves, I would expect China to have a better chance (if any) to stabilize itself."[20] Almost two years earlier, he had won accolades with a similar ex-

[20] Vandenberg, *op.cit.*, p. 532.

96

position on the power of righteousness. In his famous "get tough" speech in February 1946, he sketched the global lines of Soviet-American confrontation and came to the conclusion that the essential requirement for peace was to avoid the dangers of compromise. Principally that meant eliminating the *misunderstandings* that presumably led to war. Peace could be assured, he argued, if the United States had the courage to state its position more precisely:

> I assert my own belief that we can live together in reasonable harmony if the United States speaks as plainly upon all occasions as Russia does; . . . if we abandon the miserable fiction, often encouraged by our own fellow travelers, that we somehow jeopardize the peace if our candor is as firm as Russia's always is; and if we assume a moral leadership which we have too frequently allowed to lapse. . . .[21]

The curious part of this supposedly "tough" proclamation was that it lost the sense of any genuine conflict of interests between the United States and Russia. If Vandenberg was to be taken at his word, the major problem was one of diction. That may account for his delight in Ernest Bevin's blunt, venomous rejoinders to Molotov. To Vandenberg these dramatics of exasperation seemed to bespeak a stout-hearted sense of purpose. As for Secretary Byrnes, he feared that this former technician of Senate compromises had merely transferred his prosaic arts to the arena of foreign policy.[22]

After identifying compromise with timidity, and timidity as the bar to a forthright, positive diplomacy, it was only a matter of time until he recognized compromise as the institutional disease of the State Department. At that point, he no longer cared to believe that the State Department could actually contrive and execute a successful foreign policy. And thus, while he was willing to admit that the recovery program was conceived from a basic political and military interest, he finally convinced himself that the program was really "economic" rather than "political" in its nature.

But what exactly was meant by "economic?" After all, in the preceding twenty years the most striking changes in the Department of State had come in the area of functional specialization. Under the proprietorship of Hull the department cultivated a new sensitivity to the economic dimensions of foreign policy, and it took

[21] *Ibid.*, p. 248.   [22] *Ibid.*, pp. 243-44.

measured steps also in reshaping its own organization to deal with economic issues. For Vandenberg, however, the term "economic" came to hold two more specific connotations. First, there was the sense of something called "operations"—either the movement of materials or some actual physical work in the field. This was the type of work, it was felt, that found its usual place in private industry. The problem of reconstruction, the allocation of investment, the provision of technical advice—all seemed to suggest the very substance of private business activity. They were the activities supervised by the foreman, or the decisions made by the experienced corporate executive. Moreover, Vandenberg found support for this view among men who were closely identified with the State Department. In the Senate hearings, Ambassador Lewis Douglas explained the reluctance of the department to run the European Recovery Program on the grounds that State was not "an operating department."[23] In addition, there was a continuing body of opinion in the State Department that held to the vision of State as an exclusively policy-making organization, a haven for the generalist and the scholar rather than the expediter.[24]

[23] Senate Foreign Relations Committee, *ERP Hearings*, 1948, pp. 149, 192. See also his similar remarks to the House committee five days later. House Foreign Affairs Committee, *ERP Hearings*, 1948, p. 253.

[24] Thus, for example, when agencies like the Foreign Economic Administration and the Surplus Property Administration were transferred to the State Department after the war, Secretary Byrnes protested the role of "undertaker" for agencies undergoing liquidation. He later cast his objection in more theoretical terms:

> The State Department must be a policy-making department. It cannot be run like one which is charged with conducting a variety of operations. The amount of time a Secretary of State must give to decisions on carrying out operating functions, necessarily is taken away from the important questions of foreign policy.
>
> Because I thought the State Department should be maintained as a policy-making department, I opposed the efforts of the War Department to transfer to the State Department control of our occupation organizations in Europe and in the Pacific. The State Department is not adapted for such work. It cannot recruit an efficient organization because the appointees could at best, be promised only temporary employment far removed from their homes. If the burden of carrying on shipping, maintenance of transportation, policing, inspection and all the myriad duties of occupation forces were transferred to the State Department, its capacity to define wisely important foreign policies would be seriously hampered.

James F. Byrnes, *Speaking Frankly* (New York: Harper and Brothers, 1947), pp. 243-44.

Secondly, there was a conviction that the imperatives of the Marshall Plan were so clearly business-like in character that a combination of economic criteria and business judgment would insure the desired result. It was assumed that a firm rationality existed between the economic operations as a means and European stability as a political end. The recovery of production and trade in Western Europe would remove the economic unrest which made populations vulnerable to totalitarian appeals. It stood to reason, also, that economic recovery could be achieved more effectively if decisions were based as much as possible on the criteria internal to economics as a discipline. In Vandenberg this view could be distorted at times into a caricature, but still the argument had a certain force of common sense. That is, one did not have to assume that the economic program, and hence, economic decisions were perfectly rational in terms of the political ends, but only that they were sufficiently rational for the limited purposes of the United States in Europe. The United States had not undertaken to administer the European governments or to police the streets of the major cities. Marshall said in his Harvard speech that the Europeans would have to carry most of the administrative burden themselves and they would have to make their own internal economic decisions, while meshing them in some degree with the plans of the other ERP nations. The program was moved by the fairly simple conjecture that political stability would be threatened as long as economic unrest was allowed to continue; and that was all. It was rather limited, to say the least, as political theory, but again, it had a certain elementary strength that vastly outweighed for the moment its problematic qualities.

Vandenberg, however, went beyond this argument of limited but sufficient rationality. He identified the business approach with a whole new character for the conduct of diplomacy that promised to extend even beyond the Marshall Plan. During the hearings he insisted to Ambassador Douglas that the American people had lost their confidence in foreign policy as pursued by the State Department. What they expected now, he insisted, was a new method of achieving their diplomatic objectives:

[The American people] have a general feeling that the administration of our foreign grants and loans and aids since the war has been pretty sterile of results. . . . Therefore, they come up, in my opinion, with the new view that if they are to be happy about

99

hopefully anticipating that this is going to be a success where other things have failed, they want a new element of business responsibility injected into this formula which will give them a feeling of reliance that as a business operation this is to be conducted in a business way.[25]

Exactly how serious one could be on this matter became evident in March, when it was reported in the *Washington Post* that Will Clayton would be named as the Administrator of the Marshall Plan. Clayton had come from a career in private business to serve creditably in the Department of State as Undersecretary for Economic Affairs. Yet, as far as Vandenberg was concerned, his connection with the State Department was enough to disqualify him. Vandenberg wrote immediately to Marshall to convey his misgivings. He assured the Secretary of his regard for Clayton, but he called attention to "the overriding Congressional desire that the ERP Administrator shall come from the outside business world with strong industrial credentials and not via the State Department. . . . [T]his job as ERP Administrator stands out by itself . . . as requiring particularly persuasive economic credentials *unrelated to diplomacy.*"[26]

A short while later the President called Vandenberg to the White House and suggested Dean Acheson, who by this time had left the State Department for private law practice. But once again the same considerations applied. The President might send Acheson's name up, but Vandenberg replied rather bluntly that the Senate would never confirm him.

Willy-nilly, Vandenberg had wrested for himself the job of choosing the Administrator of the ECA. The man he finally settled upon was Paul G. Hoffman, the president of Studebaker, and one of the business members of the Harriman Committee. It was through his service on the committee, and most notably through his testimony before the Foreign Relations Committee that he came to impress Vandenberg. Hoffman had made his start in business as a used car salesman on the West Coast. What moved him up in the business world were the qualities that now brought him to Vandenberg's attention—the drive and persuasiveness of the salesman, and that invaluable feel for the concrete. Traditionally he was a

[25] Senate Foreign Relations Committee, *ERP Hearings*, 1948, p. 150.
[26] Vandenberg, *op.cit.*, p. 393. Emphasis added.

Republican, and like Vandenberg his early attitudes toward foreign policy were formed in the isolationist Midwest. But now, like many others, he supported an active and permanent role for the United States in international affairs. When he left the ECA after nearly three years of defending the program, he would be even more of a true believer. The colleagues he recruited from the business world as mission chiefs usually left after one or two years to return to their businesses. But Hoffman, as it turned out, would never go back. From the Marshall Plan he moved to a new career with the United Nations, working on the problems of investment in under-developed countries.

Fortunately, Hoffman displayed the public attitudes that were accepted as orthodox for businessmen. He was naturally wary of government intrusions into the economy, particularly as they approached the fringes of government ownership. He earnestly believed that a free economy tended to raise the standard of living and release vital human energies. He was a convinced free trader, and as several businessmen would discover somewhat painfully later, he meant it. Unlike his peers in the business world, he tinkered openly with Keynes and was willing to accept a role for the government in guiding the economy. But that was as far as he went, and for his own part he was still inclined to think that taxes were too high, and that a prime goal of the government was to reduce them. Thus his apostasy remained hardly more than parenthetical, while at the same time he possessed certain qualities of open-mindedness that seemed to suit him quite well for the task of administering the Marshall Plan. Hoffman himself was reluctant to accept the position, but Vandenberg was insistent, and Truman forced his hand in the end simply by announcing the appointment.[27]

Interestingly enough, this elevation of business competence was not confined to the Congress. Secretary of Defense Forrestal, himself a successful corporate executive, had long been advocating the virtues of "business brains," particularly for the administration for the Marshall Plan. In Forrestal, also, one could find the reflections of an older theory of politics. He wrote to John Snyder in March 1947 that "the world could only be brought back to order by a restoration of commerce, trade and business, and that would have to

[27] *Ibid.*, pp. 393-94. Vandenberg later disclosed that before he had selected Hoffman he had surveyed the opinions of over 100 businessmen. Hoffman led the rank of nominations in at least half the cases.

be done by businessmen."[28] Thirty years earlier and they might have been the words of Robert Lansing, earnestly entreating Woodrow Wilson to recede on the League of Nations. One may recall that Lansing virtually wrecked his career as Secretary of State through his tireless pleading with the President to relent on the issue of the League for the sake of hastening the treaties of peace. For Lansing the world desperately needed the restoration of peace and normal commercial intercourse. Every moment of delay merely played into the hands of the Bolsheviks by leaving the postwar world in its current state of disorganization and unrest.[29]

Although Hull was gone, there was still someone in the Administration who could fall back upon the old liberal view of commercial intercourse as conciliating, unifying, restorative. Nor did one have to go back to Europe, to John Stuart Mill or Adam Smith, to get an older statement of the argument. There were indigenous sources to draw upon, dating back at least to John Winthrop and an even more radical statement of this position in the *Agrippa Letters*. Vandenberg's views on the relevance of business were obviously caricatures, but the point is that they were reflections on a crude level of a political theory that was itself more firmly grounded and articulated. It was an outlook that was shared more widely in the government and, one would have to confess, it was a theory that still carried considerable plausibility.

III

In considering the tone of the Congressional reception, it is easy to overstate the Congressional appetite for revision, while overlooking the fact that the claims of the State Department were already significantly diminished in the Administration bill. The major departments had divided the program into spheres of influence, subject to some overall coordination with the State Department on the foreign policy issues. Of course, the focus of the program was

[28] Walter Millis (ed.), *The Forrestal Diaries* (New York: The Viking Press, 1951), p. 248.

[29] Lansing wrote later: "Those who recall the political and social conditions in Europe during the winter of 1918-19 . . . will comprehend the apprehension caused by anything which interrupted the negotiation of the peace. No one dared to prophesy what might happen if the state of political uncertainty and industrial stagnation, which existed under the armistices, continued." Robert Lansing, *The Peace Negotiations* (Boston: Houghton Mifflin Company, 1921), pp. 170, 173.

overseas, and therefore in the State Department's field. But that was not enough to give dominant authority to the State Department in decisions affecting the domestic economy, even if those decisions happened to be instrumental for the goals of the Marshall Plan. Thus the legislation that was finally sent to the Hill provided for an agency that would work within the existing facilities and the current distribution of functions. By the same token, it was admitted that the claims of the other agencies to influence the decisions of the ECA were at least as strong as the claims of the department in its own sphere. Once that admission was made, however, it became all the more difficult to justify an ill-defined State Department authority, hovering over the ECA and carrying the portents of intervention without limits.

All of the major farm, labor, and business groups gave their support to the Marshall Plan, but they all expressed concern on the issue of administration. Often they made explicit what was only implied in the legislation. In January, J. T. Sanders of the National Grange stated the argument in its most concise form:

> We feel that the European recovery program not only profoundly affects our foreign policies; but it will inevitably have a pronounced effect on our domestic economy. Obviously the State Department could not alone administer this vast program and be informed on its influence on the domestic economy. Only the Departments of Agriculture, Commerce, and Labor could constantly reflect its impact on our domestic economy in any group administering the program.[30]

Alan Kline of the American Farm Bureau Federation was willing to admit the State Department, but only as one member of a larger governing board that would represent all the interested parties; and that idea soon took hold among other groups, which were quick to recognize the possibilities for expanding their own influence.[31] Labor, however, did not join the chorus for a governing board. Union spokesmen made it clear that they expected the interests of labor to be represented in the program, but rather than tinkering with the agency, their concerns would be satisfied later by opening high-level positions in the administration to experienced professionals from the AFL and CIO.

[30] Senate Foreign Relations Committee, *ERP Hearings*, 1948, p. 1127.
[31] *Ibid.*, pp. 1117-18. See, in particular, the testimony of William Brooks for the North American Export Grain Association, pp. 1029-30.

On the policy questions, Labor was committed to a more generous and universalistic program. Phillip Murray and Walter Reuther set a liberal tone for the unions when they recommended a four-year authorization with "no strings attached." Ironically, their views brought them into concert for a moment with Vandenberg and his impulse toward a new diplomacy. In arguing for a program without conditions, and without the assumptions of a bipolar division in the world, they were refusing, in effect, to use diplomatic or political considerations in governing the distribution of aid. Murray found himself in somewhat strange company, therefore, when he confessed to the Senate committee that he was wary of having the State Department participate at all in the program lest it appear "that the aid given to the people of any nation or any groups of nations will depend at any given time upon the details of that nation's relations with our State Department."[32]

The configuration of attitudes suggested that no one was really enthusiastic about the authority of the State Department in the program. At best, some of the major organized groups were indifferent, but there were others who were obviously fearful, and who would have felt a great deal easier if the authority of the department were reduced. For in that case they would have had some assurance that the Marshall Plan would not be used to trigger a major reorganization of the bureaucracy in the areas where they presently enjoyed access.

By the time, then, that the scene shifted to the floor of Congress, the State Department had already acquiesced to a substantial weakening of its claims, the major interest groups offered either support or tolerance for any Congressional move to deflate the role of the department, and Congress found itself with a wide latitude of choice in reconstructing the plan for administration. Thus Vandenberg was free to reach out for the Brookings report and read it in a manner he found congenial.

A key phrase in the Brookings report was the assertion that "no system of interagency coordination has yet been devised that can escape the necessity of final appeals to the President as the superior authority in the event of unreconciled differences between the heads of the agencies involved." From this observation, the report skipped to the conclusion that the Administrator should be guaranteed an equal and uninhibited access to the President. We know

[32] *Ibid.*, pp. 1298, 1301.

104

from hindsight that the Brookings statement was intentionally ambiguous. Yet how could Vandenberg really be criticized if he interpreted it to mean that the State Department should not be the final and authoritative source of conflict resolution in the program? That would mean, as the Brookings report plainly seemed to say, that the department could not be allowed to stand athwart the channels of communication between the Administrator of the ECA and the President. To eliminate that threat from the State Department, two principal things had to be done: (1) The provision that the ECA would act under the "direction and control" of the Secretary of State on matters affecting foreign policy would have to be removed; and (2) the ECA would have to be given a status more nearly comparable to that of the State Department. Vandenberg now moved to accomplish both of these objectives, and on his urging they were enacted.

He turned next, however, to compensate the department and deal with its legitimate interests in the program. In requesting the Brookings report, he had written to Harold Moulton that the administrative plan had to provide essential autonomy for the ECA Administrator on the one hand, while at the same time preserving the "appropriate jurisdiction of the State Department over foreign policy." Ostensibly to serve that end Vandenberg adapted language from the Atomic Energy Act: The ECA Administrator and the Secretary of State were to keep each other fully informed on events within their spheres that might be relevant to one another. If the Secretary believed that any action or omission of the Administrator was inconsistent with American foreign policy, and if consultation did not resolve the conflict, the Secretary was given the right to appeal to the President. Actually, this addition made the situation considerably worse for the State Department. If nothing had been said, the question of whose task it was to take the dispute to the President would have remained open. But now the burden of appeal was placed clearly with Marshall and the State Department.[33] As it turned out, burdens of this kind could be quite heavy indeed,

[33] The same provisions on consultation were applied to the relations between the ECA and diplomatic missions overseas. It is instructive that Alvin Roseman, who had been following the legislation for the Budget Bureau, reported that "the legislative intent is to make the special mission relatively independent of the regular diplomatic mission." This comment came after the revision had been made in the Foreign Relations Committee. Roseman to Stone and Martin, February 17, 1948, Bureau of the Budget, Series 39.18.

and they eventually worked upon the State Department with important substantive effects.

To leave no ambiguity about the matter, Congress went on to make some very specific changes that enlarged the functions of the ECA and made its divorce from the State Department seem all the more complete.

It was accepted in the Administration bill that the head of the ECA would have to consult with the National Advisory Council in determining the balance among loans and grants. The NAC had been created in the Bretton Woods Act to coordinate all agencies making foreign loans or otherwise engaged in the area of financial transactions with foreign countries. The Secretary of the Treasury was the chairman of the governing board, which included the Secretaries of State and Commerce along with representatives of the Federal Reserve System and the Export-Import Bank. Under the formula of State Department "direction and control," the ECA was to be represented on the National Advisory Council through the Secretary of State. That arrangement seemed perfectly appropriate as long as the ECA was subordinate to the State Department, but with the move to an independent agency Congress was meticulous in leaving no symbolic relation unadjusted. The bill was amended to make the ECA Administrator a full member of the NAC. With that change, the ECA became an active partner with the chance to make its own case. And since it would be sitting in judgment of other agencies whose interests came before the committee, it figured to improve its own bargaining power substantially. By any reckoning, the alteration promised to lessen the restraints on the ECA by removing what Marshall had predicted would be the most formidable external check on the new agency.[34]

The anxiety over the shipment of industrial goods to the Soviet Union became the source of another enlargement for the ECA. Early in the Congressional discussions Senator Knowland pointed out to his colleagues that the United States was shipping about $150 million in machine tools and industrial equipment to the So-

[34] Marshall told the Senate Foreign Relations Committee that the ECA Administrator "has to assure them [the NAC]. He has to win their agreement. That is a difficult thing because each member has to act in the light of how this is going to be explained at some future date, and that imposes a very difficult situation on the individual because his freedom is very much curtailed in that respect." Senate Foreign Relations Committee, *ERP Hearings*, 1948, p. 27.

viet Union. In return, the United States was receiving $20 million worth of metals and furs. What annoyed Knowland was the apparent irony of contributing to the industrial strength of the USSR at the same time that the Marshall Plan was creating the prospect of scarcities in the United States. A few days later he brought in an amendment to restrict that trade. In its main section it provided that no exports would be allowed to European countries outside the Marshall Plan (i.e., the Soviet bloc countries) if there was any danger that the remaining supplies would not be sufficient to meet the needs of the recovery program.

Despite Knowland's anti-Communist stance, the amendment was really very moderate. It made no effort to cut off the trade with Russia or force the hand of the Administration. It merely said, in essence, that the Marshall Plan was more important to the United States than any immediate interest in trading with the Soviet Union, or as Knowland phrased it, in "building up the one nation trying to obstruct the Marshall Plan." Besides, the final decision would rest with the Commerce Department rather than the ECA, and in certain special cases Knowland was willing to permit the shipment of goods on grounds of some higher national interest.[35]

But over in the House, where Karl Mundt and his cohorts roamed, there was a far different temper. According to Mundt, it was the negligence of the Commerce Department itself that was at issue. Therefore, he responded with his own amendment, and what followed was a series of maneuvers of unusual intricacy and contrivance. In passing the Mundt amendment, what the House did, in effect, was to enlarge the ECA into an administrative monster that would integrate export controls and function outside the reach of the President. The result was to force a negotiation in conference in which Commerce would be deprived of the primacy it was given in the Knowland amendment.[36] The Senate conferees agreed to eliminate the mention of the Secretary of Commerce, but with that, also, they deleted an important support for integrated export controls in the Marshall Plan. The controls, then, would remain decentralized. If the ECA wanted to argue for its Marshall Plan needs, it would have to go before Agriculture, Commerce, the Office of Defense Transportation, and the varied lot of interdepartmental bodies.

[35] *Congressional Record*, XCIV (1948), 2297.
[36] Vandenberg reported back to the Senate that this was the one issue on which the House conferees absolutely refused to yield. *Ibid.*, 4035.

Nevertheless, the ECA emerged from the conference with a considerably higher status. To provide another check on the administration of export licenses, the Administrator of the ECA was authorized to refuse deliveries to ERP countries of certain goods that were intended for reshipment to nonparticipating countries. The test was whether those goods would be denied export licenses in the United States if they were scheduled for direct shipment to the same destinations. The significance of this provision was that it brought the ECA into the interdepartmental organization on export controls. As a result of the conference decision, the ECA was given membership very early on the Commerce Department's Advisory Committee on Export Policy (ACEP).[37] There it could act as a claimant for the needs of the Marshall Plan, even to the point of questioning the allotments to other countries that were not participants in the Marshall Plan. Thus the ECA would come a long way from that original blueprint in which the agency was seen as little more than a ward of the State Department.

Precisely how far it had come was revealed in the House discussion of the Mundt amendment. Leslie Arends raised the question of how one could expect the ECA to be any more diligent in restricting shipments to Russia than the Commerce Department had been in the past. Mundt replied that he was relying on far more than the grant of additional authority to the ECA. The intent of the amendment, he explained, was to make the ECA independent of the President and the Commerce Department. But the decisive means of enforcement lay outside that provision: They were in the requirement that the ECA return to Congress each year for authorizations as well as appropriations.[38] The administrators would have to furnish both quarterly and annual reports, and they would have to justify themselves in annual hearings before the two sets of committees dealing with foreign affairs and appropriations.

[37] See "Survey of the Economic Cooperation Administration," September 1951, p. 53, U.S. Bureau of the Budget, Series 39.32. Cited hereafter as Bureau of the Budget, *Survey of the ECA*, 1951. This was the report made after an extensive Budget Bureau survey of the organization in 1951. The basis of the report was a massive collection of interviews with the heads and other members of the ECA divisions. Since the interviews were conducted when the ECA was still in existence, they probably represent the most important single set of documents on the actual operating experiences of the ECA.

[38] *Congressional Record*, XCIV (1948), 3418.

Vandenberg himself had continually resisted the demand for annual authorizations. To satisfy Senators Wherry and Taft, he agreed to reduce the first appropriation from $6.8 billion over fifteen months to $5.3 billion for the first year of operation. Still, the two Republican leaders railed at the prospect of a four-year commitment. But for Vandenberg the difference between the one-year and the four-year commitment was the difference between relief and reconstruction, and by insisting on that point he managed to carry his position.

In the House, however, the situation had not been so manageable. As the floor manager for the bill, Congressman Vorys had to beat back three separate efforts to restrict the program to one year. Yet the doggedness of the attempts indicated something about the temper of the House; and so, when the bill was in conference, the House conferees finally pressed their counterparts in the Senate to accept annual authorizations. In no way did they disturb the original understanding that the program was intended as a four-year venture. But the importance of the change, as Karl Mundt boasted to his colleagues in the House, was that it tied the ECA more firmly to the Congress.

And if somehow, after all this, the State Department did not get the message, the point could be made crudely explicit in private conversation. A few weeks later, at the beginning of April, the ECA tried to retain those people in the State Department who had been working on the Interim Aid program. But the plan ran afoul of the appropriations committees and their redoubtable chairmen. Alvin Roseman reported that Senator Bridges and Congressman Taber "voiced strong views that the State Department should not have anything to do with the administration of ECA." Under the circumstances, it was agreed in the department that it would be better not "to appear in any institutional role in ECA operations at this stage."[39]

The Congressional decision on the relation between the State Department and the ECA was now complete. It was also unambiguous. The disparagement of the State Department seemed to have been the price the Administration had to pay if it hoped to get anything close to the type of European program it wanted. That the decision did represent a critical divide in the Congressional action

[39] Roseman to Webb, April 7, 1948, in Bureau of the Budget, Series 39.18.

was disclosed rather clearly when Senator Taft rose to make his
first comments on the bill:

> I think there is a substantial difference on the question of the role
> of the State Department [from that which appeared in the Ad-
> ministration bill]. . . . I think the great thing which has been done
> has been to take away from the State Department the adminis-
> tration of the relief program. I think the committee has done an
> extraordinary job. Regardless of the fact that the President may
> decide between the State Department, or he may not so decide,
> at any rate the man who argues with him is on an equal basis
> with the Secretary of State. So I think it is a very substan-
> tial change and one which I think makes the bill infinitely more
> acceptable.[40]

IV

Something further needs to be said about Vandenberg's decision
on the ECA and the State Department; for in addition to what it
revealed of his attitudes on foreign policy, it was a measure of his
judgment, too, on the national interest in the Marshall Plan.

In the Senate floor debate, Senator Ball maintained that
the threat posed by Russia was wholly military in character, and
for that reason an economic program alone was bound to be inadequate. What was needed, rather, was the kind of aid that
could "checkmate the onrolling avalanche of Soviet power—naked,
completely ruthless power." Senator Lodge rejoined that a military
pact might not be able to cope with the threat of subversion and internal unrest. He conceded that a program of economic aid could
not have prevented the coup in Czechoslovakia, but he contended
that countries so near the strength of the Red Army were beyond
the practical limits of American military support.[41]

What Lodge suggested, then, was that the Marshall Plan was a
response to the dangers of economic unrest, which could be ex-
ploited for political purposes by the local agents of the Soviet
Union. But what if the most pressing danger suddenly became military? Did the Marshall Plan imply a willingness to make a military
response? It was possible to infer from Lodge's words that the an-

[40] *Congressional Record*, XCIV (1948), 2539.
[41] *Ibid.*, 1984-85, 2025.

swer might be yes, but the fact of the matter was that he simply never addressed himself to that issue. Senator McClellan, on the other hand, thought the decision on the Marshall Plan should forecast something about the likelihood of a military commitment. He was convinced that economic aid by itself would not guarantee security. If the presence of aid meant anything, it signified a deeper political interest in the fate of Western Europe. One day, he warned, the United States might be called upon to back up its investment in economic resources, and a vote for ERP would mean nothing unless it foretold that future choice. No one, he declared, should vote in favor of the Marshall Plan unless he was prepared to vote later for a tighter military and political alliance.[42]

To his credit it could be said that McClellan displayed here the kind of self-consciousness that one usually hopes for in policy-making. Still, it was legitimate to view the question of national interest in a rather different light. Instead of seeing economic and military policies as parts of a seamless web, it might be desirable to accept finer distinctions among the programs. Without surrendering to pragmatism it may be possible to take a more empirical approach, in which commitments can be seen as ensembles of separate issues or as decisions reached under the strain of peculiar circumstance. One advantage in this approach is that it avoids the temptation to generalize too quickly. In the case of the Marshall Plan, this method was particularly suited to the needs of Vandenberg as he faced the resistance in his own party. Men like Taft and Wherry had not plunged from their prewar isolationism to embrace a naïve internationalism. They showed their caution at every point, seeking in turn a weaker commitment, a shorter duration, a lower aid figure. Clearly, there was no consensus yet on the American commitment in Europe. It was only natural then that the inclinations of the moment were in favor of keeping that question open. In the same way that Lodge chose to treat the military problem as a separate issue, the decision on the Marshall Plan could not be read to support anything more than a limited program of economic aid. For the time being, the Congress would merely wait and see how the situation in Europe developed. The military threat might vanish, or conditions might worsen and the American stake in Europe could become clearer; or it might be decided after all that the price

[42] *Ibid.*, 2038, 2782-83.

was too high, that it was better to cut the losses with the economic program and back away from the military commitment.

Vandenberg's own conviction that the program was business-like in character led him to view the question of commitment now in precisely this singular and highly restrictive form. If his thought patterns had followed McClellan's, the decision for the Marshall Plan should have entailed the decision for the North Atlantic Treaty. But in a revealing exchange on this issue with Senator Brewster, Vandenberg proved that he had not even begun to think in this direction. Despite his personal involvement in the Marshall Plan, he confessed to some serious doubts that the so-called Atlantic community represented a real community of interests. Even at this late date, the American relationship to Western Europe seemed far more factitious to him than the tie to Latin America.[43]

But the clearest evidence on this point was the so-called "Vandenberg Resolution," which passed the Senate on June 11, 1948. The resolution was the product of a collaboration between Vandenberg and Robert Lovett that began sometime in April. Vandenberg's purpose in the resolution was to preserve some vital collective security arrangement within the framework of the United Nations but outside the reach of the veto. The point of entry was through Article 51 of the United Nations Charter, which sanctioned acts of individual or collective self-defense until the Security Council could take the measures necessary to restore peace. In immediate policy terms, the Vandenberg Resolution encouraged the United States to participate in regional collective security pacts, which in this context meant American military support for the Brussels Pact powers. For the Administration, the resolution was the effective green light for closer military cooperation with Western Europe. Within a month, discussions would begin at the State Department that would eventuate in the North Atlantic Pact. For Vandenberg the treaty offered the recognition that "related questions of physical security should arise" in connection with the economic aid program. And yet, as much as a year later, when he admitted that " 'physical security' is a prerequisite to the kind of long-range economic planning which Western Europe requires," he was no closer to an evaluation of the military risks. "The fact remains," he wrote to a constituent, "that the problem is fraught

[43] See the exchange with Brewster in *ibid.*, 2027-29.

with many hazardous imponderables. I am withholding my own final judgment until I see the precise terms of the treaty. . . ."[44]

Apart from the concern for domestic support, it might strike one as odd that the Administration felt the need to obtain anything like the Vandenberg Resolution. It would seem even harder to account for if the Marshall Plan had already settled the issue by determining the American interest in Europe. And what of Vandenberg? Why did he enter this time-consuming and intricate project with Lovett, and why did he feel the need to make an explicit statement in June if he had already decided the matter in April? What we are faced with essentially is a problem of political vision. If Vandenberg saw the reality of foreign policy in such a variegated way, if he refused to see military and economic policies as part of a grand design of national interest, what can we do except treat that vision on its own terms? One could hardly be justified in imposing some larger theory of national interest to explain his behavior if the theory was so patently at odds with Vandenberg's own understanding of what he was doing.

If Vandenberg had agreed with McClellan, for example, he would have had a considerably harder time in holding to his view of the Marshall Plan as a "business enterprise." The move to cut the ECA off from the State Department would have labored under a heavier burden of justification. Conversely, the decision for an autonomous ECA tended to support Vandenberg's view of the national interest question now, rather than McClellan's. The organizational separation would enforce the understanding that the ECA was doing something that was not really political or diplomatic in the conventional sense. This seemingly academic subtlety would find expression in the operating code of the agency; and it would have an incalculable value later in preventing certain unusual and regrettable arrangements from gaining the force of precedent.

Thus Vandenberg's decision on the matter of organization was an accurate reflex of his position on the question of national interest. His decision for the Marshall Plan was made without a sense of political commitment, and without any final conviction that there was a vital American interest in Western Europe (if we understand "vital interest" to mean, at the least, something worth fighting for). As for a concept of American interest in terms of power, it was

[44] Vandenberg, *op.cit.*, p. 475, and see generally pp. 404-11 on the development of the Vandenberg Resolution.

never even formulated. Instead of starting, then, from a positive view of American political and military interest in Western Europe, the Marshall Plan left that question very much open. That may be an interesting point in itself for the general problem of forming an intention in foreign policy. But it is especially important to keep in mind when considering the host of specific decisions that filled out the character of the program. For in their own way these decisions represented other national "interests," and they had the chance now to preempt the definition of the Marshall Plan.

6. CENTRALIZATION AND AUTHORITY: THE PRIORITY OF THE MARSHALL PLAN AT HOME

IN ITS SIMPLEST meaning centralization implies that a set of purposes has become so important that the diversity or delay of local options is no longer tolerable. Either way, centralization involves a transfer of power. In the context of public administration, where the administrative units have come to reflect commitments to social values, and where the separate agencies are tied to different groups in the society, the centralization issue may be charged with great controversy, for the programs of the various agencies contain interests that are cared about publicly. Their status in the Executive portrays the relative standing of their ends in the government as a whole. Questions of reorganization, then, can affect the autonomy, and precedence of these agencies as well as the ends of government, and almost invariably they will activate those groups in the public which have come to invest their concerns in the bureaucracy.

If the Marshall Plan was "the" preeminent national interest, the correct administrative response would have been a thorough centralization in which the ECA was given all the authority relevant to its tasks. Conceivably one could have harnessed the entire Executive to the efficient execution of this one particular program, and perhaps even reached out to command the resources of private industry. If the Marshall Plan was not the overriding national interest of the moment, then one had to determine just how far short of that preeminence it actually fell. In some respects, of course, it was a delicate task of balancing, and some of the decisions could be deferred or left vague. But interestingly enough, the most important questions could not be avoided, because they were raised by the problem of administration itself. One could not simply declare the existence of an agency; it had to be defined and assimilated to a standing structure of administration. The Administration and Con-

115

gress were forced to work out the authoritative relations between the new agency and the regular departments, and in the course of doing that they had to consider the weight of the Marshall Plan interest in a number of highly specific decisions.

I

If the Congressional leaders did not appreciate the significance of centralization, it was stated very explicitly for them by two witnesses—Bernard Baruch, the erstwhile presidential adviser, and Raymond Baldwin, a government consultant, who was not so prominently erstwhile, perhaps, but comparably officious. Baruch and Baldwin presented the paradigms of the highly centralized ECA and the two dominant lines of thought that could have justified that solution.

Baruch saw in the economic stabilization of Europe a purpose so vital to the free world that he likened the Marshall Plan to a war emergency. An emergency of this order required urgent measures and administrative forms tailored to those ends. Baruch called then for a "global strategy" for peace: "If . . . we produce for peace as we produced for war, all-out, without interruptions, strikes, lockouts, or profit scrambling, mankind's whole lot and outlook would be magically lifted." In his plan, the United States would stand ready to buy all nonperishable raw materials "produced anywhere and by anyone in the world" for five years if those products could not find normal commercial outlets. The President's tariff authority would be continued for another three years; the Europeans would be induced to federate in a political, economic, and defensive union; and all of the European currencies would be stabilized.

At home there would be a sense of wartime emergency. A two-year production drive would be started, with longer hours and overtime where feasible. With the economy operating at a high pitch, the next critical problem would be inflation, and that too would be attacked with the seriousness of a war emergency. Food prices would be reduced in return for guaranteed crop prices. Wages would be stabilized, rent controls reinstituted, and the excess profits tax restored by 50 percent of the cut from wartime levels. Tax reduction would be postponed for two years, along with many less essential federal and state projects. Priority would go to increasing production, housing, schools, and hospitals.[1]

[1] Senate Foreign Relations Committee, *ERP Hearings*, 1948, pp. 556-57.

"By inclination," he told the Senate committee, "I am opposed to governmental controls, except in war-time." But he argued that in reality, "we have no peace today. The demobilization was done too hurriedly, without adequately considering this fact, that the peace has still to be won."

To administer a strong program the new agency would have "corporate power if not . . . corporate form." The Administrator would work under the direction of the Secretary of State and the President, and he would be aided by a board of directors that would include the heads of the major cooperating agencies. More critically, the administrative organization would recognize the fact that the European Recovery Program was *the central task* facing the government: The Administrator would handle all purchasing, even for foreign governments, in order to prevent competitive buying. He would issue directives to all federal agencies with the approval of the President, and he would control all export licenses, not only for the participating countries, but for all recipients of American exports.[2]

Baruch's onslaught left the committee overwhelmed, for it was at once too grandiose and too simple. Both labor and management had been chafing under the restraints of wartime controls. To revive those controls now, along with command direction of the economy, must surely have seemed politically untenable. It was doubly foolish to consider when there was no real evidence yet that the task of pumping goods into Europe would require such an extensive control over the economy. And besides, it *was* peacetime.

The Baruch proposal was too simple because it provided no necessary guidance in handling a plethora of smaller decisions that could still have an important effect on the character of the program. For example, was it more efficient to build up an integrated government procurement organization, or was it equally effective to work through the established private channels of trade? If there was no conspicuous advantage for government procurement on the matter of efficiency, there were good reasons in principle for favoring private channels. If one was inclined, though, to favor private channels of trade, what method could be used to document the transactions? Presumably Baruch favored speed, which might have suggested freedom from the audit of the Comptroller General. But that also removed an important instrument of Congressional control, and when Baruch urged a return to government controls, was

[2] *Ibid.*, pp. 564-65.

117

he referring really to *Executive* authority, and was it his intention to squeeze Congress out of the field? Thus the wholesale, "go all the way" approach not only lost the sense of limits, but it failed to recognize that there were important variations in the way even that full-throttled effort could be made.

The committee showed Baruch its usual courtesy, however mingled with incredulity. Vandenberg dismissed him rather sardonically with the assurance that "we are indebted to you for your message on the state of the Union and on the state of the world."[3]

Another plan for a mammoth ECA was presented with a different line of argument by Raymond Baldwin, a government consultant whose credentials included a period of government service during the war. Supposedly he had been brought before the House Foreign Affairs Committee to support Christian Herter's plan for a corporate administration. As it turned out, however, he was far less interested in Herter's corporation as a solution to the problem than as one tool in the arsenal of an "effective" administration. His real mission was to give the committee the insights of his administrative thinking.

Fittingly, Baldwin defined the question entirely in the terms of administrative theory. It was assumed that the Marshall Plan would have a set of ends, and that regardless of what those ends were, the program had to be administered effectively. Effective administration meant combating the inherent bureaucratic tendencies toward rivalry, conflict, and indecision. The answer he discovered was in the swollen authority of an administrator who could define jurisdictions—and then invade them in his supreme capacity to impose decisions. In Baldwin's view of the administrative state of nature, bureaucrats actually wanted to thwart policy. They thwarted it mainly because it was not theirs; for their basic drive was to be imperialistic, to expand their own domain and get more of the good things of bureaucratic life. The only remedy was authority, with a slight admixture of terror. For the ECA Administrator to observe

---

[3] The Baruch testimony came up a short time later in a telephone conversation between Forrestal and James F. Byrnes. Forrestal commented that "Bernie is wonderful at advocating ex cathedra [complete control of the economy] but it may not be so easy politically." Byrnes was convinced that "B.M.'s statement—so far as the Congress is concerned—made a bad impression. . . I talked to [Senator] George and somebody else on the committee—I think Vandenberg; you remember that Van said that he'd covered the waterfront? . . . And B.M. didn't like it." Walter Millis (ed.), *The Forrestal Diaries* (New York: The Viking Press, 1951), p. 428.

118

jurisdictional lines, or to be confined in his contacts to the heads of the cooperating agencies, was really to lay himself open to sabotage. Instead, the Administrator would need the authority to "go down into the working level of [an] organization, and arrange for the man in that organization who is going to do the particular functional job that he is responsible for, to get in direct contact with the other functional men that he is going to have to deal with."[4] Of course, the Administrator's own area of activity could not be exposed to such invasions from other agencies. And as a corollary to his right of unrestricted access, he was not to be compelled to seek an advance authorization, which might spell out his privileges. Baldwin argued that in most cases a previous specification of this kind would restrict the choices of the Administrator and put him at a serious disadvantage in bargaining.[5]

The reaction of the House committee to Baldwin was not nearly as definite as the Senate committee's reception of the Baruch proposal. As overblown as it was, there was at least a linkage in Baruch's plan between the administrative means and the political ends. With Baldwin, on the other hand, the argument was pegged at a very abstract level of administrative theory. Consequently, he was far too nebulous on the question of ends, and almost ingenuously blithe when dealing with the interests of other agencies. For the sake of coming down out of the clouds the committee asked him to consider the issue of export controls, which were then divided among several agencies. The introduction of departmental interests complicated the problem for Baldwin, but he had no trouble in finding his way back to familiar ground:

> It is only by the ability of the Administrator to control exports to the ERP countries, and to prevent shipments of goods to destinations, or in amounts, of which his agency has not approved, that he can prevent unauthorized encroachment upon the gross allocation of any given commodity allocated to ERP, and can be sure that shipments which are made will contribute to the recovery of Europe in accordance with a predetermined plan.[6]

The rule of efficiency called for complete centralization, and it apparently left no room to consider why the export controls were divided in the first place, or why the same argument for effective-

---

[4] House Foreign Affairs Committee, *ERP Hearings*, 1948, p. 1659.
[5] *Ibid.*, p. 1657.　　　　　　　　　　[6] *Ibid.*, p. 1670.

ness could not be used by the Departments of Commerce and Agriculture in defending their own positions. The cross-examination continued, and Baldwin was given a further chance to elaborate on his testimony. But once again he failed to leaven his administrative theory with the kinds of empirical and ethical considerations that the Committee itself would be forced to weigh in making its own decision. In this respect, the Committee was given a valuable lesson on how naïve it was to reach decisions on the strength of administrative theory alone, as though substantive questions of policy could be disguised and resolved as problems of administration.

This question of export controls, on which Baldwin proved so impressively unhelpful, was becoming the keystone of the whole centralization issue. The response of Commerce and Agriculture, as well as the major farm groups, clearly branded it as an issue that could elicit strong feelings. There were reports, for example, that the Harriman committee was split over the issue of export controls, and that a majority of the committee was determined to bring in a recommendation for a corporate ECA.

To explore the controversy the Senate committee summoned former Sen. Robert LaFollette, who headed one of the subcommittees in the Harriman group. According to LaFollette, the members of the committee were not fully decided on a corporate form, but the logic of their deliberations seemed to be pushing them in that direction. The committee started with the view that ECA should work through private channels of trade rather than establishing a large government procurement agency. But if that premise were accepted, the Administrator would have little control over what was shipped unless he had some powers of screening, or a veto over export licenses. To acquire these export controls, other departments would have to be divested of them; and, LaFollette reasoned, if the ECA was to have all these controls, then it began to look very much like a self-sufficient corporation.[7]

Unfortunately the consensus in the Harriman committee was broken by one unseemly dissenter: Averell Harriman. Along with the honor of being chairman of the committee, Harriman was also the head of the department that had the most to lose by a change in the administration of export controls. He was joined by Secretary of Agriculture Anderson in denying the need for a change and citing the superior experience of their own professional staffs. Har-

[7] Senate Foreign Relations Committee, *ERP Hearings*, 1948, pp. 1177-78.

120

riman questioned the wisdom, also, of placing the program in a corporation, where it could lose its vital contacts with other departments.[8] But that was an inverted argument, which basically assumed what others would have had him prove—that the ECA deserved to be organized in the first place as a dependent agency that would lack the primary instruments of its own policy ends.

What all this questioning did, however, was to generate support for a corporate board. Merely by raising the question of reorganization Congress induced the major farm groups to consider membership on a governing board as a form of insurance. J. T. Sanders of the National Grange thought that a governing board would be a useful device for giving all the interested parties a voice in decisions. Alan Kline of the American Farm Bureau federation was willing to uphold the generality of the principle and admit any interested group to the board as long as his own group was included.[9] As if to pick up the invitation, Harvey Brown of the Machinists' Union suggested that his group, too, expected to be consulted in this program, and, indeed, the idea now seemed to be catching on.[10]

But there were dangers of having the issue captured by people with an axe to grind. Thus, the testimony of William Brooks, speaking for a group of wheat exporters, gave the Senate committee some reason to pause and reflect on the risks of reorganization. Brooks charged that the current administration of export controls was being used to discriminate against the wheat exporters. For Brooks and his group, the Marshall Plan provided an opportune moment to reform the law and transfer the controls out of the Department of Agriculture. First, there would be a reduction of controls, as the program relied on private channels of trade. Second, export controls would be taken away from Commerce and Agriculture and centralized in a new agency that would use "non-discriminatory" criteria. Fairness would be assured by vesting decisions in a governing board composed of all interested groups, and by giving each member an effective veto over all policies.[11]

It was a strikingly candid proposal and one that was not without

[8] House Foreign Affairs Committee, *ERP Hearings*, 1948, pp. 474, 490-91, 512.

[9] *Ibid.*, pp. 1115, 1117-18.

[10] Senate Foreign Relations Committee, *ERP Hearings*, 1948, pp. 726-28. Although he favored an advisory board, Brown shared the general opposition of Labor to the idea of a corporation.

[11] Senate Foreign Relations Committee, *ERP Hearings*, 1948, pp. 1029-30.

its instructive value for the members of the Senate committee. It told them precisely what they could expect if they decided to re-open the whole question of organization. Politically, the most convenient decision was to leave the controls where they were. Neither the Chamber of Commerce nor the National Association of Manufacturers raised the issue. The anxieties seemed to be concentrated among the farm organizations, and of the major groups to take a position on the matter, all were opposed to withdrawing the controls from the Department of Agriculture.

Aside from these political considerations, still another line of reasoning developed in the hearings to support the existing arrangement of export controls. Senator Smith of New Jersey broached the subject to John Foster Dulles one day when the latter was appearing before the Senate committee. Smith was concerned at the time that the dispersion of export controls would work to hobble the ECA by subjecting the agency to a continuing veto from other departments. Dulles recalled some administrative lessons from the past that seemed to suggest, though, that the alternatives were not quite as sharp as they appeared. He noted that during the First World War the Chairman of the War Trade Board was given complete authority over export and import controls. Under the law, the Chairman was pledged merely to consult with a board of representatives drawn from Commerce, Interior, Agriculture, and State. But because it was critical to have the support of these agencies in his work, the Chairman found it essential to get a consensus on the board before taking any action. To Dulles the experience indicated that the controls could be exercised responsibly and effectively if the framework was cooperative[12]—i.e., if the agencies were so dependent on one another in their day to day work that there was a natural incentive to cooperate.

Dulles's argument was taken one step further in the House hearings by William Batt of the National Planning Association. Batt was reminded of his experience with the Combined Raw Materials Board during the war, when the board had plenary power in its operations and was not even required to consult with an advisory board. Yet, a pattern of consensus-seeking developed that seemed to exaggerate the experience of the War Trade Board in the First World War.

[12] *Ibid.*, pp. 607-608.

Theoretically [said Batt], the American representative of the Combined Raw Materials Board for the United States could take materials away from anybody. Practically, he would not have lasted down here a week, if he had gone about that ruthlessly. I learned pretty soon you can move just about as fast as they will support you, and no faster. There were times when I had a difficult time to get the Civilian Supply people in the War Production Board to go along with me. . . . Sometimes the State Department would be sticky. You have to get the majority, the ones that count, to go along with you.[13]

Where bureaucratic interdependence existed, where one agency simply needed the contributions of another, a cooperative structure was more likely to develop. Centralizing export controls in the ECA would not remove its dependence on other agencies, while it did promise to create a great deal of resentment. On the other hand, decentralized controls had worked in the past, and they were likely to encourage coordination. Therefore, accepting the status quo on export controls threatened no real disservice to the ECA. The Departments of Commerce and Agriculture had no interest in frustrating the Marshall Plan. Their major concern, rather, was to discipline the decisions on procurement with some regard for the domestic supply situation. Besides, the current arrangements had been worked out over several years and a few successive statutes; and there was no evidence to show that the reasons behind those earlier decisions had lost their validity.

Based on the arguments and precedents that were presented in the hearings, there were sound reasons, then, for Congress to make the judgment it did and leave the export controls decentralized. In the conference action on the Knowland and Mundt amendments, the conferees had another chance to make their intention clear, and they rejected even a partial integration of export controls that would have covered only the needs of the Marshall Plan. Having made that decision, it was more coherent also to reject Raymond Baldwin's advice on coordination. It made good sense now to follow the Administration bill and require the ECA to obtain the consent of the department head before it used the facilities of another agency. In this way the legislation did more than enjoin the participants to cooperate; it actually defined the structure of au-

[13] House Foreign Affairs Committee, *ERP Hearings*, 1948, p. 1156.

thority that would govern coordination. It moved beyond coordination as a general term and sought to prescribe a peculiar kind of coordination that placed certain interests before others. If the ECA stood in that scheme as a dependent agency, it was a telling judgment on the rank of the Marshall Plan interest.

II

The dispute over Christian Herter's plan for a corporate ECA must have a prominent place in any discussion of the centralization issue in the Marshall Plan. Although it was not an entirely accurate understanding, most of the discussants were prone to regard a corporation as the most extreme form of a centralized ECA. By definition, a corporation was an entity, complete, self-contained, possessing all the authority and flexibility required for its special purposes. Thus, when the Harriman committee (minus Harriman) began to consider the need for centralized export controls, it began at the same time to investigate the possibilities for a government corporation. For our present purposes the decision on the corporation contributed importantly to the articulation of the Marshall Plan. If the defeat of the corporation plan represented nothing more than another victory for the cause of decentralization, it would hardly deserve more than a passing mention. But in rejecting the Herter plan Congress established the salience of three other policy values: Congressional authority, the reliance on private channels of trade, and the restraint on bureaucratic expansion.

As the hearings would demonstrate, a surprisingly large part of the controversy could be cleared away simply by dispelling some of the confusions in the word "corporation." The problem of the government corporation was that it had come a long way—too long a way, in fact—from those early days when the Panama Railroad Company and the Inland Waterways Corporation could stand as rather unambiguous examples of the corporate concept in government. As corporations multiplied, however, through two world wars and the New Deal, they brought a large number of variations to suit their specialized purposes. The result was that the "government corporation" began to lose its integrity as a concept. Previously, it was thought that only a narrow class of "economic enterprise" could lend itself to the corporate form. But the term "economic enterprise" could now cover a huge multipurpose organization like the TVA, while operations as business-like as the Post Office and the Bonneville Dam were not organized as corporations. Moreover, the use of corporations in the Second World War showed that they did not have to be self-contained. Corporations could be employed as subsidiaries to engage in preclusive buying or the purchase of scarce materials. In these cases, they were used quite consciously as instruments of other organizations, and for ends that were clearly political.

Under emergency conditions, the pressure to get something done usually outweighed the concern for administrative form. Corporations began to appear then that lacked one or more of the traditional corporate features. It was not uncommon, for example, to find corporations that had been denied the right to issue stock or to retain their own receipts. But as they were deprived of the capacity for self-financing, they also lost the most critical supports to their corporate autonomy. If corporations were forced to get money from Congress through the ordinary process of appropriations, they would have to submit their budgets to annual hearings. Equally important, they would be subject to the audit of the Comptroller General and the general overhead controls of the Budget Bureau and the Civil Service Commission. In 1934, an Executive order imposed the auditing requirement on all corporations whose accounting procedures had been left unspecified in the law. With that order there began a steady but piecemeal attack on the autonomy of government corporations, which picked up momentum in the late 1930s with the drive for Executive integration. Subsequently, all corporations were brought into the regular departments of the government. An Executive order of 1938 extended civil service coverage to all positions in wholly-owned government corporations that had not been specifically exempted by statute. The trend was finally brought to its culmination in 1945 with the passage of the Government Corporation Control Act. The 1945 act codified the changes that occurred over the past decade and went on to place some firm obstacles in the way of a casual resort to the corporate device. By that time, the theoretical erosion of the corporation was substantially complete, and what that meant in more practical terms was that there were very few presumptions now about the kinds of features that would have to be present when a corporation was created. As Herman Pritchett noted after the passage of the 1945 act,

Every special characteristic which it is desired that a corporation should have must be specified in the statute or charter of incorporation. If it is to be free from civil service, if it is to escape the Comptroller General's audit, if it is to be allowed to adopt its own purchasing methods, if it is to be financially autonomous— then provisions to such an effect must be written into the law.[14]

By the same token, almost any desirable feature of a corporation could be given to a regular agency, and it was easier to do that than to create a whole new corporation. Thus, as Marshall pointed out in the Senate hearings, if the aim was to attract men from private industry with salaries that were higher than the regular government rates, one could simply exempt the ECA from the civil service regulations.[15] It seemed, then, that there was no special reason either to choose or reject a corporation. However, Marshall argued (and with some support from Congressman Bloom in the Foreign Affairs Committee) that the natural insulation of a corporation would remove the program from the constitutional responsibility of the President in foreign affairs. As long as that contention was credible, the advocates of the corporate plan were stuck with the burden of argument; and it was a burden they were never able to overcome.

The Congressional climate was plainly inhospitable to the notion of corporate autonomy in this particular program. The insistence on annual authorizations and appropriations should have been clear enough evidence on that point; indeed, it was clear enough to Christian Herter, for he made no claim in his own plan to avoid either the annual appropriations or the jurisdiction of the Comptroller General. In his own bill, Herter actually adopted the relevant portions of the Corporation Control Act, so he started with the model of the truncated corporation that survived the 1945 legislation. In two provisions, though, where his bill made a difference, it was found basically objectionable. One clause authorized the new organization to form subsidiary corporations under the laws of foreign countries where it might prove useful in carrying out the over-

[14] C. Herman Pritchett, "The Paradox of the Government Corporation," *Public Administration Review*, I, No. 4 (Summer 1941), p. 389. Also see his article, "The Government Corporation Control Act of 1945," *American Political Science Review*, XL, No. 3 (June 1946), pp. 495-509. Cf. V. O. Key, Jr., "Government Corporations," in Fritz Morstein Marx (ed.), *Elements of Public Administration* (New York: Prentice-Hall, Inc., 1946), pp. 236-63.

[15] Senate Foreign Relations Committee, *ERP Hearings*, 1948, p. 54.

126

seas operations. That is, three years after the Corporation Control Act, when Congress finally put a stop to the wild formation of subsidiaries, it was now presented with the vision of a free-wheeling, corporate Marshall Plan—on its own, as it were, overseas—littering the European landscape with its own subsidiaries.

Secondly, there was a provision for corporate powers of buying and selling that would be exempted from the regulations governing ordinary agencies. But this privilege collided with the Congressional preference for private channels of trade. The dual aim of that preference was (1) to preserve the place of private business activity as the dominant mode of economic transactions, and (2) to forestall the emergence of a large bureaucratic apparatus that would centralize all the procurement functions of the federal government. There was some fear that with a program the size of the Marshall Plan a centralized procurement organization would hold so much leverage that it would come to dominate the regular commercial network in foreign trade.

The Congressional intention was made explicit in an amendment introduced by Sen. Walter George that enjoined the ECA to make the "maximum" use of private channels of trade. As George explained, he was determined to prevent the construction of a mammoth agency on the order of the TVA. He thought it important to emphasize also that the commitment to private channels of trade implied the obligation to competitive bidding, and that in turn would invoke the supervision of the Comptroller General.[16] The significance of the provision for competitive bidding was that it removed one of the great advantages enjoyed by a corporation like the TVA—the capacity to negotiate with any single contractor for a lower bid. If the corporation did not get a satisfactory price, say, on a large order of cement, it had the credible threat of forming its own subsidiary and going into the cement business. But that was exactly the kind of power that George meant to foreclose to the Marshall Plan agency.

At the time George inserted his amendment the legislation still allowed the ECA freedom from the controls of the Comptroller General in the important field of offshore procurement (i.e., where goods were bought outside the United States). But in the legislative conference, the House conferees reduced even this area of autonomy for the ECA. Offshore procurement was to be documented

16 *Congressional Record*, XCIV (1948), 2470.

with such certification "as the Administrator may prescribe in regulations promulgated by him *with the approval of the Comptroller General.*" [Emphasis added.] When they reported back to the House, the conferees justified the change by pointing to the difficulties involved in getting accurate documentation in offshore procurement, especially when the trade flowed through private channels.[17] Thus, when corporate flexibility warred with either private enterprise or the interests of Congressional control, Congress had no qualms in diminishing the autonomy of the ECA.

Both the decisions on the corporation issue and those relating to the coordination of facilities responded to the prospect of a strongly centralized ECA. Centralization provided the linkage, then, and on that basis we might make several statements about the ranking of values in this phase of the program. To the extent that the strength of the national interest in the Marshall Plan was represented in the autonomy and centralized authority of the ECA, that interest was given less weight than the interests of Commerce and Agriculture in maintaining their own criteria in the regulation of exports (and, indirectly, in the management of the domestic supply situation). The purposes of these agencies were considered higher than any interest the ECA might have had in achieving the "maximum efficiency" in its allocation of materials. The interest in the Marshall Plan was seen as less important than the value of maintaining the predominantly private character of American foreign trade. It was less important than the interest in Congressional authority over the financing of the program, and less important also than the interest in assuring Congressional participation in the making of basic policy decisions. One might add, finally, that it was less important than the interest in reaching a considered judgment on the full extent of the American interest in Europe rather than having that decision prejudiced by the overseas operations of an autonomous and uncontained corporation. These were the values that the Marshall Plan would not be allowed to disrupt with a powerful and centralized agency.

III

When Congress was completing action on the bill and all the questions of centralization were thought to be closed, the issue bobbed

[17] *Ibid.,* 4062.

up again, but this time it threatened to reach into Congress itself. At a very early date Vandenberg had become committed to the idea of a special "watchdog" committee for the ECA. In February, there was a report from the head of staff in the Senate Foreign Relations Committee that the committee considered a joint Congressional group of some kind as an "essential provision of the legislation."[18] Christian Herter's Select Committee on Foreign Aid had done a creditable job in assembling a report on the Marshall Plan and in giving its members some first-hand acquaintance with conditions in Europe. The performance of the Herter group began to impress several members of the House with the value of having a permanent committee that could specialize on the Marshall Plan. Clearly, something could be said for the usefulness of a supercommittee from the standpoint of Congressional control. A program running into some $17 billion would constitute a sizable chunk of the federal budget in the late 1940s. (In the first full fiscal year under the program, the ECA took slightly more than 10 percent of the entire federal budget.[19]) Since the affairs of the ECA would range across the spectrum of standing committees, the task of surveillance could be parceled out in small and ineffective packages unless something could be done to concentrate the responsibility for oversight. With Vandenberg adding the weight of his personal interest, the Senate bill passed with the provision for the watchdog committee.

Once again, there was a different story in the House. The House leaders resolved at the outset that they would brook no such insolence, and the watchdog committee was promptly deleted. When Congressman Goff tried to reintroduce the provision on the floor, he was thoroughly chastened. John McCormack denounced what he saw as a supercommittee that might usurp the functions of the standing committees in Foreign Affairs, Appropriations, and perhaps even Ways and Means and Agriculture. Chairman Eaton of the Foreign Affairs Committee insisted that the arrangement did more than challenge the competence of the committees, but actually

[18] Roseman to Stone, "ERP Legislation—Administrative Questions Raised by Senate Committee Staff," February 2, 1948, Bureau of the Budget, Series 39.18.

[19] The figures are for Fiscal 1949. Omitting the funds spent under the China Aid Act, the ECA budget came to $4.064 billion out of a total federal budget of $40.057 billion. U.S. Department of the Treasury, *Annual Report, Fiscal Year Ended June 30, 1949* (Washington: Government Printing Office, 1950), pp. 367, 369, 377.

129

violated the Constitution. He cited the Reorganization Act and the stipulation that the committees were to "exercise continuous watchfulness of the execution by the administrative agencies concerned of any laws the subject matter of which is in the jurisdiction of such committee." If he had not believed it earlier, something in that passage apparently persuaded him now that the lines of committee jurisdiction also happened to demarcate the zones of constitutional prerogative.

Chairman Taber of the Appropriations Committee debunked the watchdog group as something that was bound to be inefficient. His wounded tone left no doubt that he would regard the move as an attempt to repudiate the chairmen of the standing committees.[20] As if that were not enough, Eaton found the very name "watchdog" repulsive. "It is a reflection," he declared, on "our integrity and our intelligence." The Goff amendment was rejected outright, without a roll call.

It must have come as a surprise then to most members when the bill returned from conference with the watchdog committee restored. Out of nine major disagreements confronting the conference, the Senate view prevailed only twice—and remarkably, the watchdog provision was one of the two. Vandenberg's report to the Senate leads one to suspect that the watchdog committee was the price he exacted for accepting the Mundt amendment and reducing the role of the Secretary of Commerce. At any rate, the House conferees accepted a watchdog committee with ten members, divided evenly between the Senate and the House. Each delegation in turn would be divided among representatives from the Foreign Affairs and Appropriations committees. If some members of the House interpreted the conference action as a retreat, Eaton quickly divested them of that notion. The watchdog committee, he told his colleagues, was more of a gesture. The conference had merely "decided to have a little imitation one to satisfy the brethren who had a hungering in that direction."[21]

As Eaton predicted, the joint Congressional committee never challenged the authority of the standing committees. The group was fortunate, though, in recruiting a competent staff, and in spite of its meager resources it turned out some of the most impressive papers in the intellectual history of the Marshall Plan. On at least one im-

---

[20] *Congressional Record*, XCIV (1948), 3851-52.
[21] *Ibid.*, 4064.

130

portant occasion it managed to reverse the direction of ECA policy. But if the watchdog committee never encroached upon the jurisdiction of the regular committees, that did not mean that the Congressional power over ECA was in any way diminished through the absence of a centralized instrument. If anything, the decision to work within the existing committee structure enhanced Congressional control by saturating the program with inspectors. In their trips to Capitol Hill, Hoffman and his executives would often circulate among the committees on Commerce, Merchant Marine, and Small Business, in addition to their regular sessions with the Foreign Affairs and Appropriations committees. However, the critical point is that there *was* a decision on the issue of committee jurisdiction, and one that provides a meaningful postscript to the account of centralization. For most of the Congressional leaders the national interest in the Marshall Plan was not of such an order that it deserved to extend itself into the legislative branch and reorganize the committee structure. It was not so compelling a national need that it was justified in overturning a set of relationships which was considered—apparently by many others in addition to Charles Eaton—as bound up in some way with the character of the regime itself.

131

7. THE REACH OF AUTHORITY OVERSEAS I: PLURALISM AND THE GOAL OF INTEGRATION

IN THE SAME WAY that the character of a polity is determined by the distribution of authority, as well as the ends for which power is used, the relations of authority between the United States and the European countries carried obvious meanings for the character of the Marshall Plan. On the immediate question of distribution there had to be some authoritative system for allocating aid. But that in turn raised the question of what the ends of the program were, and what kind of enforcement would be necessary to achieve them. Once again, there was an intersection between power and ends, and though the correspondence was far from perfect, there was a noticeable connection between the contending views of authority and the conception of ends in the program. In clarifying the choices, then, it might be helpful to sort out the different strands of thought on the problem of authority.

We can distinguish, at one extreme, the inclination to a more hierarchical relationship. In this view, the United States would stand as the superior in a clear chain of command. Decisions would be made unilaterally, without consultations, and the directives would be immediately binding on the Europeans. Again the correlation was by no means complete, but by and large the preference for hierarchy went along with attitudes that were highly conservative on domestic issues, and very nearly isolationist on the question of an American commitment in Europe. For those who defined the American system in terms closer to laissez-faire liberalism, there was a fear of contaminating the United States through a new intimacy with European socialism. If there was to be a program with this magnitude and involvement, it was imperative to provide some basic insurance against the erosion of American values. The appropriate prescription then was for strict hierarchical authority. In

132

place of a rich exchange in ideas and policies, the United States would dominate the flow of transactions. In the last analysis it was only by avoiding the need to associate—the need to bargain on occasion and harmonize one's interests with others—that the United States could hope to escape the danger of corruption.

There may be a distortion, however, in characterizing the spokesmen for this position entirely in terms of the attachment to hierarchical authority. There was no drive here to impose American rule on the outside world, and the society valued by these men was anything but hierarchically organized. Their ideal was an economy of private ownership, regulated primarily by market forces. Their polity was one of local options, a strong federalism with a weak central government and an even weaker federal bureaucracy. It would probably be fairer, therefore, to use the term "unilateral," since it expresses their attitude on organization without exaggerating their motives. It is probably more faithful, also, in conveying the ex parte nature of their concerns and their extreme sensitivity to matters of narrow self-interest.

As the polar opposite we can identify a preference for "non-hierarchical" or "pluralist" organization. At its extreme, pluralism could utterly reject the claims of self-interest. There was a preference for criteria of a universalistic character, for standards that refused to make distinctions between friends and enemies, as though there were genuine conflicts of interest in the world. The pluralists took a generous course by favoring a large commitment of funds with no conditions and, above all, no American authority in regulating the program.[1] But in some respects this, too, could be a caricature. The most common and essential attribute was the acceptance of a world with multiple centers of power. There was a willingness to deal with a variety of regimes, showing diversity in their economies and ideologies, and still treat with them in a spirit of tolerance and respect.[2] The idea was expressed quite well by Dean Acheson in 1950:

[1] See, for example, the recommendations of Phillip Murray and Walter Reuther of the CIO in Senate Foreign Relations Committee, *ERP Hearings*, 1948, pp. 1298, 1301.

[2] In this sense "pluralism" seems to have acquired a currency in our everyday language. Thus, not too long ago, Henry Kissinger used the term as a matter of course in some testimony before the Senate Foreign Relations Committee. Nor did the account in the press make any special explanation in reporting his statement. Discussing American alliance policy in Western

Two antithetical concepts of foreign relations are loose in the world. One concept is that no state is friendly which is not subservient. . . .

The other concept is that no state is unfriendly which in return for respect for its rights, respects the rights of other states. This concept is one which permits and encourages variety, which demands only that conflicts of interest be resolved by peaceful means.[3]

The most exaggerated proposal for the universalistic approach came from the Wallace left. Taylor in the Senate and Marcantonio in the House condemned the program as a tool of American monopoly capitalism. The design, they charged, was to dump American products in Europe and use economic penetration as a political lever for destroying European socialism. As an alternative, they sponsored identical measures calling for a program of $25 billion to be administered entirely through the United Nations. Contributions would be based on the ability to pay, while benefits would be distributed according to the extent of war damage at the hands of the Axis powers. No other political considerations would intervene. In short, it was a formula through which the United States would bear the bulk of the costs, while the Soviet Union stood to receive the lion's share of the benefits.[4]

The proposal, however, failed to elicit a response. Even without the bias in favor of the Soviet Union, Congress was no longer in the mood for such altruism. Since the experience with the UNRRA, Congress had become soured on the use of permissive and universalistic criteria. Not only was it accepting the fairness of political tests now, but it was insisting also on the exercise of American supervision overseas, including a veto on the local disbursement of funds.

Still, that did not mean there was a general movement to divide the world into two camps and jettison all the international agencies.

Europe, "Kissinger commented that he was becoming more worried about 'the excessive concentration of decision making' power. Hence he said he favored 'pluralism,' felt it 'safer' to have a federated Europe rather than a unified Europe. . . ." *Washington Post*, June 28, 1966, p. A18.

[3] U.S. Senate, Committee on Foreign Relations, Hearings, *Extension of European Recovery—1950*, 81st Cong., 2nd Sess., 1950, pp. 13-14. Cited hereafter as Senate Committee on Foreign Relations, *Hearings on Extension of ERP*, 1950.

[4] See *Congressional Record*, XCIV (1948), 2448-49, 2454-55, 3874.

There were many liberals who supported the Marshall Plan, but who were alarmed at the growing tendency to circumvent the United Nations. There were some, like Fiorello LaGuardia and Chet Holifield, who were moved to vocal opposition over the unilateral character of the Greek-Turkish program, and they were not without a political following. Furthermore, as Vandenberg himself showed, even the old isolationists had not given up on the United Nations. In fact, some of them needed the United Nations far more than the liberal internationalists; for if the United Nations system could still take hold, there was reason to hope that the United States might yet be relieved of these new international responsibilities. It seemed vital then that some way be found to use the facilities of the United Nations if it was at all possible. But for the moment, the focus of pluralism narrowed from the interest in "one world" to the aim of enlarging cooperation in Western Europe.

In his speech at Harvard Marshall called for a new level of coordination in Europe's plans and resources. It was assumed that there *was* a natural economic entity called "Europe," though for a while no one wanted to inquire too deeply into the boundaries of that European community. Eastern Europe, as a source of food and raw materials, was very much a part of the traditional pattern of intra-European trade, but whether Eastern Europe or even the Soviet Union would participate in the program was still an open question after Marshall's Harvard speech. The Paris conference deadlocked on June 30, 1947, when Molotov apparently discovered that the United States and Britain were adamant on the requirement of divulging economic data and exchanging information on investment decisions. A week later *Tass* announced that Poland, Yugoslavia, and Rumania could not attend the larger Paris conference called by Bevin and Bidault. The situation seemed to have reached a point of finality at the beginning of October when the Cominform was organized in opposition to the Marshall Plan and "United States imperialism." Only then did the matter seem settled; but even so, the continued trade with Eastern Europe in the first two years of the Marshall Plan offered at least some faint hope of healing the split in Europe.

Although the precise definition of Europe was unsettled, there was a feeling that a reduction in the barriers to the movement of goods and persons would have a generally integrative effect. Benelux and the United States seemed to stand as the models to emulate,

135

but how that integration was to be brought about—what particular barriers would be lowered, how much and how soon—presented another order of questions. There were still conflicting economic interests to reconcile, particularly in agriculture. More basically, the British and the Scandinavians had commitments to full employment that presented obstacles to the removal of controls and trade quotas. That made it even more difficult, therefore, to arrive at a common policy on tariffs. Thus, in addition to the negotiations on tariffs, there was clearly a need for some other inducements to the Europeans. In the Congressional hearings and debates, three different approaches to the problem of integration stood out as especially noteworthy. The response to each one of them would affect the character of ECA in very distinct ways.

1. *Action on the Level of Political Institutions*

Early in the floor debates, Sen. William Fulbright urged an explicit commitment to European *political* integration—in essence, a United States of Europe. His modest proposal was to add the words "political unification" to the section listing the objectives of policy. Fulbright's argument, as it remained throughout the Marshall Plan, was a direct assault on the functionalist thesis: Economic cooperation would not necessarily lead to political union or peace. Europe had been prosperous before the war, and yet prosperity did not establish political harmony. The reliance on the American experience, he concluded, was usually misconceived, because it was not the American market that had integrated the separate states, but the existence of a common government.

However, Senator Barkley feared that Fulbright's amendment would be interpreted as political intervention. He argued that a political move of this nature was beyond the competence of the delegates who gathered in Paris to form the Committee on European Economic Cooperation. Fulbright accepted the objection, but he replied that the American Constitutional Convention of 1787 had risen above its own limited instructions on behalf of a higher end. The Founders had reached beyond their mandate to perform a creative political act. Similarly, he thought, the mission for the United States in the present crisis was to act as a force for political change and "encourage the creative act of unification" in Europe.

Vandenberg interjected to join Barkley. He, too, showed his prime concern with the effects on public opinion. What he feared

136

now was an overt step that might confirm the theme of Communist propaganda, that the Marshall Plan was a device for gaining political control of Western Europe. As Vandenberg commented to Fulbright, "It would be a source of maximum embarrassment to at least a few of the more exposed European countries if there were anything in the bill which partakes of a political or military character." Nor was Vandenberg simply conjuring up a phantom issue. Particularly in the early months of 1948, responsible men were beginning to treat this matter seriously. Thus, for example, Pope Pius endorsed the Marshall Plan on June 30, 1947; yet, on July 26 *L'Osservatore Romano* warned the statesmen of Western Europe to pay some regard to the fears of the Russians that the Marshall Plan would threaten the sovereignty of the member nations. From the perspective of the present it is easy to underestimate the potential division of opinion in Europe at this time. The Communist parties and trade unions were in active opposition, and one may tend to forget that the Cominform was a party-to-party rather than a government-to-government organization. The French and Italian governments might have adhered to the Marshall Plan, but the Communist parties of France and Italy were just as firmly integrated into that rival political system represented by the Cominform. It was worth considering, also, that the Italian elections were coming up the next month, in April 1948.

At any rate, Vandenberg's objections were reasonable enough to persuade even a Fulbright supporter like Scott Lucas of Illinois. After a while a consensus seemed to form, and the Fulbright amendment was discarded.[5] Moreover, the Senate leadership was to hold to this position with scrupulous consistency. When the House sought to clarify American goals by adding the adjective "political" at several points in the declaration of policy, the Senate conferees insisted on deleting even these innocuous references.[6] With the support of the State Department, a similar motion to add political unification to the list of goals in the legislation was defeated the following year, and another attempt in 1950 failed in

[5] See *Congressional Record*, XCIV (1948), 2030-35.

[6] The italicized words were removed from this statement: ". . . The restoration or maintenance in European countries of principles of individual liberty, free institutions, and genuine independence rests largely upon the establishment of sound economic and *political* conditions, stable international economic and *political* relationships, and the achievement . . . of a healthy economic independence. . . ." *Ibid.*, 3886.

conference.[7] It was not that anyone denied the value of political integration. In fact, from the earliest discussions in the hearings there were demands for devising some tests for cooperative behavior,[8] and Congress, in 1950, conditioned part of the aid on the progress made in liberalizing trade and payments under the new European Payments Union.[9] But in successively reaffirming the original decision, Congress continued to support a definite persuasion in the ECA: Integration could be pursued in a number of ways, including the strengthening of those institutions that encouraged freer intercourse. But integration was not necessarily achieved any better by advertising its political connotations. The belief was to remain with the ECA that it was not its place to court obviously political contacts, or to clothe its disputes with local governments in the public rhetoric of politics.

2. *Covert, Organizational Incentives*: *The Special Ambassador*

The goal of European integration seemed widely shared in the American government. But any effort to direct the Europeans bore the traces of domination. The dilemma was raised in the Senate hearings by Charles Taft (the brother of the Senator) even before anyone seemed aware that a dilemma might have existed.

Instead of approaching the question as one of pressuring the Europeans, Taft proposed to view the issue entirely as a problem of American administration. The first question, he suggested, was what the United States could do on its own for European integration, regardless of what the Europeans were willing to do for themselves. Was there some better way, for example, in which the United States could order its own administrative affairs that would make the commitment to European integration that much more meaningful? Taft did subscribe to the view that Europe represented a coherent focus of interest for the United States. He believed that the problems of Europe were regional rather than simply national; beyond that, he felt there was a definite "regional view" that could

[7] William Adams Brown, Jr., and Redvers Opie, *American Foreign Assistance* (Washington: The Brookings Institution, 1953), p. 162.

[8] John Foster Dulles, for example, thought that aid should be adjusted to *degrees* of cooperative behavior. Senate Foreign Relations Committee, *ERP Hearings*, 1948, p. 589. J. T. Sanders of the National Grange suggested that assistance be terminated upon a finding of "willful failure" to cooperate. House Committee on Foreign Affairs, *ERP Hearings*, 1948, p. 1387.

[9] Brown and Opie, *op.cit.*, pp. 162-63.

not be had in the separate country missions and that could not be reproduced merely by collecting all the cables from the American embassies. He maintained that the separate missions in Europe were like the spokes of a wheel unconnected by the outer rim. If the United States was sincere about European cooperation, it could register that commitment by connecting its own diplomatic sensors in Europe. It could start by organizing its diplomacy as though "Europe," as a regional entity, actually existed.

As an immediate organizational measure, Taft recommended a regional conference of American diplomats. The conference would be a continuing organization with its own administrative staff, and as it gained in strength it could play a vital role in making policy and coordinating diplomacy on the European level. But even more practically, as far as Vandenberg was concerned, Taft found a nucleus for this organization in the present legislation, in the provision for a Special Representative in Europe.

The valuable point was that these changes in the organization of American diplomacy could be justified entirely by the legitimate interests of any government in perfecting its own organization. It did not depend on the existence of the Marshall Plan, and it could not be denounced credibly as imperialism. Yet these simple organizational changes might act as incentives for parallel changes on the part of the Europeans. If critical decisions were being made in this active regional center, and if the central American mission dealt mainly with the permanent organization of the European states, there would be a clear interest among the Europeans in strengthening their own common agency. By its own moves, then, the United States could create a structure for the program that not only promoted cooperation, but encouraged the building of central institutions. Thus Taft commented:

> [The] suggestion that the European nations themselves have an international staff at the same place as the European-recovery program European office is not one which Congress can implement. That is their job. But if you will provide for a truly regional office of the United States Foreign Service, you will be encouraging that development.[10]

It remained, however, for Arthur Vandenberg to bring the administrative provisions into closer congruence with Taft's ideas. On

[10] Senate Committee on Foreign Relations, *ERP Hearings*, 1948, pp. 1298, 1301.

the Senate floor, Senator Brooks tried to reduce the role of the State Department even further by eliminating the joint authority of the Administrator and the Secretary of State over the Special Representative. He proposed to change the name of the officer to the "Agent General of the Administrator" so that there could be no doubt that he was under the exclusive authority of the ECA Administrator. Vandenberg accepted one part of the Brooks amendment and agreed to give the Special Representative the authority to coordinate the overseas missions. In that way, also, he drew out the qualities of the office as a regional center. But on the crucial point, he refused to change the dual character of the Special Representative as a member of the ECA and the State Department. In holding fast here he underscored a new meaning for the Office of the Special Representative as something more than another arm of the ECA. His reply to Brooks is worth quoting, because it established the significance of this feature beyond question:

> In spite of all the emphasis upon the indispensable economic independence of the Administrator, despite that economic necessity, there is another contact inevitably involved in this enterprise if we are to hope to succeed with it, namely, the creation of a new governmental coordination in Europe, which is not a matter of economics at the top, even though it is at the bottom. Therefore the top representative abroad must not only be economically sufficient unto the occasion, but he must also be in a position to deal at the top level with the heads of government in the 16 CEEC nations if we are successfully to pursue our desire to create constantly expanding contacts between them, and to create, so far as possible, what Mr. Bevin has called a Western Union or something comparable.[11]

In the Administration bill, the Special Ambassador had merely been the representative assigned to the permanent organization of the European countries (the Organization for European Economic Cooperation, as it came to be called later, or the OEEC); and the overseas units of the ECA were fully subordinate to the heads of the local diplomatic missions. But now Congress transformed the office by creating a powerful coordinating center in Paris that would exercise primary authority over the local missions of the ECA. As a result of these simple changes in the law, the Office of

[11] *Congressional Record*, XCIV (1948), 2536-38.

the Special Representative (OSR) would come to look very much in practice like the vigorous regional center envisioned by Vandenberg and Charles Taft. Requests from the country missions would be funneled into the Paris office, where they would be screened and then sent along to Washington with a covering recommendation. Similarly, the Paris office would take the full plan hammered out in the OEEC, and add its own revisions and recommendations before passing the plan on to central headquarters.

To perform these functions, of course, the OSR had to build up some rather large staff resources of its own. For those who were unaware of the special ends represented by the OSR, the full extent of these resources could often appear startling. In 1953, when the overseas operation had been running for five years, and the Marshall Plan had given way to the Mutual Security Program, a Senate investigating unit visited Paris and came back righteously appalled. To the staff assistants of the committee, who apparently had no knowledge of the original purposes of the OSR, the size of the Paris establishment seemed to present a bald case of bureaucratic expansion. They charged that when the office was formed, "the theory was that this coordinating task would be performed ... with a small staff of 30 or 40 highly qualified specialists who would concern themselves with questions of policy and would not intervene in the detailed operations of the missions." But as of March 31, 1953, they noted, the personnel levels in the office had risen to include 630 Americans and 825 "locals," for a combined total of 1,455. The Office of the Special Representative alone was taking almost 50 percent of the administrative costs for the entire European operation.[12]

But the outrage of the committee staff stemmed from a fundamental misunderstanding. After the committee hearings and the action in the Senate, the OSR was never meant to be a mere staff or service unit of 30 or 40. There was a danger here of generalizing from the initial stages of the ECA. The personnel buildup was especially constrained in Europe by the ordinary difficulties one would expect in recruiting staff, transferring them and their belongings, and setting up administrative services overseas. Thus, on June 30, 1948, after the Marshall Plan completed its first quar-

[12] For Fiscal 1952 the figures were $10,511,000 for the OSR, against a total of $21,980,060 in administrative expenses. U.S. Senate, Committee on Appropriations, Investigative Division, *Report, Foreign-Aid Program in Europe*, 83rd Cong., 1st Sess., 1953, p. 20.

ter, there were still only 63 full-time ECA people in all of Western Europe. In contrast, there were 378 people in the Washington office. Within one month the European figure had almost quadrupled to 242.[13] By the end of the *first* year of the Marshall Plan, the distribution of administrative costs had already reached the proportions that jolted the Senate staff in 1953. Projecting estimates for the last quarter of the first full year, the ECA offered the account of its administrative expenditures overseas that appears in Table 1.

TABLE 1. Direct Administrative Expenses for European Operations for Period April 3, 1948 to April 2, 1949 (as estimated in February 1949)

	Dollar Cost	Local Currency in Dollar Equivalent	Total
16 ECA Missions	2,869,116	3,255,636	6,124,752
Office of the Special Representative	2,646,260	2,543,618	5,189,878
Total	5,515,376	5,799,254	11,314,630

Source: Senate Foreign Relations Committee, *Hearings on Extension of ERP*, 1949, p. 116.

That is, even before the first year of the program had ended, the OSR was taking nearly half of the administrative costs for the overseas operations. It was not a case, then, of administrative imperialism; it was a function, rather, of the larger meaning that was attached to the Paris office, and which was present from the very beginning.

Almost from the outset, the OSR posed organizational problems for the central headquarters, and before the end of 1948 the Washington office requested a formal study by a Budget Bureau task force. Deputy Administrator Bruce reported that a unique organizational problem had been created by "the existence in Paris of what is almost a second headquarters, exercising general direction over the country missions."[14]

With Averell Harriman as Special Ambassador, it should have been clear that the OSR was something more than a clerical staff;

[13] The figures were given in a letter from Howard Bruce, Deputy Administrator in the ECA, to James Webb, the Director of the Budget Bureau, August 9, 1948. Bureau of the Budget, Series 39.18.

[14] Bruce to Webb, December 13, 1948, Bureau of the Budget, Series 39.27.

and when the ECA missions contained such strong personalities as David Bruce in France, one could have predicted that a sense of separateness would arise between the overseas operations and the Washington office. It was no wonder that the OSR began to view itself as a "theater command" with a wide area of discretion in policy decisions.

To this extent, Charles Taft's thinking had an important impact on the character of the ECA. Paradoxically, however, his theory concerning the effect of the OSR on European integration turned out to be inverted. It was not the vitality of the Paris office that strengthened the OEEC and the tendencies toward supranational institutions. Instead, it was the decline of the OEEC, notably in its programming functions, that brought a concomitant loss of stature in the Office of the Special Representative. One of the critical signposts here was the announcement by the OEEC in 1951 that it would not even attempt to provide its usual projections of national trade and production—the integrated program that had been used in the past as the basis for allocating Marshall aid.[15]

The annual estimates of the OEEC by which national plans had been merged, had always been rather problematic. Even more so was the projection of trading patterns in Europe that underlay the successive payments agreements leading to the European Payments Union. As William Diebold later argued, "only in a period of widespread shortages can an important trading country count on selling abroad, at remunerative prices, all the goods it plans to export." The problem was even more complex if one tried to forecast not only the level of foreign trade in general, but the volume of exchange with specific countries. Here one had to add the mixture of planned and unplanned trade, rationed commodities against those available on the free market, and the contrasting pressures on price that resulted from different levels of demand and subsidy among the several countries.[16] Although the estimates were always faulty, they were still helpful in bringing some minimal order to the prob-

[15] A Budget Bureau report took notice of this failure of the 1951 statement to include "any real analysis or pulling together of the programs of its member countries." Consequently, it was noted, this was the first time that the submission of the OEEC "was not a significant factor in ECA programming." Memorandum on interview with Sam Van Hyning, Special Assistant to the Deputy Administrator of ECA, July 29, 1951, p. 3, Bureau of the Budget, *Interviews in Survey of ECA*, 1951, Series 39.32.

[16] See William Diebold, Jr., *Trade and Payments in Western Europe* (New York: Harper and Brothers, 1952), p. 54. See also pp. 117-18.

lem, and to some degree they were useful learning devices. But the Korean War altered the situation radically. There was a worldwide scramble now to acquire raw materials before prices soared. Restrictions on imports became harder to maintain, and the trading patterns in Europe became skewed. With a large rearmament program apparently imminent in the West, the OEEC threw in the towel:

> [W]hen the time came for the present report to be written, it was realised that while for some countries the material was most full and up-to-date, for others the quantitative material contained in the submissions relating to the future was based on plans which had been rendered out-of-date by the march of events, and that an analysis based on this material would be misleading. . . .
>
> The structure of this report has thus to be adopted to the ineluctable facts of the present world situation. . . .[17]

For the Marshall Plan, the period of major commodity transfers was substantially over. The emphasis switched to raising productivity, and that was pursued mainly through the support of key industrial projects and an intensive effort in technical assistance. But in these activities the principal need was for a group of mobile engineers or technical consultants, preferably people who could work out of the country office and be on the spot to evaluate projects. In this new scheme, the OSR found its main function as an administrative backstop to the local missions. Consequently, when the opportunity arose to redistribute personnel for Fiscal 1951, the OSR was slated for a drop from 518 to 488, while the missions were scheduled to rise, in the aggregate, from 630 to 653.[18] It was evident by then that the center of gravity in the overseas operations had shifted to the country missions.

To a great extent, therefore, the eclipse of the OSR was a result of basic changes in the content of the Marshall Plan. The Paris office was a victim, too, of its own lack of conspicuousness as a symbol of European integration. As an instrument for promoting

[17] Organization for European Economic Cooperation, *Economic Progress and Problems of Western Europe*, June, 1951, p. 4.

[18] See U.S. House, Subcommittee of the Committee on Appropriations, *Hearings, Foreign Aid Appropriations for 1951*, 81st Congress, 2nd Session, 1950, pp. 414, 424; and more generally on the personnel shifts for Fiscal 1951, see the testimony of William Foster, pp. 408 ff.

integration, it was already being superseded by such functional organizations as the European Payments Union and the Coal and Steel Community. When these institutions were added to NATO and the impending movement toward military integration, the co-operative tendencies in Western Europe were moving well beyond that vision of subtle inducements held out by Charles Taft. Yet it was also arguable that the OSR might have remained more vital— and would have been able to vitalize the OEEC in turn—if other decisions had been taken at the outset to make the OEEC a more significant organization. Here again it was a matter of decisions that could have been taken by the United States alone, and it presents another dimension of the response to the pluralist alternatives.

3. *Incentives of Administrative Power*: *The OEEC*

The theory behind Charles Taft's proposal for the OSR had been that self-interest would move the Europeans into closer forms of cooperation if the significant decisions in the Marshall Plan were made by central institutions in Europe. In that event, there was an incentive for the Europeans to organize as a more effective means of influence, and the target in question was the OSR. But the argument could be taken one step further: The incentives could be multiplied if a common European organization, and only that organization, would make the actual decisions on aid and supervise the operations.

In the Congressional hearings, this argument had its spokesmen in David Lloyd of the Americans for Democratic Action and Charles Dewey, a former Congressman and Assistant Secretary of the Treasury. Lloyd translated his preferences into specific operating procedures before the House committee:

> We can help in the process [of promoting European cooperation] by dealing with the participating nations *as a group rather than separately*, by asking them to pool their resources and requirements, to divide scarce supplies equitably among themselves, and otherwise to act in concert.[19]

The object then was to construct a framework in which the contenders for American aid would have to confront the demands of their competitors. Rather than approaching the United States sep-

---

[19] House Committee on Foreign Affairs, *ERP Hearings*, 1948, p. 924. Emphasis added.

arately with their individual requests, the members would have to justify their interests in a wider regional context.

Charles Dewey would have filled out the scheme by assigning the entire responsibility for overseas operations to the European organization. The OEEC would draft the comprehensive economic plan and submit it to the member nations before it was sent on to the ECA for final approval. Once it was initiated, the plan would be supervised and executed by the European organization itself. As for the Administrator of the ECA, he would work only with the European organization and not with the separate governments. The ECA missions overseas would have no contacts at all with the local governments; they would serve exclusively as channels of communication between Washington and the local missions of the OEEC. The Special Ambassador would stand in the middle of this network, offering facilities to the OEEC, the ECA missions, and the Administrator in Washington, but he would have no relations with the constituent governments.[20]

Thus there was a clear set of policies for fostering cooperation and eliminating the incidents of American intervention. But the propositions also had their important obverse meaning—the essential abdication of enforcement. Any meaningful enforcement of conditions would have to act upon the individual recipient country, and yet, in the pluralist scheme, enforcement had to be directed against the group as a whole. If the United States could single out the members for penalties, the basic cooperative structure would be disrupted. Common decision-making would lose its meaning if the United States could overturn an allocation, for example, in a bilateral maneuver.

However, the Administration could not accept these purer models of pluralism, and it was not simply because of a trend toward "toughness" in foreign aid. Rather, the commitment to enforcement arose from the commitment to European cooperation itself. Marshall was insistent on the point that only a coherent program with thorough coordination could work. It was the commitment to a new degree of cooperation that would make the Marshall Plan different, and therefore the major thrust of the Harvard speech was that either there would be cooperation in the program or there would be no program at all. But if integration was vital to

[20] Dewey's proposals were incorporated in a memorandum to the Senate Committee on Foreign Relations. See *ERP Hearings*, 1948, pp. 1353-54.

146

the program, it followed that the ERP would have to be "closed" at least on that essential point. The program could not be left defenseless against those who might join and then refuse to cooperate by providing information. More important than the prospect of withholding information, though, was the danger of an obstructionist nation that could block the efforts of the other countries to cooperate among themselves and integrate their economies. If the United States was serious then about promoting integration, there had to be some means of regulating membership. And rather than letting the whole program stand or fall on the risk of one obstructionist, it was better to have some capacity either to discipline or to expel a disruptive member. Thus, in addition to a multilateral pledge, the United States would require a bilateral agreement with each of the member countries as a means of holding them responsible individually.

Moreover, once it was determined that integration was a cardinal policy, and that some basic enforcement would be necessary in the program, a good case could have been made for conceding a share of authority to the United States. First, it was not inconceivable that planning in the OEEC might result in a crude form of log-rolling as well as an "optimal" or just distribution of resources. In fact, log-rolling did appear, and by the third year of the program it became visible enough to induce cynicism in Washington.[21] Second, there was the problem of Germany. As we have seen, Marshall was convinced that the recovery of production in Germany was the key to recovery in the whole of Europe.[22] Yet it was reasonable to expect that the other members of the OEEC would tend to be less than generous with Germany, especially when it meant diverting Marshall aid from their own recovery. Third, there was the natural drag of separate national interests. Despite the rhetoric of Ernest Bevin, for example, every step toward integration in Europe found the British in opposition. They furnished the main resistance to reform in the European payments system, and they refused finally to join the Coal and Steel Community. In most cases the British had good reasons for their reluctance, and it was not to be supposed

[21] See Bureau of the Budget, *Survey of the ECA*, 1951, p. 11.

[22] See Marshall's speech before the Chicago Council on Foreign Relations, November 1947, in U.S. State Department, *State Department Bulletin*, XVII, No. 439 (November 30, 1947), p. 1027. Cf. *ibid.*, No. 442 (December 21, 1947), p. 1204.

that they were the only ones whose interests might brake the movement toward integration.

Since it was American resources that were being spent, the United States had a material interest in reducing its own expenses and achieving the kind of distribution that promised to be most efficient in promoting European recovery. As a nation that had not been occupied by Germany, the United States could view the problem of German economic recovery with somewhat more detachment. As a participant in the occupation of Western Germany, and as the major source of foreign assistance, the United States was also bearing the costs of German weakness. It could be more sensitive then to the consequences of dismantling industrial plants for reparations deliveries. Thus, on several counts the United States might have been in a better position to express the interest in German recovery than the Europeans themselves. It is revealing, in this connection, that there was only one instance in the first year of the program when the ECA actually raised an aid allotment beyond the level requested by one of the members. That was for the French zone of Germany, where the French were not providing the same type of relief program for "disease and unrest" that the United States was administering in its own zone. To reduce the disparity in living standards between the two zones, the ECA raised the allocation from $110 million to $115 million, although the French had not seen fit to recommend the additional aid.[23] In other instances, it was evident that some members of the OEEC could be remarkably uninhibited in pressing their own interests at the expense of Germany, perhaps because they knew that the charges were ultimately being shifted to the United States.[24]

Early in the preparations for the Marshall Plan it was also discovered that the Europeans could be distracted with alarming ease. At the initial sessions in Paris it was complained that the Euro-

[23] Senate Committee on Foreign Relations, *Hearings on Extension of European Recovery*, 1949, pp. 304-305.

[24] With some annoyance, General Clay recalled the time he tried to bring surplus American tobacco into Germany as an incentive good. Greece and Turkey protested in the OEEC, claiming that the American shipments intruded upon the traditional markets for their own tobacco. Although it meant higher prices, they argued that Greek and Turkish tobacco should be favored for the sake of bolstering the European economies. "To alleviate their resentment," Clay later wrote, "we did purchase more tobacco than the German economy could afford." Lucius D. Clay, *Decision in Germany* (Garden City, New York: Doubleday and Company, Inc., 1950), pp. 224-25.

peans were giving too little thought to the organization of the program at their end, or to the precise forms that cooperation might take (as, for example, in the pooling of currency). Instead they seemed to be more concerned with drawing up "shopping lists" for the United States. To bring some order to the process, the United States informally conveyed the concept of a joint effort for reconstruction and the need for a continuing administrative body to recommend allocations. The Europeans were then "advised" to adopt the statement on cooperative goals by September 23.[25]

Thus, one could argue that there was an integrative role here that the United States was best qualified to fill, even if that meant some resort to hierarchical authority on behalf of the goals of pluralism. On several grounds there were reasons to believe that the United States could have equally valid insights into the interests of European recovery. If the Europeans did not hold a monopoly on that vision, then it was at least possible that a tension might arise between the inclinations of the OEEC and the genuine interests of European recovery. If one conceded, further, that the United States was in a peculiar position to contribute some sound advice as to what those interests were, then the American sharing of authority had all the justification it required.

In the Administration bill, assistance was conditioned at the outset on the adherence to a multilateral agreement in which the members pledged themselves to certain cooperative goals, like the promotion of industrial production, the furthering of currency stabilization, and the reduction of barriers to trade. Much as David Lloyd would have had it, Section 115(b) declared that assistance was based upon *continuous* cooperative efforts to accomplish a joint recovery program "through multilateral undertakings and the establishment of a continuing organization for this purpose."

And following very quickly, Section 115(d) moved in the direction of Charles Dewey's recommendation:

> The Administrator shall encourage the joint organization of the participating countries . . . to ensure that each participating country makes efficient use of the resources of such country, including any commodities, facilities, or services furnished under

[25] Sheppard to Webb, "Present Status of the Marshall Plan," September 19, 1947; also, Staff paper, "Outline of Memorandum on Marshall Plan," n.d. [September 1947?], Bureau of the Budget, Series 39.18.

this title by observing and reviewing such use through an effective follow-up system approved by the joint organization.

Accordingly, one of the first acts of the ECA was to invite the OEEC itself to work out the initial distribution of aid. Commodity specialists convened to estimate national needs and agree upon a joint program; and as Lloyd and Dewey anticipated, something close to the model of a cooperative framework began to develop. Years later, Frank Figgures of the OEEC observed that the delegates seemed to become "denationalized." To win the confidence of the group, "people had to demonstrate that they were not cheating in favor of their own countries or showing undue partiality."[26] The delegates were compelled to defend their estimates before their colleagues, and soon the ingredients of a group code began to appear. Each government was expected to alert the others to any action of its own that might affect them adversely. In this setting, instructions to delegates had to be more flexible, and as a result of the deliberations national policies were often modified.

Any assessment of the OEEC as an agency of integration would have to give a central place to the European Payments Union, for it was in the management of the EPU fund that the OEEC came the closest to resembling a genuine supranational authority. In 1950, for example, Germany had fallen into a deep deficit with the EPU. Four-fifths of the deficit came from debts to the sterling and franc areas, both major sources of raw materials. Instead of imposing quotas, the German government preferred to attack the import surplus indirectly by discouraging the expansion of credit and making speculation more costly. The EPU assigned two experts to the case, both of whom concluded that harder control measures would be necessary. Implicitly, the investigators tended to support the view arising at the time that the German government was showing far too little courage in restricting consumption. Thus the EPU refused the German request for a larger payments quota. Instead, the Germans were offered a special credit, along with recommendations for stiffer fiscal and credit policies. In the meantime, the Managing Board of the EPU kept up the pressure. It criticized the German program of March 1950, for failing to recognize the urgency of new taxes. In May, the OEEC Council insisted that the Germans not issue any more import licenses until they made a sig-

[26] Quoted in Harry B. Price, *The Marshall Plan and Its Meaning* (Ithaca: Cornell University Press, 1955), p. 294.

nificant improvement in their EPU position. The council also urged that governments with healthy credit positions take steps to limit exports to Germany before June 1, particularly in goods that had contributed to the deficit. William Diebold noted a short time later that the efforts of the Managing Board to spell out the principles governing German imports was the first attempt on the part of the OEEC nations collectively to decide the terms under which one of their members would be allowed to depart from the standards of trade liberalization.[27]

Later, a Mediation Group of three independent experts was appointed to work out a program of import licenses in order to help the Germans out of their balance of payments difficulties. Germany accepted the program, although it contained some important disadvantages. By allocating their purchases according to the schedule drafted by the Mediation Group, the Germans were prevented from concentrating their purchasing power. They were forced to buy more than they otherwise would have from countries with an EPU deficit, and relatively less in the way of raw materials from the sterling and franc areas, which were large EPU creditors.[28]

Thus, within a circumscribed area of economic decisions the OEEC was able to bring specialized knowledge to bear on behalf of wider European interests; and at times it could achieve the effectiveness of a supranational authority. But the ambitious plan laid out by Charles Dewey never became a reality. The decision to have ECA missions abroad destroyed the rationale for giving sole administrative responsibility to the OEEC. The OEEC never did enter the field of end-use inspection. It never succeeded in coordinating intra-European investments or the allocation of resources. It had some effect in coordinating country programs, but largely through the dissemination of information that had previously been withheld by the national governments. The OEEC contributed marginally to rationalization through its exhaustive economic analyses and its recommendations for the distribution of assistance. It was a matter of no slight importance that there was a central organization in Europe that continued to produce rational plans for the regional level. Perhaps, then, the real significance of the OEEC was here, in the supranational tendencies it helped to sustain, rather than its own evolution as a governing body. The vital political responsibility in Europe was still, after all, in the nation-state.

[27] Diebold, *op.cit.*, pp. 115-16, 120-21, 124.
[28] *Ibid.*, pp. 123, 127-28, 130.

Part I

In a period when economic reconstruction was widely regarded as an opportunity for social change, there were sharp limits on what the national governments were willing to surrender to a supranational body in the area of economic policy.

This failure of the OEEC to develop further as a supranational authority reflected the boundaries placed by the Europeans, as well as the Americans, on the elasticity of self-denial. The OEEC estimates would continue to be screened and approved both by the Office of the Special Representative and by ECA/Washington. Even so, the United States did not take the necessity of American authority as a premise on which to bias the program toward hierarchical control. On the contrary, starting with the device of counterpart funds, the United States was able to reconcile the demands of hierarchy and pluralism, and in a manner that gave the advantage to liberality.

8. THE REACH OF AUTHORITY OVERSEAS II: UNILATERALISM AND THE CLAIMS OF SELF-INTEREST

I

THE MOST coherent and extended statement of the unilateralist position was made by Henry Hazlitt, the highly conservative columnist of *Newsweek* magazine. To Hazlitt, the fundamental threat facing the United States was not only the Communist movement, but socialism and inflation: Freedom was abrogated with every government control on business activity and the working of the free market. "Targets of production," he told the Senate committee, "are fundamentally totalitarian mechanisms." With this analysis one could share Congressman Ralph Gwinn's conviction that there was no essential difference between the British Labour Government and the Soviet regime. They both stemmed from Marxism, Gwinn declared, and "what sense is there in making fine distinctions between [British] socialism and outright communism?" But for Hazlitt socialism was not merely totalitarian; it was inefficient as well. In destroying the market system, socialism removed the incentive to produce and thus hampered economic growth. To funnel aid through European socialist governments, then, was not only ethically dubious, but ineffective.

To achieve a thorough economic recovery in Western Europe, it was essential to enlarge the use of business criteria and avoid the corrupting influence of the socialist systems. In Hazlitt's view, it was better for the Marshall Plan to deal directly with private firms rather than going through the local governments, for in that way the program could be used to bolster the free sectors of the European economies. Further, when loans were given to private enterprises, the government would have to give a pledge against nationalization. Loans to nationalized industries were to be dis-

153

couraged, but where they were unavoidable they were to be granted
only where the state-owned industry was not running a deficit. To
Hazlitt, apparently, it was too much to ask of the United States
that it step in to save an experiment in nationalization that was on
the brink of ruin.

Relief aid would also be distributed without the agency of the
local government. Instead of assigning the aid to the government
for sale and distribution, the assistance would be administered directly by the International Red Cross or another version of the
American Relief Administration. Letting the European governments ration and sell the food merely worked to give them a profit.
For all anyone knew, the money could be used to reduce their taxation while American taxes remained high. More cunningly, these
governments might use the proceeds "to pay a deficit on some
state-owned enterprise."

The unilateralists could justify this circumvention of the local
governments by holding socialism itself as contrary to human nature, and therefore illegitimate in some basic sense. Human beings,
they were convinced, had a natural desire for freedom, incentives,
and acquisition. Their natural economic environment was one of
unfettered competition rather than controls. Thus, no people, except in rare moments of pressure and confusion, would freely
choose a socialist system. For the most part, the socialist governments in Europe owed their existence to postwar bewilderment,
and they would survive only as long as it took their respective publics to regain their right reason. It was important for the unilateralists then that the period of darkness should not be prolonged. Aid
was to be addressed to the people rather than their alien governments. Congressman Gwinn emphasized that the plan "must contact the people as distinct from their temporary socialist overlords.
. . . I think we could loan money to the Ford Company in England,
and it would be much better than loaning it to Bevin's
government."[1]

But to bypass the socialist predators was not enough. One had
to deal with business in a business-like way, by using standards and
practices that were familiar to businessmen. There was a need to
condition the program with costs in order to provide the basis for
calculation. Thus one would give loans rather than grants, and
scale them to the capacity to repay. Some organizations, like the

[1] House Foreign Affairs Committee, *ERP Hearings*, 1948, pp. 1799, 1805.

Export-Import Bank, customarily used procedures that were closer to these business methods. It seemed only logical then to expand the role of these agencies that promised to give the widest play to business criteria. Or, as the case was made for the technocratic ideal, the program would be sliced into zones of expertise. The International Monetary Fund would take over the problem of currency reform, for example, while the International Bank for Reconstruction and Development concentrated on long-term capital loans. As the argument was stated by Carl Fritsche, an engineer, the goals were clearly technical and economic, so there could be no legitimate grounds for the intrusion of political criteria. The tests of achievement would be technical rather than political: Would the program put men to work? Would it divert students toward the more necessary arts and encourage them to "give up the classics and turn to engineering and science?" These were questions that were too important to leave to the people themselves or even to their governments. A "decadent leadership" could sabotage the plan through its own unwillingness to "sacrifice its personal political ambitions for the welfare of all."[2] Only the technicians could know the true public interest, and only they had the rectitude to govern.

However, even Fritsche could not escape the problem of discretion. He admitted that there was room for judgment in selecting a strategy for modernization, and he conceded that it might be necessary at times to convert a short-term loan into a long-term investment, or to replace either one with a grant. But, the argument ran, if discretion could not be eliminated, there were still some better and worse ways of reaching these decisions. At the very least, one could restrict the play of political criteria, and again, some agencies were more likely than others to evade the political quagmire. In this respect, the State Department seemed to be one of those agencies that was bound to err in the wrong direction and pile political considerations on top of the slightest economic issues. As Senator Robertson of Wyoming reasoned, it was more likely that the State Department would compromise before it would allow a mere dispute over economics to color its relations with another country.[3]

In this manner, the conservative outlook could lead to some very specific ideas on organization, and not surprisingly, the Hazlitt

[2] *Ibid.*, pp. 1257-59, 1262-65.
[3] *Congressional Record*, XCIV (1948), 2540.

model became the point of reference for other schemes that joined the preference for business-like or technical criteria with an opposition to the State Department. In varying degrees they combined administration by corporate boards, tightly defined business criteria, and direct industry-to-industry contacts. Appropriately enough, the most emphatic opposition came from Labor leaders like Walter Reuther and Phillip Murray, who were able to identify themselves with European socialism. Their opposition at times took distorted ideological outlets.[4] But it might have been said in their defense that the ideological response was really the most appropriate in this case. Labor had a vital interest in seeing that welfarism was not discredited abroad in these highly industrialized societies. It would have been a disastrous precedent if it were accepted now that the progress of recovery in Europe required the docility of labor and a rollback in the welfare state.

Thus the debate over forms of administration acquired ethical overtones, and in considering the alternatives, Congress was implicitly facing a choice among competing philosophies. Whether the British Labour Government was illegitimate, for example, was a matter it would be forced to pass judgment on when it came to decide the question of working *through* or *around* the local governments.

The pivotal decision came with the adoption of counterpart funds. Here Congress simply reenacted a procedure that was followed in the UNRRA program. But fortunately for our present purposes, the issue had been consciously drawn in that earlier decision, so the Congressional leaders were aware now of what they were choosing. The UNRRA foreshadowed the Marshall Plan in the use of commercial facilities and in the accumulation of local currency from the sale of relief goods. A question naturally arose at the time over who would have control of these local funds. The

---

[4] Reuther, for example, condemned Herter's corporation proposal as a "corporate franchise for world imperialism." The corporation would be a "glorified holding company board of directors, and they will have the power to determine not only how much relief each country gets, but they will have the power also to dictate how the internal economy of that country shall be operated, whether they shall have rationing, price control, material allocation." See Senate Foreign Relations Committee, *ERP Hearings*, 1948, pp. 1385, 1394. The Herter plan did anticipate the exclusive control of American funds abroad, but it was nowhere near the monster suggested by Reuther. In fact, as we have seen, it was not even intended to be free from Presidential control.

156

United States took an advanced position by supporting full multi-lateral control through the UNRRA. The British thought this to be an impractical approach, however, as well as a serious invasion of national sovereignty. As a compromise it was decided that the governments receiving aid would be allowed to control the funds, but on the condition that they would consult with the UNRRA in spending "an equivalent amount for relief and rehabilitation programs within a reasonable period." Subsequently, the procedure was repeated in post-UNRRA relief, the Interim Aid effort, and the civilian supply program for Germany.[5]

If we neglect for a moment the precise forms of payment (which could become a bit complicated if the country was low on foreign exchange and required a special account), the procedure worked roughly like this: An importer in the recipient country might place his order for goods with suppliers in the United States. He would deposit with his own government an amount of local currency equivalent to the price of the American goods. The government would retain that local currency and then draw on its own foreign exchange in order to pay for the goods in dollars. If the transaction was approved by the ECA, the dollar cost would be placed on the country's ECA account, which meant that the recipient government would be reimbursed for its own outlay of dollars. In return for picking up the dollar costs, the ECA would share authority with the local government in determining the use of that currency which had been deposited with the government by the local importer. Under the usage that developed earlier, 5 percent of these local currency proceeds were retained by the United States to cover administrative expenses or the cost of critical materials that might be made available to the United States by the national government. The remaining 95 percent could be used in further relief programs, in the financing of reconstruction projects, or simply in debt-retirement. The non-use of the fund could also contribute importantly to recovery by accumulating currency, and thereby taking it out of circulation in a time of threatening inflation.

The important point in principle was that the control of these funds was shared by the United States and the recipient country. Neither the unilateralist nor the pluralist models were accepted in their pure form. The local governments would not be circumvented, but neither would the United States be sealed off from events with-

[5] William Adams Brown, Jr., and Redvers Opie, *American Foreign Assistance* (Washington: The Brookings Institution, 1953), pp. 79, 188.

157

in their territories. In principle, counterpart funds represented an important sharing of power between the recipient countries and the United States on matters that were traditionally considered internal for the ERP nations. Yet the practical administration of the counterpart funds was weighted in favor of the Europeans, and it was not because the administrators happened to be liberal or permissive. Instead, as we shall see more clearly later, it resulted from a combination of other factors, including the organizational character of the ECA, the advanced industrial nature of most of the ERP countries, and the inherent limitations in the counterpart device.

II

The unilateralists might have lost on the basic issue of authority, but their values did not simply vanish from the scene after the decision was made on counterpart funds. In their own curious way they were linked to persuasions that were more enduring in the American system. Otherwise it would be hard to explain why separate themes in the unilateralist position seemed to have a wider currency, and among men who could not really be labeled as coreligionists. Thus, for example, Wayne Taylor of the Export-Import Bank (who would later become Assistant to the Administrator of ECA) urged Congress to proscribe the use of aid funds in acquiring property rights for the American government overseas. His fear was that a practice of this sort would emulate the Soviet model and establish a precedent that could eventually make government ownership at home more palatable.[6] Allan Kline of the Farm Bureau Federation leaned more heavily on a plain conservative bias in tying his support of the Marshall Plan to the level of expenditure. Still, his position reflected something more than a calculation of tax rates. Kline insisted that the American interest in the European Recovery Program should diminish as the first year appropriation left the $4.5 billion mark and approached a figure of $6.8 billion. He was convinced that the higher figure would represent such a drain on the American market and the creation of such scarcities at home that the government would soon have to restore economic controls. In that event, controls could become so familiar in the United States that they would begin to describe a

---

[6] House Foreign Affairs Committee, *ERP Hearings*, 1948, p. 1444.

158

normal pattern of operation that was not confined to wartime emergencies.

It would be misleading to characterize these men merely as zealots for private property. Doubtless some of the more popular clichés about big government were present, but for many of these men who were concerned about the effects of the program on an economy of private ownership, something vastly more important was involved. These practices were thought to imply principles that were central to the institutions of the American political-economic system. If we consider the concept of regime in a fuller sense as involving the character of a community or its way of life, then the institutions underlying the economy are as fully implicated in the definition of the regime as the institutions that define the political order. And if these practices of the business world were attached in some way to the nature of the regime, they were also bound up with the character of social life. Thus, the preference for loans instead of grants could not be entirely understood as the symptom of a miserly conservatism. The debate on this point tapped some older strains of social theory. At its worst, it revived the perennial dialogue from New Deal days on whether it was corrupting for the individual to receive outright grants of money.[7] At its best, however, it raised some pertinent questions about social cohesion and the consciousness of ends. A sophisticated argument could be made that simply giving aid in the form of gifts was likely to be a wasteful and distorting system of allocation. By separating the acquisition of goods from the consideration of costs, a grant system might relieve the Europeans of the necessity of reasoning out their own schedule of values. If that touchstone of costs were absent, there would be no necessary limit on demands, and no basis therefore for adjudicating among them. Instead of a cooperative process, there would be atomization. Each country would go off on its own in an effort to pry more aid out of the United States. In this way, rather than promoting integration, the altruist might end up destroying the mainsprings of cooperative behavior.

In the 1949 Senate hearings, Hoffman illustrated the value of distributing Marshall Plan goods through normal commercial transactions. Because the goods carried prices, they would be ordered in the conventional means by importers, who would put out their

[7] See the exchange between Congressmen Judd and Monroney in *ibid.*, p. 1891.

own money or credit. The goods would then be placed in the hands of people who had the facilities for distributing them profitably. Hoffman's explanation, though admittedly homely, was a rather accurate statement of the rationale behind the ECA procedure.

> . . . We have been singularly free up to now of any misuse of supplies we finance. . . . It is not because we are smart, because if we had been giving away $4,000,000,000 worth of goods to people throughout Europe I would say that a considerable percentage of those goods might have gone to uses which had no relationship whatever to recovery.
>
> In other words, as human beings we love to get things free. If I can use a homely illustration, several months ago I came home with two or three bottles in my hand. . . . Mrs. Hoffman said to me: "What is that?"
>
> I said: "There are some bottles I have, some medicine to stop athlete's foot."
>
> She said: "Have you got athlete's foot?"
>
> I said: "No, but I might have it some day, and this was free."
>
> We cannot resist taking things that are free. So all through Europe, I think if we had been giving this away we would be in trouble. But we have not. Every person who has gotten one blessed thing, practically speaking, through ECA financing, has paid for it through local currency. It does not make any difference whether it is food they pay for, or machinery, they paid for it. And that has been the self-policing, and Congress figured that out. We did not.[8]

In most of these provisions, then, which happened to refer to economic transactions (whether in the preference for private channels of distribution or in the desire to enlarge the use of loans) one can find a common set of concerns that was more than a crude sympathy for business. There was some apprehension, first, for the effect of the program on the economic systems in the United States and Europe. It was not a matter of indifference that the administration of the Marshall Plan might promote the use of controls, or that it might lend indirect support to the nationalization of key industries. Even the preoccupation with business-like practices was related in a rough way to some more general assumptions about

[8] Senate Committee on Foreign Relations, *Hearings on Extension of ERP*, 1949, p. 81.

160

human nature. These were not necessarily pessimistic assumptions; they simply recognized that any system of distribution carried its own biases—that it could bring out certain traits of character (like acquisitiveness and selfishness) or that it could repress others (like the willingness to consider the interests of others), depending on which way the incentives were turned. It was recognized, too, that these distortions could imperil the ends of the program, both in the search for a viable pattern of recovery, and in the hope of placing interstate relations in Europe on a new level of integration.

Thus, there is a sensible basis for treating these provisions as a coherent set and applying some tentative or summary term to them in our later discussions. A convenient label might be "economic pattern maintenance," an adaptation of a term used by Talcott Parsons.[9] One difficulty, though, is that "pattern maintenance" has become associated with an analytical scheme elaborated by Parsons, and for that reason it may suggest connotations that are out of place here. However, the primary and simple meaning of the words comes closest to describing this collection of preferences without overstating the case: "System maintenance" would be far too ambitious and final; it would suggest that the traits of business activity alone can define the system. On the other hand, "pattern maintenance" can encompass that artless defense of the familiar, as well as the conviction we have been emphasizing thus far, that the pattern was somehow integral to the character of the regime.[10]

As we have seen, the preference for private channels of trade was shared more widely within the Administration and Congress. An explicit amendment on this point had been introduced by Walter George, who clearly did not fit the unilateralist mold. Similarly, the unilateralist preference on loans acquired support from some of the

[9] Talcott Parsons, "Some Highlights of the General Theory of Action," in Roland Young (ed.), *Approaches to the Study of Politics* (Evanston, Ill.: Northwestern University Press, 1958), pp. 282-301, at 293.

[10] Moreover, Parsons himself used the term "pattern maintenance" to refer to the basic institutions of society, including the institutions of the economy: "It has been said that a social system is always characterized by an institutionalized value-system. The first functional imperative of any such system then is the maintenance of the integrity of that value-system and its state of institutionalization. . . . The tendency to stabilize these values against pressures to change through cultural channels may be called the 'pattern maintenance' function. . . ." *Ibid.*, p. 293. For the application of the concept to both the polity and the economy see pp. 295 ff.

most ardent backers of the Marshall Plan, who were nevertheless anxious about the effects of outright gifts. Congressman Vorys, who managed the bill in the House, was uneasy over the prospect of having the same man make the decisions on loans and grants. Vorys feared that the pressures on him for grants would be intense. In this respect he coincided with Carl Fritsche, who had warned the House committee earlier that the existence of discretion would open the program to political influence. The Congressional response was to follow the lead of the unilateralists and reduce the discretion of the Administrator. In separate but parallel steps Congress *guaranteed* that loans would be used, and that business-like agencies would be included in the program. First, in making his decisions on loans and grants, the Administrator would have to consult with the National Advisory Council, an adjunct of the Treasury. Next, the Senate accepted an amendment requiring a minimum of $1 billion out of the first year authorization of $5.3 billion to be disbursed in the form of loans—and further, the loans would be administered through the Export-Import Bank.

It was also a critical part of Hazlitt's own recommendations that the administration be parceled out in this way to standing institutions. For one thing, agencies like the Export-Import Bank and the Red Cross were considered apolitical. But beyond that it was even more important to him that the program not be used as an excuse for creating new administrative machinery; for here was the central phenomenon that accelerated the movement to larger government and more extensive controls: a burgeoning government bureaucracy. In the tradition of Weber and Von Mises, Hazlitt was invoking the "domination" aspect of bureaucracy, the vision of an insulated, continuing body that would stand against society with all its advantages in technical knowledge and discipline. It was the machine-like Leviathan, spreading its "disenchanting" effects throughout the society until it brought every sector into its own routine and dissolved all politics into questions of administration. But for this, Hazlitt did not need the inspiration of German (or even Austrian) theorists. He was simply acting within the radical tradition of hostility to bureaucracy, which became a permanent part of the American idiom of politics with the Revolution. Hazlitt could carry his ideological equipment, then, as an heirloom. It came down to him from Richard Henry Lee and the anti-Federalists; it picked up continuing support from Jefferson and the nineteenth century Democracy, and carried on through to the American

162

Right of the post-New Deal period. For Hazlitt now it could serve as a practical guide to the problem at hand; and for our later analysis of the ECA it is a matter of some importance that there was a body of opinion that could accept the Marshall Plan grudgingly, and still maintain that part of the national interest in the program was that there should be no ECA. The ECA would be conceived as a temporary agency. The presumptions would stand against the enlargement of those facilities under the exclusive control of the ECA, or the addition of full-time personnel. The administrators would have to give constant proof of their aversion to bureaucratic expansion by demonstrating a progressive effort to phase the program out. This anti-bureaucratic vow would have a profound effect on the character of the ECA. It would be the source of a steady, constricting pressure that would alter the capacities of the agency and tighten its range of choice. And to a greater extent than anyone realized at the time, it would transmit itself outward to affect the Marshall Plan countries themselves.

III

The effort to mold the administrative structure of the ECA was the most important outlet the unilateralist argument could take. But it was not the only form in which the unilateralists could campaign for self-regarding interests. The bilateral agreements between the United States and the recipient countries constituted the legal basis for enforcing American conditions on the Europeans. In defining those bilateral conditions, the members of Congress had the chance to insert a veritable catalogue of provisions for special American interests. When it was all over they discovered, perhaps more than anyone allowed, that they were all pluralists, and they were all unilateralists.

Congress took steps almost immediately to broaden the protections to the American economy by enlarging the scope of the Administration bill on the matter of scarce materials. In Section 115(b), it authorized the transfer to the United States, by sale, exchange, or barter, of goods that were both strategic and scarce, but which were not strictly needed for stockpile. In Section 112, Congress called upon the ERP nations to establish a schedule of minimum availabilities for materials in which the United States became deficient as a result of the Marshall Plan. But here, as elsewhere, the self-serving thrust of the provision was softened by a merging of the pluralist and pattern maintenance values. The access to these deficient materials would be guaranteed to American industry rather than the government, and instead of granting access on conditions of advantage, the guarantee would extend only to equal treatment in the use and development of resources. The Administrator, finally, was permitted to accept these goods in repayment of loans.

Not everyone, however, could see these references to American industry as a moderating provision, or even as a reasonably modest condition for American aid. To Adam Clayton Powell, the combination of treaty rights and business privileges bore the traces of imperialism. As an antidote he quickly served up a "Powell amendment"—this one to prevent the expenditure of program funds with firms that discriminated in their hiring practices on the basis of color. There was no perceptible enthusiasm in Congress for inserting the race issue, but in his attack on the acquisition of rights for American business Powell soon found some allies.

The reactions were triggered by the problem of oil. Since the war, Europe had been undergoing an expansion of its oil-consuming equipment. Railroads were converted from coal to oil in France; fishing fleets were replaced with motor boats and oil-burning trawlers in Portugal; motorboats increased in Holland and Italy; and there was an expansion generally of highway transportation. However, the American oil reserves at the time hardly seemed excessive in terms of the long-range planning of American strategic interests. Forrestal had visions of a seventy-group Air Force, which accounted in large part for his mania on the Palestine issue, for he was convinced that the American access to supplies of oil in the Middle East would now become urgent. The Krug Committee sounded a note of caution on the oil supply, and Krug himself saw an outside chance of rationing fuel oil during the coming winter, with or without the Marshall Plan.[11]

If the expansion of oil-consuming machinery in Europe were impeded, there was a risk of braking the process of modernization. Yet, if the United States attempted to supply European needs, both its domestic and its strategic requirements would be strained. In that event it would be ever more important to cultivate good diplomatic relations with the Arab states. The legislation tried to embrace all these considerations. First the Administrator was told to

[11] See House Committee on Foreign Affairs, *ERP Hearings*, 1948, pp. 566-67.

164

discourage the expansion of oil-consuming equipment where other fuels were available; and here, in fact, Congress had a better case than it chose to make. There was some evidence that the switch to oil in Europe had been accelerated needlessly. As the United Nations *Economic Survey* pointed out in 1948, given the general state of Europe's industrial plant, it was still more efficient in many places to use coal. That was especially true under postwar conditions. The combination of shortages and monetary instability distorted the market allocations of manpower. In 1948 France had a larger portion of its work force in the commercial and distributive occupations than before the war.[12] Both Britain and France were hampered by underemployment in mining, a condition that also marked the weakness in basic industrial production. Thus, to inhibit the trend toward oil was another way of encouraging the Europeans in the kinds of measures that should have been part of the attack on the structural problems in their own economies.

As a second directive to the ECA, Congress urged the Administrator to procure petroleum and petroleum products outside the United States as much as possible. Hopefully, two ends would be served: (1) the charge on American supplies would be lessened, while (2) the Europeans would reduce their dependence on the dollar area. But it also implied a new diplomatic concern for the Middle East, which would undoubtedly receive support from the American companies that operated in the region. The implications were not lost on pro-Israeli congressmen. Representative Isacson accused the Administration of patronizing American oil companies, and he followed through with an amendment to prohibit the use of ERP funds to purchase Middle Eastern oil. The amendment was defeated only after Congressman Jackson cited Forrestal's testimony on the state of American strategic needs. Ultimately, however, the situation never became so desperate. American oil production soon developed surpluses that relieved much of the pressure on the domestic economy. But the logic of the dollar theory still lent its force to offshore purchasing, and there would be a continuing interest in directing the Europeans to sources of supply outside the dollar area.

Congress moved next to the aid of more identifiable American groups. Agriculture had enjoyed some patronage during the

[12] Howard S. Ellis, *The Economics of Freedom: The Progress and Future of Aid to Europe* (New York: Harper and Brothers, 1950), p. 30.

UNRRA program with the purchase of surpluses, and now the farmers stood to receive some important benefits in the Marshall Plan as well. Senator Aiken brought in an amendment that synthesized some earlier proposals by Senators Thye, George, and Magnuson. The new version also had the consent of the Departments of Agriculture and State, and with the most interested parties having come into agreement, the amendment was readily accepted.

For the segment of the program dealing with agriculture, both the standards and the authority were tilted to the side of the Department of Agriculture. The Administrator would not be permitted to buy agricultural commodities abroad without the approval of the Secretary of Agriculture. The Secretary was to allow the purchase of foreign goods only on the condition that it would not create harmful surpluses in the United States or cause injury to American producers. Apologists hastened to emphasize that the Administrator still had the choice of products; he was not compelled to buy every item in surplus.[13] But the fact of the matter was that the legislation had established a presumption against purchasing foreign goods when American products were in surplus, and they would be in surplus during most of the program. That meant that in certain critical instances the ECA might not provide the financing that could bring European agricultural goods back into the market and stimulate production. It also meant a more expensive program, with a greater outlay of dollars (as opposed to local European currency).

The interest of European agriculture, then, was downgraded in the program. A similar decision occurred in the matter of shipping, where the claims, however, were far more ambiguous. Shipping services can represent an important part of those so-called "invisible" receipts in the overall balance of payments accounts. For countries like Britain and Holland, shipping was traditionally the source of income that enabled them to overcome their deficit in intra-European trade. With their earnings from shipping they could afford to run deficits in their European trade, and as they spread their debts throughout Europe, those debts could become a form of currency that allowed them, particularly the British, to play an integrative role. Through their position in shipping they could keep the cycle of exchange going, and they could maintain the network of trade that connected Europe to the outside world.

[13] *Congressional Record*, XCIV (1948), 2709, 2715, 2720.

British shipping receipts had actually increased somewhat since the war, but Norway and the Netherlands had lost half their merchant fleets. For the Dutch the situation was aggravated by the division of Germany. They not only lost an important part of their German export market, but also much of the transit traffic on the Rhine. By contrast, the United States expanded both its dry cargo and its tanker tonnage during the war through an almost incredible production effort. At the end of the war the American fleet was five times its prewar size.[14]

The Administration estimated that it could cut dollar costs and increase the earning capacity of the ERP countries if the United States transferred about 300 unused vessels for foreign chartering. Very early, though, the issue was tagged as a "hot" one in the Administration. The State Department and the Maritime Commission were anticipating a great expansion of postwar trade, foreshadowed perhaps by the large American export surplus for 1947. Both agencies called for increased construction in shipping, but others were more skeptical. R. W. Stokely in the Budget Bureau figured that in the previous several years approximately 70 percent of American exports on the basis of weight were in coal and grain. Total exports were forecast at 80 million tons for 1947, with coal taking about 40 million, and grain and flour together accounting for 16 million. But as production revived in Europe, there surely figured to be less need for American coal, and possibly also, less need for wheat.

Nor was the shipping industry inclined to be as optimistic or liberal as the Maritime Commission. Stokely reported that "American shipping interests" were opposed to the loan or charter of United States ships abroad on the grounds that it would cut into their current revenue. The Marshall Plan was expected to employ 1.7 million deadweight tons of American vessels in berth services between the United States and Western Europe. That compared to 1.46 million deadweight tons foreseen by the Maritime Commission in its postwar plan, and only 1 million deadweight tons that were actually employed in 1938. Yet the plan was not acceptable to the industry because it appeared to represent a "residual, less-than-50 percent

[14] Economic Cooperation Administration, *Recovery Progress and United States Aid* (Washington, 1949), pp. 40, 46-47, 240-41. For figures on British "invisibles" for 1938, 1946, and 1947, see Senate Foreign Relations Committee, *Hearings on Extension of ERP*, 1949, p. 154B.

share of a hypothetical total trade which is generally regarded as inflated."[15] The 50 percent formula was now a familiar one in legislation dealing with shipping, and by this time it seemed to have acquired a certain legitimacy of its own. At any rate, the Maritime Commission was willing to settle on that figure and grant American flag vessels at least 50 percent of the export-import trade.[16]

Meanwhile, union leaders brought in some alarming estimates that showed a future drop in the American percentage of international shipping.[17] Figures of decline came from the Pacific coast, with portents of unemployment and labor unrest. Shipping state Senators, like Knowland of California and Magnuson of Washington, responded with a spray of amendments. Congressman Bland of Virginia, one of the fathers of the Merchant Marine Act of 1936, forecast a signal catastrophe if the American ships were transferred. Some rather stringent ratios for the protection of American shipping were introduced, and although they were ultimately loosened to leave some discretion with the ECA, the alterations were important. "Merchant vessels" were eliminated from the list of commodities that the Administrator could procure on his own judgment. After considering various proportions of guarantee, the familiar 50 percent formula was finally adopted. It was provided that 50 percent of the gross tonnage of all cargo *procured in the United States* had to be shipped in American flag vessels. This was a modification of an earlier amendment that would have applied the 50 percent provision to *all* cargo procured under the program.[18] But to leave no mistake about the Congressional intent, the transfer plan involving 300 vessels was deleted.[19]

[15] R. W. Stokely to Schwartz, "Implication for the United States program of merchant marine promotion of Initial Report on European Cooperation," October 24, 1947, Bureau of the Budget, Series 39.18.

[16] *Ibid.*

[17] However, in his memorandum on the merchant marine, Stokely also noted that the share of world shipping among the Marshall Plan countries had dropped from the prewar figure of 60 percent to a level of 40 percent in 1947. It was a rather strange interpretation of American interest at this point that the United States should retard the efforts of the Europeans to regain one of their most natural and important sources of exchange earnings.

[18] *Congressional Record*, XCIV (1948), 2461. Also, the section was further qualified by requiring the Administrator to use American ships in this ratio "so far as . . . practicable," and to the extent that the ships were available at market rates.

[19] *Ibid.*

On its face, the shipping provision promised to raise ERP costs significantly because of the higher cost of American shipping and labor. In 1949, when the ECA was feeling the squeeze of this provision, American rates were approximately $11.15 per ton, as against $8.75 for foreign vessels. The difference of $2.40 per ton was enough to reduce the competitiveness of American coal,[20] and it was expected to add approximately $13.5 million to the cost of ERP during the first half of 1949. More than that, the delivered price of American coal affected the price of European coal. Higher American prices for transportation led to higher prices for British and Polish coal, and in this way the shipping provision made its own unsolicited contribution to the problem of European inflation.[21]

Senator Connally, for one, recognized that the shipping clause would raise costs for the ECA and place burdens on European recovery. But on the other side of the issue was the desirability of protecting the jobs of American seamen and maintaining the merchant marine. The cause of the merchant marine was one of the strongest points in the argument, and indeed, the shipping provision might have looked much less like a case of special pleading if one considered its antecedents.

The problem of the merchant marine was first posed with some urgency during the Spanish-American war, when the Navy was forced to purchase or charter foreign vessels in order to supply its forces in the Philippines and maintain the blockade of Cuba. In the next year, with the Boer war, the British were forced to withdraw large numbers of their ships from the North Atlantic trade. The effects on freight rates and services put a serious strain on the American export trade, and the results were even worse in 1914 with the outbreak of the war in Europe. American flag ships were active largely in the coast trade, extending as far as Canada and the Caribbean; but for trade with Europe and the Middle East (and even for most of South America) American merchants were dependent mainly on the shipping of Britain, France, Germany, and Italy. With the withdrawal of ships from the belligerent countries, American trade and shipping were thrown into a crisis, and the les-

[20] See Senate Foreign Relations Committee, *Hearings on Extension of ERP*, 1949, pp. 374-75.

[21] Bureau of the Budget, "Staff Memorandum on Shipping Provisions of ECA Legislation," January 27, 1949, Series 39.18.

sons of vulnerability were brought home once again in a painful way.[22] Through a series of acts beginning in 1916 and culminating in the Merchant Marine Act of 1936, the federal government established its commitment to the merchant marine and the subsidy of the shipping industry. It might have been said, in fact, that the successive pieces of legislation on the subject had raised the status of the merchant marine as a national commitment, and that it came to the proceedings on the Marshall Plan as a matured national interest.

Still, the issue was not as clear as one or two among the old ECA hands would insist. Critics pointed out that very little American trade before the war or the economic crisis was in the bulk cargoes of coal and grain. It was largely on that account that there was no provision in the Merchant Marine Act for subsidizing tramp vessels. Ship owners themselves were unwilling to go into this type of construction, but preferred to rent vessels from the government.[23] Because the need for tramp service was not expected to last beyond the present crisis, there seemed little point in starting a subsidy program. Moreover, many of the operators benefiting from the program had not even been part of the American merchant marine. They had operated foreign flag vessels in the past, and they were likely to continue that affiliation in the future.[24]

The shipping provision remained one of the most odious of the special interest requirements. One of its immediate side effects, too, was to alter the tone of the Congressional proceedings. The gates were opened, and everyone with a pet interest to protect rushed in to reserve a place in the Marshall Plan. Amendments were accepted for the procurement of by-product feeds, fish, canned goods, and corn. A certain percentage of wheat was required to go out in the form of wheat flour as a sop to the millers. As an illustration of how far this kind of thinking could extend, it was provided that the procurement of tobacco under the program should reflect the ratios among the various types of tobacco grown in the United States. This feature came to be known in the Administration as the "Barkley" provision, and its purpose widely understood as a form of insurance for Kentucky tobacco.

[22] See Samuel A. Lawrence, *United States Merchant Shipping Policies and Politics* (Washington: The Brookings Institution, 1966), pp. 33-34, 38.

[23] ECA, *Recovery Progress and United States Aid*, pp. 240-42.

[24] Bureau of the Budget, "Staff Memorandum on Shipping Provisions of ECA Legislation," *loc.cit.*

170

Much to their credit, though, the Senate-House conferees displayed a toughness that became important in principle. Corn, canned goods, and fish were knocked out in conference. John Vorys reported to the House that the products were not barred from future acquisition. It was decided, rather, that they should not be enumerated in the legislation, lest they create a moral obligation that could seriously hamstring the ECA.

And yet, despite the show of toughness, the action in Congress left the impression of an indiscriminate openness to special interests. In the Budget Bureau, Ralph Burton commented, "As I read the ECA act and sense the general legislative and administrative environment it seems that it is intended that U.S. commodites shall be available to European countries only insofar as it will work no hardship on any domestic consumer or industry."[25] There was a danger of slipping into cynicism and characterizing the whole by reacting to the most egregious parts. Nevertheless, the concern for special provisions was so pronounced that one could hardly blame Burton for drawing the most uncharitable conclusions. "In other words," he wrote, after reviewing the legislation, "I doubt that the soft drink or sardine industry will be allowed to take a beating for European recovery."

I have argued that as the Congressional leaders faced the problem of administration, they initiated a chain of inquiry that raised some of the most fundamental questions of national interest. When they diminished the role of the State Department, there was a drive to impart a new character to American diplomacy. As they tried to resolve the question of centralization they had to determine a relative ranking for the Marshall Plan within the Executive—and with that, the relative weight of the Marshall Plan interest among the host of competing interests represented by the regular agencies and their clientele publics. Potentially, the issue could have resulted in a vast reorganization of the Executive branch, as well as the two houses of Congress.

Decisions on operating procedures were regarded with some gravity as precedents that could have long-term consequences for the relationship between government and the economy. In defining the relations of authority with the Marshall Plan nations, the

[25] Ralph Burton to Royden Dangerfield, July 7, 1948, Bureau of the Budget, *loc.cit.*, p. 5.

United States was presented with one of those moments in which a nation is given a chance to articulate something of its own character through the medium of its foreign policy. The choice between the pluralist and unilateralist alternatives was significant in principle, and it was reflected also in the conditions that the United States was willing to impose on the ERP countries. In that category of "conditions," I have tried to suggest the relative weights that were assigned to various group interests, as for example in agriculture and shipping. One could go on and on in this vein, listing the relations of the different interests to one another; but the question is: Are we faced here simply with a catalogue, or is there some basis on which we could pull all these separate decisions together to form a coherent statement? Do we have some common reference by which we could give a relative weight to these decisions and arrange them in a hierarchy? If we did, we could distinguish the features that were more or less important, the primary from the secondary. If we had such a hierarchy of features we would be in a position to define the essential character of the Marshall Plan. In addition to making sense out of the program, that would give us some vital standards to apply in testing the performance of the ECA and the character of the Marshall Plan in practice. Obviously I think we do have that common measure, and I believe it was contained in the legislation itself. In the following chapter I shall try to set out this method of analysis and show how it might be applied to the Marshall Plan.

Part II

9. PRESUMPTIONS AND POLITICAL THEORY

I

No ONE TODAY would deny that administration inevitably brings discretion about important policy questions. The fact that decisions must continue to be made in applying rules to particular cases, and that the choice over means will often create a choice over ends, is all quite familiar to us now. The hope of anticipating every situation of choice seems obviously futile, and there appears to be more skepticism, too, about the possibility of identifying all the relevant value premises in advance. Only the positivists may still cling to the hope of building an administrative science by resolving all value questions ahead of time and translating the solutions into fixed operational terms.

However, even if it were possible in fact to define all of one's values rigidly in advance, the result may still be ethically undesirable. If values were operationally fixed once and for all, we would deny ourselves the need to test them in concrete cases. There would be no basis, then, for that discourse on values that permits one to explore their rational content and thereby, perhaps, lay the foundations for their rational change over time.[1] Only the true totalitarian system can be so much the prisoner of its own theory that it can pride itself on being blind to empirical circumstances and the possibility of special cases.

We know that value choices are inescapable, and that the administrator often has room to follow his own predilections. Yet if we utterly denied Frank Goodnow's separation of politics and administration, there would be a disquieting lack of predictability in the world, and in the things that matter. There would be freedom for the venal bureaucrat to violate his public obligation and subvert the program he is charged with administering. Even more

[1] A good example of the "post-positivist" critique can be found in R. M. Hare, *Freedom and Reason* (London: Oxford University Press, 1963).

disturbing is the case of the administrator who might be personally committed to a policy, but finds himself in one of those in-between situations where the formal policy statement provides no direction. His intentions are good, but they offer no guide, and he finds himself floating, as it were, in a sea of values. In this respect the problem of the administrator is really an enduring problem of political action more generally: How can we assure *principled action* when decisions normally have to be made under conditions of uncertainty? How can our practice reflect our essential values when we may not know entirely what all the important values are, when our knowledge of the facts is probably incomplete, and when we have only a dim vision, at best, of the future course of affairs?

Fortunately, the world is not so unmanageable for us. The very fact that we can have awareness of the problem of principled action may imply that we are willing to do some serious deliberating on the subject of ends. That willingness alone might indicate that we have more sophisticated equipment for dealing with the problem than is commonly suggested by such techniques as "satisficing" or "muddling through."[2] With these latter approaches, it is sufficient if we simply match the preference with the selection of a "good." In some instances we may compare alternatives at the margins. In others, we may simply choose the option giving us more goods for our resources, or perhaps even more resources. But it is not the concern of these approaches necessarily that the best or optimal decision be made. The individual choice presents no occasion for reconsidering the shape of the utility schedule itself. If there is an exchange involved, it is the quick, once-and-for-all transfer across the counter. What the concepts of "satisficing" and "muddling through" seem to rule out is that the application of a preference may be only the beginning, a method of entry that provides the initial definition of the problem rather than the final decision. What

[2] See Herbert A. Simon, *Administrative Behavior* (New York: The Macmillan Company, 2nd ed. rev.; 1957), pp. xxv-xxvi: Simon writes that "while economic man maximizes—selects the best alternative from among all those available to him; his cousin, whom we shall call administrative man, satisfices—looks for a course of action that is satisfactory or 'good enough.' Examples of satisficing criteria that are familiar enough to businessmen . . . are 'share of market,' 'adequate profit,' 'fair price' " (p. xxv). See also Charles E. Lindblom, "The Science of 'Muddling Through,' " *Public Administration Review*, Vol. XIX, No. 2 (Spring 1959), pp. 79-88.

may follow, then, is not the immediate accumulation of goods, but the start of a rather prolonged period of discussion. In the images associated with "satisficing" or "muddling through" we lose, in short, the sense of administration as deliberation. Perhaps this suggests how much our vision is still shaped by Goodnow's categories —politics versus administration, Executive versus Legislature, *execution* versus *deliberation*. It reveals how far we have come from Weber's fundamental understanding of bureaucracy as the peculiar administrative structure of rational-legality—or even the distance we have come from Goodnow's own recognition that administration includes adjudication.

The satisficers and their relatives leave us with administrators who have a collection of values but no value structure. If the participants bring nothing more to the problem of choice than a set of disjointed "likes," it is evident that they come only to buy and not to deliberate or argue.

But perhaps to a greater extent than we recognize, people are able to bring order to their choices through the use of consistent biases or operating presumptions. It is quite common to act under conditions of imperfect knowledge, and what most of us try to do under those circumstances is manage the area of doubt by stacking our presumptions in favor of one alternative rather than another. We create rules of thumb that may take forms like "When in doubt . . ." or "All things being equal, it is better to . . ." or "Presume in favor of. . . ." And their referents may be numerous. For example, when in doubt, "do not invest," or "take the umbrella," or "do not publicly attribute a quotation to someone." Our knowledge of the empirical world is not sufficient to tell us, in these instances, whether a business venture is sound, or whether it will rain today, or whether someone actually said what we think he said (although we have strong reasons to believe he said it). But if our knowledge is insufficient, we can still make a decision by casting the issue in more general terms. We may be conservative and think that it is better not to act than to act without deliberation when financial risks are involved. We decide it is better to say nothing, and possibly accept a duller piece of writing, rather than take the chance of misquoting someone or misrepresenting his position. In each case a decision is made ultimately in terms of a preference that is closer to the form of a general rule. Since the situations are apt to recur, it is likely that the presumption followed the first time will

177

be followed in the future. The rule might have been intuited on the spot, but it acquires more than *ad hoc* relevance because it is rooted in a more stable set of preferences.

As these examples illustrate, we create operating presumptions in our daily lives, and they impart some of our more characteristic values even to small decisions. I use the term "operating" here because the very creation of the rule is sparked by the need to act in the real world. The terms "bias" and "presumption" are connected. By "bias" I mean the literal significance of the term as an "inclination" or a "leaning." "Bias" is especially apt because it signifies that the crude working assumptions we use are able to provide us with little more than an entry into the more complicated issues. An inclination is clearly different from a completed act or a matured judgment. "Bias" implicitly recognizes that many questions are left to be explored, and if a decision has to be taken now, on the strength of bias alone, it is likely to be problematic, and for that reason discussion would continue to be appropriate.

By applying a bias we are *presuming* in favor of one class of outcomes. We might as easily say that we are "assuming in favor" of something, or that we are using a "working assumption," and that would be fair enough. But the term "presumption" carries certain connotations from its legal usage that add a valuable dimension to this analysis. When we fix presumptions in law, as we do, for example, when we presume someone innocent until proven guilty, we do something more than register a preference (in this instance, that it is better for the guilty to go free than for the innocent to suffer unjustly). Our presumption defines the framework of the hearing, and although it may give an advantage to the defendant, it is not enough in itself to decide the case. It is only the beginning. It establishes certain guides for the area of doubt, but it presupposes that there will be issues to consider—that evidence will be presented, that in the framework created by the presumption, the presumption itself can be rebutted in a reasoned decision.

Thus, to take an example outside the courtroom, liberal Democrats in the Senate could confront the issue of a communications satellite with a bias against private ownership. Consistent with their own inclinations, they could assign the burden of proof to those who favored private operation or something less than full government control. For a small band of liberals, the burden of argument was never carried. But others found some intervening considerations persuasive, so eventually they were able to overcome their predilections and vote for a mixed stock arrangement.[3]

Operating biases, then, can provide a useful tool in organizing a problem of decision. More than that, the inclinations they convey can be inclinations about some of the highest things, about relations of authority or the conditions of the public good. As they form themselves into presumptions, and as they are confirmed in practice, they foster a linkage among preferences. In that way, the presumptions come to form a coherent operating code. Inclinations become rooted in stable principle and, however roughly, they manage to impart the character of the actor to the disconnected episodes of the empirical world. Burke understood the essence of this long ago when he defended "prejudice" in the sense we use "bias" or "presumption" today:

> Prejudice is of ready application in the emergency; it previously engages the mind in a steady course of wisdom and virtue, and does not leave the man hesitating in the moment of decision, sceptical, puzzled and unresolved. Prejudice renders a man's virtue his habit, and not a series of unconnected acts. Through just prejudice, his duty becomes part of his nature.[4]

II

The very purpose that calls forth the operating presumption is the desire to affect practice. At a very common sense level, then, operating presumptions involve power, or the capacity to realize one's will. But the question is, what kind of power do operating presumptions represent? Do they distribute some commodity or "power" that originates elsewhere, or do they themselves generate a specific kind of power? The answers would be clearer if we looked first at the forms that operating presumptions can take, and the peculiar kinds of burdens they create to support their effectiveness.

[3] More recently, Senator Cooper of Kentucky explained his decision on the nomination of Abe Fortas to succeed Earl Warren as Chief Justice: "I went upon the presumption that the nomination to such an important position by the Chief Executive deserved the approval of the Senate and my vote, unless there was evidence to the contrary. . . . [B]ut my presumption, as we went forward with the evidence has been overturned." *Congressional Record*, CXIV (October 1, 1968), S11684 (Daily Edition).

[4] *The Works of Edmund Burke*, Vol. III: *Reflections on the Revolution in France* (London: Henry G. Bohn, 1845), p. 110.

Starting at the least articulate level, an operating presumption may assign a burden of explicitness and attention. Probably the most familiar example here is that of the subordinate who receives an unwelcome order from his superior. Rather than openly disobeying, he decides simply to do nothing and gamble that the issue will be forgotten. To revive the order, the superior will have to assume the burdens of detection for the sake of determining, in the first place, that the original order had not been enforced. After that, he will of course have the additional bother of raising the matter again and issuing another order. Lacking a decision, nothing is done and inertia works to maintain the existing policy. We might say that the situation naturally contains a presumption in favor of continuing the current policy and, conversely, that the burden of effort is shifted to the side of those who would seek change.

This technique of evasion has become closely identified with bureaucracies; yet, it may be found in almost all relations involving the element of authority, and what is more important, the presumption underlying the technique may be raised to a level of explicitness and conscious design. It made a significant difference, for example, that the crews in the SAC bombers presumed that they would turn back *unless* they received a definite signal to go on to their targets. The alternative would have been to set the presumption in favor of going on to the attack until the plane was recalled. The differences should be fairly obvious: In the one case, the presumptions worked to prevent an air strike unless it was deliberately intended. In the other case, the major risks were given over to the side of avoiding accidental war. To choose a working presumption here was to choose, in effect, a clear rank order of preferences. It was a means, also, for setting inertia in the service of one goal rather than another, while reducing the risks of doubt and inadvertence.

An important variation is the arrangement for interpreting silence or inaction. What did it mean, for example, when Congress failed to take action either to sustain or reject President Truman's seizure of the steel mills in 1952? Congress failed to act because it could not produce a majority on either side of the question; but did that mean that Congress disapproved the seizure because it failed to approve, or did it mean that Congress approved the action because it failed to disapprove?[5] By way of contrast, this is exactly

[5] Some members of the Court majority were altogether too blithe in

the sort of difficulty that was eliminated in the field of administrative reorganization with the Reorganization Act of 1939. Under the terms of the act, a reorganization plan could be promulgated by the President to take effect within sixty days unless it was overruled by a majority vote in both houses of Congress. That is, in the absence of Congressional action, the reorganization measure was presumed to have passed. The burden of forming a Congressional majority was transferred now to the side of those who would have rejected a specific organization plan, rather than those who would have supported one. Once again, through the arrangement of presumptions a definite preference was registered in the decision rules themselves —in this case, that it was generally better to reorganize than not, and to reorganize faster, when the Executive found it necessary.[6]

The burdens of explicitness may also be complicated by enlarging and formalizing them. There may be more arguments to make, and in written form, where the requirements of style may be more exacting and the argument itself becomes increasingly public. In his study of the OPA, Victor Thompson suggested that the government was probably prepared to grant additional fuel oil during the war to anyone who was prepared to argue long enough for it. But to argue for an additional ration could be very trying. That was particularly true when it involved a trip or repeated visits to a central office, when it required an elaborate application form with seemingly endless categories, and when, finally, the whole case might seem to hinge on the persuasiveness of an oral argument. As Thompson discovered, the procedures were fearsome enough in most cases to discourage people from making the additional demands.[7]

On the other hand, when the government wants to get maximum compliance, as for example in paying income tax, it may try to reverse the burdens and make that extractive operation as painless as possible. It may be willing to gloss over fine distinctions and reduce

---

assuming that the first inference was the only sensible one. See 343 U.S., 601, 603-604, 631-33, 637-38.

[6] Compare the argument advanced by Samuel Huntington to apply a similar arrangement to the area of taxation and fiscal policy. Huntington, "Congressional Responses to the Twentieth Century," in David B. Truman (ed.), *The Congress and America's Future* (Englewood Cliffs, N.J.: Prentice-Hall, 1965), pp. 22-25, 29-31.

[7] See Victor A. Thompson, *The Regulatory Process in OPA Rationing* (New York: King's Crown Press, 1950), pp. 27-29.

the number of categories in the tax form. The result will be a simple form that most people can fill out with a minimum of error, and with the costs of error borne by the government. If that is not enough, counselors may be provided and offices can be kept open later to accommodate stragglers. It becomes a case, then, of reducing and simplifying the acts that people must perform for themselves and, in some instances, giving them free help in doing what remains.

The burdens, in all these cases, are burdens of speaking, deciding, acting. To summarize them simply as "inconveniences"—like standing in line—is far too gross, and it surely misses the point. These burdens are much heavier and much more difficult to manage than the discomforts inherent in moving bodies. They are the burdens of committing oneself in public, of taking responsibility, of making a decision and speaking out. But beyond that, and at the highest level, they are the burdens of offering reasons and justifying decisions. We might say, in summary fashion, that presumptions distribute burdens of reasoned argument. When we presume in favor of one alternative, we presume against another, which is to say that we assign a burden of proof to the opposing side. To argue for a rival position now is not to act any longer in an unstructured situation, where the issue may be open or undefined. It is to argue, instead, where premises have been established and preferences have already congealed. Very often it is to argue after a considerable amount of discussion has already taken place, at a time when intuition and hunches are no longer sufficient to carry the decision.

What I am suggesting, in sum, is that the burdens of explicitness and argument may be extraordinarily heavy ones to carry. The structure of presumptions itself creates difficulties, and it may be toughened by a host of special requirements and discouraging techniques. The shift of presumptions makes the burden heavy even for someone with a good argument or a zeal for dissent. But for the man who is diffident, who is not quite sure he has all the facts he needs, and who may well have to argue before committed and responsible men, this structure of discourse may simply be too forbidding to enter.

A particularly good illustration is provided by Richard Neustadt in his account of the situation in Washington when General MacArthur advanced into North Korea and found himself facing a Chinese intervention. MacArthur, of course, had been subject to directives from Washington, but those directives gave him a wide measure of discretion. In early October of 1950, when Chinese intervention was recognized as a possibility, the modified directive still permitted him to "continue the action as long as, in your judgment, action by forces now under your control offers a reasonable chance of success." As much as a month later, when MacArthur was instructed not to bomb Manchuria, and while the State Department explored the prospects for a settlement, MacArthur was still told that "he should be free to do what he could in a military way." Since it was not clear that the Chinese would intervene in force, or that the situation would be clarified by stopping MacArthur's advance, there was considerable doubt in Washington over what should be done. In the meantime, MacArthur had succeeded brilliantly at Inchon, and there was the chance that he might succeed now. Under the conditions of uncertainty in Washington, the military directive essentially shifted the presumption in favor of MacArthur as the commander in the field. The presumption was enforced by Truman's administrative theory, which favored "unity of command" and full responsibility to the subordinate.

When the debacle came on November 28, as Richard Neustadt noted, it was not completely unanticipated; it was what many people in the government had feared for a long time. The question then was, Why were MacArthur's orders left unchanged? "Poor intelligence, or poor evaluation," wrote Neustadt, "may account for MacArthur's conduct, but it does not suffice to explain Washington's behavior in the days before his victory march." Neustadt's own explanation is worth quoting at some length:

> By mid-November some of these men [in the Pentagon] felt virtually certain of the real Chinese location and were becoming worried lest MacArthur fail to concentrate his forces. Before those forces marched, the worry . . . was intense in Bradley's mind and Marshall's and in Acheson's. . . . Pentagon unhappiness about [MacArthur's separated columns] grew apace, and [MacArthur] was practically implored to show more caution. When he demurred, as under his instructions he had every right to do, the Chiefs of Staff lacked courage (*lacking certainty*) to seek their alteration from the President. Despite the worry, no one went to Truman—and that outcome turns on matters more complex than poor intelligence.

No one went to Truman because everyone thought someone else should go. Before November 25 the men who had concluded two weeks earlier that Truman should not change MacArthur's orders were agreed, it seems, in wishing that he would. . . . When worry grew, the military chiefs deferred to State; let Acheson, as guardian of 'policy,' ask Truman to reverse MacArthur. But Acheson, already under fire from the Capitol, was treading warily between the Pentagon and that inveterate idealist about generals, Harry Truman. . . . As for the Secretary of Defense, he had preceded Acheson in State and had been Army Chief of Staff when Bradley was a subordinate commander. Since his return to government Marshall had leaned over backwards not to meddle with the work of his successors in their jobs. . . . What Acheson and Bradley were not ready to initiate, Marshall evidently felt he could not take upon himself.

For Cabinet members and for military chiefs, a decision to go to the President is something like a government's decision to go to war; it is not something done each day on every issue. When the issue is reversal of established plans on grounds of sheer conjecture, men of prudence and responsibility may pause. . . .[8]

The President had shifted the burdens of proof and made it more difficult for people to come to him with a different policy. Even if no basic change in policy would have been made, it would have been valuable to place the burden of justification on MacArthur. At least policy would have had to proceed then through positive decision, and wherever doubts existed, they would have been made to work against the danger of sliding unconsciously into a disaster.

What happened, then, was that operating presumptions arose and defined a structure for the flow of policy disputes. The presumptions were never formally stated, but they effectively conditioned access to the President, and for all practical purposes, they distributed power with a bias toward one set of ends.

Now it is often said that political science has nothing comparable to the "money" of economics, in the sense of a currency that can represent generalized power. Certainly political science has nothing

[8] Richard Neustadt, *Presidential Power* (New York: John Wiley and Sons, 1960), pp. 144-46. Emphasis added. For a strikingly similar account, see Arthur Schlesinger's memoir on the Bay of Pigs affairs in *A Thousand Days* (Boston: Houghton Mifflin, 1965), pp. 240, 255, 259.

comparable to money as a counter for measuring transactions. Yet even money changes in value, and not all the concerns of economics can be reduced to numerical terms. On the other hand, distributing burdens of reasoned argument through the use of presumptions can be very powerful, and it is one of the most common of social phenomena. Presumptions are employed everywhere, in the household and the office as well as in the government. But perhaps even more important, the meaning of "presumption" is fixed in our established usage. As a concept, it is known to us in our ordinary language, and for that reason it informs our natural understanding of events, including our natural understanding of politics.

Still, with the device of money, economics can lay claim to an impressive social science, even though it starts from assumptions that are surely as exaggerated as any assertion we might make about the responsiveness of human beings to reasoned argument. It would be hard, in fact, to decide which proposition is more distorted and which more generally true—that men are naturally acquisitive, that they can be relied on to buy cheap and sell dear, or that people are commonly impressed by an informed statement. In this respect, the recent survey studies of "deference" and democratic elitism merely illustrate what Mill was able to see long ago: that people ordinarily recognize a gradation of skills; they understand that legislating is not merely different from brick-laying, but that, in some significant sense it is higher, and that it requires skills that are not evenly distributed in the population at large. Clearly, everyone does not have the ability to engage in reasoned discourse on a fairly high plane, but it was still assumed in this older and more traditional view that most people were capable of recognizing intelligence when they saw it, and wise enough, at least, to recognize someone more informed than themselves.[9] Again, it would simply be natural in this view to be affected by a reasoned statement, and by the same token, it is only natural for most people to be deterred from the serious intellectual effort involved in reasoned argument.

It might be said, then, that presumptions reflect values, but that they themselves create power in a peculiar currency. They create and allocate power, as we have said, by distributing burdens of proof or reasoned argument.[10] In the case of Truman and Mac-

[9] See, for example, John Stuart Mill, *Considerations on Representative Government* (Indianapolis: Bobbs-Merrill, 1958), pp. 135-37.

[10] To contend that burdens of argument may present us with a currency

Arthur, the presumptions were unarticulated. They were brought about by a combination of things, including the directive to Mac-Arthur and the conviction, held by Truman, that the subordinate taking responsibility should be given as much discretion as possible. But there are also occasions when the presumptions are stated explicitly in formal procedures or find their roots in the organizational structure itself. Two of the best examples here figured prominently in the history of the ECA—the European payments agreements and the Congressional action in separating the ECA from the State Department.

1. *The Payments Plans*

As the Europeans turned to the problem of postwar construction, the critical materials they required were available in large quantities mainly in the United States and the dollar area. To get them, one needed dollars or other hard currencies. But until production could be revived, the Europeans were not in a position to earn the necessary volume of dollars through their own export of goods and services. Under these tight conditions, their economies were highly vulnerable to the direction taken by private decisions on imports and investment. The management of foreign exchange thus became crucial, and governments soon responded with import licensing, quotas, controls on capital flight, and restrictions on the use of exchange reserves. The object was to get gold or dollars; the worst thing was to accumulate European currencies, for they would contribute little to the acquisition of basic reconstruction goods. As a consequence, though, the Europeans seemed to fall into a primitive autarchy. Each nation was reluctant to hold the currency of the others, and several countries began to demand repayment in dollars from their European trading partners. A good index of the problem was that the British showed an export surplus with the

---

or medium of exchange is not to say, however, that they provide us with coinage. The burdens of argument do not themselves contain measurable units. Still, that does not prevent us from measuring their effects, or even from making some rough predictions. We may not be able to report the exact weight, for example, of the burdens involved in obtaining a larger quota of rationed oil. But we can determine the amount of appeals that were actually made and the volume of oil that was distributed above the quotas. In testing for the results of operating presumptions, then, we would have to vary our techniques and find the methods most appropriate to the case at hand.

186

Continent. Traditionally, the British trade deficit had provided some valuable liquidity by dispersing sterling debts throughout Europe. Now, however, one country could not use its favorable balance of trade with another nation to pay its debts to a third. The result was that intra-European trade was reduced to a collection of bilateral barter deals.

By the end of 1947, over 200 bilateral agreements had been concluded in Europe. If they appeared to symptomize the tendencies toward disintegration in Europe, it was nevertheless true that they provided a basis on which some form of multilateral trade could go forward. The agreements specified the exchange of particular commodities along with ceilings, and they included a very critical provision in which the contracting parties agreed to hold each other's currency up to a certain level—at which point a country would have to start discharging its debts in gold or dollars (these were later called the "dollar points").[11] Thus, although the bilateral agreements were important integrative measures, they were bound to have a constricting effect on intra-European trade. Each nation would have to keep a close watch on its bilateral accounts and take care not to exceed the dollar points. Imports from creditors would have to be cut back, and instead of the free search for comparative advantage and expansion, trade was constrained in the bilateral mold. Intra-European trade in 1947 was still only 56 percent of the prewar level, while imports from overseas were already 6.5 percent higher.

The aim of the various payments agreements that followed in annual succession from 1947 was to overcome this inhibiting character of bilateralism. The immediate need was to provide more international liquidity, but the long-run goal was to eliminate the bilateral structure itself and place European trade on a firm multilateral basis. A limited payments agreement was outlined at the CEEC conference in the summer of 1947, and after much negotiation, a modified version was approved in October. The character of the agreement could be seen in the two major operating procedures. First, each country would report monthly to a central office on its debtor or creditor positions. The office would determine the multilateral compensations or "offsets" that could be made without increasing any balances. For example, if country A

[11] William Diebold, Jr., *Trade and Payments in Western Europe* (New York: Harper and Brothers, 1952), pp. 16-17. And here, I think, one could hardly do better than to rely on Diebold's excellent account.

187

owed $3 million to country B, B owed country C $5 million, and C owed A $4 million, the central office would simply cancel A's debt to B, lower B's debt to C to $2 million, and C's debt to A to $1 million. These initial offsetting moves were called "first category" compensations. The second procedure concerned multilateral compensations that involved an increase in any balance. It was in this operation, the "second category compensations," that the tension between multilateral payments and the bilateral structure became manifest. The bilateral structure made unrestricted compensations perilous when they were carried out on a multilateral basis. Let us assume, for example, that Belgium was holding $4 million in sterling, and that the British agreed to convert the Belgian sterling holdings into dollars when they reached $5 million. With free multilateral transfer, Norway might be able to pay off its debts to Belgium with any sterling reserves it happened to hold. If Norway paid Belgium $2 million in sterling, the transfer would raise Belgian sterling holdings to $6 million and force the British to begin paying out dollars. However, the initial payments agreements avoided this problem by requiring the consent of all the interested parties before a multilateral compensation was permitted. The British then could veto the Norwegian remittance in sterling, and as the system actually operated, even secondary or indirect debtors might be able to interpose a veto. Thus, at the time of the first clearing, the eleven participating countries had debts among themselves that totaled $762.1 million, and yet only $1.7 million, or 2 percent of the total, was cleared. During the entire life of the agreement, the total clearings came to only $51.6 million.[12]

The aim of the succeeding payments agreements was to broaden the sphere of multilateral transfers. The payments agreements of 1948-49 incorporated American aid with the concept of "drawing rights." Each pair of nations would actually negotiate its "estimates" of bilateral transactions, including "invisibles." The expected creditors would then extend "drawing rights" or credits to their individual debtors for the amount of their estimated surplus with each nation. In turn, the United States would supply the creditor nation with an equivalent amount of dollar aid. European trade would be facilitated, and at the same time, the creditors were rewarded for their contribution by gaining increased access to dollar sources of supply.

[12] *Ibid.*, pp. 21, 27.

The system of drawing rights was also tolerable because it was safely bilateral. The credits were created only in bilateral transactions, and they were valid only in the relations between the creditor and its particular debtor country. But if the drawing rights had been transferable, if one nation could have used its credits from France, for example, to buy goods in Belgium, then the British troubles would have been aggravated. The British were deeply in debt to Belgium, and since Belgium was one of the strongest creditor countries on the Continent, transferability promised to build up Belgian reserves. As the Belgians accumulated sterling, the British would have been pressed to provide dollars. Therefore, it was understandable that the British would form the center of opposition to any broadening of the transferability provisions.

The movement to a multilateral payments system became a widely shared goal, but it was still possible to insist that transferability take place only in a framework that guaranteed bilateral controls. Here the British found stronger support than usual among the other members. If balances could be transferred, the creditor nations stood to lose dollars in conditional aid. Thus they came to agree with the British in creating an operating rule that rooted the clearing process in the bilateral structure: Multilateral transfer was considered the last resort. A debtor could ask the Council of the OEEC to transfer its drawing rights to a third country, but only after it bore the burden of proof and demonstrated that it could not use its drawing rights profitably in the creditor nation. Moreover, the council would work on the principle of unanimity in recommending the change to the ECA—which meant that each creditor would still have a veto on what was done with its credits. This structure of operating rules proved so formidable a deterrent to multilateral clearances that no country even bothered to petition for a transfer of its drawing rights.[13]

For the next year, the ECA urged a major step ahead, with the use of drawing rights anywhere in Western Europe. It was a declaration, in effect, for the full transferability of credits on a multilateral basis. Nevertheless, only one-quarter of the funds were to be allowed outside the bilateral mold. The conditions attached to those multilateral funds provide an interesting example of the way in which operating presumptions can be used, not only to affect results but to discipline behavior.

[13] *Ibid.*, pp. 44, 60.

189

One-fourth of the drawing rights were clearly permitted for multilateral transfers. However, some conditioning rules were attached, and their effect, again, was to establish the dominance of the bilateral framework. The main operating preferences were these:

—The transferable drawing rights could not be used until the bilateral drawing rights were exhausted. (The bilateral drawing rights referred to that three-fourths of the credits which could be used only in the country granting the credits.)

—Nor could the transferable drawing rights be used until the debtor exhausted all of its "existing resources" in the currency of the creditor country—i.e., in addition to the requirement of using the bilateral credits first.

—Drawing rights left over from any of the previous agreements would also have to be exhausted before one could use the transferable credits.

The operating presumptions were further reflected in the organizational procedures. The use of bilateral drawing rights was automatic. The Bank of International Settlements recorded the transaction or adjusted balances whenever its calculations showed that they were necessary. But when a nation sought to use its multilateral drawing rights, it had to make that intention explicit. No multilateral transfer was simply to be assumed. Departures from bilateralism would have to be conscious and intended, not inadvertent.

Clearly, the agreements of 1949-50 took a decisive step toward multilateral payments, but that aspiration was subject to the terms of bilateralism. The operating presumptions were not designed to prevent the multilateral use of drawing rights; they were meant to discourage only an indiscriminate use which might not be responsive to the national interests represented in the bilateral framework. In that case, one may ask, what were the results, or as some might phrase it, what was the "behavior" that flowed through the structure created by the operating rules? The total multilateral drawing rights established under the 1949-50 agreement came to $172.4 million. (This was the sum of those 25 percent portions of the drawing rights that were set aside by all the creditors.) Of this, $153.2 million was used, and out of that figure, only $62.9 million was used under the transferability provisions. There were only six instances of multilateral rights being used where no previous bilateral privileges had been created. Thus, out of funds that were

190

marked off explicitly for multilateral transfer, only a little more than a third was actually used outside the bilateral pattern.[14] The priorities expressed in the operating rules were successfully conveyed into practice. The bilateral framework was protected, and in the meantime, the participants were left free to experiment with further steps toward a more flexible system of multilateral exchange.

2. *The Autonomous ECA*

In the Administration bill, the ECA Administrator was to act under the "direction and control" of the Secretary of State on matters affecting foreign policy. It was Marshall's expectation that the State Department would determine what was a matter of foreign policy and the ECA would simply comply. But under Vandenberg's leadership the Senate Foreign Relations Committee removed the "direction and control" formula and provided for the independence of an ECA with Cabinet status. Further, the committee went on to specify a right of appeal to the President for both the ECA Administrator and the Secretary of State. Where the situation had previously been in doubt, it was evident now that the burden of appeal would rest with the Secretary of State.

As Neustadt observed, going to the President was not something done casually, and certainly it could not be done every day. The appellant was forced to choose his issues well, for it would be folly to bring trivial matters, and it would be even worse to bring important matters and then lose. In any given instance there would be a presumption against making an appeal and in favor of husbanding one's credits instead for the really important issues of principle. If this interpretation is correct, we might hypothesize that with the decision on organization, Congress created an operating presumption for the State Department that might have been expressed in this way: "In any given situation, accept a compromise rather than appeal; and if a compromise cannot be had, concede the point rather than take it to the President. (Take something to the President only in unambiguous cases, where the alternative is to give up an important policy position.)"

We do not have the kind of statistical evidence here that we had in the case of the payments agreements. But there are times when the study of signal incidents may be quite as reliable for our pur-

[14] *Ibid.*, pp. 71-72, 75.

poses as the massing of numbers. To prove the existence of these hypothetical operating presumptions—and with that, the important changes in behavior that resulted from a change in the structure of authority—we would have to establish at least three separate points:[15]

1. that at some time, preferably earlier, the State Department effectively renounced any intention to wage an active campaign of appeals to the President. The point would be documented if we found that no major appeals, or only a negligible amount, were made. If the department gave up its chance for high level appeals and seemed to content itself with coming to terms with the ECA on a lower level, it would tend to confirm the operating rule. It would appear then that the department preferred to concede or compromise rather than appeal to the President. Still, that would not be conclusive, for it might only indicate that the department was perfectly satisfied with the performance of the ECA. To complete the test we would have to show, in addition:

2. that the State Department was not satisfied with the arrangement; and

3. that there was a major policy conflict in which the State Department lost out to the ECA. If Marshall's "direction and control" formula meant anything, it was intended to get compliance on major foreign policy issues without question. But if the department failed to achieve even this minimal goal, there would be strong grounds for inferring that the change in organizational authority had something to do with the outcome.

1. On the first point, we have some interesting evidence in the form of a commitment of administrative resources. A great deal of the burden in appealing to the President may be removed if the President is given special staff resources that can be concentrated on the task of arbitrating conflicts. In April 1948, the President was given these resources for the exclusive end of overseeing the

[15] In testing for the operating presumptions in this instance we are faced, as we often are, with the problem of affirming the consequent. Even if we demonstrated that the predicted effects actually occurred, we would be open to the rejoinder that they would have occurred anyway. There is really no way out of the problem, because we will never know how the original provisions might have worked. In this kind of situation, all we can do is cite the evidence and let the reader judge. It may be sufficient if the resulting behavior was so flatly in contradiction to the pattern sought by the State Department that the organizational changes stand out as the most obvious and compelling explanation.

relations between the ECA and the State Department. On April 27, Frederick Lawton of the Budget Bureau was appointed to the White House staff as a special assistant to the President for administrative coordination in the Marshall Plan. It was significant that Lawton's transfer was not a "detailing," but a permanent appointment. Although it was expected that he would return to the Budget Bureau eventually, it was also assumed that his duties in the White House would be full-time during the life of the Marshall Plan.[16] But contrary to expectations—and quite revealing for the situation of the State Department—Lawton returned to the Budget Bureau in six months, claiming that he had nothing to do at the White House. Unless the people at State were fully content with matters as they were, the removal of the President's staff resources deprived them of the most important lever they had in maintaining an effective appeals program. In point of fact, no major appeal would be brought to the White House by the State Department. Lawton's departure in the fall of 1948 meant that as early as the second quarter of the program, Hoffman was assured that any high level friction with the State Department was likely to be only sporadic. The department had evidently given up whatever potential it might have had for the continuous initiation of policy disputes.

2. The State Department was outwardly quiescent, Hoffman was satisfied, and Marshall, for his part, saw nothing in the department's setback in Congress that was very perturbing. Marshall was willing to let the ECA go its own way in the short time it had, but there were others in the State Department, especially in the career levels dealing with administration, who were far more committed to the department as an institution. For them, the legitimate claims of the State Department were not to be surrendered with such detachment.

On this matter of dissatisfaction within the department, we nec-

[16] For short term projects the agencies usually resort to the device of "reimbursable loans." In this arrangement the department loaning the personnel continues to pay their salaries, and it is reimbursed in turn by the borrowing agency. Lawton's transfer was a full and formal separation from the Budget Bureau rather than a reimbursable loan. See Bureau of the Budget, Office Memorandum No. 220, April 27, 1948. Here, as in many other instances, I am grateful to Mrs. Hope Grace, the Archivist of the Budget Bureau, for locating this document in the bureau archives. An explicit discussion of the reasons for the special staff assignment appears in Roseman's memorandum to the Director, April 20, 1948, Bureau of the Budget, Series 39.18.

essarily fall back on more impressionistic evidence. In this regard, one very illuminating incident was recalled by a man who was, at the time, one of the top executives in the ECA. Early in 1948, he was invited to an interdepartmental meeting at the State Department. Like many others in the ECA, this administrator had come to the Marshall Plan from another agency, and since his earlier work involved foreign operations, he attended many previous meetings of this kind, with some of the same people. Thus, when he appeared at this coordinating session in 1948, it was understandable that the people at the State Department would not identify him instantly with the ECA, but would tend to associate him instead with his old agency. Without any awareness, then, that there was a member of the ECA present, the chairman of the meeting launched into what was remembered as an unusually long and bitter diatribe against Congress for taking the Marshall Plan and the ECA away from the State Department. What was scheduled as a technical conference lapsed into a rambling critique that consumed the better part of the meeting, which itself lasted over an hour and a half. Finally, in a flourish that was apparently stamped with vividness in the mind of our respondent, the chairman vowed that the department would right this wrong if it took ten years! Clearly, the arrangement was a source of continuing spite in the State Department, and as much as twelve years later, Dean Acheson could still be moved to a fit of sarcasm when he recalled the incident.[17] It seems safe to conclude, then, that if the people at State gave up their prospects for an active appeals policy, it was not because they were delighted or even satisfied with the new arrangements.

3. As for a major policy conflict, it occurred on the issue that came to represent, perhaps, the highest-order goal of the ECA— the building of permanent collective institutions for the OEEC countries. The disagreement was particularly acute on the European Payments Union, which was one of the proudest creations of the ECA period.

The ECA inherited the original State Department aversion to putting public pressure on the Europeans for political integration. But Marshall's Harvard speech and the multilateral pledges of the OEEC included the goal of reducing trade barriers in Western Europe and achieving a new coordination of resources. As the second

[17] See Dean Acheson, "The President and the Secretary of State," in Don K. Price (ed.), *The Secretary of State* (Englewood Cliffs, N.J.: Prentice-Hall, 1960), p. 50.

year of the program drew to a close, the ECA executives grew more desperately aware that their own time was running out. And like Dr. Johnson's prisoner, who knew he was about to be hanged, that awareness concentrated their minds wonderfully. They became more anxious than ever that something permanent be left behind when the ECA ended.

With a sense of urgency, Hoffman flew to Paris in October 1949 to put the matter directly on the line to the OEEC. In a speech that unsettled the State Department, Hoffman told the Europeans that immediate recovery had been achieved, but that basic structural changes would be necessary in order to hold the gains that were made and ensure continued progress. The task was to create a new system with a larger market, which could expose industries to the cost-pressures of competition. But that effort, said Hoffman, would require "nothing less than an integration of the Western European economy."

Nor was Hoffman lacking in recommendations. He urged more coordination on national fiscal and monetary policies, new means of adjusting exchange rates, and an immediate attack on quotas, dual pricing, and other trade restrictions. He observed that the program could be accomplished through existing institutions, but he held out the possibility that new institutions could be created to meet the need. In any event, he forcefully "advised" the Europeans that some notable accomplishment was expected early in 1950.[18]

The result was to add impetus to the negotiations for a European Payments Union as the culmination of the previous payments agreements. In place of the network of bilateral accounts in the previous agreements, the EPU would have a true multilateral framework. All surpluses and debts would be set off against one another, leaving each member with a net surplus or deficit with the EPU itself. The EPU would use a schedule of credits, with provisions for converting a portion of one's debts to gold or dollars whenever they exceeded certain critical points along the scale. On the whole, it was a vast improvement. The creditors had incentives to expand their trade, and the debtors were induced to balance their accounts. The scheme was not so dependent as the previous agreements were on bilateral negotiations, and more important, it could function without American funds. Therefore, it was an institution that promised to survive the Marshall Plan.

[18] *New York Times*, November 1, 1950, p. 22.

For Hoffman, the Payments Union was a necessary part of the attack on quotas and trade barriers. He put the weight of the ECA behind the movement, and he secured a fund of $600 million from Congress as a form of marginal aid, which turned out to be very useful for the EPU in its formative stages. But oddly enough, this initiative was taken against the firm opposition of the State Department. From the earliest point, in the original outline of the recovery program, the State Department had opposed the suggestion of the CEEC that Marshall Plan dollars be used in a European clearing system. First, the department thought that American influence could be enhanced if the ECA itself would finance procurement from one country to another. Second, the department still adhered to a rigid free-trade view, and it continued to subscribe to the principles of the International Trade Organization. On those grounds, the department opposed all efforts to restrict trade—and discriminate against American goods—by closing off regional blocs.[19] On the other hand, the ECA faced the problem of reducing dollar costs in order to help the Europeans out of their balance of payments difficulties. Consequently, the ECA became more willing to accept discrimination against American goods if it was the price of increased trade and integration in Western Europe.

If the ECA had been under the authority of the State Department, it is inconceivable that it would have taken the position it did on integration and the EPU, and it is highly doubtful that Hoffman would have made his famous prodding speech to the OEEC in October 1949.[20] If Marshall's preference for "direction and control" had not been meant to cover these issues, which the State Department considered vital policy questions, it is difficult to see what meaning it might have had.

The actual experience of the Marshall Plan tends to bear out the pattern described in the operating presumption. The State Department withdrew from any effort to assert its position in appeals to the President. Instead, it resigned itself to bargaining for what it could get in interdepartmental conferences on an ad hoc basis. It was a marked difference from the position of legitimate authority

[19] See Diebold, *op.cit.*, pp. 30, 240.

[20] The only concession Hoffman made to the point of view of the State Department was a warning in his speech that smaller customs unions should not destroy the possibilities for wider trade relations.

196

over the ECA that was contained in the original legislation; and while it was always possible to say that "coordination" had been achieved, the play on words merely concealed what everyone recognized as a very substantial transfer of power. If the department withdrew from any effort to contest the decisions of the ECA, it was certainly not because it was satisfied either with the administrative arrangements or the substantive policies. It was a result, rather, of the organization itself, and it flowed from the logic of the structure created in Congress.

III

There is a final quality of operating presumptions that comes through in the case of the payments agreements, and makes them particularly useful for the analysis of the Marshall Plan. There is a capacity in these presumptions to arrange an order among policy values—to determine what is primary and secondary in the relation between two values, and beyond that, at times, to establish a relation of dependence between one policy commitment and another.

In the payments agreements, operating presumptions were used to reconcile two policy values that were in some tension with one another: the protection of the bilateral structure and the commitment to a multilateral system of transferring payments. Both values were seen as critical, and so both had to be followed to some extent. The reconciliation, as I have suggested, took this form: Bilateralism was established as the base value, and that was made to regulate in turn the conditions on which further advances could be made in multilateral payments. The revised payments agreements of 1949-50 expressed this priority in a set of operating presumptions, and as a result, only one-third of the funds earmarked for possible multilateral use were actually employed in transactions that were outside the bilateral pattern.

The commitment to move toward a multilateral payments system was genuine, but for the moment it had to be understood as a secondary interest. It was important to recognize that it could be advanced with safety only when there was a favorable balance in the bilateral patterns of international trade. What I have tried to show is that the operating presumptions registered this understanding in a very precise way: They fixed the commitment to multilateralism in a dependent and secondary status, and while they permitted the

197

expansion of multilateral payments, they worked to discipline that movement by making it responsive, in the first instance, to the national interests contained in the bilateral framework.

In this way, the Europeans compromised on a measure that allowed some expansion of the multilateral transfers, but gave them more time, also, to test the course of events. And only one year later, they would refute the notion that current performance is the most decisive test of character. In constructing the European Payments Union, the OEEC countries would not merely enlarge the scope of multilateral payments; they would replace the bilateral framework itself with one that was truly multilateral.

I would not want to burden the case by piling example on example, but the function that operating presumptions performed here might be illustrated more clearly if we could leap widely for a moment and take a less technical case, involving sharper alternatives. One of the most interesting examples that comes to mind involves Lincoln and his reconciliation of two discordant policies: the rejection of slavery and the acceptance of the Fugitive Slave law. Upholding the Fugitive Slave Act was an important part of Lincoln's promise not to interfere with slavery in the areas in which it already existed, for the law required the free states to enforce the right to property in slaves that originated in the slave states. As Lincoln conceded, the Fugitive Slave Act had its basis in the Constitution, and for that reason he felt obliged to support the federal enforcement legislation.[21] The constitutional basis of the provision seemed to rule out the validity of hostile state legislation, but there was room for argument over other legal methods. In his first debate with Douglas at Ottawa, Illinois, Lincoln suggested the grounds for a possible reconciliation:

> When [the slave states] remind us of their constitutional rights, I acknowledge them, not grudgingly, but fully, and fairly; and I would give them any legislation for the reclaiming of their fugitives, which *should not, in its stringency, be more likely to carry a free man into slavery, than our ordinary criminal laws are to hang an innocent one.*[22]

[21] *The Collected Works of Abraham Lincoln*, ed. Roy P. Basler (New Brunswick, N.J.: Rutgers University Press, 1953), Vol. II, pp. 131-32, 386, and see also pp. 317, 334.
[22] *Ibid.*, p. 15. Emphasis added.

198

The criminal law presumed in favor of the innocence of the accused. In doubtful cases, it would work to free the defendant rather than take the chance of sending an innocent man to jail. Similarly, Lincoln now seemed to accept the enforcement of the Fugitive Slave law, but under a comparable shift of presumptions. The base value was the denial of human slavery. The secondary value was the acceptance of the Fugitive Slave law. It was the operating presumption that reconciled the two and assigned the Fugitive Slave Act to its secondary status. The burden of proof would fall upon those who claimed that any particular slave was a fugitive. If ten cases were brought, and seven of them were doubtful, the presumptions would work in favor of the accused and prevent more than three slaves from being returned. Thus, slaves would be delivered up as the Constitution prescribed, but only when their fugitive status was unmistakably clear—and when it was not, the processes of the free state would not act to consign a man to slavery.

We might say, then, that the rejection of slavery was the primary policy value; the commitment to enforcing the Fugitive Slave law was the secondary value; but as the two were connected through the medium of presumptions, the enforcement of the Fugitive Slave Act was also placed in a *dependent* status: that is, its area of effectiveness would always be circumscribed by the primary commitment against slavery.

In all instances, the operating presumption becomes the link. If we could tell where the presumptions have been placed in the conjunction between policy values, we would be in a position to say something more definite about the way in which the different policy values have been ranked and related among themselves. Of course the measurement of results would be important, but again, it may be enough to determine what is higher or lower, primary or secondary, without establishing that relation with numerical exactness. As in the case of Lincoln, the language may provide all the evidence we need for imputing an intention to shift presumptions, and in some cases, the language may be sufficient in itself to tell us which values were given primacy in practice, and which ones were subordinated.

In the way of summary, operating presumptions may combine a set of ethical postulates and empirical theories. They are able to join preferences together in a coherent order, and because of that,

199

the values they convey to action are not merely isolated expressions of taste, but actual preferences, which are part of a characteristic pattern. What the presumptions impart to practice, then, may be the essential character of an individual, a policy, or even possibly a political regime. They provide the actor with a working code or an ordering of preferences, which may offer some guide to decision when choices have to be made. In that way, too, they might furnish the standards for adjudicating between policy goals when major lines of policy come into conflict. It is in this respect that operating presumptions may supply the foundation for principled action, particularly after the decline of positivism and the recognition that in administration, as in politics generally, the question of ends can never be fully closed. In a rather unique way, the language of presumptions reflects the understanding that administration requires deliberation as well as commitment. If the task of reconciling those two qualities raises hard conceptual problems for social scientists, it usually raises no such problem for practitioners. On a very common sense level, most administrators are able to reconcile the two, largely because they are free from social science and free, for that reason, to understand the situation more precisely in the concepts given to them in their ordinary language.

Operating presumptions may be designed consciously in advance and stated explicitly, perhaps, in formal procedures. But they may also be created implicitly in decisions on organizational structure. In that case, the presumptions themselves become important parts of the total structure of action, and as the relations between the ECA and the State Department suggested, the operating presumptions may be imposed by the logic of the administrative structure, whether the actors are conscious of them as explicit rules or not. If that is correct, it would suggest the approach we might take in using presumptions as a means of analyzing the Marshall Plan. It should be possible to read the legislation, with a mind also to its historical context, and reconstruct the operating presumptions that were either stated or implied. If we could do that, we could recreate the hierarchy of policy values that gave the Marshall Plan its essential meaning. At the same time, we would have a theory of the Marshall Plan that we could test against the history of the ECA.

10. THE OPERATING RULES

BY THEIR very nature operating presumptions must be expressed in terms that are immediately intelligible to the actor. As we try to formulate these rules from a reading of the legislation, then, it is very important that we start from the most obvious themes and the most explicit language. The first step would be to demonstrate the presence of a policy theme by citing explicit statements outside the legislation, but preferably in the hearings and floor debates. We might follow David Easton and call these "associated statements" as a means of marking them off from the legally "authoritative statements" in the legislation itself.[1] Within the legislation, it makes further sense to distinguish between a hortatory statement and a provision that has some direct bearing on the structure of administration.

Thus, in extracting the policy themes and formulating the rules, the object is to start from the most explicit and authoritative statements, and work our way outward to the more implicit and speculative. The best source would be an explicit provision in the legislation on administrative structure, and one that happened to be stated in the form of an operating rule. After that, we might infer operating preferences from other parts of the legislation, on some occasions, perhaps, from the convergence of two or more themes. Finally, we might be able to fill in the ellipsis and suggest other rules that would seem to be consistent with the overall network.[2]

[1] David Easton, *A Systems Analysis of Political Life* (New York: John Wiley and Sons, 1965), pp. 352-54, 357-59.

[2] One reservation needs to be made: The rules are not necessarily "operational" according to the strict canons of social science. An operational definition must actually spell out the precise terms in which the data are collected or the proposition is tested. The ECA, for example, could work under the presumption of phasing out the program in four years, but the rule was not translated into operational terms until the agency decided to use the per capita consumption figures of 1938 as a base and seek standard reductions in the annual country programs. On the difference between nominal and "operational" concepts, see Hans L. Zetterberg, *On Theory and Verification*

Part II

It is probably unnecessary to burden the reader with the complete body of textual citations in every case. But for the sake simply of showing how an analysis of this kind would work, it might be helpful if we reproduced the fuller sources for two of the most important policy themes: pluralism and the concern for self-regarding interests.[3]

1. *Pluralism*

The pluralist orientation respected diversity and tolerated many centers of power. Its process was bargaining or accommodation rather than hierarchical control. In the Marshall Plan specifically, it opposed a policy of intervening in the domestic affairs of the ERP countries. Aid with "strings attached" was offensive in principle, and it was especially odious when it worked to restrict the freedom of the local governments in arranging their own social and economic policies. But even apart from the partisans of European socialism, there was support for the pluralist approach on the conservative side as well. Marshall's own emphasis was on the practical limits to American responsibility overseas, and there was an interest, shared more widely by liberals and conservatives alike, to escape the charges of Soviet propaganda—that the Marshall Plan was largely an American device for undermining national sovereignty and attaching the Europeans to an imperialist camp.

ASSOCIATED STATEMENTS:

Marshall's Harvard speech: "It would be neither fitting nor efficacious for this Government to undertake to draw up unilaterally a program designed to place Europe on its feet eco-

---

in Sociology (Stockholm: Almqvist and Wiksell, 1954), p. 30; Hubert M. Blalock, Jr., *Social Statistics* (New York: McGraw-Hill Book Company, Inc., 1960), pp. 8-11.

Despite that, the word "operating" still seems appropriate here. First, it indicates that the issues have been phrased in terms that are sufficiently empirical that the administrators would know what preference to follow in any concrete case (e.g., when the ECA was told to "facilitate and maximize the use of private channels of trade"). Secondly, and at the same time, it avoids a misplaced sense of finality; it cautions us against any premature judgment that we have already found the hard, operational rule for the particular policy we are dealing with.

[3] After that, the documentation on the remaining themes can be found in Appendix C. The section numbers in the legislation are drawn from U.S., *Statutes at Large*, LXII, Part 1, 137-59.

nomically. This is the business of the Europeans. The initiative . . . must come from Europe."

Marshall testimony for Interim Aid (November 10, 1947):

". . . [W]e will be working with sixteen nations each of which is sensitive as to sovereignty and some of which are in delicate political balance. Consistently our daily cooperative actions must proceed on a premise that each nation in self-reliant manner is seeking its own political solutions. Seasoned judgment must constantly guide us against improper intrusion and against unfriendly distortions of our activities."

Rejection of the Fulbright amendment to urge the participating countries to seek political unification—rejected out of fear of lending credence to Soviet propaganda

Conference decision not to add Spain to the program, but to leave the matter of membership to the Europeans themselves (Vandenberg's explanation)

AUTHORITATIVE STATEMENTS AND DECISIONS:

". . . [A] joint recovery program based on self-help . . ." (Section 102 (a))

The goal of making the program itself unnecessary, so that the Europeans might become "independent of extraordinary outside assistance (Section 102 (a) and (b); Section 115 (b) (1))

To encourage the joint European organization to monitor the use of assistance by the participating countries (Section 115 (d))

The presumption of a four-year commitment (Section 112 (a))

Counterpart procedure: The local governments would not be circumvented, but instead, they would share authority with the United States in determining the uses to which the proceeds of American aid would be put. (Section 104 (a), Section 115 (b)(6))

To require only $1 billion out of the first authorization of $5.3 billion to be distributed in the form of loans (Section 111 (c) (2))

The transfer of certain scarce materials to the United States for stockpiling or other purposes

by sale, exchange or barter—and not simply given to the United States as a condition of American assistance, and transfer of materials only "after due regard for reasonable requirements for domestic use and commercial export of such country" (Section 115 (b)(5))

The transfer of materials in lieu of dollars in the repayment of loans under terms *agreed to* by the European country (Section 111 (c)(1))

The production of these materials may be encouraged through development programs *financed by the United States* with Marshall Plan funds. (Section 117 (a))

To alleviate scarcities in the United States, the countries must prepare schedules of minimum availabilities for materials that might be delivered to American industry.

But deliveries will be made for payment as normal commercial transactions, and what will be demanded will be only equal access for American industry, and not special advantages. (Section 115 (b) (9))

No requirement of compensation for American investment or property that may become involved in nationalization, but only a more modest requirement of submitting the matter to international arbitration boards (Section 115 (b)(10))

Termination of assistance

when a country is not adhering to its agreement, or is diverting materials from the purposes of the program, and when, "in the circumstances remedial action *other than termination* will not more effectively promote the purposes" of the program (Section 118, emphasis added) (Operating Presumption: Presume against termination and in favor of the participating country; use more limited penalties first—perhaps [we might speculate] a reduction in aid or a warning.)

when conditions have changed in such a way that assistance is no longer consistent with the national interest of the United States (Section 118)

We have one clear operating presumption here: that the termination of aid would be a last resort rather than a first response. That seemed to indicate that ambiguous cases would be decided in favor of the participating countries. It did not mean that assistance could never be ended, but that termination carried a heavier burden of proof. The provision on cutting off aid in the event of changed

204

circumstances seemed to contemplate a sudden and unmistakable change, like a Communist takeover. But once the program was joined, and the Europeans accepted the minimal conditions of membership, a reciprocal commitment began to apply on the part of the United States. At that point the American interest in European recovery seemed to demand, at the very least, that the program not be dismantled for casual reasons.

The presumptions on terminating aid may thus stand as a boundary-defining feature, and the related sections in the statute seemed to etch out the basic character of this approach. The uniform preference was in favor of shared authority and consent. As a matter of policy, equity was preferred to favoritism or special benefits for the United States; and in general there was an aversion to imposing conditions, particularly at the cost of removing resources from the Marshall Plan countries and slowing the pace of recovery. It may be premature to draw any operating rules from these provisions, but when combined with the presumptions that do emerge here, they seemed to support the view that pluralism was more important than hierarchical control and self-regarding interests.

Congress made its obeisance to the demands for business-like methods when it required $1 billion worth of aid to be disbursed in the form of loans. But the very act of stipulating the amount of loan aid reduced this preference for loans from the status of a general rule. Once the $1 billion limit was reached, it was apparently legitimate to use the balance of the funds entirely in grant aid. Which is to say, that as far as 80 percent of its first year funds were concerned, the ECA was given a virtual license to follow a liberal course and presume in favor of the sincerity of the recipient countries. Given the dominant cast of presumptions in the program, it was more than likely that the license would be used. That is, the odds were considerably higher that the ECA would incline toward the use of grant aid, and that it would take no gratuitous steps in advancing the loan program. And if that indeed were the case, then pluralism was given a much higher rank in the program than the preference for "business-like" activity.

This reading would gain additional support from two further provisions in the legislation. First, in authorizing the loan program, Congress clearly anticipated the limits of this financial instrument. At the end of the authorizing passage,[4] Congress warned that the

[4] See Section 111 (c)(1).

decision on whether to require repayment should turn on "the character and purpose of the assistance and upon whether there is reasonable assurance of repayment considering the capacity of such country to make such payments *without jeopardizing the accomplishment of the purpose of this title*." (Emphasis added.) This hedging clause actually embodied the warnings of Administration spokesmen, who argued from the grounds of "a cure rather than a palliative." In this view it was folly to enlarge the debts of the Europeans at a time when their debt load was already running very high, and when their efforts at recovery were encumbered by balance of payments problems. It was the same reasoning that Congress would accept a year later in abandoning the loan requirement; and it seems significant in retrospect that this line of reasoning was already contained in the provision that brought the loan program into being.

Second, when Congress sought to enlist the efforts of private investors, it authorized the ECA to provide guarantees of *convertibility* on the income derived from these investments in Europe. It was merely an assurance that the investors would receive their normal returns in dollars, even when the Marshall Plan countries were not in a position themselves to convert their currencies into dollars. Congress put a ceiling of $300 million on the guarantees the ECA could issue, but more revealing was the fact that the guarantees would be deducted from the $1 billion loan fund. The important point in principle was that private investment was not to be enlarged at the expense of the grant program. That was enough to dispel any notion that the ECA was to expand the loan program until it defined the entire aid effort. Loans were not to displace grants; they were supplementary, and they would apply only in the limited areas that the grant program could safely leave to them. In relation to the grant program, to the pluralist view, and to the priority of a thorough recovery in Europe, the loan program was clearly assigned to a subordinate place, along with the preference for "business-like" methods.

2. *Hierarchical Control and Self-Regarding Interests*

ASSOCIATED STATEMENTS:

Arguments of Hazlitt and Gwinn (and to a lesser extent, Fritsche) to circumvent the national governments and disassociate the United States from socialist programs in Europe

206

Concern of Krug and Forrestal for shortages of oil

Concern of Hazlitt, Taft, and others for inflationary pressures on the American economy as a result of supplying goods to Europe

Taft amendment to reduce the first year authorization to $4 billion—for the same reason

Demands of spokesmen for various groups that their interests be considered in the administration of the program—e.g., J. T. Sanders of the National Grange, Harvey Brown of the International Machinists—and in the case of the maritime unions, demands for specific benefits

AUTHORITATIVE STATEMENTS AND DECISIONS:

Annual authorizations and appropriations (Section 114 (c)) (Besides qualifying the four-year commitment, this provision was also expected to keep the ECA responsive to Congress.)

Counterpart funds (Section 104 (a), Section 115 (b)(6)) (In providing shared authority over decisions, the adoption of the counterpart device signaled the rejection of an extreme attitude on permissiveness and noninvolvement, and it particularly rejected the preference for "no strings attached.")

Overseas ECA missions (Section 109) (Unlike the procedure in the UNRRA program, the United States would have representatives on hand to oversee the uses of aid and participate in planning.)

ECA Administrator will "review and appraise the requirements of participating countries for assistance. . . ." (Section 105 (a)(1)) (That is, the authority would not be abandoned to the permanent organization set up by the Europeans themselves.)

Creation of a Public Advisory Board with twelve members "selected from among citizens of the United States of broad and varied experience" (Section 107) (A more formal means of interest group representation)

Bilateral agreements with the United States as a basis for enforcing obligations (Section 115 (a))

Capacity to revoke assistance to any specific country and cancel all scheduled shipments (Section 118)

207

Bilateral conditions

> Transfer to scarce materials to the United States for sale, exchange, or barter (and possibly for repayment of loans)
>
> Access of American industry to scarce materials
>
> Authority to promote the production of these materials with ECA funds

To "minimize the drain upon the resources of the United States and . . . avoid impairing the fulfillment of vital needs of the people of the United States" (Section 112 (a))

> Procure petroleum and petroleum products "to the maximum extent possible . . . outside the United States" (Section 112 (b))
>
> Miscellaneous provisions to guarantee the procurement of wheat flour (Section 112 (c)) and "encourage utilization of surplus agricultural commodities" (Section 112 (f)), along with the provision already made in Section 111 (a)(2) to require 50 percent of the gross tonnage of commodities to be shipped in American vessels

The priority of American agriculture:

> The existence of an agricultural surplus in any commodity is "determined" by the Secretary of Agriculture
>
> The Administrator, after this determination, "shall authorize the procurement of any such surplus agricultural commodity *only within the United States . . .*" (emphasis added)
>
> > except if the administrator determines, in consultation with the Secretary of Agriculture, that procuring the commodity from a participating country will further the purposes of the Marshall Plan "and would not create a burdensome surplus in the United States"; or if the commodities are not available in the United States in sufficient quantities to supply the needs of the Europeans (Section 112 (d) (1))
>
> (Operating Presumption: Presume against the procurement of goods abroad when there are actual or potential surpluses in the United States.)
>
> Centralized authority for the Secretary of Agriculture in providing for the use of agricultural commodities: When the Secretary "determines" the existence of a surplus "he

shall so advise all departments . . . of the Government"
that are involved in administering foreign aid. Thereafter, those agencies are to procure "such quantity of
such surplus" commodity "to the maximum extent practicable. . . ." (Section 112 (e)) (Operating presumption)

The clearest presumptions here are on the priority of American
agriculture. The men who drafted and altered the legislation were
well experienced in the techniques of distributing power through
the careful use of legislative language. When they said that the
Secretary of Agriculture would "determine" the existence of a surplus and then simply communicate this finding for enforcement,
they left no mistake that the Secretary's decision represented a conclusive finding of fact. On the other hand, when they preferred to
withhold such conclusive authority they knew how to do it with a
comparable clarity. Then they would say, "when the Secretary of
State [or the ECA Administrator] *believes*," and they would go on
to provide for "consultation" and recognize "differences of view"
that had to be adjusted. Conversely, when they replaced "believes,"
with "determines," when they recognized no conflict and provided
no procedure for consultations or appeals, there could be no doubt
as to where the presumptions lay. Thus, even when the Administrator carried the burden of argument, it was not enough for him to
cite a compelling need of the ERP countries. He had to justify his
decision also against the interests of American agriculture by showing that a "burdensome surplus" would not be created. In this sector of the program, then, the health of American agriculture would
stand as the base value or the first-order commitment. European
agriculture would be aided only after the prior commitments to
American producers were fulfilled.

In the same spirit, Congress provided in the appropriation act
that the ECA would have to exhaust the stocks of wool surplus held
by the Commodity Credit Corporation before it could buy wool
elsewhere. But with the exception of these agricultural surpluses
the commodity provisions shared the same liability as the $1 billion
loan requirement. They were not specifications made in illustration
of a general rule. For that reason they indicated nothing about the
presumptions that were likely to be followed in the procurement
of other commodities.

Moreover, the general heading under which most of these specifications appeared was the goal of lessening the drain on American

209

resources. The example attached to this section called for the off-shore purchase of oil. Thus, in a possible tension with the special interest clauses, there was a more general imperative at the very head of Section 112 that told the ECA, in effect, not to take goods off the American market when they were not in surplus. If there was an interest in benefitting specific groups, there was an even stronger and more widespread concern to avoid a new round of domestic inflation and the prospect of moving once again to the brink of price controls. The important point, therefore, was that even the most explicit provisions for self-regarding interests were affected with a critical ambivalence. Beyond their patently selfish concerns they supplied an operating presumption that could also be used to support the pluralist outlook and reduce the incidence of narrow self-serving.

The provisions for counterpart funds, overseas missions, and the review of country estimates presented rather clear marks of ECA authority. But again, they said nothing about the presumptions under which that authority was to be exercised. Together they did not seem to generate any operating presumptions, and nothing, certainly, that could offset the commitments arising out of Section 118 on the termination of aid. As we noted earlier, that section established the minimal commitment of the American position— that in some fundamental way the United States would have to presume in favor of the Europeans once they entered the program on American terms. If that commitment held, its implications were bound to flow over into other areas; and in particular, they were bound to leave their imprint on the exercise of authority.

In addition to these two major themes, which I have chosen for the sake of illustration, there were several other policy strands that contributed in varying degrees of importance to the character of the program. We can probably dispense here with the elaborate reproduction of the sources,[5] but the policy themes themselves, and the operating rules they supported, deserve at least a brief explanation.

3. *Economic Pattern Maintenance*

Economic pattern maintenance took its prime reference to an economy organized predominantly under private auspices. The

[5] The textual sources for these remaining themes, along with the associated and authoritative statements, can be found in Appendix C.

central concern was to prevent the Marshall Plan from revising that essential pattern by creating a state trading organization, undercutting private channels of trade, and building up new federal programs that might compete with private business. A logical correlate of this position was the desire to expand the role of private investment in bringing about European recovery. Without subsidizing industry, it was still possible to offer incentives for business participation. In addition to any financial help the government might provide, the climate for business activity promised to improve if the Marshall Plan used methods that were more familiar to business operations. Initially that meant an accent on the use of loans and the recruitment of people with business credentials. But this emphasis on business expertise could also command the involvement of federal or international agencies that had some claim to a special competence in the field of investment or the management of economic affairs.

At any rate, the injunction to "facilitate and maximize the use of private channels of trade" was one of the clearest operating rules to come out of the legislation. But Congress took a further step and extended the potential application of the rule to areas outside procurement. A similar provision was attached to the end of Section 112, and the Administrator was urged to use private channels of trade "to the maximum extent" possible, not only in procurement, but in all the principal activities of the ECA—in the processing, storage, and transfer of materials; in the furnishing of technical advice; and in the allocation of commodities and services. (See Section 112 (h)) The presumption, then, was firmly fixed, and its relevance was general.

4. ". . . a cure rather than a mere palliative"

The phrase comes from Marshall's commencement address at Harvard, and it conveyed his insistence that a piecemeal program of relief was no longer adequate to the crisis in Europe. According to Marshall the United States was prepared to commit itself to a large-scale effort and put up the sums that were needed in a major reconstruction. But in turn the Europeans would have to commit themselves to a new system of cooperation, both in the planning of investments and the sharing of resources. Membership in the program would begin with adherence to a multilateral pledge, and the continuance of aid would depend upon the "continuous effort of the participating countries to accomplish a joint recovery pro-

211

gram through multilateral undertakings." Those multilateral efforts would be directed toward the goals of reducing trade barriers, raising production, stabilizing currencies, and balancing budgets; and the desire to cooperate could be shown most tangibly through participation in a "continuing organization" of the member nations.

The insistence on membership in a joint organization seemed to suggest that there was something desirable in organization itself as a means of making joint activity continuous. There was some partial recognition in the legislation that there was an American interest in extending short term aid even to noncooperating countries, if for no other reason than to prevent a worsening of the situation in Europe. But it was determined also that the aid would in fact be short term and minimal, so that no one could hope for large scale assistance without accepting the commitments of membership. In this respect, the provision established another one of those boundary-defining features: It rejected the view that any program was better than none. Instead, it registered the basic preference that it was better not to have any large scale program at all than to launch an ambitious project without some serious commitments to integration.

5. *ECA Autonomy*

Perhaps the most important single consequence to arise from the demand for a business-like program was the separation of the ECA from the State Department. It was Vandenberg who made the connection when he condemned the previous administration of foreign assistance programs and held out the prospect of a new agency that could contribute some distinct brand of economic rationality. The separation from the State Department could be marked off in a number of ways: through the design of the appeals process; through Cabinet status and separate membership in the National Advisory Council [on international monetary and financial problems]; and through the control of the overseas missions by the central ECA office in Washington, rather than the local embassies.

But aside from this organizational divorce from the State Dement, the concept of ECA autonomy became considerably weaker. In handling its major substantive activities, the agency was limited at the outset by the emphasis on private channels of trade and the reliance on other government agencies. Even where Congress was willing to grant some administrative flexibility, it usually subordinated that freedom to other requirements. The use of a corporation was allowed, but Congress refused to permit the kind of insulation from Congressional control that had been eliminated three years earlier in the Government Corporation Control Act. In the case of offshore procurement, Congress insisted on the authority of the Comptroller General—along with the Administrator—in drafting regulations (Section 111 (b)(1)). Nor were these restrictions confined to the weightiest issues. In a matter as prosaic as the disposing of goods, the ECA was instructed to transfer the goods first to another agency rather than develop its own facilities for disposal.[6]

One could argue, then, that the autonomy of the ECA was valued more highly than the interests of the State Department in running the program; but at the same time, that autonomy was clearly subordinate to the concern for Congressional authority and the desire to limit the bureaucratic commitments of the ECA. The succeeding themes would tend to support these conclusions.

6. *Decentralization*

In his testimony at the Interim Aid hearings, Marshall maintained that the program would require only a fairly simple agency, since most of its operations were "now being performed by a number of government agencies in cooperation with business, agricultural, and labor groups." Of course, a case could always be made on the grounds of "efficiency" for centralizing authority and transferring more functions to the ECA. But there were serious political costs involved in threatening to rip functions out of the existing agencies and administer them with a wholly new set of criteria. The separate agencies had interests of their own at stake, and all things considered, there were sound political reasons for leaving the current distribution of authority as it was. The result, though, was to force the ECA into a closer dependence on other agencies, particularly in the use of export controls and the procurement of food. In the event of conflict, the interests of the ECA were being devalued apparently in favor of other agencies. Whether the ECA would gain access then to the instruments it needed would depend thereafter on the acceptance of its policies by other departments.[7]

---

[6] It was possible for the ECA to dispose of some commodities under its exclusive authority, but only when that was a means of averting a complete loss due to spoilage. Section 113 (b).

[7] In a subtle way, too, Section 111 established some preferences about the conditions of cooperation between agencies. With agreement on purpose, collaboration could begin immediately; it would not require the formal

When they were accumulated, the various provisions for decentralization seemed to describe some general preferences: If any services needed by the ECA could be performed by another agency, they ought to be; and if new functions must be added, an attempt should be made first to transfer them to other agencies. Admittedly, the support for these preferences was only indirect. As a firmer base they required some preference for keeping the ECA smaller, and that preference could be found in the related efforts of Congress to resist the growth of bureaucratic commitments.

7. *Debureaucratization*

In the literature on administration, "debureaucratization" has come to stand for a process of resisting or removing certain practices that are distinctly bureaucratic.[8] Here the term is useful in summarizing several different perspectives that were held by people with radically opposing ideologies, but which managed to converge in a preference for nonbureaucratic features. More precisely, the theme of "debureaucratization" covered the preferences for: (a) a temporary, rather than a permanent agency, (b) a smaller, more dependent and controllable unit, (c) an agency inclined to divest itself of functions, and (d) an agency geared to phasing itself out of existence, rather than seeking its own perpetuation.

The central decision under the debureaucratization theme was that the program would not last more than four years, and might even terminate sooner. It was a manifest of Marshall's view that the program would be extensive but thorough, so that the ECA could withdraw from the field after a relatively short period. And to Congress especially, the existence of a timetable seemed to have the further advantage of convincing the Europeans that the United States meant business.

The use of personnel ceilings was but another means of symbo-

---

authorization of the President unless one of the agencies refused to lend its facilities. But in that case, the burden of appeal was clearly on the ECA.

[8] The term was used, for example, by S. N. Eisenstadt in a study of the Israeli bureaucracy to describe the absence of routine and the tendency of public employees to develop more affective and personal relations with their clients, as opposed to the bureaucratic ideal of impersonal and functionally specific contacts. S. N. Eisenstadt, "Bureaucracy, Bureaucratization, and Debureaucratization," *Administrative Science Quarterly*, Vol. 4, No. 3 (December 1959), pp. 302-20. Also, see his piece with Elihu Katz, "Some Sociological Observations on the Response of Israeli Organizations to New Immigrants," *ibid.*, Vol. 5, No. 1 (June 1960), pp. 113-33.

lizing an agency that would not be allowed to grow. When seen from this view, the access to other agencies and the privilege of using consultants were simply alternate ways of avoiding the build-up of permanent staff. If the exemptions from the Civil Service restrictions offered flexibility, it was also true that they withheld the assurance of permanent tenure.

What eventually proved to be the most interesting part of the debureaucratization theme, however, was the support it received from values other than decentralization. In the very beginning, for example, Marshall had already made the connection to pluralism: As early as the Interim Aid hearings he had warned that a larger, more powerful agency would also have a greater potential for intervening in the domestic affairs of the Europeans. In the same sentence, he declared that a strong ECA would be "a threat to private enterprise in this country." The subsequent emphasis on private channels of trade and the facilities of existing departments came to be understood quite clearly as a preference for restricting the administrative resources of the ECA. Thus Marshall's testimony called attention to the linkage among pluralism, decentralization, and economic pattern maintenance. It was the first recognition that the policies associated with economic pattern maintenance, instead of projecting an imperialist capitalism abroad, actually served to strengthen the pluralist features of the program by reducing the capacity of the ECA for intervention.

When we combine these imperatives to debureaucratization and decentralization, the following presumptions seem firmly established:

— In any given case presume against an expansion of activities or an enlargement of full-time administrative resources. Rely as much as possible on the facilities of other agencies or private industry.

— Treat new functions first on a temporary basis, possibly with the use of consultants or temporary employees. If new activities cannot be avoided as full-ime concerns, try first to transfer them to other agencies (or even to private industry) before taking them over as exclusive functions of the ECA.

8. *Congressional Authority in Foreign Policy*

It was the Congressional demand for a larger role in foreign policy that eventually separated the program from the State Department and led to a more autonomous ECA. As one might have expected, though, the same interest in Congressional influence could also work in the direction of restraints on the ECA. When Congress attached the controls of the Comptroller General to the ECA, it demonstrated rather conclusively that its enthusiasm for an independent ECA did not extend to an ECA that was too independent of Congress.

Doubtless this concern for Congressional power was one of the chief supports to the autonomy of the ECA. But after securing the independence of the ECA, the principal effect of this new Congressional assertiveness was to support the tendencies toward debureaucratization. This point came out clearly enough in Sections 121 and 122 of the legislation. In the former, Congress granted discretion to the President in transferring ECA functions to the United Nations, even without the consent of the ECA Administrator. Section 122 permitted the President to transfer functions from the ECA to regular government departments (again without the consent of the ECA). If that discretion, however, was exercised before the fixed termination date, the President could act only after Congress had passed a joint resolution. Congress had no objection, therefore, in seeing the ECA dismantled; in fact, it was the hope of the Congressional leaders that it *would* be dismantled on a precise schedule. Their concern, rather, was that Congress should participate in the decision when it was going to result in additions to the government bureaucracy. For the benefit of our later analysis, then, we may assume that apart from the initial separation of the ECA from the State Department, the Congressional power interest would find its principal reflection in the political consequences that flowed from debureaucratization.

9. *Bipolarity and Universalism*

In the Marshall Plan the United States was determined to apply some elementary policital tests and integrate the member nations in a common organization. The nagging question is whether this search for commitment actually hardened the division in Europe by giving it an organizational substance. Was the program, in fact, grounded in assumptions of bipolarity? By insisting on organizational commitments did the United States really take the final steps that consummated the Cold War?

It would be foolish, of course, to deny the central place of the Communist threat in the minds of American decision-makers. Yet there was a real difference to be drawn between a prudent recogni-

216

tion of bipolarity and a willingness to take the responsibility for making that breach conclusive. In this respect, one of the most revealing qualities of the discussion in Congress was that the argument for bipolarity was hardly ever stated. The closest approximation came in some vague remarks by Senator Ball on the prospects for converting the United Nations into a rump military organization, or, at another moment, in Senator McClellan's contention that the economic program would have to imply a military commitment as well. But there was nothing in the legislation itself about cutting off relations with Eastern Europe. In fact, the official American line was quite the opposite: The Administration was maintaining at this time that East-West trade in Europe could be a valuable means of reducing dependence on the dollar area, and thus contributing to the ends of the Marshall Plan. Even Senator Knowland's amendment was designed merely to tighten up on the shipment of industrial goods to the Soviet Union; it was not meant to eliminate even that trade entirely.

The real test of Congressional intentions came on the issue of export priorities and the transfer of responsibilities to the United Nations. In Section 112 the presumptions were placed firmly against exports to nonparticipating countries if any doubt arose on the ability of the United States to meet the requirements of the Marshall Plan. The interest in the Marshall Plan was judged superior, then, to any interest the United States might have had in trading with other countries. Congress held out the possibility, though, that there was a higher national interest that could warrant shipments to nonparticipating countries in particular circumstances. That alternative was allowed, but in the context of Section 112, it seemed to carry the burden of justification. Thus, while the Marshall Plan had an evident priority, it did not exhaust the definition of American foreign policy or force the understanding of American goals into a rigid bipolar cast.

Section 117 seemed to go the farthest in representing American interests in a bipolar world. The government was already developing criteria for restricting the shipment of strategic goods to the Soviet bloc, and the Administrator was now directed to enforce those criteria on the Europeans. Implicitly, it meant that limits were placed on the extent to which the Europeans might cultivate nondollar sources of trade. But on the whole it was a modest and unprovocative move, and one that the Europeans should have been able to accept.

Finally, the provisions for shifting functions to the United Nations rounded out the Congressional view. In contrast to the conditions for transferring programs to other government agencies, it was made uncommonly easy to dismantle sections of the ECA in favor of the United Nations. The President could do it at his own discretion, without the consent of the ECA and without the necessity of getting Congressional approval. To that extent the universalistic interest was given a higher status in the program than the autonomy of the ECA. If, in the course of events, the conditions of bipolarity happened to recede or lose their force, the organization of the ECA could be modified very quickly in response. Instead of being treated as a matter of administration for the ECA, though, the decision was reserved to the President, which seemed to indicate that the change would have to come about as part of a basic decision on foreign policy. Thus, the ground was prepared for future changes in administration, but quite plainly it was the universalistic approach that carried the heavy burden of argument.

On the basis of the more explicit statements alone, I think we can put together a body of more general preferences at this point that outline the character of the program. With the addition of some amplifying and explanatory comments, it would run something like this:

—There is an American interest in providing at least a relief program that can prevent a further retrogression in Europe.

—But it is better not to have any large-scale program of assistance unless it is accompanied by European commitments to cooperation.

—If those commitments represent a basic condition, they should be enforced, at the very least by removing obstructionists from the program. But once those minimal American conditions are accepted, the American interest in a thorough European recovery makes it preferable to keep the program going, and to presume against disbanding it precipitously.

Faced in any given instance by an apparent failure of one country to cooperate, it is better to presume in favor of the ERP country and extend the benefit of the doubt. Rather than cutting off assistance, it would be better to apply more limited penalties first; and it would be better to rest the termination of aid on a *pattern* of obstruction, or on the occurrence, perhaps, of a political change as profound and sharp as a change in regime.

—The interest in the Marshall Plan is more important than any immediate interest in trading with other countries—if it comes to a matter of making a choice in the export of scarce commodities.

—The interest in a rapid and thorough recovery, in "a cure rather than a mere palliative," is more important than the access of the United States to scarce materials—if that means taking resources away from the Europeans or their dependent territories that might be used better in their own recovery efforts.

And although it seems to enlarge the cost, it may be better to presume in favor of the intentions of the Europeans and allow most of the aid to be given as grants rather than loans.

—(But loans clearly have their place and should be used. They may be helpful in smaller doses, especially when they are used to finance specific industrial projects.)

Nonetheless, the interest in raising European trade and production quickly does not sanction the reshipment of products made with American goods to nonparticipating countries when those products would be denied export licenses in the United States on grounds of national security.

—The strength of the American economy is the basis of the American capacity to supply tools to Europe. To maintain the stability and vigor of the American economy, then, should be one of the fundamental conditions of the Marshall Plan.

If goods are scarce in the United States, or their removal from the domestic market would create serious dangers of inflation, it is better to procure the commodities outside the United States.

If, however, surpluses are available in the United States (notably in agriculture) those surpluses should be exhausted before the same commodities are purchased outside the United States.

In particular circumstances it might be appropriate for Congress to require the use of specific American commodities or services.

—The maximum reliance should be placed on private channels of trade. The program should be careful not to undermine

219

these channels, either by creating a huge state trading apparatus or by constructing new units that may duplicate the services of private industry.

For that reason we would reserve some place in the program for nongovernmental assistance. We would encourage recovery efforts through the normal commercial processes in the form of private investment.

An enlarged agency would also pose a formidable threat to the sovereignty of the ERP nations. Even though some form of American intervention is implied in the concept of sharing authority with the United States, there are still important degrees of intervention. Certain agencies are constitutionally less likely to stretch their activities into gross and "improper intrusions."

—Less activity abroad is generally better than more activity.

—A smaller administrative organization is preferable to a larger one.

Similarly, there seems to be little warrant in transferring functions from standing agencies to a temporary administrative unit, especially since there were reasons for distributing those functions to different agencies in the first place.

Thus, the interest of the Marshall Plan in a powerful, centralized agency must be subordinated to other interests:

—the interest in respecting the sovereignty of the Europeans and limiting our intrusions;

—the interest in maintaining an economy characterized predominantly by private transactions;

—the primary interests of the regular Executive agencies in their own areas of jurisdiction.

—The ECA will contribute something distinctive to the foreign aid program, principally in bringing a greater emphasis on economic rationality and business judgment.

The interest in strengthening that approach to foreign aid outweighs any interest the State Department may have in controlling the agency and grafting "diplomatic" considerations on to the management of the program.

But that autonomy of the ECA is less important than the legitimate interest of Congress in controlling appropriations and having a share in the making of foreign policy.

That autonomy is less important, finally, than the interest in transferring ECA functions to the United Nations in the event that the current crisis subsides and the bipolar structure begins to dissolve.

We have a rather clear ranking of preferences here, and it might be even clearer if we return to our list of themes and try to make it a bit more manageable by separating the various strands into primary and secondary commitments, or independent and dependent values. We shall treat themes as independent if they are distinct, if they do not seem to depend for their weight on the strength of other policies, and if the presumptions seem to be turned in their favor in their connections with other policy values. (It is possible, too—and worth noting—that policies that are independent in their separate origins may become ranked as primary and secondary among themselves, especially as they become related to one another in the course of administering the program. Of this we shall see more later.) By these standards, five themes stand out as having an independent force. They are:

1. Pluralism
2. The commitment to "a cure rather than a palliative"
3. Economic pattern maintenance
4. Decentralization
5. Congressional authority

Dependent policy strands would be those that were established as secondary, that seemed to be placed in a subordinate position by the operating presumptions, and that consequently depended for their strength on the area that was allowed them by the more fundamental policies. These would be:

a. ECA autonomy
b. The "business-like" approach
   (1) Loans
   (2) Private investment
c. Hierarchial control and self-regarding interests
   (e.g., the American enforcement of cooperation, or the American insistence on receiving scarce or strategic materials from the participating countries)
   Within this context, however, certain interests *specified* by Congress could be given the priority of independent commitments.

221

    d. Universalism:
       (1) the removal of political tests for entrance into the program and the receipt of Marshall aid
       (2) the export of scarce materials from the United States
       (3) the transfer of responsibilities from the ECA to the United Nations

Beyond this, the presumptions contained in the legislation make it possible to offer some hypotheses, also, about the relations among the independent themes. The most striking relation to emerge is the apparent tendency of these policy strands to converge in support of the pluralist theme. When taken together, economic pattern maintenance, decentralization, and Congressional power seemed to mold the ECA into the character of a dependent agency. They promised to limit both its resources and its life expectancy, and make it that much less likely that the ECA would undertake any major new commitments. By restricting its administrative capacities, these policy values worked to reduce the capacity of the ECA for deeper intervention in the ERP countries. Although Congressional power figured to be a useful instrument for the self-serving interests of American groups, the commitments to a thorough "cure" and to offshore purchasing could serve as a strong antidote. It was recognized that there was a competing American interest here in reducing the dollar costs of the program and curtailing the export drain on the American economy. Cutting dollar costs was also at the heart of the balance of payments problems—at least for the short run, before Europe could build its capacity to compete in dollar markets. Thus the ECA would have some legitimate doctrines within the definition of American self-interest that could actually be used in turning back the special claims of American groups.

If this analysis proves correct, we would find pluralism as the central value in the program. That is, we would find that pluralism and the commitment to making Europe "independent of extraordinary outside assistance" were higher values than pattern maintenance, Congressional power, and the more self-regarding American interests. The way to test these hypotheses, of course, is to view the actual record of the ECA and determine the ways in which the operating presumptions were turned in practice.

As for the working presumptions themselves, we have started from the base of the most explicit language in forming a skeleton set of rules. Beyond that, we have been able to add to the list by drawing inferences from the merger of two or more policy themes. And finally, as we intimated earlier, we may find it possible to fill in the ellipsis by suggesting some additional rules that might have been implied in the overall network. We would advance one such set of rules here, in which the prime emphasis in decision-making would be placed very consciously on the side of economic rationality. It would be accompanied by a thorough deemphasis of political considerations, or at least a tendency to withdraw from overt political disputes. Rules of this character could prove highly consequential for the performance of the ECA, and they would draw their rationale from several important sources. First, the insistence on "a cure rather than a palliative" prescribed a full rein to economic rationality. It was a preference shared by the partisans of a business-like approach as well as those practical men who simply urged the involvement of specialized economic agencies like the Export-Import Bank. Second, there was a concern, both in Congress and the Executive, to avoid the charges of Communist propaganda. It would not do to create the ECA in the image of an aggressive political arm of the United States, and for that reason it was prudent to soften the political overtones in the work of the ECA.

Furthermore, this understatement of the political had an important relation to Vandenberg's own understanding of the national interest. We have argued that Vandenberg did not reach a full decision on the national interest in the Marshall Plan, particularly on the appropriate military policy. If that interpretation was correct, the question of national interest was still open, and it included an interest in deciding the question on its own merits, rather than having a decision simply forced upon the government by the commitments of the ECA.

To lessen the play of political criteria, then, was a convention that could appeal at once to isolationists on the order of Henry Hazlitt and unreserved pluralists like Phillip Murray. On every count, it described a style that was more appropriate to the station and responsibility of the ECA. If we tried to summarize these considerations in the form of a directive to the ECA Administrator, it might have read something like this:

"In disagreements with the Europeans do not force issues to the level of overt political contest. Base your own decisions as much as possible on economic reasoning. You are free to challenge the

Europeans, and quite vigorously, but question them largely on the basis of economic reasoning. If they can provide a reasonable defense of their action in those terms, that may be enough. (We need not inquire too deeply into their political motives; it satisfies our interest if they merely have some good economic reasons for what they are doing.) Thus, the best thing to do is to presume in their favor. Do not impute political motives to them where another explanation is available. Bringing the issue to a head as a political dispute is a last resort, and it is more properly left to the President and the Secretary of State."

If we were now to add these presumptions to our complex of rules, the ECA Administrator would have his fuller directive:

—The purpose of the Marshall Plan is to provide a thorough recovery that will make Europe "independent of extraordinary outside assistance" in no more than four years.

　—That goal will require a new level of coordination among the Europeans themselves in raising trade and production, and stabilizing their currencies. It is not to be supposed that the inclinations of the ERP nations will always move them to compromise their national interests for the sake of cooperative ends.

　　—It will be necessary, then, to enforce some minimal conditions in the program. Because of its special interest in the success of the program—but at the same time, because it enjoys a certain detachment from the situation of the Europeans—the United States would appear to be in an especially fitting position to enforce these obligations.

　　—At the very least there must be a capacity for removing an obstructionist nation from the program. The legitimate basis of this power will be in a bilateral agreement signed by each participating country with the United States.

　　—Adherence to that bilateral agreement, as well as to the multilateral pledge with the other participating countries, may constitute prima facie evidence of a willingness to cooperate.

　　　—That presumption would be strengthened also if a nation participated in any joint organization formed by the ERP countries. (Since organizations tend to perpetuate different forms of cooperation, there may be a positive interest in extending the number and range of these supranational institutions.)

—Once the Europeans have joined the program and accepted their minimal obligations, it becomes the interest of the United States to guarantee the stability and duration of the program.

    —Therefore, in any ambiguous instances of noncooperation on the part of any participating country, resolve the doubts on the side of the Europeans.

        —Act only where there is a clear *pattern* of obstruction, and presume against cutting off aid unless there is a radical change in the behavior of the government in question. Generally, respond with more limited penalties first (perhaps a reduction in aid, or a warning).

        —In disagreements with the Europeans do not force issues to the level of overt political contest. Base your own decisions, as much as possible, on economic reasoning. Challenge the decisions of the Europeans largely on economic grounds; do not impute political motives where other explanations are available. Bringing an issue to a head as a political dispute is a last resort, and it is more properly left to the President and the Secretary of State.

—That interest in a rapid and thorough recovery means enlarging the resources available to the Europeans, while trying to reduce their dollar costs.

    —Do not insist on the delivery of scarce materials to the United States if it may impede the recovery of European production or trade. (For the same reason, encourage the interested parties in Europe to forego their removal of reparations from Germany in the form of industrial equipment.)

    —Accept the possibility of short-run costs to American producers by purchasing goods outside the United States—*except where Congress makes specific provisions to the contrary.*

    —Presume in favor of grant aid, rather than burdening the Europeans' balance of payments with heavy dollar liabilities for the future.

225

—But within that predominant emphasis on grants, loans may be used without creating balance of payments problems. Thus, where it can be done safely, expand the use of loans, perhaps in connection with specific industrial projects.

—In the event of scarcities in export goods, where the satisfaction of other demands threatens our capacity to supply goods under the Marshall Plan, do not hesitate to claim precedence for ERP needs.

—However, it is flatly unacceptable for the Europeans to use American goods in order to produce strategic commodities for Soviet bloc countries. Discourage this trade, and if necessary, refuse delivery of the basic commodities.

—Presume against adding new and permanent administrative commitments to the federal bureaucracy. Nor should you undermine private channels of trade by duplicating facilities that can be found outside the government.

—"Facilitate and maximize the use of private channels of trade"—not only in procurement, but in any of the regular ECA activities.

—In this same vein, encourage private investments and gifts as another form of aid to Europe.

—Presume against an expansion of activities or administrative resources. Rely to the greatest extent possible on the facilities of other agencies.

—Treat new activities as temporary measures. Handle them by contracting with private consultants, or by hiring personnel (perhaps from other agencies) on a temporary basis.

—If it appears necessary to pursue any activity as a full-time concern, you should try first to transfer it to another agency for the duration of the program. Only if that does not prove practicable, or if the head of the agency objects, should you take the function under the exclusive authority of the ECA.

—The same presumptions do not necessarily extend to international organizations, particularly the United Nations. Whether conditions have changed sufficiently to permit a transfer of functions to the United Nations must depend on a more basic political decision. And

226

much like the matter of raising political issues among the Marshall Plan countries, that decision, too, is more properly left to the President and the Secretary of State.

No one would urge that Paul Hoffman, or anyone in the ECA, sat down and compiled this set of operating rules before the work of administering was begun. But as in any instance of launching a new agency, the people who set up the ECA in Washington were guided first by the language in the statute. We need only recall, too, that agencies commonly employ a general counsel for the precise purpose of advising them as to what they may or may not do under their authorizing legislation. The construction of this list then would represent nothing more ambitious than the sorts of things that agencies normally do for themselves in the course of administering their programs. The question, as we have said, is whether these particular operating rules were the ones that really characterized the agency; and what we have to establish now is whether the ranking of values we have attributed to the program was actually confirmed in practice.

11. THE DEPENDENT AGENCY

I

THE ECA began its life as it lived it—heavily in debt to other agencies. The difficulties in Europe did not arrange themselves conveniently to suit the legislative schedule in the United States or the delays involved in such proprieties as appointing an Administrator and setting up an organization. A group in the State Department was keeping the aid pipeline going, and even before the Congressional action ended, Commerce and Agriculture had worked out a supply program for the first five weeks. Around the time Paul Hoffman was appointed Administrator in early April, a rough program for the entire April–June quarter had been substantially completed. Within a week of his appointment Hoffman had to make a full-scale justification of ECA estimates before the appropriations committees of Congress, and it was the same combination of departments now that presented him with his elaborate brief. The new office on Connecticut Avenue was still being set up when the State Department relayed some anxious cables from overseas: A vessel was reported as having left Galveston on April 14 loaded with supplies and headed for the Netherlands. Two or three other ships were rumored to be on the high seas bound for France. The local embassies were urgently trying to find out if someone was supposed to meet the ships—and if so, who was it, and what was to be done?[1]

Thanks to the State Department there was someone to give signals in Washington, and someone waiting at the pier when the shipments landed. Some indirect thanks was due to the department, too, for losing the original argument with Treasury over private channels of trade. The Treasury had also preferred an arrangement for paying suppliers more directly with drafts drawn on American banks, rather than having the separate vendors apply for reimbursement. There was some added advan-

[1] Roseman to Pace, March 29, 1948; Southworth to Stone, April 16, 1948; Bureau of the Budget, Series 39.18.

228

tage in that plan in reducing the interference of the government in private transactions, but the main point was to speed up the pace of procurement. Of course, as one would expect, there were costs that came along with the advantages: The burden of finding errors and violations fell upon the ECA itself in a "post-audit," i.e., after the deliveries had already been made, when it was too late to affect the shipment of materials, and when all the ECA could do in response was to seek a rebate. Nevertheless, it was a price the people at ECA were willing to pay for the sake of moving goods more quickly. Or at least it was a price they could accept more easily as long as they did not have to start from scratch in working out the arrangements for letters of commitment and establishing accounts with banking institutions. Fortunately, that effort too had been spared them. By the time the ECA was starting operations, the procedures had already been drafted in joint meetings among State, Commerce, Treasury, the Export-Import Bank, and a group of bank officials in New York—all of which seemed to confirm the image of the ECA as a creature of other agencies.[2]

At the end of the first quarter it was calculated that other agencies were distributing approximately a third of the program expenditures charged to the ECA—$70 million, on the monthly average, as against $147 million spent by the ECA itself.[3] It was understood by everyone at the beginning that the ECA would rely primarily on other agencies for specialized services. The Army would take charge of procurement in occupied areas. The Labor Department would compile a handbook of labor statistics and manpower analyses. Interior would bring in studies of mineral resources; the Public Health Service would provide medical services for ECA employees and lend its facilities for a health program in Greece; and Commerce would supply the ECA with export statistics. But the offer of services could also turn itself into a virtual bombardment of claims on the ECA, so the Budget Bureau was finally called in to act as a referee during this formative stage. The bureau succeeded in condensing some of the more extravagant claims,[4] but the essential dependence of the ECA was a fact of ad-

---

[2] Hefner to Roseman, March 12, 1948; Lynch to Taylor, April 16, 1948, Bureau of the Budget, *loc.cit.*

[3] Bruce to Webb, August 9, 1948, Bureau of the Budget, *loc.cit.*

[4] See Bureau of the Budget, "Administrative Expense Estimates for Other Federal Agencies Under the Economic Cooperation Administration" (Photostat), April 11, 1948; Bruce to Ewing (of the FSA), March 28, 1949;

ministrative life.[5] Thus the ECA found itself paying the FBI to have itself investigated, and in what was perhaps the consummation of this whole logic, the Department of Agriculture was paid approximately $180,000 for compiling a list of surpluses, which the ECA was then forced to use.[6]

The State Department took what was by far the largest reimbursement to any agency—over $650,000 during the first quarter. For anyone who had heard the original arguments for separating ECA from the State Department, there must have been some heavy irony in these early operations. According to those initial arguments, the State Department was exclusively a "policy" organization; it was not suited to the task of administering "operations," especially those involving practical business judgment. But what, in fact, was the State Department doing for ECA at this time? In most cases, it was exactly the kind of hard, practical, and even manual work that the department was supposedly incapable of doing. Through one or another of its divisions, the department was preparing budget estimates and field expense formulas; it was developing personnel regulations for overseas staffs; and it was arranging for such special services as hospitalization and insurance. In addition, counseling services were extended to the families of ECA personnel who had to be sent overseas at once, and in one section of the Foreign Service Administration, the department was doubling its manpower in order to help its new employees overseas in acquiring such earthly goods as luggage, appliances, food, and medicine. All of this might have seemed unusual for a "policy" agency, which was not supposed to know very much about mundane matters. But it was not really so surprising for an agency that had to train, transfer, and maintain personnel overseas.[7]

Finan to McCandless, "Economic Cooperation Administration Request for Allocation of Funds for Administrative Expenses to Public Health Service," June 10, 1949; Finan to McCandless, ". . . Allocation of Funds to the Department of Labor . . . ," June 8, 1949, *loc.cit.*

[5] In its first quarterly report, the ECA announced that "formal agreements have been signed with the Departments of State, Agriculture, Commerce, and Post Office, and the Export-Import Bank of Washington, War Assets Administration, and the Federal Bureau of Investigaton," ECA, *First Report to Congress*, p. 43.

[6] Roseman to the Director, "Allocation of Category 'A' Funds for State and Agriculture for Fiscal Year 1949 for ERP Expenses," April 26, 1949. Bureau of the Budget, *loc.cit.*

[7] In fact, ECA and the State Department seemed to switch roles. The

With the State Department involved so extensively in the affairs of the ECA, it was virtually assured that conflicts would arise, and one of the first abrasions to occur happened also to illustrate the connection between administrative structure and operating rules. Following its vision of a tightly corralled agency, Congress imposed a ceiling on the administrative expenses of the ECA for Fiscal 1949. When Congress moved then to provide for reimbursements to other agencies, it seemed to imply rather strongly that the charges would be made directly on the ECA account. That is, the ECA would not be able to enlarge its functions indirectly by distributing the charges to other departments. The Budget Bureau came to the same understanding of the legislative intent, and it quickly warned the participating agencies not to seek additions to their own budgets for the Marshall Plan expenses.

But under the pressure of cost ceilings, the elementary problem of defining an administrative expense became highly consequential. "Direct administrative expenses" were those incurred immediately in providing services that were specified in the legislation. For the most part this category seemed clear enough, as in the case, for example, of the Department of Agriculture, which was expected under the legislation to determine the existence of surpluses. However, the participants also acknowledged a category of "indirect expenses." These were the costs of secondary or supporting activities, which seemed to arise in the course of providing the primary services to the ECA; and when an agency became as deeply engaged in operations as the State Department was, the boundary between direct and indirect expenses could be somewhat blurred. The definition of "necessity" often merged with the imperatives of agency style, and even on very technical issues it was not always clear, for example, how many additions to full time personnel were really required by the heavier workload. In April, the Budget Bu-

---

ECA people would issue instructions as to what they wanted shipped, and the Despatch Agency would take it from there. It was found in some cases that the regular vendors did not even know how to pack goods for export or that they packed too slowly. In those instances, the purchase clerks in the Despatch Agency had to step in to make the arrangements for packaging, which often required the hand-processing of orders. Department of State, Office of Budget and Planning, "First Quarter Charges for Services Rendered the ECA—Second Quarter Estimates for Services to be Rendered to the ECA" (for Fiscal 1949), December 1, 1948 (Mimeo), pp. 10-11, 16-17; copy in Bureau of the Budget, *loc.cit.*

231

reau reduced the claims of the State Department by two-thirds on the grounds that State could handle the increased volume of work without a significant expansion of its facilities. State argued, in turn, that when any agency was assigned responsibilities in the statute, the ECA was obliged to honor all the expenses that might emerge. The obvious difficulty, though, was that the ECA would have no control over a process that threatened to fritter away its administrative funds.[8] In the circumstances, the response of the ECA was probably predictable: It began to require an extraordinary amount of documentation on the part of other agencies in justifying these indirect expenses. What ECA tried to do, in effect, was make the issue of doubt work against the claim for reimbursement by throwing the burden of proof on the other departments. Still, that was a burden which the other agencies did not have to accept, and in most cases their reaction was to cut back on their services to the ECA.[9] But at the same time, that suited Hoffman and the ECA quite well, for they were beginning to find it quite preferable now that none of the other agencies should do anything more than it was explicitly asked to do. As a result, the original decisions for decentralization and containment came together to imprint a strangely antibureaucratic character on the ECA. What we hypothesized earlier came to be established rather firmly as an operating rule: Untrue to bureaucratic fashion, the ECA would not use the facilities of other agencies as a means of expanding its own functions. The presumptions were clearly in favor of limitation, not expansion.

This same pressure of administrative resources had other effects that modified some of our hypothetical operating rules. Thus, for

[8] A Budget Bureau paper noted that "considerable difficulty is being experienced by the ECA and the requesting agency in reaching agreement on the amount of . . . funds to be allocated. ECA feels that it is not in any position to judge the validity of such requests, that it is financing activities and projects from which it receives no direct benefits and that the tightness of the administrative expense limitation, as a result of the Congressional cut, makes it necessary that all available funds be used for direct administrative costs of the ECA operation." Bureau of the Budget, "The Problems of Agency Costs Arising from ERP," n.d. [It was apparently written shortly after the passage of the appropriation act for Fiscal 1949], *loc.cit.*

[9] *Ibid.* For the argument of the State Department see Department of State, "Legislative Authority for Availability of Foreign Aid Appropriation Act Funds to the State Department for Services Not Specifically Requested by ECA," in Bureau of the Budget, *loc.cit.*

232

example, the ECA had been given some national security responsibilities in the field of export controls. One important duty was to cut off the reshipment of strategic goods to the Soviet bloc from the ERP countries. The difficult job here was in determining that commodities which were otherwise unobjectionable were being used to produce goods of a more strategic nature for sale in the Soviet bloc countries. On its face, it seemed an impracticable task. It was even more unmanageable for an agency that was morally bound to limit its intrusions overseas, and which had been denied, for that very reason, the kind of administrative resources it would have taken to carry out such a meticulous and continuing surveillance. The ECA, of course, had its country missions and its agents on the local scene. But aside from a few spot checks on the piers, inspection was performed largely in the mission offices, where the Controller's department could monitor vouchers. The missions lacked the ability to follow shipments through their respective countries; nor was it feasible to track supplies to the factories and watch closely as the materials were being processed.

The ECA needed a simpler procedure and a clearer set of standards. What it finally did was to adopt the list of prohibited commodities that had been established already in the Commerce Department. Then, where ERP nations were found shipping these commodities to nonparticipating countries, the ECA would refuse to permit the export of the constituent materials.[10] As an administrative solution it was faithful to the original premises of the legislation—that recovery should not come at the expense of strengthening one's adversaries, or that it was at least unreasonable to ask the United States to subsidize recovery that depended on trade of this type. It succeeded in putting pressure on the Europeans, but it also gave them the guidance of clear standards, and it foreclosed any intricate meddling by the United States in their separate economies.

A difficult assignment was made unworkable, then, by the character of the ECA itself; and unless basic changes were made in the authority and ends of the agency, the assignment had to be modified. The ECA was compelled to accept the implications of its own character, but what is equally important for our concerns here, it managed to find a solution within the guidelines of other policy values. Without distorting the intent of Congress the ECA drew

[10] Burton to Dangerfield, July 7, 1948, Bureau of the Budget, *loc.cit.*

back from its authority, but did it in a manner that strengthened the goals of decentralization and pluralism.

A similar shift in strategy and working rules occurred in the field of export priorities, where Congress authorized the ECA to act as a claimant for Marshall Plan needs. In many ways, though, the assignment of export priorities could be far more onerous than the exercise of regular export controls. In an economy of private transactions, it meant persuading or threatening private businessmen, and inducing them to ship to one place rather than another. Exporters were reluctant to serve the priorities upon their suppliers, and there was considerable noncompliance among the suppliers themselves when they were faced with quotas. The Commerce Department encountered so much resistance, in fact, that by the eve of the Marshall Plan the program was virtually abandoned.[11] There was some preference at this time to wait for the Marshall Plan before activating the program again, but there was no reason to expect that the fundamental situation would be changed with the advent of the recovery program. Establishing and enforcing a priority was not something one ventured to do without being asked. Before the Marshall Plan it was the State Department that had to make the request explicit. Now it was the function of the ECA, and with the presumptions still stacked against the use of priorities, it became that much more of a burden. To get a priority meant going before one or more interdepartmental groups, and as a report in 1951 noted, "Such a request requires elaborate justification, and involves a great deal of time of the commodity experts." The response of the ECA was to transfer the burden to the participating countries and raise its claim only when the need seemed clear or urgent. As the Budget Bureau survey noted, "The ECA claims for priority assistance primarily on an ad hoc basis, usually when it is under pressure from one of the participating countries."[12] Here again the ECA found it either too troublesome or too costly to exercise an advantage that Congress had been willing to grant in principle. Again the tautness of administrative resources was a factor, but the ECA cer-

[11] The Office of Materials Distribution had only two items under priority control—tin plate and nitrogenous fertilizer. The program in tin plate involved 14 percent of annual production in the United States, and the fertilizer only 8 percent. R. L. Hirshberg, Memorandum, October 6, 1947, Bureau of the Budget, *loc.cit.*

[12] Bureau of the Budget, *Survey of the Economic Cooperation Administration*, September 11, 1951, p. 31, Series 39.32.

tainly had more choice in this matter of export priorities than it had in the field of strategic commodities. What the people at ECA chose to do in this instance was of a piece with what they were beginning to discover about their own resources in relation to the Europeans—that the most effective weapon they had was the weakness of the agency itself. Hoffman and his top executives emphasized time and again that the ECA was a temporary agency, that it was going out of existence precisely at midnight on June 30, 1952.[13] Thus when they told the Europeans that reforms had better come now, while Marshall aid was still available, their words seemed to carry more force. Similarly, when faced with the need to phase out their operations on schedule, they could convert this obligation into a form of leverage with the Europeans by making annual reductions in the country programs. And when they put the burden of justification on the Europeans for export priorities, they served the same end. No one was going to receive export priorities casually in this program, as Hoffman in his anecdote had accumulated a stock of unneeded remedies for athlete's foot. For the ECA, it was another means of assuring that allocations were responding to more basic needs; and at the same time, it was a method by which the dependent and temporary status of the agency could be turned into an asset.

II

Until letters of commitment could be established in private American banks, the initial procurement in the program was necessarily in the hands of the participating governments. A letter of commitment was issued by the ECA to a bank in the United States and provided the credit covering specific procurement authorizations. After importers in the ERP countries deposited local currency with their governments, they were able to draw upon the credit estab-

---

[13] See, for example, the remarks by Hoffman and Howard Bruce, the Deputy Administrator, in Senate Foreign Relations Committee, *Hearings on Extension of ERP*, 1949, pp. 78 and 332. These views were reiterated two years later by Richard Bissell, Assistant to the Deputy Administrator, who, as the head of the ECA's "brain trust," was more significant than his title might have indicated. See U.S. Senate, Committees on Foreign Relations and Armed Services, 82nd Cong., 1st Sess., *Mutual Security Act of 1951, Hearings* (Washington: Government Printing Office, 1951), p. 157. Cited hereafter as Senate Foreign Relations and Armed Services Committees, *Hearings on Mutual Security Act*, 1951.

lished in the United States. The ECA moved immediately to get the accounts started, and from the very first it showed a scrupulous regard for the legislative command to "facilitate and maximize the use of private channels of trade." After nearly a year of operations, Hoffman reported to the Senate Foreign Relations Committee that 84 percent of ECA procurement was through private channels of trade, while only 16 percent was in the form of government procurement through the Commodity Credit Corporation (CCC). The CCC held the surplus agricultural stocks, and the only items ECA was buying were coarse grains and corn. Remarkably the ECA was about to switch even those transactions to private channels until the President intervened and ordered the ECA to continue its purchase of surpluses. ("[B]ecause of reasons he felt were sufficient," was Hoffman's only comment.[14]) Agriculture, of course, presented the only commodity group in which the government could offer an alternative source of supply. Thus the practical test of adherence to the priority on private channels was here, in the record in agricultural procurement (and this was true even though the ECA took products that otherwise would have ended up in government stocks). That record shows that the reliance on private sources of supply was not only maintained, but that the preponderance of private over public stocks was increased. In the last quarterly report of the ECA, the cumulative figures through June 30, 1951 indicate only $128.9 million worth of goods as having been bought from government stocks. The figure for private procurement was $3,716.1 million—almost 97 percent of the agricultural purchases, and approximately a third, in dollar value, of all the money spent in the Marshall Plan.[15]

Working through private channels was no liability to the ECA. Despite some early forebodings, it was not clear that this was more costly than government procurement. The samplings in the postaudit revealed few mistakes, and if there was something lacking in the documentation, it was always possible to request additional information.[16] Also, the ECA frequently found it less troublesome to deal with private companies. There were fewer sources of fric-

[14] Senate Foreign Relations Committee, *Hearings on Extension of ERP*, 1949, p. 97.

[15] ECA, *Thirteenth Report* (Quarter ending June 30, 1951), p. 94.

[16] ECA, *Recovery Progress and United States Aid*, p. 109. Also, see Hoffman's comments in Senate Foreign Relations Committee, *Hearings on Extension of ERP*, 1949, p. 97.

236

tion and, strange to say—or perhaps not so strange to say—it was often easier to get information from private organizations than from other government agencies.[17]

Nor did the ECA really suffer because of its reliance on other departments. For the most part, the regular government departments were well experienced in their own fields, and the procurement agencies in particular were quite efficient. The CCC had participated in two foreign assistance programs already, and it had a reputation for moving goods successfully without a high administrative overhead. Under the Lend-Lease program the CCC delivered food at a cost of only 8 mills to the dollar, and it promised to perform at something close to that level for the ECA.[18] With the ECA able to call in this way upon the specialized services of other departments, the Marshall Plan enjoyed a great deal of output at a rather low administrative cost. The result was that the ECA was able to operate fairly consistently with administrative costs running at less than one-half of one percent.[19]

The picture we get, then, is of an agency with administrative resources held taut. The tendency of the ECA was to restrict commitments, and even where it did not delegate a task entirely to another department, it still found itself highly dependent on the special skills or authority of the regular agencies. Moreover, this dependence was even further exaggerated in the early stages of the program, when the ECA was still in the midst of recruiting staff.[20] In all, it is a sharp contrast to the images drawn in the hearings of a free-wheeling, autonomous agency that was to go out in the field and reorganize Europe on a business-like basis. If ECA seemed to lack anything but the rudiments of its own self-control in the first

[17] Bureau of the Budget, *Survey of the ECA*, 1951, p. 29.

[18] The CCC had "slipped" somewhat under the UNRRA program, when it ran the rate up to 8.6 mills, but there was a smaller dollar volume in that program and a number of more specialized purchases, such as seeds, livestock, and vitamins. See Memorandum to George Newman from Agriculture Department, "CCC Participation in the Marshall Plan," October 7, 1947, Bureau of the Budget, *loc.cit.*

[19] U.S. House of Representatives, Subcommittee of the Committee on Appropriations, 81st Cong., 2nd Sess., 1950, *Foreign Aid Appropriations for 1951, Hearings* (Washington: Government Printing Office, 1950), p. 415. Cited hereafter as House Subcommittee on Appropriations, *Hearings on Foreign Aid Appropriations for 1951* (1950).

[20] Herbert A. Simon, "Birth of an Organizaiton: The Economic Cooperation Administration," *Public Administration Review*, Vol. XIII, No. 4 (Autumn 1953), pp. 227-36.

three to six months and, indeed, if it remained largely a dependent agency throughout its life, the natural question is, What happened to European recovery while all this was going on? The answer is that it kept advancing as the State Department maintained the pipeline of aid, and that it was practically achieved in its most immediate and elementary form by the time ECA finally got possession of itself. In a major report on the first year of operations, the ECA admitted that it was not until October 1948 that it was "able to appraise more carefully and accurately the needs of the European countries for aid." Up to that point, the ECA was still relying on the initial program set up by the State Department, and it was not until mid-summer of 1948 that it succeeded in turning the OEEC countries to the job of constructing an annual program.[21] Yet, in the same report, issued only four months later, the ECA was able to announce that the first phase of recovery was substantially completed.[22] As it came out of the early discussions within the Executive, the first phase of recovery was defined as the restoration of production to prewar levels, with 1938 taken as the base year. That goal was actually more impressive than the term "first phase" might have indicated. It referred, after all, to basic production, and although 1938 was a recession year in the United States, it represented only a slight downturn in Europe from a relatively prosperous year in 1937. Of course, Europe now had about twenty million more in population than before the war, so the recovery of 1938 levels might not have seemed that crucial. But when set against the near breakdown conditions of 1946-47, it was significant that the counter-trend had set in, and that the reciprocal cycles of trade and production had revived. Figure 1 shows the curves in industrial production for the major ERP nations at this time. Table 2 gives a wider representation and expresses the change in terms of the numerical index.

According to the figures, shortly after *Recovery Progress and United States Aid* was released in February 1949, almost all the Marshall Plan countries had exceeded the 1938 production levels. The notable exceptions were Austria, Greece, and the Bizone of Germany; but they were also the places that showed the sharpest improvement in the first year (as seen in the percentage of change).

[21] ECA, *Recovery Progress and United States Aid*, p. 66.
[22] *Ibid.*, p. 2.

238

FIGURE 1. Industrial Production Curves, 1946-49

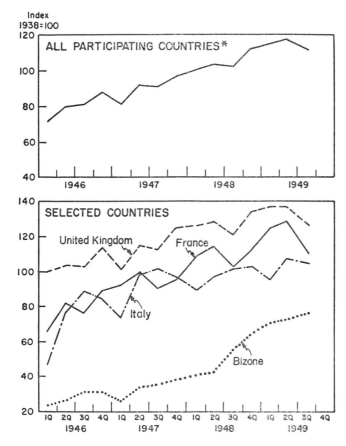

*Total excludes Luxembourg, Portugal, Switzerland, and Turkey.

Source: ECA *Sixth Report* (Quarter ending September 30, 1949), p. 15.
No adjustment has been made for seasonal variations, so that the graphs
show seasonal downturns for the third quarter of 1949.

Agriculture was recovering more slowly. Production generally
exceeded the 1947-48 period, but was still slightly below prewar.
The coal situation improved, and with the exception of Britain and
Germany production was up to prewar levels. The most striking
growth occurred in the heavy industries, where operations ran beyond the 1938 rate and were closer to the higher figures of 1937.[23]

[23] *Ibid.*, pp. 4-5.

239

Part II

TABLE 2. INDEX NUMBERS OF INDUSTRIAL PRODUCTION

	Indexes (1938 = 100)			Percent Change Second Quarter 1949 from Second Quarter 1948
	Second Quarter 1948	Third Quarter 1948	Second Quarter 1949	
Total	103	101	117	+14
Austria	75	77	99	+32
Belgium	114	113	119	+ 4
Denmark	132	124	132	0
France	115	103	129	+12
Bizone of Germany	43	56	73	+70
Greece	71	77	90	+27
Ireland	138	132	144	+ 4
Italy	98	102	108	+10
Netherlands	110	113	121	+10
Norway	133	110	138	+ 4
Sweden	143	143	146	+ 2
United Kingdom	128	121	137	+ 7

SOURCE: ECA, *Sixth Report* (Quarter ending September 30, 1949), p. 13.

Recovery in production was given some critical assistance, also, by the rapid reconstruction of the railways and the expansion of electrical power. Freight traffic rose to a third above prewar, while electric power production showed a gain of 65 percent.[24]

Ironically, though, the United States was not injecting vast supplies of capital goods, which might have been used directly in churning items off the production line. The delivery of machine tools took a long time, so the ECA simply concentrated in this early period on the repair of existing facilities. In the first quarter, machine tools constituted only 7 percent of the supplies. The emphasis was on raw materials (22 percent) and the combined group of food, feed, and fertilizers (33 percent).[25] By the end of the first full year, machinery and equipment accounted for only $435.3 million out of a total commodity expenditure of $4,481.3 million.

[24] In France, for example, the quarterly average of net ton miles was 4.537 billion in 1938. In the second quarter of 1948 (at the very start of the Marshall Plan), it had climbed to 7.115 billion. ECA, *Second Report*, Appendix A, Table 7, p. 135. At the same time, the output of electricity in the ERP countries rose from a quarterly average of 29.9 billion kilowatt hours in 1938, to 40.4 billion. See Table 3, p. 131.

[25] ECA, *First Report* (Quarter ending June 30, 1948), p. 25.

240

In comparison, raw materials and semifinished products totaled $1,314.7 million and the food–feed–fertilizer group $1,673.4 million.[26]

What the ECA was finding, then, was that the United States did not have to rebuild the entire industrial plant of Western Europe in order to raise production. It could be equally important to supply raw materials to feed the manufacturing process. Marshall Plan assistance was hardly more than 5 percent of the combined national incomes of the ERP nations, but it was critical at the margins and capable of having a multiplier effect of three or four times its value. For Hoffman, a relevant analogy came from his own experience in the auto industry. A few hundred dollars worth of metal was processed by machinery and labor, with each component adding its costs, until a product finally emerged that was worth about $2,000. Thus, Hoffman admitted to the Senate Foreign Relations Committee that his own understanding of the substantive problem had undergone a change.

> MR. HOFFMAN. . . . In some cases I think the very No. 1 recovery item is a little more food to get a little more work out of people. They cannot work without food. . . .
> SENATOR LODGE. Do you think if you gave everybody in Europe a steak three times a week it is just as much a capital investment as giving them machine tools?
> MR. HOFFMAN. No sir, I do not. . . . I do think that giving them a steak perhaps once a month might be an incentive. I think it is a recovery item.
>
> .   .   .   .
>
> I am responsible for drawing [the distinction between relief and recovery]. I say that I am now less sure of the distinction. I found last year that supplying cotton, for example, for mills that did not have cotton, was just as much a recovery item as perhaps machine tools to some company that needed machine tools.[27]

However, this recovery of production was still, as the ECA said, only the first phase. The Marshall Plan was addressed to an economic problem that was fundamental and structural. Western Eu-

[26] ECA, *Fourth Report* (Quarter ending April 2, 1949), Appendix B, pp. 104-105.
[27] Senate Foreign Relations Committee, *Hearings on Extension of ERP*, 1949, p. 75.

rope was dependent on the dollar area for raw materials, and that dependence was now accentuated by the division of Europe, which separated Western Europe from a traditional source of supply in the east. The costs and destruction of the war had forced the liquidation of overseas assets, as in the case of Britain, or reduced the capacity for dollar earning, as in the case of Norway with its huge losses in merchant marine. The scarcity of foreign exchange made it hard to acquire materials needed for production, and as production and trade declined, it became that much more difficult to produce for domestic demand while still providing the export goods that could earn foreign exchange. The balance of payments, to this extent, was a useful index of the more basic problem. In the calendar year 1948, the total deficit of the ERP countries in their international accounts declined 22 percent to $5.6 billion. However, the ERP countries were able to pay for only 63 percent of their imports from their own earnings.[28] Perhaps it was the British, with their relatively impressive record in the index of industrial production, who made the overall situation in Europe look considerably better than it was. As *The Economist* took pains to point out, the British were the only ones in the Marshall group who actually showed a gain from 1938 to 1948-49 in the percentage of imports covered by export earnings. (See Table 3.)

TABLE 3. IMPORTS FROM AND EXPORTS TO THE DOLLAR AREA

	Trade with Canada and USA, April 1948-March 1949		Proportion of Dollar Imports Covered by Dollar Exports		Change from 1938 to 1948-49
	Imports (millions of dollars)	*Exports (millions of dollars)*	*1948-49 (percent)*	*1938 (percent)*	
Belgium	355	138	39	55	—16
Denmark	125	15	12	18	— 6
France	594	82	14	39	—25
Italy	595	95	16	73	—57
Netherlands	355	39	11	42	—31
Norway	120	35	29	46	—17
Sweden	160	74	46	64	—18
Switzerland	231	114	49	80	—31
United Kingdom	565	559	36	27	+ 9

SOURCE: *The Economist*, Vol. CLVII, No. 5529 (August 13, 1949), p. 331. Reprinted here with the permission of *The Economist*.

[28] ECA, *Fourth Report* (Quarter ending April 2, 1949), p. 6.

It was necessary, of course, to cultivate sources of supply outside the dollar area, but clearly that was not sufficient. In the long run the Europeans would have to compete and earn in the dollar area itself. That would mean modernizing industry as well as simply raising production, and it would require more than new equipment, but a radical change in managerial practices and a new concern with the techniques of marketing. As Hoffman and the ECA saw the matter, the way to make industries competitive in the dollar area was to expose them to more competition in Europe. Therefore, the attack on trade barriers and the press for a multilateral payments system became important parts of the ECA program for the second phase of recovery. Increasing economic integration would promote rationalization and knock out the inefficient producers. In this next phase, technical assistance would be moved to the center of ECA's interest. For the Marshall Plan countries themselves, the ECA insisted that the priority would have to be on modernizing through basic investment. The ideal was to devote about 20 percent of GNP to investment and hold consumption below the prewar level. Naturally, the formula could not apply to Turkey, where the main problem was in developing the nascent forms of industrialism, rather than repairing an established industrial system that had suffered temporary disruption. Greece would be able to advance a step into Turkey's position once the civil war was ended —and the turning point in the war would come in the middle of 1949. For Belgium and Ireland, at the other extreme, the problem was no longer one of raising production or enlarging investment. These two countries faced a considerably more refined problem of adjusting their trading positions in order to achieve a better overall balance in their international accounts. They would find their place in the ECA scheme through the program for freeing multilateral trade.[29]

Thus while no one would contend that the more basic problems of the Marshall Plan were all conquered during the first year, it was nevertheless striking that the ECA was able to turn to them so quickly. As early as 1949, then, immediate recovery had been achieved and the ECA was preparing to move the program into a higher gear.

But what was the nature of this agency, which seemed to be presiding now over a startling success in Europe? We can accept the

[29] ECA, *Recovery Progress and United States Aid*, pp. 2, 20-21, 59.

fact that it was a rather dependent agency, but still, where were those heralded "operations" that were cited so prominently in the past to justify an ECA outside the State Department? Certainly they did not involve the moving of goods, and as we have seen, they were not even present in the procurement of commodities. The ECA merely *authorized* Marshall Plan financing for goods that were scheduled for delivery to the participating countries; and yet even here, in this fairly modest function, the ECA was eventually forced to recede in futility. For even if the ECA refused to sanction the purchase of any commodity, it was entirely possible for the Marshall Plan country to buy the item anyway with its own foreign exchange.[30] Unless the United States was prepared to take the critical step and impose a complete system of controls on the private sector in foreign transactions, there was no practical way to enforce a control on commodities. By the end of the first quarter, then, the ECA was compelled to withdraw from commodity screening and to begin authorizing procurement in terms of broad commodity groups, such as fuel, fertilizer, and machine tools.[31]

But if the ECA was forced to retreat, at the center, from the most elementary form of control over operations, did that have to be true of the local missions as well? The rationale for the missions, after all, was to have some operating arms abroad that could inspect the use of aid. Despite its connotations of field work, though, end-use inspection was essentially a clerical task: It was entrusted to the Controller's office in each of the country missions, and it proceeded largely through the sampling of vouchers.[32] Whether the ECA was checking for violations in the procurement rules, or whether it was merely certifying that a given shipment was sent to a given factory, what was actually inspected was the central collection of statistical reports.

To some extent, of course, the size of the Controller's office in Greece was a fair measure of American influence in guiding the Greek bureaucracy. In certain cases, the end-use investigators were

[30] On this point, see Simon, *loc.cit.*, p. 232.

[31] ECA, *Recovery Progress and United States Aid*, p. 60.

[32] Bureau of the Budget, *Survey of ECA*, 1951, pp. 11, 29-30. Memoranda on interviews with Howard Wright, Special Assistant to the Controller of ECA, June 20, 1951, pp. 4-5, and with Edward Kunze, Director of the Program and Methods Control Division, June 20, 1951, *Interviews in Survey of the ECA*, 1951. Bureau of the Budget, *loc.cit.*

in a position to affect the strategic materials program and East-West trade, and for that reason, it was not unusual to find some missions in which the Controller became the top staff adviser to the mission chief.[33] Even so, this prominence of the Controller's office seemed much less a sign of veiled strength than a deflating commentary in itself on the nature of ECA power and the status of the ECA as an "operating" agency. And as the Marshall Plan reached its full stride, there was no denying the prominence of the Controller's office. In January 1950, that office embraced 174 out of 938 permanent employees in ECA/Washington, which is to say, not far from 20 percent of the entire headquarters staff.[34]

In addition, if we took the figures for ECA/Washington from January 1950, we would find 522 people—well over half the employees—in units we would identify as "administrative" in the narrowest sense. That is, they were units engaged in administrative overhead, management, and related services, as opposed to either substantive programming or operations.[35] Less than 10 percent of the staff was grouped under an Assistant Administrator for Operations.[36] Yet even with that modest representation, there was something suspect about the labeling. Subsumed under this office were divisions for Small Business, Transportation, Strategic Materials, and Technical Assistance.

As its critics would later point out, the ECA Small Business Division never did anything more than distribute information or hold counseling sessions. The Transportation Division was concerned almost exclusively with ocean shipping, particularly with the enforcement of that provision in the law that required 50 percent of the tonnage to be carried in American vessels. But Arthur Syran, who served as Chief of the Transportation Division, emphatically

[33] Memorandum on interview with Howard Wright, *loc.cit.*, pp. 9-10.

[34] Roughly the same proportion applied to the sixteen country missions. At the time of the Budget Bureau survey in 1951, the Controllers' offices represented 120 people out of a combined mission total of approximately 650. *Ibid.*, p. 9; House Subcommittee on Appropriations, *Hearings on Foreign Aid Appropriations for 1951* (1950), p. 424.

[35] They included, for example, the Office of the Administrator (Central Secretariat and Assistant to the Administrator), Controller, Director of Administration (Organization and Management, Personnel, Administrative Services Budget), General Counsel, Statistics and Reports, and Information.

[36] House Subcommittee on Appropriations, *Hearings on Foreign Aid Appropriations for 1951* (1950), p. 424.

245

denied that his unit was engaged in operations. His own job, he insisted, involved little more in the way of operations than the drafting of one-page policy memoranda. According to Syran's estimate, over 90 percent of the work in his division was concerned with water transportation, which meant that inland transportation in Europe, with all its importance in distributing American aid abroad, received little direct supervision by the ECA.[37]

If anything done by the ECA deserved the name "operations," it would have been found in the technical assistance and strategic materials programs, for at least they were faithful to the images of field work. But even after 1950, when the ECA became more genuinely interested in the strategic materials program, the personnel commitment in Europe had a permanent core of only five engineers, and these men formed a consultants' pool in the Paris office. By the time of the final quarterly report to Congress, the cumulative expenditures for the development program were less than $60 million.[38]

As for technical assistance, it did not really take hold as a priority program until the later phases of the Marshall Plan. In Fiscal 1949, it commanded only $2.4 million, as compared to its growth to $20 million by Fiscal 1952. But the program maintained the character of a "farmed out" operations (in some instances, quite literally). Experts on productivity were naturally found in private industry and the labor unions, and again they were usually unavailable except for short-term assignments. The Director of the Technical Assistance Division told a House subcommittee in 1951 that "we use the Agriculture Department almost exclusively. There is not a single project in the agricultural field that is not either actually implemented by the Department or on which we have not had the fullest discussions with them. . . ."[39]

---

[37] Memorandum on interview with Arthur Syran, Chief, and James Kirwin, Transportation Division, ECA, June 18, 1951, Bureau of the Budget, *Interviews in Survey of the ECA*, 1951.

[38] ECA, *Thirteenth Report* (Quarter ending June 30, 1951), pp. 86-89, 127. Also, the ECA found it difficult to recruit full-time technical specialists to go abroad. Eventually it was forced to hire engineers on contract from private organizations, or on a reimbursable and temporary basis from government agencies like the Bureau of Mines. Bureau of the Budget, *Survey of the ECA*, 1951, p. 44.

[39] House Subcommittee on Appropriations, *Hearings on Foreign Aid Appropriations for 1951* (1950), p. 401.

Thus the rules of decentralization worked in this area as well, and they kept the technical assistance program as something less than an ECA operation. That seemed all the more true, too, when the initial contract for services did not end the delegation. In 1949, for example, a small training project brought a group of Dutch farmers to the United States. As one might expect, the program was delegated to the Department of Agriculture, but Agriculture, in turn, gave it over to the Extension Service. The Extension Service, finally, let contracts to several private farmers, who were paid for housing and instructing the foreign visitors, and who presumably could have claimed a hand now in managing the "operations" of the United States in foreign policy.[40]

When the time came to plan for Fiscal 1951, the ECA found itself in a unique bind. According to the logic of debureaucratization, the agency had to show a progressive reduction in program expenditures—which it did. But that also seemed to suggest the appropriateness of parallel reductions in personnel and administrative costs. The ECA did manage to show a net reduction in overall costs, but with the programs added by Congress since 1948, and with the special needs arising in the latter phase of the Marshall Plan, the ECA actually could have used a slight enlargement of personnel. As it was, the ECA had to reshuffle its administrative resources and hope that Congress would accept a plan that kept personnel levels substantially where they were. If one accepted the ideal of debureaucratization, a curve representing the trend in personnel levels from 1949 through 1951 should have shown a consistent slope downward and to the right. Of course, most of the twenty-five identifiable subunits in Washington did not conform to this ideal curve, although they did share the general downward trend. What is revealing, though, is to notice the units that struck off in dramatic counterpoint to the main trend—that is to say, the units for which the administrators were willing to brave the Congressional winds and order consistent increases in personnel. Since this was also the time when the ECA was becoming more anxious about pushing the Europeans into basic reforms, it is even more interesting to consider where the priorities were placed in the use of personnel.

[40] Bruce to the Director, April 14, 1949, Bureau of the Budget, Series 39.18.

247

There were only five of these units that were given annual incre-ments in staff. One was the Technical Assistance Division, which has already been discussed. A second was the Information Divi-sion, which was now being enlisted in the productivity drive. The purpose was to enlarge the active advertisements for economic in-tegration and the introduction of new production techniques. Third was the Controller's Office, and William Foster, the Deputy Ad-ministrator of ECA, was frank to acknowledge that the large in-crease in this unit was to cope with increased auditing, accounting, and price-checking—and generally, "to permit an even more care-ful check abroad of the end use of ECA-financed commodities."[41] The fourth and fifth were the divisions for Program Coordination and Administrative Services. Thus, aside from the technical assist-ance program, these were changes that emphasized administrative or program management rather than operations.

For those who had been living with the ECA, there was nothing extraordinary in this discovery. None of the division heads inter-viewed in the Budget Bureau survey would admit that his own unit had anything to do with operations if, indeed, anyone could ade-quately define the term. But those who had heard the original argu-ments in 1948 could have been forgiven some confusion. Certainly Congressman Rooney could have been forgiven some bewilder-ment when he learned, as he said, that the ECA was actually "increasing the general's department" at the same time it was claiming a shortage in personnel. William Foster, who would later succeed Hoffman as Administrator, had to explain that the ECA was dealing now with more specialized skills and "coordinating" functions. "Our activity," he told Rooney—perhaps the first time anyone came out and said it—"is pretty much a general's depart-ment. It is not an operating agency."[42] Two years after the rather muddled discussion of "operational" capacities and the State De-partment's supposed lack of them, it was perhaps fitting that some-thing along these lines be said. The virtue now, however, was that it could be said from experience, and by someone who could speak for the "other" ECA—not that dynamic organization in the mind of Vandenberg, which would venture out and rationalize Western

[41] House Subcommittee on Appropriations, *Hearings on Foreign Aid Appropriations for 1951* (1950), pp. 412 and 424, and see generally, p. 408 ff. for an explanation of ECA personnel changes. My own analysis is based on the tables and discussions presented in this section of the testimony.
[42] *Ibid.*, p. 428.

Europe, which would somehow avoid every previous fault in foreign aid and replace every misadventure with technical brilliance. It was appropriate now that someone should speak for that constrained and dependent agency that was created by the same Congress, and in the same set of decisions.

12. A CURE RATHER THAN A PALLIATIVE

I

IF THE "business-like" approach never came to define the essential Marshall Plan, it was not because it lacked faithful adherents within the ECA. Vandenberg knew exactly what he wanted when he chose Paul Hoffman, and Hoffman's own predilections were never in doubt. In 1950 Hoffman told the Senate Appropriations Committee:

> I do not believe we are ever going to have sound relations with other countries abroad until those relations are on a business basis where they are earning the dollars they need, directly or indirectly for the goods they buy from us and paying for those goods on the barrelhead. We will get rid of a great many unfortunate influences in the American system as well as unfortunate tensions in relationships between the United States and foreign countries once we get the relation on a business basis.[1]

Yet, after the program had been running for nearly a year, Hoffman was forced to admit that the response of private business to the convertibility guarantee had been "very, very disappointing." There was a $300 million ceiling on the guarantees, and $25 million had been made available for the first year. By April 1949, however, only $2,625,000 worth of guarantees had been issued. Rather than stimulating new investment, the guarantee program elicited interest only among firms that had already developed a large volume of business in Europe, in some cases because they had

[1] U.S. Congress, Senate, 81st Cong., 2nd Sess., Committee on Appropriations, *Foreign Aid Appropriations for 1951, Hearings* (Washington: Government Printing Office, 1950), p. 215. Cited hereafter as Senate Appropriations Committee, *Hearings on Foreign Aid Appropriations for 1951* (1950).

250

already established plants overseas. Moreover, all of the first year investment was in Britain.[2] What little private capital was made available, then, was not very venturesome.

Hoffman was naturally disappointed, but as a businessman he was not surprised. Despite the inducements, private investment was not likely to trickle out until the political uncertainties in Europe began to subside. Thus Hoffman was forced to conclude that private investment would not be the primary instrument for generating European recovery; its presence would indicate, rather, that basic recovery had already been attained. "The thing we have got to do first of all," Hoffman told the Senate Foreign Relations Committee, "is to have a more secure Europe. In other words, if ECA succeeds, then it is my hope that . . . the conditions will invite American capital."[3]

Setting aside $25 million for guarantees left $975 million in the fund Congress reserved for loans during the first year. The ECA followed Congressional orders, and in one way or another it managed to get rid of almost all of the loan money. But having disposed of the money, it quickly appealed to the escape clause in the legislation and urged Congress to drop the loan requirement. For the new loans were merely adding to the debt load of the Europeans, which was already burdened by the war settlements and postwar credits. The ECA estimated in fact that, in 1948-49, the interest and amortization payments to the United States would be equivalent to one-eighth of the dollar earnings of the participating countries.[4]

Furthermore, assessing the ability of a nation to repay its loans was not quite comparable to gauging the capacities of a private firm within a specialized area of operations. This issue arose very early in the ECA, when the loan program was in the hands of some former members of the Export-Import Bank staff, who had followed Wayne Taylor into the Marshall Plan agency. The Export-Import Bank was already scheduled to administer the ECA loans; its erstwhile staff members sought to make the alignment more complete now by adopting the formulas used by the Bank in its own postwar loans. Within a matter of weeks, though, the new people at ECA

[2] ECA, *Fourth Report* (Quarter ending April 2, 1949), pp. 56-57.
[3] Senate Foreign Relations Committee, *Hearings on Extension of ERP*, 1949, p. 32.
[4] ECA, *Recovery Progress and United States Aid*, p. 113.

251

found themselves locked in a dispute with Treasury, State, Commerce, and the Budget Bureau. On the surface, the ECA seemed to be urging flexibility by resisting a uniform loan policy, but in reality it was advancing a more rigid program. The terms of the Export-Import Bank allowed a range from 18 months to 30 years, and from 2⅜ to 3½ percent interest. The inherent problem with this arrangement, as the critics pointed out, was that the loans were geared to specific commodities or projects—e.g., 18 months for cotton, which was processed and sold in a fairly short period, as against several decades for development projects. Roger Nelson of the Budget Bureau argued that the program was dealing with countries as wholes, instead of dividing them into commodity sectors. The interest, then, was in the total capacity of a given country, and in its general strength as measured in the balance of payments. As the Budget Bureau contended, this generalized capacity was more relevant to the ability of any country to pay off a collection of loans in the future.[5] Until recovery had progressed at least far enough to make the balance of payments deficit manageable, it seemed illusory to rank countries as credit risks and allocate loans on that basis. Under those conditions, the countries most qualified for loans would be the ones that were far less in need of American aid. Thus, as the balance of payments approach came to be accepted, the view of the other agencies finally prevailed.[6]

Later Hoffman acknowledged the wisdom of the original decision when he remarked, "The only way you can take the loans you have made and make them good loans . . . is through the success of the recovery of Europe. If the recovery effort succeeds, then

[5] Roger Nelson to Arthur Smithies, April 20, 1948, Bureau of the Budget, Series, 39.18.

[6] Looking back on his own experience in the ECA, Herbert Simon suggested that the relative descent of Wayne Taylor in the ECA hierarchy represented the decline of the Export-Import Bank approach, and that the Bank approach failed because it was not considered appropriate or effective. See Herbert A. Simon, "Birth of an Organization: The Economic Cooperation Administration," *Public Administration Review*, Vol. XIII, No. 4 (Autumn 1953), p. 233. It bears adding, though, on the basis of the evidence presented here, that it was not simply the case of an approach that did not work out, and the result did not depend on a conflict among groups and agencies. Whatever conflict occurred was due mainly to the fact that the people at ECA were rather late in understanding a position that had been worked out already, and whose reasoning they themselves would find persuasive.

252

... the chances of repayment of the ECA loans are very good indeed. ...."[7]

What this meant in practical terms was that the ECA would treat loans as supplements, rather than alternatives, to grant aid, and the results were sometimes disconcerting. Some of the most ardent supporters of the business-loan theory were astonished to learn at the end of the first year that the countries receiving the largest shares of the loan program were also the ones who were getting most of the grant aid. Britain and France together, for example, accounted for half the dollar value of all the loans combined (see Table 4). Senator McClellan professed to be shocked that the British were receiving such a large share of the loans, when it was the ineffectiveness of the previous loans to Britain that helped to bring on the Marshall Plan. "How can you hope for her to ever repay?" he asked Richard Bissell. "She cannot repay what we have already

TABLE 4. ALLOTMENTS TO PARTICIPATING COUNTRIES FOR APRIL 1948 TO MARCH 1949, BY TYPE OF AID (Millions of dollars)

Country	Total	Loans	Direct Grants	Conditional Aid
Total	4,953.0a	972.3	3,478.0a	502.7
Austria	231.6	—	231.6	—
Belgium–Luxembourg	206.7	57.4	3.0	146.3
Denmark	103.0	31.0	68.2	3.8
France	1,084.9	172.0	905.8	7.1
Greece	177.5	—	177.5	—
Iceland	8.3	2.3	2.5	3.5
Ireland	88.3	88.3	—	—
Italy	585.9	67.0	490.8	28.1
Netherlands	473.9	146.7	323.1	4.1
Norway	82.8	35.0	37.0	10.8
Sweden	40.0	21.6	—	18.8
Trieste	13.8	—	13.8	—
Turkey	40.0	38.0	—	8.0
United Kingdom	1,316.0	313.0	773.8	229.2
Western Germany:				
Bizone	388.1	—	356.1	32.0
French Zone	94.4	—	83.4	11.0

a Includes a reserve of $11,400,000.
SOURCE: ECA, *Fourth Report* (Quarter ending April 2, 1949), p. 38.

[7] Senate Foreign Relations Committee, *Hearings on Extension of ERP*, 1949, p. 70.

253

lent her." "Your judgment on that, Senator," said Bissell, candidly, "would be as good as mine."[8]

With the loan requirement removed, the ECA let the program atrophy. From the high point of almost one billion dollars that Congress specified for the first year, loans to the ERP countries fell to $143.7 million in the second year and $16.2 million in the third.[9] The results, then, tend to bear out our earlier hypothesis that the loan program was given a secondary status, and that the outcome was foreshadowed in the statute itself.

However, there was nothing in the eclipse of the loan program that implied any lessening of Hoffman's own commitment to the value of business and business standards. In fact, Hoffman and his staff were able to find a justification within the premises of the business approach for their decision to abandon loans in the short run. Hoffman pointed out in 1949 that private investors and international lending agencies would be sensitive to the piling of further claims on the Marshall Plan countries by the United States. At the same time, the ECA was arguing in *Recovery Progress and United States Aid* that:

> The addition of a further large debt to Western Europe's present dollar charges might absorb so much of its capacity to borrow as to throw serious obstacles in the path of private American investment in Western Europe at the end of the program, when such investment should play a strategic role.[10]

Thus when the ECA was forced to step away from a previous policy commitment, it was not subverting the definition of its program. Instead the decision could be defended in terms of other prominent policy values, like the business approach itself, or the preference for a cure rather than a palliative. These were the grounds on which the agency could appeal to Congress to eliminate any provision for the mandatory use of loans, and on those terms Congress found the request unexceptionable. The understanding

[8] Senate Appropriations Committee, *Hearings on Foreign Aid Appropriations for 1951* (1950), p. 291.

[9] ECA, *Thirteenth Report* (Quarter ending June 30, 1951), Appendix B, p. 12.

[10] ECA, *Recovery Progress and United States Aid*, p. 113. For Hoffman's parallel comments see Senate Foreign Relations Committee, *Hearings on Extension of ERP*, 1949, pp. 77-78.

was reflected more precisely in the report of the Senate Foreign Relations Committee after the 1949 hearings:

> Testimony indicated that the Administrator would plan to extend aid in the form of loans to certain countries which clearly would have the capacity to repay dollars without undermining their financial position after the end of the program. The committee was impressed with the validity of the consideration advanced and decided to require no fixed amount of the appropriation to be used in the form of loans. At the same time the committee clearly expressed its view that loans should continue to be an integral part of the programs and should be used whereever they can be made on a sound basis.[11]

The hearings and the report leave no mistake about the understanding between the committee and Hoffman. For prudential reasons the loan program would be reduced, but in no definitive or "operational" sense had the commitment to the premises of the program ended. The operating rule was still intact; only its exercise had been abridged, and for the moment, possibly, deferred. It is revealing, in this respect, that in 1950, when the ECA was prodded into a more earnest effort in the strategic materials program, it presumed in favor of loans rather than grants in financing the development projects. In this way it was able to use about $1 million worth of loans during Fiscal 1950 for technical assistance projects in Turkey. Generally speaking, the total funds expended in loans were unimpressive after the first year, but the significant thing was that they were used at all—and that there was an effective standing presumption to use them wherever they were remotely relevant.

Similarly, the investment guarantees came to slightly more than $40 million for the entire program, a figure that hardly threatened the ceiling of $300 million. Yet with all the disappointments of the initial year, the trend of the program was one of growth. More important, it was growth in fields that mattered—in chemicals, in heavy earth moving equipment and machine tools. The industrial investments soon surpassed the guarantees for informational media, and by the end of June 1951, industrial investments accounted for three-fourths of all the guarantees.[12]

---

[11] U.S. Congress, Senate, Committee on Foreign Relations, *Report, Extension of European Recovery Program*, Report No. 100, 81st Cong., 1st Sess., 1949, p. 18.

[12] ECA, *Thirteenth Report* (Quarter ending June 30, 1951), Appendix B,

Finally, even though the loan program itself was going into decline, the presumption in favor of loans was able to affect other areas of policy. In 1948, for example, the Brussels Pact powers devised a payments plan that would have earmarked a portion of each country's counterpart funds for a common pool. The common fund would be used in financing exports and breaking away from the constraints of the bilateral accounts. But the most important creditor country in Europe was Belgium, and because Belgium was in such a relatively healthy state, the priorities of ECA prescribed loans rather than grants. Only grants, however, could generate counterpart funds; and thus the very countries that would have been able to support the multilateral trade would not have the grant proceeds available to earmark as credits.[13] Of course, the ECA and the Marshall Plan countries would later move toward the same end with a system of drawing rights and conditional American aid. But that does not disturb the essential point: that in spite of the decline of the loan program, the standing presumptions on the use of loans were capable of restricting the choices before the ECA and the Marshall Plan nations, and in some of the most important areas of policy.

The loan program might terminate, and the ECA might pledge itself to apply loan financing where it could, but still that did not necessarily end the issue. It was possible to find certain secondary options that were more or less consistent with the spirit of the business approach. Senator George insisted to Hoffman in 1949 that currency stabilization and budget balancing would be even more important "when we are as I understand now going away from any loan idea" in administering the program.[14] If the American taxpayers were generous enough to give large sums of grant aid, the least the Europeans could do was to guarantee that the money was not being used in a prodigal way. The United States, the argument ran, should not be asked to underwrite budgetary deficits, espe-

---

p. 122. Instead of being confined to Britain, the new investments spread out geographically to include France, Germany, Italy, the Netherlands, and Norway. At this date, in fact, investments in Germany and Italy had already exceeded the guarantees assigned to Britain.

[13] William Diebold, Jr., *Trade and Payments in Western Europe* (New York: Harper and Brothers, 1952), pp. 32-33.

[14] Senate Foreign Relations Committee, *Hearings on Extension of ERP,* 1949, p. 36.

cially when they might create an inflation that could undermine the effectiveness of American aid.

The notion of secondary goals was actually contained in the legislation. Section 115 (b)(6) described the arrangement of counterpart funds and went on to list a few ends that might be pursued with these local currency proceeds. The very first activity mentioned, ahead of stimulating production and exploring for strategic materials, was that of promoting "internal monetary and financial stabilization." That goal was quite compatible, also, with the ECA's emphasis on austerity, with the restriction of consumption for the benefit of investment, and with the aim of achieving convertibility among the European currencies as a means of expanding intra-European trade.

Counterpart funds required the recipient government to deposit the local currency equivalent of American aid, so they had the immediate and anti-inflationary effect of taking money out of circulation. In addition, the ECA could make the release of counterpart funds contingent upon the adoption of stabilization measures. In France, for example, in 1948, the government enlisted the help of the ECA in financing the Monnet Plan. Its only alternative was to go to the central bank, which would have meant more deficit financing, however, and a confrontation with the Chamber of Deputies. As chief of the ECA mission, David Bruce agreed to finance the investment plan, but in return the French government was forced to promise stabilization measures, which included additional taxation and quantitative controls over private credit.[15] In Britain, over 90 percent of the counterpart releases was used in retiring public debt. At the end of the first year of the Marshall Plan, the ECA had approved the release of counterpart funds that were equivalent to more than $435 million. Of this, $433 million was used for debt retirement, and only about $2 million for the promotion of production.[16]

Thus, when the loan program was suspended, the ECA did not find itself roaming aimlessly, or with unlimited discretion in its choice of policy alternatives. And paradoxically, the effect of the seemingly more selfish decision to clamp down on the Europeans and press for stabilization was to support the pluralist features of

[15] Harry B. Price, *The Marshall Plan and Its Meaning* (Ithaca: Cornell University Press, 1955), pp. 104-105.
[16] ECA, *Fourth Report* (Quarter ending April 2, 1949), Appendix C, p. 122.

the program. Counterpart agreements were highly superficial as instruments of penetration. Money could be taken out of circulation, commitments to stabilization could be accumulated, and yet nothing prevented a country from using other budgetary devices to go out and create more debt. For example, if we take the price levels of 1937 as equal to 100, the wholesale price index in France during the month of Marshall's Harvard speech was at 904. In January 1948, it was 1,463. The stabilization agreement with the ECA was worked out in the summer of 1948, but the wholesale price index kept rising. By September it was at 1,791.[17]

To put the matter another way, what little leverage the ECA could command in the use of counterpart was essentially dissipated if the funds were used for debt retirement. When they were devoted to production, it was at least possible for the ECA to argue about the relevance of the project or the size of the investment. But to insist on debt retirement as a priority goal was to choose, in effect, the alternative that was most likely to disarm the ECA in its relations with the local government.

Ironically, also, the effects often ran counter to the conservative impulses that inspired these stabilization measures. Largely as a result of the wartime bombings, for example, housing represented one of the most critical shortages in Europe. In Britain, the damage to residential housing was considerably more extensive than the destruction in industrial buildings. Any anti-inflationary program, then, had to give a central place to rent controls. But rent controls, in turn, tended to discourage private builders from undertaking the new construction in housing that was sorely needed. Four hundred seventy thousand houses had been destroyed through enemy action, and as late as 1949, a half-million houses had been classified as unfit for habitation. Since private developers were not responding to the need, the Labour government began its own construction program. Thomas Finletter, the chief of the ECA mission in Britain, reported back to the Senate Foreign Relations Committee that the permanent houses built under public authority represented 83

[17] ECA, *Second Report* (Quarter ending September 30, 1948), Appendix B, p. 136. Taking a later ECA index that used 1948 prices as the base, the wholesale price index in France was 104 in September 1948, and after a brief period of stabilization in early 1949, it rose to 152 by June 1951. See ECA, *Thirteenth Report* (Quarter ending June 30, 1951), Appendix A, p. 104.

percent of new construction in 1948.[18] It was not a figure that was particularly relished by the committee, but the members seemed to understand that it was a situation they would have to live with as long as they remained committed to their own policy premises.

II

The dominant facts of life for the ECA were those expressed in the themes of "a cure rather than a . . . palliative" and debureaucratization. The goal was to bring about a radical improvement in Europe's balance of payments situation, and do it with an organization that was gradually curtailing its operations over four years. For those reasons, the ECA grew restive under any provisions added by Congress that were not really central to the recovery effort, but that nevertheless worked to consume scarce dollars and administrative resources. All things being equal, the ECA preferred to acquire goods and services in Europe rather than paying dollars and higher prices in the United States. At the same time, the fact that many of the ECA people knew that they were leaving the government within two or three years made them that much less fearful of antagonizing any specific group that might have been out to exploit the program.

Of course, one could find numerous efforts to pawn off specific commodities on the ECA. There were times, quite often, when Hoffman's exchanges with the Senate Foreign Relations Committee sounded like a sales meeting. Senator Hickenlooper of Iowa expressed his apprehension to Hoffman one day that ECA was not as active as it might have been in promoting fats and oils. "I have the impression," he added, "that the purchasing agencies are not doing all they could to take up the surpluses."[19]

But incidents of this kind also disclosed the essential weakness of the farm "lobby," which was never as overbearing or effective as its publicity suggested. The demands were almost always fragmented. They came in the form of isolated requests to buy more of one commodity or another, much in the way that Hickenlooper's discussion with Hoffman eventually centered on fats and oils. Even if the demand was satisfied, no general rule emerged. If more flax-

[18] Senate Foreign Relations Committee, *Hearings on Extension of ERP*, 1949, p. 161.
[19] *Ibid.*, p. 63.

seed was bought, it did not necessarily indicate anything about a priority on barley. For that matter, it did not even suggest that more flaxseed would be bought in the following year. The fact that the pressure was so visible, and that it came chiefly from Congress, was merely another part of the weakness. Each demand required Congressional initiative; there was no persistent pressure coming from within the Executive, either from the ECA itself or from the Department of Agriculture.

The largest single commodity group in the ECA program on agriculture was grain, with bread and coarse grains ultimately accounting for over $2 billion. Yet, the head of the Grain Division in Agriculture at this time was a man named MacArthur, who happened to be a close personal friend of D. A. Fitzgerald, the head of the Agriculture Division in ECA. As a friend, MacArthur was not inclined to take advantage of his relationship with Fitzgerald for the sake of pushing one commodity or another on the ECA. Two incidents recalled by Fitzgerald probably give a more measured sense of the situation of agriculture in ERP. Fitzgerald remembered a call from MacArthur one day, telling him of some dried eggs that were available at a cut rate. A sizable dried eggs industry had been built up in the United States during the war, largely to supply Britain. On the thought that the British might still have their interest in this food, Fitzgerald decided to take the eggs. As it turned out, the British, too, recognized a good deal when they saw it, and the eggs proved useful.

In another incident, Fitzgerald and a member of the ECA Paris mission were summoned to Capitol Hill for a conference with several farm state Congressmen. There, as Fitzgerald recalled, they were surrounded by a few Senators and several Congressmen, all of whom had apparently come to the conviction that sorghum syrup was the key to European recovery. The domestic market for this product had fallen far short of expectations, and since it was an election year, the alarm was being conveyed to Washington with rather high fidelity. Fitzgerald pledged to do what he could, though he insisted, also, that he would not buy the product unless some of the ERP countries actually wanted it. Back at his office, he checked on the nations that had previously imported sorghum syrup and that might have been interested again. He then sent a circular out to the ECA missions and suggested that they mention to their respective governments that the product was available. It was not, however, to be pressed upon them. Eventually, the ECA did receive orders from Norway and Sweden, so in some small way it was able to help; but still, according to Fitzgerald's recollection, all the orders together came to little more than $10,000.

If we examine the cumulative figures through June 30, 1951, (see Table 5), we would find a significant drop-off in the magni-

TABLE 5. AUTHORIZED PROCUREMENT OF SURPLUS AGRICULTURAL COMMODITIES FROM UNITED STATES GOVERNMENT STOCKS AND DOMESTIC COMMERCIAL STOCKS APRIL 3, 1948 TO JUNE 30, 1951

Commodity	Procurement from Commercial and Government Stocks		Procurement from Government Stocks	
	Value (millions of dollars)	*Approximate quantity (thousands of metric tons)*	*Value (millions of dollars)*	*Approximate quantity (thousands of metric tons)*
Total	3,716.1	—	128.9	—
Cotton	1,437.8	1,811	—	—
Wheat and wheat flour	1,105.7	13,494	—	—
Tobacco	445.9	414	—	—
Corn	285.5	4,610	—	—
Grain sorghums	86.0	1,589	—	—
Cheese	65.2	79	—	—
Peanuts	57.0	195	49.8	174
Flaxseed	34.0	176	26.0	129
Oilcake and meal	30.3	450	—	—
Rye	23.2	300	—	—
Oats	21.4	342	—	—
Barley	19.1	290	—	—
Wool	12.5	9	12.5	9
Dried eggs	11.2	8	11.2	8
Dried beans and peas	10.1	62	—	—
Wood rosin	9.8	70	—	—
Dried whole milk	9.5	10	—	—
Linseed oil	8.1	16	6.8	14
Gum rosin	7.5	52	—	—
Raisins	7.1	62	3.7	26
Frozen eggs	7.0	18	7.0	18
Prunes	6.7	44	4.5	32
Gum turpentine	3.7	21	3.3	21
Nonfat milk solids	3.3	13	3.2	12
Wood turpentine	2.8	17	—	—
Pork	2.6	5	—	—
Tung oil	1.7	4	—	—
Hemp fiber	.7	2	.3	1
Flax fiber	.1	(b)	.1	(b)
Mohair	(a)	(b)	—	—

(a) Less than $50,000.
(b) Less than 500 metric tons.
SOURCE: ECA, *Thirteenth Report* (Quarter ending June 30, 1951), p. 94.

tude of purchases after the four leading commodities—cotton, wheat, tobacco, and corn. These were all major crops, and both the economic and political markets in the United States were highly sensitive to their fate. As one would expect, they were also the products that benefited from the most consistent attention in Congress. Wheat was mentioned in the legislation itself, and tobacco was inserted by indirection with the Barkley amendment. As for cotton, Fitzgerald was called before a Congressional committee at one time when the ECA threatened to buy a few hundred dollars worth of long-stapled cotton in Egypt. Congress played its role as advocate for these commodities with a vigor and persistence that was nearly embarrassing. In the end, the ECA did manage to buy the cotton in Egypt, but as Fitzgerald later observed, that could never have occurred on a significant scale or as a matter of regular practice. If the ECA had tried, he added after the shortest of reflections, "we would have had legislation."

But even without the political protection, these were the products with the greatest usefulness in the Marshall Plan, and they promised to be used in large quantities in almost any event. Cotton, after all, was the critical raw material for the European textile industry. Wheat and corn had become even more essential for basic food requirements with the contraction of supplies from Eastern Europe. Even tobacco was in heavy demand in Europe, and it would prove highly important as an incentive good. In short, it is difficult to argue that these products were, in any meaningful sense, foisted on the Europeans. Of course, France had regained her position of near self-sufficiency in bread grain, and production was generally on the rise, but domestic production as a percentage of supply was still below prewar levels in non-Communist Europe. In 1934-38, these nations produced 78 percent of their total needs in bread grain. In 1948-49, the comparable figure was 70 percent.[20] Moreover, there was not even any hope of saving dollars and lessening the dollar drain on the Europeans by purchasing wheat outside the United States. When the ECA was prevented from moving wheat out of the country in 1949 because of a maritime strike, the only place where the commodity was available in large enough quantities was in Canada. For Britain, Germany, Belgium–Luxembourg, Italy, and the Netherlands, only 363,000 tons of wheat could be obtained from nondollar Latin America in 1949. In con-

[20] United Nations, Department of Economic Affairs, *Economic Survey of Europe Since the War* (Geneva, 1953), Appendix A, p. 274.

trast 8,449,000 tons were supplied to them from the dollar area. While these countries were able to get 389,000 tons of wheat within Western Europe itself in 1934-38, they could procure only 8,000 tons in 1949.[21]

These major commodities were being supplied almost entirely from the United States. Out of a total expenditure on cotton that approached $1.5 billion, only $300,000 worth of orders slipped out of the United States. American cotton undoubtedly cut into the supplies from other areas, but a major consumer of raw cotton, such as Britain, was still getting the bulk of its cotton outside the dollar area.[22] At times, especially during the recession year of 1949, there was valuable political capital for the ECA in showing that 25 percent of the wheat, cotton, and tobacco produced in the United States was being purchased by Marshall Plan countries, or that the same nations were taking over 60 percent of American cotton exports.[23] In comparison with the first year, when, as Hoffman remarked, "we actually were taking it out of our hide to send abroad the wheat and the steel and other things in this economy when we had shortages," it was excellent salesmanship for him to point out in 1950 that one could "substantially complicate things in the American economy" by curtailing aid too quickly. "[L]ooking at this thing strictly as a business proposition," said Hoffman, "the withdrawal of aid from Europe any faster than we are now withdrawing would destroy our chance to rebuild in Europe a consumer of American goods."[24] When phrased in these terms, the leadership of the ECA could be rather blithe in taking credit for a situation they would have been quick to disclaim had someone been callous enough to point out that they were confirming the Communist line of attack on the Marshall Plan.

At the same time, this method of selling the program often concealed the effectiveness of the ECA in restricting the claims of special interests. As production revived in Europe, and the Europeans took steps to reduce their own expenses in the dollar area, they received some very strong support from the ECA in their efforts to cut back on purchases in the United States. Thus from the peak of $248.3 million in the third quarter of 1948, bread grains declined to $32.2 million by the third quarter of 1950. The legislation

[21] *Ibid.*, p. 284. [22] *Ibid.*, p. 294.
[23] ECA, *Seventh Report* (Quarter ending December 31, 1939), pp. 60-61.
[24] Senate Appropriations Committee, *Hearings on Foreign Aid Appropriation for 1951* (1950), p. 293.

263

had required that 25 percent of all wheat shipped out of the United States be in the form of flour. But since milling capacity in Europe was quite ample, the provision came to be seen by 1949 as an outright subsidy for American millers. When Hoffman succeeded in demonstrating that the subsidy added $8 million to the cost of the Marshall Plan, Congress found the argument for cancellation persuasive.[25]

With coal production increasing in Europe, American coal producers began to face rigid ECA quotas on American exports. The bituminous coal industry had come out of the war with its productive capacity built up to about 14 million tons. Instead of a post-war decline, domestic demand was sustained, while the foreign assistance program raised exports to Europe to a peak of 40 million tons in 1947. Around the beginning of the Marshall Plan, however, coal experts began to drop off, and the decline was deepened by lagging demand at home. As a recession developed in the United States, the industry found itself with excess production, and its argument now was that American coal could produce power, gas, and steam at a lower overall cost, although it was higher in price. In this way, it was contended, the costs of European recovery could be lowered, while the additional purchases in the United States could stimulate the industry. Daniel Buckley of the Coal Exporters' Association complained that the coal industry was not being given the consideration it deserved, despite the fact that he himself had had several interviews with heads of the various ECA divisions.[26] He insisted that an export quota of 1 million tons per month was one-half of what it should have been. And he was not beyond suggesting, finally, that the priority in the program should go to American coal.[27]

When matched by the resistance of the ECA, Vandenberg's own reaction conveyed the strength of the "cure rather than a palliative" theme:

[25] A compromise was finally accepted in which the requirement was halved to 12½ percent. In substance, the ECA had won its point. Under the new arrangement the millers would get little more than their traditional share of wheat exports, which usually ran from 5 to 10 percent. Roseman to Stow, "ECA recommendation regarding 25% wheat-flour provision (section 112 (c)) in Public Law 472," March 2, 1949, Bureau of the Budget, Series 39.18.

[26] Senate Foreign Relations Committee, *Hearings on Extension of ERP*, 1949, pp. 370, 376.

[27] See *ibid.*, pp. 375-76.

264

I quite agree that, *other things being equal,* American surpluses should be used, but I could never agree that we would be remotely faithful to the purposes of ECA, or even fair to the countries from whom we are demanding increased production, if we were arbitrarily to insist that the things they can produce they shall cease producing, and that that trade shall be transferred to our own domestic producers.[28]

In this view, the demands of the coal producers threatened a direct charge on the Marshall Plan that could only retard the pace of recovery. Thus, despite the recession and demands of the coal producers, the trend of coal exports continued downward. They accounted for $275.9 million during the first quarter of 1949, around the time Buckley testified. Two quarters later, the figure dropped to $2.9 million, and for a year and a half thereafter the ECA would finance no coal at all.

Although machine tools were in consistent demand throughout the Marshall Plan, the incident with the coal producers was replicated in this field as well. The machine tool industry was also plagued by the recession, and it was only natural that the National Machine Tool Builders Association would raise a protest in public when the ECA placed an order of $150 million for machine tools in Britain. Much the same arguments were used: on the one side the health and contributions of American industry; on the other the value of pumping funds into European production. The dispute was given a bit sharper point here, however, by the fact that American machine tools *were* cheaper, they *could* be delivered more quickly, and rather than preventing the encroachment of American firms, the order for Britain actually cut into a traditional American market. But even here, the accent on building European resources prevailed over the claims of an American group.[29]

What makes the case of the machine tool industry particularly worth mentioning is the fact that it displayed Hoffman's working assumptions about free trade and competition, and it showed how those assumptions were being used now to restrict the access of American groups to the trough of the Marshall Plan. The argument advanced by the machine tool industry rested on a view of a traditional American market that was currently under invasion. Instead

[28] *Ibid.,* p. 379, and see also p. 378. Emphasis added.
[29] See *ibid.,* pp. 469-77, especially p. 474.

of the Europeans "usurping a large part of the normal market of the American machine tool industry," spokesmen for the industry urged that a division of labor be worked out. Since the Americans could supply machine tools more efficiently, the argument ran, let the Americans take over this market while the Europeans concentrated on other products. The philosophy here was much closer to the older theories of free trade than to the modern views of comparative advantage. It smacked more of Richard Cobden and the Anti-Corn Law League than of Paul Hoffman and the ECA. To the old free traders, the division of labor would be worked out in gross portions. If Britain, for example, developed textiles, Germany would not compete in this line, but would turn to other products, preferably in a different category of production, such as agriculture. Following this plan, the world of commerce would be sectioned off into spheres of influence, nations would become ever more dependent on one another, and with interdependence would come peace. And this was not simply because nations would become too dependent to risk the disruptions of war, but because the irritant of economic competition would also be removed. The scheme was free trade and competition, but the underlying vision was still the liberal model of natural harmony.

Hoffman, however, was neither a classic liberal nor a modern social scientist with an enthusiasm for "conflict models." He saw nothing incompatible between an active, harmonious trade relationship and vigorous competition. To Hoffman competition was a general good. It tended to drive down costs and make producers more efficient; and with a more efficient productive base, output could be increased and the standard of living raised. For Hoffman, then, the tendency of competition was to expand the good things of life and distribute them more widely; and working from these convictions, he was more willing than others to accept competition on a broad variety of fronts. He saw no reason, for example, to restrict the British production of cars or harass their efforts to market them in the United States. There was always room for one more product, for there was always the possibility of creating a new market for a novel commodity. When a Congressional committee warned that he might be using American funds to modernize the competitors of American industry, Hoffman replied,

As far as I am concerned [the] more prosperous they are the better I like it because the better customers they will be, and all our

266

history shows that we have had our largest volume of trade with those nations which were our toughest competitors, and along with it, our biggest customers. . . .[30]

As Hoffman pointed out to the Senate committee, it would take something like fifteen years to modernize the British textile industry. But even if it were possible to modernize overnight, he thought the American textile manufacturers would "still have left the thing that gave them their great advantage, and that is their great resourcefulness." If machinery was equalized, then the issue, he was convinced, would turn on other factors, like plant layout, managerial practices, or marketing techniques. If Senator George could not dispel his anxieties for the textile industry, Hoffman could only repeat, with a nonchalance that must have been disconcerting: "Sir, I cannot tell you how little concerned I am about European competition." And when Senator Hickenlooper worried about the possible danger to the fine cutlery and fine steel industries in the United States, Hoffman fell back on the logic of the commitment to "a cure rather than a palliative":

> I would like to say this. It has been my assumption that it was the Administrator's job to take these dollars put up by the American taxpayer and invest them in European recovery so that for every dollar we will get the maximum recovery in Europe. That is the basic concept we have, and I [do not] think that if there are special situations in America where, as a result of unexpected success on our part, Europe becomes resurgent and becomes a danger, that you ought to protect those special situations and get them not to 'resurge.'[31]

We suggested earlier that the combination of two preferences—(1) giving full throttle to European recovery under the "cure rather than a palliative" theme, and (2) treating the problem of recovery in terms of the dollar theory and the balance of payments—would probably have to manifest itself in some operating rule that made the ECA more willing to accept disadvantages to American business in the short run. The behavior of the ECA toward outside groups would lend weight to this hypothesis. But Hoffman's testimony at various times before the Senate Foreign Relations Committee provides us with an explicit confirmation, which was often

[30] *Ibid.,* p. 421.   [31] *Ibid.,* p. 423.

cast in the language of operating presumptions. In one instance, he revealed in 1949 that the ECA was screening requests for the sake of dollar savings, but that it was giving no consideration to the possible effects of these exports in strengthening American competitors overseas.[32] Nor did he seem greatly troubled by the implication. As he had told the Senate committee earlier, "The stake in recovery in Europe is so great for every industry that whatever slight risk might be involved in a *temporary abdication* . . . of the market, it is not a matter of concern to me."[33]

When a controversy arose over the administration of the "50 percent provision" in shipping, Hoffman explained that the presumptions had been set in favor of reducing costs. The burden of justification was assigned then to anyone who would have raised costs in the program by favoring American industries:

> We do feel that *unless we are otherwise directed* we should try to buy everything . . . at the lowest possible price. We should not spend one dime we do not have to spend. . . .
>
> That means that if Congress for any reason . . . wants us to give particular support to any segment of the American economy, and thus make this somewhat of an American recovery program, all we ask is that we be given *very specific and direct instructions, because if you do not give us those instructions we are going to buy where we can buy at the lowest price.* If that is not the way you want the program run, *we want to be told that.*[34]

As a conservative estimate, the shipping provision cost the ECA an extra $10 million from April through December 1948. Using a more liberal estimate of the difference between American and foreign flag rates, the extra cost could have been as much as $25 million. The legislation said that American ships were to be used to the extent they were available at "market rates." If that could have been interpreted to mean *world* market rates, Hoffman could have had a legitimate basis for transferring more of the business to the Europeans. But what Hoffman now put before Congress—and he put the matter directly—was that Congress should tell him openly if it wanted him to pay four dollars more per ton in freight rates, or if it was positively in favor of subsidizing the shipping industry.[35]

[32] *Ibid.*, p. 430.
[33] *Ibid.*, p. 68. Emphasis added.
[34] *Ibid.*, p. 54. Emphasis added.
[35] See *ibid.*, p. 55.

If the Congress insisted on saddling the administrators with policies they considered unjustified, then it was told now that it would have to carry the burden of explicitness and responsibility in each case. Thus there could be no real doubt as to Hoffman's purpose in regard to the shipping provision.[36] The placing of the presumptions clearly marked the priorities being followed by the ECA. The only mistake was in underestimating how obdurate Congress could be— or even had to be—when challenged so overtly. Not only did Congress direct Hoffman to follow the American market rate instead of world market rates, but it extended the application of the 50 percent provision to cover each *class* of cargo. (The old provision referred only to gross tonnage.) Moreover, the ECA failed to anticipate the wrath of Congressman Bland when his pet project, the merchant marine, was assaulted so flippantly. Bland brought in an amendment to require 50 percent in American shipping for every single commodity, and for shipments to each ERP country. Although the amendment was softened, one of his proposals lingered: To make certain that the ECA would not be laggard in enforcing the shipping provision in the future, a special Congressional committee was formed to oversee this aspect of the program. Thereafter, the Transportation Division of the ECA had the unique distinction of being the only subunit of the agency that was followed by its own watchdog committee.

In most other matters, though, where Congress was not as closely engaged, the ECA was able to employ the device of shifting presumptions with considerable effect. In 1949, for example, Senator Wherry joined Wright Patman in sponsoring a bill to promote the

[36] It seems incredible, in the light of all the evidence available, that there are individuals today who contend that Hoffman definitely favored the shipping provision, and that he went before the Senate committee merely to get assurances that he could spend the money. The complaints directed at the shipping provision abound in the records. Hoffman's own testimony in 1949 indicates that he did not credit the view that the subsidy was essential to the life of the merchant marine. (See *ibid.*, p. 54.) A Budget Bureau report at this time reveals that some estimates put the cost of the shipping provision as high as $50 million. Carrol Hinman of the Budget Bureau reported: "ECA officials appreciate fully the extra cost and economic undesirability of the 50-50 shipping provision. Their reluctance to suggest any change is due solely to a tactical judgment that it would be difficult to get the restriction liberalized. They feel that the chief danger is that it may be made more severe, that the best they can hope for is to hold the present line. . . ." Carrol Hinman, "Comment on Changes in ERP Authorizing Legislation as Proposed by ECA," Bureau of the Budget, January 25, 1949, *loc.cit.*

269

participation of small business in the Marshall Plan. The reaction within the Administration was rather cynical, and to the ECA it presented just another way of tying down administrative resources that could be used to better purpose elsewhere.[37] It was found, however, that the agency could avoid using up more than seven full-time positions if it made good use of voluntary help and restricted the program to an information service. The ECA enlisted the aid of private bankers, who would act as voluntary "counselors" for small businessmen interested in entering the export field. In addition, a regular contingent of ECA people would travel from city to city, recruiting counselors and holding its own counseling sessions.

On the surface, the ECA seemed to be in the throes of a feverish effort to whip up sales for small business. It could point to stacks of pamphlets and circulars, and even its critics were somewhat diffident in charging that the ECA was not really sincere. But the crux of the matter was that all the burdens in the program were being shifted to the potential applicant. One simply did not jump into export sales, after all; one had to make connections first with export agents and foreign importers. The newcomer encountered a formidable mass of government export regulations and customs procedures, which often proved discouraging, and in many cases the expenses involved in brokerage and legal services were prohibitive. It was unrealistic to expect much of a response unless the ECA was willing to relieve these businessmen of the inconveniences and actually provide them with minute counseling all along the way. The design of the ECA program, however, was quite to the contrary. The businessmen were not sent the information; it was their task to seek it out, and what they were likely to receive when they contacted the ECA was a host of literature that warned them against making the effort. One principal pamphlet, "The ECA and Small

[37] See Rupley to Garber, December 2, 1949, Bureau of the Budget, *loc.cit.* The author commented: "Every so often the vague, but nevertheless potent, symbol known as 'small business' is taken out from the attic and given a whirl on the merry-go-round. In the war years it rode under its own colors with Maurey Maverick at the wheel; subsequently the [Bureau of Foreign and Domestic Commerce] was saddled with the old girl and as a result had to pay a pretty heavy price in the way of lost face with chambers of commerce, manufacturers' associations and business people generally, not to mention a good section of the Congress. Now, it is the ECA which is the one which gets hooked. . . . [T]he ECA people know that it is just a lot of hogwash. . . ."

Business," which was circulated widely, admonished the business-man that "selling to ECA countries for payment in ECA dollars is *not* simple." Before entering the market the businessman was asked to decide several questions for himself, which presented an almost insuperable task for anyone who was not experienced in the export market. The businessman was told to decide that his product was "essential to the ECA countries *under existing conditions* [italics in original]"—that there was a market for his product, that the product was "desirable from every angle—performance . . . price . . . quality . . . delivery . . . repair and service facilities abroad . . . spare parts stocked abroad . . . [and finally, that one's] manufac-turing capacity or source of supply justifies the seeking of export outlets."

It was hard to avoid the impression that the ECA was trying to discourage applicants, and the agency itself did nothing to dispel these suspicions when it stalled on the counseling program. It was over a year before the ECA disclosed the identity of the volunteer counselors to the local offices of the Commerce Department. When a roster was eventually sent to Dallas, for example, it was marked "Restricted," with the result that the Commerce field office was prevented from divulging the information. Commerce complained that it was receiving about 100,000 inquiries per month, but it had no information to dispense, and the ECA was apparently doing nothing to follow through.[38] Before long, these complaints were taken up by Budget Bureau field offices in the West and Midwest, and as they accumulated in Washington, the charges of negligence were beginning to raise suspicions of something more studied and deliberate. A request went up in the Budget Bureau for a formal meeting to determine just exactly what the ECA was up to. A meet-ing was finally held, but the ECA simply pointed to its faultless record in mailing circulars. And who, faced with that record, was prepared to press the matter?[39]

Confined by the tautness of their own administrative resources, and yet responsible at the same time for producing dramatic results in European recovery, the administrators at the ECA were develop-

[38] Mitchell to Garber, March 1, 1950; Bozman to Schwartz, February 15, 1950; Givson to Garber, January 27, 1950; Mitchell to Garber, January 16, 1950; Rupley to Garber, January 24, 1950; Bureau of the Budget, *loc.cit.*

[39] Pillsbury to Finan, March 14, 1950; Pillsbury to Lawson, May 10, 1950; Bureau of the Budget, *loc.cit.*

ing their own subtle defenses. By rearranging their operating presumptions they could ward off the Congressional attempts to bog them down in special interest projects. Where Congress left them room, they could also choke off the capacity of American groups to exploit the program for their own ends. Admittedly, something was bound to be lost in the process. When the ECA leadership stacked the presumptions against self-regarding interests, they could also shut themselves off from an assortment of claims and arguments that they might have done well to consider more thoughtfully. But in the press of their own administrative time, they could devote that much more of their resources to a thorough recovery of trade and production in Europe. If that seemed to be a case then of aligning priorities to serve the pluralist ideal, it was not wholly an act of altruism. It happened also to be the best strategy this somewhat harried agency could afford.

13. THE IMPERFECT INTERVENTIONIST

I

THE ECA was the despair of those people who were most apprehensive in their concern for American self-interest. To the former isolationists, foreign adventures always threatened to ignite that old strain of American utopianism; every involvement abroad carried the risk of losing that valuable sense of limitations, and that sober regard for the requirements of national strength. After the experience with the UNRRA, there was virtually no support in Congress for a program of foreign aid without conditions or reciprocal obligations. Marshall was taken quite seriously when he promised that the program would not be another dole, and that proved to be a critical selling point among the conservatives in Congress. But still, there were others in Congress who were far more vigorous in asserting American interests, and who were not content to stop with the assignment of minimal conditions. For them, the huge outlay in American resources provided some justification for the United States in laying down the law to the Europeans and dictating terms on a take-it-or-leave-it basis.

And with Congress acting upon the ECA authorization every year, the law could be laid down with a tiring frequency. Amendments were introduced at various times to create a timetable for European political integration, to cut off all aid to countries that continued to nationalize basic industries, and to refuse funds to countries whose dependent territories discriminated against American business.[1] But with every amendment to tighten up on the Europeans, the ECA and the Administration would launch a rearguard action that would usually eliminate the amendment, either in committee or in conference. When an amendment passed, the ECA would often circumvent it by putting the presumptions on the

[1] William Adams Brown, Jr., and Redvers Opie, *American Foreign Assistance* (Washington: The Brookings Institution, 1953), pp. 164-65.

side of the Marshall Plan nations. Faced with the practical task of administering the program, the heads of ECA could not afford to be as casual in ordering the termination of aid. In the short time they had they were not going to disrupt the program on impulse, and in taking this line of argument, they could contend, quite legitimately, that they were being faithful to values that were part of the program from the very beginning, but which the Congress was now tending to neglect. Thus, when doubts arose, they were willing to presume in favor of the ERP nations and take their chances.

The British, for example, had refused to join the Coal and Steel Community, and they were the single most important source of obstruction in the efforts to construct a broader system of multilateral payments. They went out of their way to cultivate trading relations with Russia, Czechoslovakia, and other Eastern European countries. They concluded a bilateral agreement with Argentina that Hoffman reportedly condemned as "the kind of bilateralism which we are trying to do away with."[2] If anyone had demonstrated the kind of behavior that called for the termination of assistance, it surely might have been the British. Yet they were the most important American ally and the country whose difficulties had done the most to inspire the Marshall Plan. Privately, the ECA could remonstrate; publicly, it could only hope that the frictions, as well as the tendencies toward bilateralism, would begin to disappear with the advent of the European Payments Union.

This was a good example, in fact, of a general ECA adjustment in operating priorities. The threat of terminating aid was too blunt a weapon for coercing the Europeans into closer forms of cooperation. What the ECA did instead was to put its weight behind the movement toward supranational institutions. When the Coal and Steel Community emerged as a European initiative, the ECA intervened very quickly to press for its adoption. After his speech to the OEEC in October 1949, Hoffman made it clear that the formation of the European Payments Union would be taken as evidence of the commitment of the Europeans to the goal of integration. Institutions seemed to represent something permanent and solid. They represented the kind of concrete achievements that Congress seemed to appreciate, but beyond that they could become the great hope of the Marshall Plan: What the ECA could not accomplish in its own short life in such problem areas as trade liberalization

[2] House Subcommittee on Appropriations, *Hearings on Foreign Aid Appropriation for 1951* (1950), p. 351.

might be achieved in the long run by the institutions it left behind. Thus, for example, although the ECA induced the Europeans to lower their trade quotas 50 percent by the spring of 1950, the results in the short run were still disappointing. The rules applied only to imports from other OEEC countries. They depended, therefore, on the proportion of foreign trade in any country that was tied up in European trade. For Belgium, Ireland, and Switzerland, the liberalization policy removed quotas on 40 percent of their total imports by the spring of 1950. But at the same time, the comparable figure for Britain and France was only 10 percent. In terms of their signficance for the entire national economy, the liberalized imports accounted for 12 percent of Belgium's gross national product, as opposed to 2 percent for Britain, Ireland, and Italy.[3] However, there was some evidence that the liberalization did tend to increase trade. Germany and Denmark increased their imports, while France and Italy attributed a rise of exports to the removal of the quotas. The OEEC claimed that the rate of trade accelerated in 1950, whereas all the expectations were in favor of a slowdown. The actual rate of increase in intra-European trade was about 60 percent above the increase registered in 1949.[4] There were good reasons to believe, then, that the creation of institutions in Western Europe would do more to achieve the long range goals of the ECA than anything it might accomplish in the short run by means of coercion.

In an earlier chapter we recounted the practical difficulties that the ECA faced in applying restrictions on exports to the Marshall Plan countries for goods that threatened to find their way into the Soviet sphere. Even apart from the problems involved in inspecting deliveries, the ECA had a natural interest in raising production in Europe, and it was understandably reluctant to restrict the shipment of any material unless the case for embargo was unexceptionable. It was not so surprising, in that case, that it took the Korean war and the demands of an agitated Congress before the ECA could be prodded into a tougher course of action on the shipment of strategic material.[5] With a stiff enforcement policy, American exports

[3] William Diebold, Jr., *Trade and Payments in Western Europe* (New York: Harper and Brothers, 1952), pp. 88-89, 182.

[4] *Ibid.*, p. 184.

[5] The definition of strategic material could also produce some petty aggravations for the ECA. David Mayer of AID, who was then in the Nether-

to Eastern Europe were almost completely eliminated by 1951. But within the context of a more severe export control, it was significant that the ECA and the Administration were still able to resist the Congressional pressures to force the same policy on the Europeans. The difference in the two policies may be seen in Table 6. For

TABLE 6. Exports of Western Europe and the United States to Eastern Europe (Millions of dollars at 1948 prices, f.o.b.)

Exporting Country or Area	Year	Machinery	Other Manufac- turers	Total All Products
Prewar Germany	1938	145.4	343.4	569.6
Western Germany	1951	17.6	44.9	73.3
Other Western Europe a	1938	96.2	314.1	719.2
	1951 b	166.9	184.2	535.8
United States	1938	82.8	89.9	251.0
	1951	0.3	0.5	2.3

a Belgium–Luxembourg, Denmark, Finland, France, Italy, the Netherlands, Norway, Sweden, Switzerland, and the United Kingdom.
b Reparation deliveries by Finland to the U.S.S.R. are excluded.
SOURCE: UN, *Economic Survey of Europe Since the War*, p. 111.

Western Europe apart from Germany, the total value of exports to Eastern Europe did decline, but neither in relative nor absolute terms was the drop equal to that of American exports. In the category of machinery, in fact, there was an actual increase in exports from Western Europe over prewar.

In a concealed way, the same orientation of the ECA was at work on the matter of oil. To conserve American supplies, the legislation advised the Administrator to procure as much oil as he could outside the United States, and to discourage the expansion of demand for oil in the participating countries. The presumption in favor of offshore purchase was clear, and it seemed easy enough

---

lands, recalled that the Dutch wanted to peg their definition of strategic materials to several "horizons," depending on when the United States estimated that war was likely to break out. If the war was expected within a year or two, they would not ship rifles to Eastern Europe, but they would continue to send research material, such as graph-making equipment. If the war was expected in ten years, they would not send the research equipment, but they would send the rifles, since the rifles would be obsolete by the time the war came. Incidents like these continually raised the question of the kinds of tools available to an agency like the ECA when a clientele nation insisted on complicating the issue, perhaps tendentiously, perhaps not.

to fulfill. By the end of June 1951, the ECA had allowed only $310.5 million to be spent on the procurement of American oil, which was less than one-quarter of the total value of petroleum or petroleum products financed by the Marshall Plan.[6] Moreover, the imports of oil into Western Europe from the dollar area dropped from 11.3 million tons in 1938 to 7.4 million in 1951. Concomitantly, supplies from the overseas sterling area increased from 3.9 million tons in 1938 to 5.3 million in 1948 and 27.5 million in 1951 (see Table 7). Nevertheless, this apparently healthy trend did

TABLE 7. IMPORTS OF PETROLEUM PRODUCTS BY SELECTED WESTERN EUROPEAN COUNTRIES[a]. (Millions of tons [crude equivalent])[b]

Area of Origin	Year	Crude Petroleum	Refined Petroleum	Total
Dollar area	1938	5.7	5.6	11.3
	1948	2.8	4.2	7.0
	1951	3.3	4.1	7.4
Overseas sterling area	1938	3.9	1.0	4.9
	1948	5.3	1.7	7.0
	1951	27.5	1.4	28.9
Dependent overseas territories	1938	0.8	6.1	6.9
	1948	1.2	7.9	9.1
	1951	1.1	5.0	6.1
Other overseas areas	1938	0.2	3.3	3.5
	1948	5.2	5.4	10.6
	1951	18.2	2.5	20.7
Eastern Europe	1938	0.1	2.3	2.4
	1948	—	0.2	0.2
	1951	—	—	—
Total from outside Western Europe	1938	10.7	18.3	29.0
	1948	14.5	19.4	33.9
	1951	50.1	13.0	63.1
Western Europe	1938	0.1	0.4	0.5
	1948	—	0.2	0.2
	1951	—	1.7	1.7
Not allocated	1938	1.1	0.4	1.5
	1948	0.9	0.7	1.6
	1951	1.0	0.9	1.9
Total imports from all sources	1938	11.9	19.1	31.0
	1948	15.4	20.3	35.7
	1951	51.1	15.6	66.7

a France, Western Germany (whole of Germany for 1938), Italy, the Netherlands, Switzerland, and the United Kingdom.
b Refined petroleum converted into crude equivalent on the basis of 1 ton of refined oil for 1.11 tons of crude oil.
SOURCE: UN, *Economic Survey of Europe Since The War*, p. 91.

6 ECA, *Thirteenth Report*, Appendix B, p. 109.

277

not achieve the original purpose of lowering dollar costs. The reason was that the production of oil in the non-dollar areas was controlled by a network of international companies. The most important of them were under American ownership, and notwithstanding their location, they demanded dollars in repayment. Even where the ownership was not American, and might instead be under British or Dutch auspices, the transactions still required a sizable expenditure of dollars, mainly because of the need to pay royalties, buy equipment, or hire tankers in the United States.[7] Thus the UN Economic Survey could report in 1953 that "petroleum has become the largest single element in Western Europe's total dollar disbursements."

The fact hidden by the surface figures on offshore procurement was that the ECA had done little in the way of following the statutory directions to discourage the use of oil. In 1951, Britain and France together accounted for almost two-thirds of the increase of oil imports into Western Europe since 1938. Much of this result, of course, was out of the hands of the ECA. The enlarged importation of crude oil, for example, was directly related to the expansion of refining capacity in Western Europe, which rose from 19 million tons in 1938 to 24 million tons by the end of 1948.[8] Still, it was rather curious that out of some $29 million in guarantees issued by the ECA for private investment in industry, $19 million was allocated to oil refining in Italy.[9] The example of Germany had already demonstrated that one could run a modern industrial system without such a heavy reliance on liquid fuels. In 1951, the inland consumption of petroleum in Germany came to 4.3 million tons, compared to 10.6 million for France, and 17.2 million for Britain.[10] But the German emphasis on indigenous sources of fuel was also

----

[7] In fact, a spokesman for a group of small American oil companies charged that the provision for offshore purchase of oil had turned out to be nothing more than an indirect subsidy for the seven largest American oil firms. See the testimony of L. Dan Jones, representing the Independent Petroleum Association of America, in Senate Foreign Relations Committee, *Hearings on Extension of ERP*, 1949, pp. 461-69. For a rather good picture of how this situation continued to baffle the Senate Foreign Relations Committee see *Hearings on Extension of ERP*, 1950, pp. 48-70.

[8] UN, *Economic Survey of Europe Since the War* (Geneva, 1953), pp. 90-92.

[9] ECA, *Thirteenth Report* (Quarter ending June 30, 1951), Appendix B, p. 122.

[10] UN Survey, *op.cit.*, p. 91n.

278

part of a more traditional policy of autarchy, which the ECA was flatly unwilling to accept. The commitment of the Marshall Plan was to integrate Western Europe and enlarge the volume of transactions among the member states. If the choice was between modernization and dependence on outside fuel sources on the one hand, as against dollar savings and less dependence on the other, then the ECA did not hesitate in choosing modernization.[11]

One of the most notable cases in which the ECA was caught shifting the presumptions to favor the ERP countries arose on the very important matter of acquiring strategic materials. Aside from the goal of getting nondiscriminatory access to scarce materials for American industry, the ECA had two principal statutory assignments. First, it could arrange for the transfer of scarce materials to the United States for stockpiling or other purposes, either in exchange for goods, or as a form of repayment on loans. Second, it could promote the production of scarce materials through development grants or loans.

The ECA was already encountering a host of problems in its efforts to lure private investment into the field of strategic materials development. The problem of convincing the member nations themselves to develop or deliver these materials was far trickier, and the ECA found the task even more uncongenial. Fortunately, the legislation seemed to offer an escape. Section 115 (b)(5) called for the transfer of materials, but only "after due regard for reasonable requirements for domestic use and commercial export of such country." We conjectured earlier that the pluralist bent of the ECA would have inclined it to make use of this provision and take a more permissive line in enforcing the obligation to deliver materials. And that is essentially what occurred. C. Tyler Wood, the Administrator for Operations in ECA, justified the position of his agency in what seemed to be an elaborated echo of the legislation:

[11] The ECA admitted in 1950 that it had financed automotive equipment, which included trucks, busses, tractors, Diesel engines, and some other mobile equipment used in construction work and mining. "The use of such equipment," the agency acknowledged, "contributes to expansion in petroleum consumption." But it added, without apology, that "in screening and financing these items the ECA recognizes that their use is necessary for increasing production and productivity in the participating countries. The use of alternative fuels in such equipment is, in our opinion, not satisfactory." Economic Cooperation Administration, *A Checklist of Operations* (Washington: Government Printing Office, 1950), p. 24.

We have adopted what seemed to us a sensible position, which is that it is not sound to pull toward this country a very large quantity of strategic materials if, at the same time, in order to carry on European recovery, those same materials might have to be produced and procured in the United States and shipped to Europe for use in factories there.[12]

Deputy Administrator Bruce announced at the end of the first year that the ECA had purchased about $23 million worth of strategic materials, but that it was still in the process of negotiating on the other issues, i.e., development projects and the schedules of minimum availabilities.[13] However, in March 1949, a report was issued by the Congressional watchdog committee, charging that the ECA was purposely dragging its feet on the strategic materials program.[14] The committee found that an initial sum of $25 million had been set aside for the promotion of production in strategic materials, but after a year of operation the fund had never been used. In addition to that, the ECA had already announced that it was not going to ask for repayment of loans, either in whole or in part, by the transfer of strategic materials. The arrangement had been given "careful consideration," Hoffman wrote to Styles Bridges, when the latter was still head of the Joint Congressional Committee, but "the provision was strongly opposed by some of the participating countries."[15] And finally, for the same reason, the agency had held back from negotiating a minimum schedule of availabilities.

[12] House Subcommittee on Appropriations, *Hearings on Foreign Aid Appropriation for 1951* (1950), p. 382.

[13] Senate Foreign Relations Committee, *Hearings on Extension of ERP*, 1949, p. 333.

[14] Space does not permit us to do full justice to the committee report, which was surely one of the most thoughtful and devastating critiques of ECA performance. The report traced the development of the national strategic materials program through fourteen statutes to a level of complexity and importance that ultimately involved the work of sixteen separate agencies. Thus the committee sought to establish at the outset that the strategic materials program represented a matured national interest and not something that was simply appended to the Marshall Plan as an impulse of the moment. See U.S. Congress, Joint Committee on Foreign Economic Cooperation, 81st Congress, 1st Session, Senate Report No. 140, *ECA and Strategic Materials*, March 1949. Cited hereafter as Joint Committee on Foreign Economic Cooperation, *ECA and Strategic Materials*, 1949. The report was delivered by Senator McCarran as head of the committee, but it was apparently written by Charles Dewey, who was the principal staff aide to the committee.

[15] Hoffman also argued that "since any material delivered to the United

The Joint Committee declared that the leaders of the ECA had "staged a complete retreat from the position originally taken by the executive branch," and they had done it in large part by shifting the presumptions on three important points of policy interpretation. First, the ECA was allowed to retain 5 percent of the local counterpart funds in any country for administrative expenses, and it was authorized in the legislation to make use of that fund in acquiring strategic materials. However, the ECA had interpreted the legislation to say that the 5 percent figure was a *ceiling,* and on that premise it claimed to limit the dimensions of the program. But as the committee observed, the legislation had said "not less than 5 percent." There was nothing preventing the ECA from using the authority it already had in the release of counterpart funds to negotiate for a larger outlay on strategic materials.[16]

Second, the ECA confined its demands to those materials in which the ERP nations, collectively, had a net surplus, and which were part of their traditional exports to the United States. Howard Bruce wrote to the Joint Committee staff:

We doubt if Congress intended that the United States Government should endeavor to secure for the benefit of American industry an agreement to supply an agreed percentage or absolute quantity of a material produced by any one of the participating countries if no part of such production normally flows to the United States and if the European economy is itself a net claimant on the world supply.[17]

States under the loan agreement would be in lieu of dollars, the inclusion of such a provision would not result in any saving in dollars to the United States government." But as the committee pointed out, that argument rested on the assumption that the debtor country would have dollars available for repayment on the due date. Either that was true or it was not. If it was not, then the loan would have to be extended. Meanwhile, "the failure to provide for payment of loans in strategic materials may result in the recovery of neither materials nor dollars." *Ibid.,* p. 34.

[16] Whether the committee knew it or not, Secretary Forrestal had made the same argument to the ECA a few months earlier, when the ECA had solicited his suggestions for changes in the legislation. The materials most needed by the United States were available in adequate quantities only in the dependent territories of Britain and the Netherlands. But aid to these countries had not been generating a significant amount of counterpart funds for use in strategic materials development. The choices, then, were to expand the amount of counterpart available or to get a more flexible arrangement that could permit the use of counterpart outside the host country. See Forrestal to Hoffman, December 1948, Bureau of the Budget, Series 39.18.

[17] Bruce letter to Charles Dewey, reproduced in the appendix of the

Part II

The difficulties here were somewhat similar to those of historians and political scientists today in identifying "traditional" political systems. It was not clear where the tradition began, or which tradition was relevant. The sources of supply in these strategic materials were constantly changing. The United States had been an exporter of copper before the war, but now it was a larger importer. Also, a nation could be a net claimant on strategic materials for reasons other than the lack of materials. Low production could be attributed to the high costs of shipping from overseas territories to processing plants in the mother country. Or, as the committee suggested, it might have been easier for these countries to spare themselves from the effort of attacking the problem and simply "claim dollars from us [while they left] their own ores and concentrates in the ground." In August 1948, the Secretary of the Interior had warned the ECA that the previous patterns of international trade might reflect only the "conditions existing at that time, and that a sounder method of determining mineral availabilities would be on a basis of each country's mineral *potentialities*."[18] Thus the committee was forced to reject the contention that there was any such thing as a "normal" market in these goods. By holding to that concept, it argued, the ECA was merely reconciling itself to the preservation of the status quo.

Third, the committee discovered that the ECA had turned all the presumptions in the fact-finding process to serve the preference for delay in constructing a schedule of availabilities. Under the procedures evolved by the ECA, all a nation had to do was object to a proposed schedule of materials, and that was enough to stall the whole venture in a rambling fact-finding mission. A team of geologists would be appointed to make a survey, and no action would be taken until conclusive evidence had been presented on each point of a rather lengthy program of investigation. Before a schedule could be worked out, information would have to be collected to satisfy all these tests:

1. A determination of *all* principal world sources
2. For each material and each country, the assembly of the following information as completely as possible—

committee report. Joint Committee on Foreign Economic Cooperation, *ECA and Strategic Materials*, 1949, pp. 55-56.

[18] Quoted in *ibid.*, p. 37. Emphasis added.

a. Undeveloped reserves
b. Present capacity for exploitation of reserves
c. Present production
d. Present internal consumption
e. Present exports and destinations
f. Present imports and sources
g. Analysis of bottlenecks, limitations, and unusual circumstances
h. Present quantity available for United States stockpile
i. Quantity available for United States stockpile assuming development of reserves
3. The grouping of sources into ECA and non-ECA countries
4. A breakdown of United States stockpile objectives into allocation between ECA and non-ECA countries
5. A breakdown of the ECA portion into fair allocation by countries[19]

As the committee noted, "all of this information is to be gathered and analyzed antecedent to the opening of negotiations. When, if ever . . . these proposed negotiations can reach the closing stage is not apparent." What was especially revealing in this shift of presumptions was that the ECA had required no such detailed information as a basis for piping billions of dollars of Marshall aid into Europe in a relatively short period of time. As the committee recalled, the ECA itself had acted on nothing more than rough estimates—later described as "shopping lists"—but once, in a space of two weeks, it had authorized grants totaling over $58 million. The committee observed rather caustically that "the lack of speed with which ECA has operated and its insistence upon precise and comprehensive data with respect to strategic materials are in sharp contrast with its activity as a disbursing agency."[20] If shopping lists were good enough for the Europeans, the committee reasoned, they were good enough for the United States; and with this thorough reprimand the committee instructed the ECA to get on with the job of collecting these strategic materials.

In the period following the report of the watchdog committee, the ECA demonstrated how operating presumptions could be quickly reversed with a simple change in the organizational struc-

[19] *Ibid.* It took the ECA until October 1948 merely to negotiate this program to govern the fact-finding process.
[20] *Ibid.*

ture of decisions. In ordinary technical assistance projects, an engineering report had to make its way through the ECA channels by starting in the local mission. There it would attract criticisms and comments, which in turn would impel further discussions before a decision was finally reached in Washington. But contracts for development projects were now exempted from this procedure. The ECA removed the requirement of initial screening by the country mission, and instead, the engineering report was sent directly to Washington for the approval of the Materials Development Division. The Budget Bureau survey in 1951 disclosed that approval in Washington was virtually automatic if the engineering report was at all favorable.[21] Thus the ECA showed that it knew how to rearrange both its presumptions and its organizational structure when it became imperative for certain things to be done more quickly. It is perilous, of course, to attribute precise causes when there are so many variables at work. But the graph of project approvals shows a striking change in the record of the ECA, which just happens to coincide with the report of the watchdog committee and the change of working presumptions in the ECA (see Figure 2). In Fiscal 1949, the ECA committed only $622,000 to strategic material projects, but within the first six months of the year beginning July 1, 1949, it spent almost $5.5 million.[22]

FIGURE 2. STRATEGIC MATERIALS DEVELOPMENT PROJECTS CUMULATIVE COMMITMENTS, APRIL 3, 1948 - JUNE 30, 1951 (Millions of dollars and dollar equivalents)

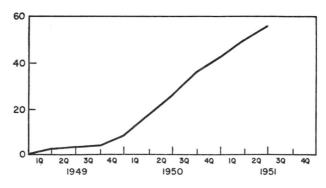

SOURCE: ECA, *Thirteenth Report* (Quarter ending June 30, 1951), p. 87.

[21] Bureau of the Budget, *Survey of the ECA*, 1951, p. 44, Series 39.32.
[22] See House Subcommittee on Appropriations, *Hearings on Foreign Aid*

284

On the most important matters of self-regarding interests, then, the tendency of the ECA was to turn the presumptions to the benefit of the ERP countries, and therefore to subordinate the more narrow conceptions of American self-interest. In the case of strategic materials, it required a very astute Congressional staff and a trenchant written report before the ECA could be made to change its direction.

II

If it was meaningful at any time to speak of ECA intervention, it seems generally agreed that it was more likely to occur in instances where the ECA had the choice of financing specific projects.[23] Brown and Opie have suggested further—and the suggestion would seem to make sense—that the United States had the greatest opportunity to affect investment decisions in those cases where the ECA was committing dollars of its own, rather than merely agreeing to the release of counterpart funds. Where it was spending its own dollars, the ECA could choose to support projects that were closer to its own ideals for the program, i.e., basic investment, and perhaps projects with a transnational character, like the Austro-German hydroelectric power plant in Braunau, Austria.[24] Here again, ECA dollars could enter at a strategic place and support contributions to the European economy that were many times the size of the American expenditure. Even if we disregard the more extended value of these projects for the economy, the ratio of the overall worth of the investment projects to the actual expenditures of the ECA was still impressive. By June 1951, the ECA had obligated $565 million of its own funds, and it was supporting projects

Appropriations for 1951 (1950), pp. 377-78. Out of the $6 million committed from July 1948 to December 1949, $3.6 million was allocated to France and $2.1 million to Britain. In terms of commodities, the largest single expense was for lead and zinc ($3.9 million). The program was subsequently expanded to include bauxite, chrome, and diamonds among the materials attracting the larger investments.

[23] See, for example, Brown and Opie, *op.cit.*, p. 237. This view was supported also by Glenn Craig, the director of the Industry Division of the ECA in 1951. Bureau of the Budget, "Interviews in Survey of ECA" (Interview with Craig, June 8, 1951), Series 39.32.

[24] See ECA, *Thirteenth Report* (Quarter ending June 30, 1951), Appendix B, p. 121.

totaling about four times the value, or $2.25 billion. By project type, the largest allocations went to manufacturing ($1.348 billion), and to a combined group for transportation, communications and utilities ($550.7 million).[25]

But the thesis that American intervention enjoyed its greatest advantage in this area of financing suffers from many ambiguities. From what one can gather in interviews and from comments scattered through the files of the Budget Bureau, the choice of whether to charge a project to counterpart funds or the ECA dollar account was often a budgetary exercise. Apparently, there was nothing that fundamentally distinguished the projects under the two accounts, apart from the fact that one project might have required equipment from the dollar area. And even in that case, if the United States refused to underwrite the sale, the recipient country could buy the materials anyway with the dollars in its own reserve. The Austro-German power plant was still the only "international" project that the ECA could cite in its final quarterly report, and the projects supported with counterpart funds showed no less of an accent on basic productive investment (see Table 8). Moreover, the projects were usually designed within the recipient country, so the ECA did not find itself at liberty to plunge in, take over the projects, and rework them.

The very fact that the American contribution was at the margins might be an indication of the relative bargaining power that the United States was able to muster in these decisions. Thus, for example, in terms of the total value of projects aided by ECA dollars, France would seem to have been the prime beneficiary. But as Table 9 shows, the ECA contributed only $148.4 million, or approximately one-fifth of the French total of $751.1 million in industrial projects. In Britain, where the projects totaled $421.4 million, the Marshall Plan contribution was less than one-eighth. The largest portion of ECA financing in a sizable program occurred in the Netherlands, where the ECA allocated $170.9 million to projects estimated at $435.6 million. But if that gave the United States any greater capacity for intervention, it was not apparent to the people in the ECA mission at The Hague. Despite some occasional departures, the Dutch were still maintaining their extensive controls on economy, and that alone made it far more difficult for

[25] *Ibid.*, pp. 53-54, and Appendix B, p. 120.

outsiders to intervene. Under the German occupation, the major segments of the economy were formed into syndicates and incorporated into the familiar Nazi organizational net. With the passing of the war, the decision was made, however, to keep these organizations rather than dismantle them. Both industry and government found some advantages in working through this rationalized structure, which offered a convenient mixture of private ownership and public guidance. The problem for the ECA, though, was that the public and private sectors were locked together too conveniently, and the total bureaucratic complex was simply too formidable to penetrate. Where it was able to nudge the Dutch government into more adventurous policies, it was with the help of guaranty funds for venture capital, or through the encouragement of licensing arrangements with American firms. But industrial projects did not provide an avenue for significant American intervention, and as one member of the ECA mission observed, that was even truer when the American agency, like all the other ECA missions abroad, was hardly more than a "mailbox" operation.[26]

And what of the industrial projects that the ECA supported with counterpart funds? In total dollar value they presented a far larger commitment of resources than the outright dollar grants. Perhaps the best place to gauge their significance is in the cumulative figures for the period through December 1949. These were the figures that were available to the ECA when it planned its changes in personnel and program for Fiscal 1951, the beginning of its "interventionist" period. The emphasis now was in pushing the Europeans into those basic changes that would enable them to produce for active competition in the dollar area. Along with further efforts toward economic integration, the program involved a broad assault on the obstacles to larger and more efficient production, whether they came in the form of antiquated machinery, backward manufacturing techniques, or even managerial ideologies. A year later, when the ECA was on the eve of termination, its final efforts would be focused on the productivity program as the summary of its own most ambitious goals. It was at that time, too, that the policy would receive its most extravagant interventionist statement. William Foster, who succeeded Hoffman as Administrator in 1951, declared that the

---

[26] I am grateful to David Mayer of AID for some of the most detailed and helpful recollections of ECA work in the Netherlands at that time. The "mailbox" metaphor belongs to him.

TABLE. 8. USE OF COUNTERPART FUNDS TO PROMOTE PRODUCTION
(Dollar equivalents in millions of dollars)

Purpose	All Participating Countries	Austria	France	Germany	Greece	Italy and Trieste	The Netherlands	Other Countries
Electric, gas, and power facilities	956.0	50.6	724.5	166.6	2.7	—	—	11.6
Transportation, shipping, and communications	781.3	96.9	281.3	56.1	47.9	269.9	13.7	15.5
Agriculture	623.9	44.1	203.9	70.5	40.8	99.5	138.9	26.2
Coal mining and other mining and quarrying	452.4	17.3	340.2	82.4	2.1	—	—	10.4
Primary metals, chemicals, and strategic materials	332.8	38.4	195.1	52.6	4.2	20.6	21.9	—
Machinery	164.2	9.4	10.4	61.0	.2	83.2	—	—
Light industry	64.7	28.7	10.8	24.0	1.2	—	—	—
Petroleum and coal products	22.0	—	11.7	10.3	—	—	—	—
Technical assistance	20.3	.5	—	4.6	6.6	5.6	.1	2.9
Other and undistributed	452.1	14.9	157.4	101.3	45.1	113.1	5.9	14.3
Total	3,869.7	300.8	1,935.3	629.4	150.8	591.9	180.5	80.9

SOURCE: Opie and Brown, *op.cit.*, p. 237, figures compiled from ECA, *Thirteenth Report* (Quarter ending June 30, 1951), Appendix C, pp. 128-29.

TABLE 9. INDUSTRIAL PROJECTS AS OF JUNE 30, 1951[a]

(Millions of dollars and dollar equivalents)

	Total ECA-approved Industrial Projects				Raw Materials Extraction				Manufacturing			
Country	Total cost	ECA cost	ECA authorizations	ECA paid shipments	Total cost	ECA cost	ECA authorizations	ECA paid shipments	Total cost	ECA cost	ECA authorizations	ECA paid shipments
Total projects, all countries	2,250.0[b]	565.4	473.8	260.0	260.8	39.6	32.9	20.5	1,348.6	344.7	289.7	176.7
Austria	81.8	37.0	32.7	20.2	8.1	3.1	2.9	1.6	73.7	33.9	29.9	18.5
Belguim	50.0	15.2	9.8	8.8	—	—	—	—	50.5	15.2	9.8	8.8
Denmark	9.5	5.1	3.5	2.6	—	—	—	—	—	—	—	—
France	751.1	148.4	132.4	73.8	147.0	10.8	8.3	5.9	398.8	104.6	96.8	54.8
Germany (Federal Republic)	10.7	2.5	1.9	.5	—	—	—	—	10.7	2.5	1.9	.5
Greece	112.9	32.5	16.3	2.3	10.2	3.9	1.6	.2	8.8	4.3	2.9	1.1
Iceland	15.9	7.6	5.5	1.3	10.1	3.4	2.8	.7	4.7	2.6	1.0	—
Italy	435.6	170.9	154.5	74.6	—	—	—	—	314.4	100.3	85.8	46.9
Netherlands	68.0	26.9	18.2	8.4	—	—	—	—	47.0	23.5	14.8	5.5
Norway	29.7	5.1	4.0	2.1	29.7	5.1	4.0	2.1	—	—	—	—
Portugal	28.5	9.2	8.7	.9	—	—	—	—	11.2	5.3	5.3	1.9
Turkey	205.9	53.5	45.4	25.3	55.8	13.3	13.3	10.0	7.4	1.4	1.0	1.4
United Kingdom	421.4	51.0	40.0	39.4	—	—	—	—	421.4	51.0	40.3	39.4
Internationale	28.6	.5	.5	—	—	—	—	—	—	—	—	—

a Excludes technical assistance projects, strategic materials, and counterpart fund projects. Allocations to overseas dependent territories included in the figures for the mother countries.

b Totals shown are sums of unrounded figures, and hence they may vary slightly from the totals of the rounded amounts.

c Austro-German hydroelectric power plant in Braunau, Austria.

SOURCE: ECA, *Thirteenth Report* (Quarter ending June 30, 1951), Appendix B, p. 120.

ECA was now ready to go beyond the goal of increasing production. Within the short time left to it, the ECA would not only press for reforms in industry, but for a wider distribution of the benefits as well:

> We are going to work not only through and with the governments as we have in the past but will go down to the plant, to the village, to employers, it is our hope that we will have, before we undertake the specific increases in production and productivity, an agreement that they will share any of the fruits of that increased production and productivity not only with the workers, but also with the consumers. . . .[27]

If the United States was in fact determined to intervene more extensively, it seems highly probable that the effort would have been reflected somewhere in the distribution of administrative resources, particularly in the use of personnel overseas. One should recall, again, the peculiar situation in which the ECA found itself in 1950, and which made the question of personnel changes even more revealing. Under the commitment to phase out the administrative staff, the ECA was reducing its administrative budget from $16.5 million to $15.2 million, and its personnel totals from 1,148 to 1,141 in Europe and 988 to 956 in Washington. Yet, within this overall trend, the agency was actually enlarging some of its overseas missions (see Table 10); and as we have already shown, those changes overseas were tailored to the special needs of the Marshall Plan in this final stage of the program. If the capacity to intervene was related directly to the amount of counterpart funds available for investment in projects, and if the personnel changes for Fiscal 1951 were aimed at enlarging American intervention as a necessary part of achieving the new program goals, then there should have been some relation between the two items—the increase in personnel and the percentage of counterpart devoted to production. That is, if the United States had more leverage in those areas where there were more counterpart funds to be spent, then the changes in personnel should have been concentrated in the same countries—if, in fact, it was the purpose of the ECA to make use of this leverage to expand its influence.

[27] U.S. Congress, Senate, Committee on Foreign Relations and Committee on Armed Services, *Hearings, Mutual Security Act of 1951*, 82nd Congress, 1st Session, 1951, p. 79.

290

TABLE 10. Status of ECA Employment—Europe[a] as of January 31, 1950

	Net Employment	Budget Estimate, 1951
Office of the Special Representative	518	488
Country missions:		
Austria	42	45
Belgium	20	27
Denmark	26	25
France	113	96
Germany	56	59
Greece	54	48
Iceland	1	1
Ireland	11	12
Italy	77	90
Netherlands	34	33
Norway	23	29
Portugal	15	22
Sweden	25	24
Switzerland	4	5
Trieste	7	8
Turkey	39	36
United Kingdom	83	93
Total country missions	630	653
Total Europe	1,148	1,141

[a] Includes accessions less separations.

Source: House Subcommittee on Appropriations, *Hearings on Foreign Aid Appropriations for 1951* (1950), p. 424.

To review somewhat, counterpart funds were generated only through grant aid, and not through loans. They did not have to be spent on factories or on projects related more directly to production; they could also be used in retiring debt or in constructing public buildings. Table 11 takes account of these issues and shows how the figures on productive investment fit into the overall scheme. In the way of explanation for the general layout of the table, the first column shows the total allocation to a given country. The next two columns list the proportions available in direct grants, which could then generate counterpart funds. The fourth column indicates the amount of those counterpart funds spent on production projects. The fifth shows the total spent on projects as a percentage of the counterpart releases actually approved at the time. The effect is to exaggerate the proportion of aid used in project

TABLE 11. PROPORTION OF AID USED IN "PROMOTION OF PRODUCTION" THROUGH DECEMBER 31, 194
(Dollar equivalents of local currency, in millions of dollars)

Country	Total Allotment	Direct Grant	Percent in Grants	Promotion of Production		As percentage of counterpart released	As percentage of total allotment	Percent change in ECA mission personnel for 1950
				Total				
Austria	396.4	276.9	69.9	118.5		70.1	29.9	+ 7.1
Belgium–								
Luxembourg	461.4	3.0	0.7	—		—	—	+35.0
Denmark	187.0	90.1	48.2	—		—	—	− 3.8
France	1784.1	1131.7	63.4	1038.6		83.9	58.2	−15.0
Germany	848.7	516.1	60.8	191.3		56.7	22.5	+ 5.4
Iceland	13.2	2.5	18.9	—		—	—	—
Greece	301.0	191.7	63.7	47.1		32.3	15.7	−11.1
Ireland	117.6	—	—	—		—	—	+ 9.1
Italy	940.1	553.7	58.9	136.2		71.6	14.5	+16.9
Netherlands	789.1	413.1	52.4	21.9		24.2	0.0	− 2.9
Norway	164.0	49.6	30.2	—		—	—	+26.1
Portugal	10.0	—	—	—		—	—	+46.7
Sweden	79.0	—	—	—		—	—	− 4.0
Turkey	90.2	—	—	—		—	—	+ 7.7
United Kingdom	2317.7	963.0	41.6	1.4		0.2	0.1	+12.0

SOURCES: House Subcommittee on Appropriations, *Hearings on Foreign Aid Appropriations for 195*
pp. 424, 645-58; ECA, *Seventh Report* (Quarter ending December 31, 1949), Appendix D, pp. 146-4

financing, and with that, the alleged capacity for American intervention.

Starting from the most striking aspects of this table, we would notice that Britain, with the largest total allocation of aid, was using less than .2 percent of its counterpart in these productive investments. The bulk of the counterpart releases in Britain was devoted to debt retirement, which presumably furnished no basis for intervention. Yet the British mission was scheduled for a 12 percent increase. In contrast, France, with the largest percentage in productive investment (over 83 percent), was also the scene of a significant reduction in ECA personnel (15 percent). Eight of the countries had either no counterpart available, or had none of it allocated to production projects.[28]

For the sake of argument, let us assume that there was an opportunity for effective intervention where productive investments

[28] In Denmark, $50,000 was used in technical assistance.

292

accounted for only 40 percent of the total counterpart expenses. If we take even this modest view, we would have to exclude Greece and Turkey, where Americans were actually involved in running the national bureaucracies. (Interestingly enough, personnel levels in these two countries were cut back.)[29] Only four countries would qualify for American intervention under this formula—Austria, Germany, Italy, and France. For Austria and Germany, the presence of occupational forces made the subject of intervention somewhat academic. Still, the investments in projects accounted for little more than a fifth of the total aid to Germany. In Austria, where the percentage was greater, the investments were half the size of those in Germany and almost insignificant when compared to France. Over 70 percent of Italy's counterpart was used in the promotion of production, but the figure was still less than $200 million, and what is more important, it constituted only about 14 percent of the total American aid in Italy.

The interventionist argument here would have to center on France, where over a billion dollars in counterpart was approved by the end of December 1949, and where over half of the total aid was used in projects. But here the Monnet Plan was the dominant factor. France either had the projects staked out or had full control of the administrative machinery that was developing them. According to informants who were in France as members of the ECA mission, the American role was usually one of providing an official source of financing for projects that, for one reason or another, could not be included in the French budget. In this vein, a former member of the ECA program staff in Paris recalled a request he received from one of the French ministries engaged in economic planning. The French did not have the funds available to cover a modernization project in a certain coal mine. The ECA was asked if it would simply put the item on its own books as a Marshall Plan project, and as a matter of course the ECA agreed to do it. In no meaningful sense was the pattern one of ECA participation in the drafting of the projects.[30]

[29] The scale of intervention in Greece was quite apparent in the distended allocations to "public administration" under the technical assistance program. Through June 30, 1951, the ECA had spent $1,755,000 on public administration in Greece out of a total program expenditure of $2,311,500. The nearest rival to Greece in this field was naturally Turkey, but even there the cost was only $246,300. See ECA, *Thirteenth Report* (Quarter ending June 30, 1951), p. 119.

[30] The story is also told—although I have not been able to document it—

293

If counterpart funds provided any leverage for intervention, then, it was only among the weakest of the ERP nations. To that extent it would have been merely a subtle projection of the situation in Greece and Turkey. But that meant, in turn, that the capacity for intervention had the least significance in the countries whose economic performance mattered most to the success of the Marshall Plan—Britain, France, Belgium, Italy, and the Netherlands. Of course the question arises: What happened *after* January 1950, when the personnel changes were made and the new policies were put into effect? The answer is: Nothing very much different. As Table 12 shows rather graphically through the use of rank-order correlations, the distribution of aid followed much the same pattern in the second phase of the program that it did in the first. Furthermore, there were strong correlations among the various measures of aid, although interestingly enough none of them revealed anything other than a negative relation to the changes in mission personnel.

In the first phase of the program, countries that ranked higher in the overall allotment of funds were likely to rank higher, also, in the receipt of grants (not only in absolute terms, but as a percentage of total aid as well). Countries that ranked higher in grant aid were likely to rank higher, in turn, in the size and percentage of funds used in production projects; and the countries that were farther advanced along this scale of project financing by the end of

---

of a group of visiting Congressmen in Paris who wanted to see some of the concrete results of American aid. The clerk at the ECA mission looked into the files and found a coal mine project that had been financed, apparently, in the same manner as the one described above. The Congressional delegation then traveled to the mine and burst in upon its director. The tendency among Congressmen at that time was to solicit expressions of gratitude from the recipients of American aid. The mine director insisted, though, that he had never even heard of the Marshall Plan. As the Congressmen persisted, the man became more and more heated, until finally he yelled that he didn't know what they were talking about or what they wanted of him or, for that matter, what they were all doing down in his mine. And with that, he chased them out.

I have been told also of one instance when the ECA account books arrived just in time to save the director of the nationalized railways in one country. The director, it seemed, had started postwar reconstruction immediately after the end of hostilities. The only problem was that he had neglected to get an appropriation from the Treasury to cover the new debts. His efforts were all illegal until the ECA happened along.

TABLE 12. GRANT AID, PRODUCTION PROJECTS, AND PERSONNEL CHANGES IN THE OVERSEAS MISSIONS OF THE ECA: RANK-ORDER CORRELATIONS FOR FOURTEEN MARSHALL PLAN COUNTRIES, 1949-51a

	(a)	(b)	(c)	(d)	(e)	(f)
(a) Total aid allotment, 1948-49		.624	.740	.444b	.454b	—.203b
(b) Percent of aid in grants, 1948-49			.895	.662	.829	—.579
(c) Percent of aid used in production projects, 1948-49				.736	.793	—.370b
(d) Increase in allocations to production projects, 1950-51					.790	—.508b
(e) Rate of increase in the funding of projects (d/a)						—.846
(f) Personnel changes in the ECA missions, Fiscal 1951						

a Except where otherwise noted, the correlations in the matrix are significant statistically at the .01 or .05 levels. Correlations of .544 or above are significant at the .05 level; those at .715 or above are significant at the .01 level.
b Not significant statistically.

1949 were the countries, by and large, that experienced the greatest increase in this area in the final stage of the program. Moreover, this correlation becomes stronger even when we consider the *rate of increase* in the funding of projects [item (e) in the table] and compare the advances of 1950-51 against the total allotments of aid through 1949 (a procedure, by the way, that should have weakened the correlation).[31]

It may be risky to place too much reliance on rank-order correlations in these circumstances, but fortunately we do not have to lean on the positive correlations in the table. It so happens that the negative findings in the data may be even more useful for our pur-

[31] The only places where the correlations fell below the level of statistical significance were in the relations between the total allotments of aid, 1948-49 (a), and the two measures of increase in project financing, (d) and (e). Some decline was to be expected here, but even so, on a closer examination of the figures it appears that the decline was due entirely to the movement of Britain in the table—a "movement" that occurred largely by indirection. The British had never devoted more than a slight portion of their counterpart funds to specific projects, and in the latter part of the program they simply failed to fund additional projects, while the other countries were enlarging their own. The British could remain stationary then, but their relative position slipped markedly. Thus, if we eliminated the British from the comparison, we would find that the correlations between (a), (d), and (e) fall back into place and become statistically significant.

295

poses. Thus, for example, it seems firmly established that there was no positive relation between the personnel changes of 1950-51 and the degree of project financing. In fact, as we noted earlier, the correlations with personnel change were all negative, and they were statistically significant in only two cases: in relation to the size of grants and the rate of increase in productive investment. And yet, these were the two places in which positive correlations would have had to appear—if grants and projects were really a source of leverage for the United States, and if the changes in staff overseas were really conceived for the purpose of enlarging American influence. Therefore, one of the two things must have been true: Either the funding of projects failed to act as a vehicle for American influence, or the shifts in personnel overseas were part of no design to further American intervention.

In the last analysis, it is hard to place any other interpretation on the changes in personnel apart from the very brief explanation given by the ECA itself in 1950. Leland Barrows, who was Executive Officer in the Office of the Special Representative in Paris, told a House subcommittee that "the main change is a shift in personnel, using more in country missions and not so many . . . in the OSR [Office of the Special Representative in Paris]. . . . That is primarily because of the productivity drive, the export drive, in the overseas territory, where we want to focus on country missions. . . ."[32] The substantial personnel increases, as Barrows pointed out, were in Belgium, Italy, and Britain. What the ECA was doing, then, was concentrating its technical assistance resources in those developed areas where American advice might produce the most dramatic results in the shortest time. As William Foster told a Senate committee the following year, the ECA favored "existing establishments where considerable improvement can be gained from relatively small new investment." Even more preferable were projects that could actually come to fruition within the life of the ECA.[33]

It was admitted that this latter phase of ECA operations would require an increase in end-use inspection. But as we noted earlier,

[32] House Subcommittee on Appropriations, *Hearings on Foreign Aid Appropriation for 1951* (1950), p. 425.

[33] Senate Committees on Foreign Relations and Armed Services, *Hearings on Mutual Security Act of 1951* (1951), pp. 85, 87. But more directly, see Paul Hoffman's remarks in Senate Foreign Relations Committee, *Hearings on Extension of ERP*, 1949, p. 61.

the locus of that activity was in the Controller's office in Washington, and that unit was slated for an expansion in its permanent employment from 174 to 185. If anything fit the label of "interventionist," it had to be end-use inspection; and yet, as it was carried out in the Controller's office through the sampling of vouchers, this was intervention of the most distant and superficial kind.

The interventionist rhetoric was in the technical assistance program—in Foster's promise to get down into the plants and work directly with labor and management. To be sure, productivity teams came to the United States, and consultants were sent overseas. But that was a distinctly different matter from assigning personnel permanently to a given plant or industry in a foreign country. And in much the same way that the ECA was given to hiring the services of outside agencies, it was able to find a large portion of its technical consultants in the recipient countries themselves. In fact, in the most critical parts of the program, those dealing with industrial and agricultural productivity, the foreign experts accounted for a greater part of the technical assistance budget than the Americans (see Table 13). Where the American effort was predominant was in areas like public administration, where the figures were swollen by the unusual involvement in Greece. The figures also suggest that it was the Greek program that took most of the American costs in industrial and agricultural productivity. American experts must have accounted for almost all of the $2,671.9 thousand spent in the industrial productivity program in Greece, and yet the total expenditure on American consultants in the industrial field was only $3,048.9 thousand, or only $300,000 beyond the costs of the Greek program. It is very likely, then, that the American activity in the more industrial countries was even more subordinate than the figures would seem to indicate.[34]

While the ECA did encourage contacts between American management-labor teams and their European counterparts, it came under the attack of the old unilateralist argument in its first year of operation. For even here, in the technical assistance program,

[34] The Greek figures, again, account for the predominance of American consultants in transportation and communication. Aside from these categories, the only significant preponderance of American over foreign consultants occurred in the area of overseas development. But there the category explains itself. The Americans were out of the home territory of the recipient country, and they were dealing with surveys rather than investment decisions in matured developments.

TABLE 13. Technical Assistance Authorizations by Field of Activity, Recipient Country, and Type of Assistance, Cumulative through June 30, 1951 (Thousands of dollars)

Recipient Country and Type of Assistance	Total Authorizations	Field of Activity								
		Industrial productivity	Agricultural productivity	Manpower utilization	Public administration	Transportation and communication	Development of overseas territories	Marketing	Tourism	Program management
Total of all countries	28,775.3	13,908.1	4,371.1	2,512.2	2,311.5	2,047.9	914.4	464.6	187.8	2,057.8
United States experts	10,032.5	3,048.9	1,162.5	420.0	1,964.9	1,335.0	806.8	286.1	85.1	923.5
Foreign experts	9,738.1	4,485.3	2,085.6	589.9	345.7	712.6	107.2	174.9	102.7	1,134.3
Technical materials	5,564.2	5,193.5	367.0	.4	.9	.3	—	2.1	—	—
Basic surveys	1,832.6	582.8	746.0	501.8	—	—	.5	1.5	—	—
Services of international organizations	1,000.0	—	—	1,000.0	—	—	—	—	—	—
Services of U.S. Government agencies	607.7	597.7	10.0	—	—	—	—	—	—	—
Austria	657.3	529.7	60.0	33.1	.9	.3	—	4.1	—	29.2
Belgium–Luxembourg	330.1	112.2	22.2	13.2	1.0	—	175.7	1.5	—	4.3
Denmark	985.0	472.5	449.0	10.8	4.1	9.4	5.3	10.2	—	23.6
France	2,764.3	1,937.4	250.3	96.7	4.3	22.7	78.4	37.0	—	337.6
Germany (Federal Republic)	1,069.2	510.8	198.3	66.0	73.5	99.3	—	25.3	—	96.0
Greece	7,529.9	2,671.9	1,260.1	466.0	1,755.0	999.4	—	279.7	42.0	55.7
Iceland	124.8	45.8	62.4	12.4	2.3	—	—	—	—	2.1
Ireland	1,266.8	189.0	77.8	—	8.4	21.1	—	.1	59.5	911.0
Italy	1,568.6	694.8	122.3	456.4	99.0	62.7	5.5	10.5	5.6	111.8
Netherlands	658.4	352.4	168.1	23.0	3.0	—	3.7	2.6	—	105.7
Norway	847.7	668.5	124.5	8.5	—	4.0	—	—	—	42.2
O.E.E.C.	3,321.2	1,467.2	273.1	1,122.2	81.2	192.7	5.0	18.3	70.0	91.5
Portugal	720.9	200.0	4.2	—	5.0	—	507.0	—	—	4.7
Sweden	134.6	53.3	29.2	17.5	.5	2.0	—	8.8	—	23.4
Trieste	30.0	30.0	—	—	—	—	—	—	—	—
Turkey	2,387.2	687.8	774.5	—	246.3	560.4	—	—	8.5	109.8
United Kingdom	3,601.8	3,192.2	127.3	11.6	1.6	9.3	133.9	22.1	2.2	101.7
U.S. Government Agencies	777.6	92.7	368.1	174.8	25.4	64.7	—	44.5	—	7.4

the ECA followed the pluralist rules of shared authority and refused to circumvent the local governments. All technical assistance programs were subject to the approval of the host government. Contacts among businessmen and unionists were organized under government auspices, as in the case of the Anglo-American Council of Productivity; and under the rules finally adopted by the ECA, even the working contracts had to be approved by the local government.[35] The unilateralist objection was expressed by Roy Gifford of the Detroit Board of Commerce, who managed to sustain the attack throughout the program. His central point was that it was self-defeating to conduct productivity programs through socialist governments, which were basically hostile to the prospect of efficient and vigorous management in the private sector of the economy. "If you can deal only with the British Government first," Gifford told the Senate Foreign Relations Committee, "you have hamstrung industry completely."[36] What particularly aroused Gifford was that the action of the ECA seemed gratuitous. There was nothing in the legislation that required this particular decision on how to proceed. In Gifford's eyes it was entirely a matter of being soft on the Europeans. He made no allowance, apparently, for the simple phenomenon of acting "in character." One suspects it would have been futile to suggest at the time that this particular decision of the ECA had simply been implicit in the character of the agency all along—that it derived from the same core of decisions that had given rise to the procedures on counterpart funds.

By 1950, then, the precedents were set in favor of working through the local governments. Despite the hope voiced by William Foster for departing from that pattern, the departures were never to be regarded as anything other than exceptions to the standing rule; and there is no evidence that any aberrations of this kind actually occurred. Further, with the emphasis placed on quick results, the ECA was forced to abandon any hopes it might have had for exercising a strict regulation of the technical assistance projects in terms of a coherent overall plan. The Budget Bureau survey found in 1951 that once the project applications passed the scru-

[35] Harry B. Price, The Marshall Plan and Its Meaning (Ithaca: Cornell University Press, 1955), pp. 107-108; Bureau of the Budget, *Survey of the ECA*, 1951, p. 44, Series 39.32.

[36] Senate Foreign Relations Committee, *Hearings on Extension of ERP*, 1950, p. 233. See also his prepared statement of the previous year in Senate Foreign Relations Committee, *Hearings on Extension of ERP*, 1949, pp. 545-49.

tiny of the engineers, they were approved on a first-come-first-served basis. Once again, the initiative was left to others. There was no schedule of priorities among the projects, and certainly no attempt to confront the Marshall Plan nations with the conception of an integrated program.[37]

Intervention, for the ECA, was a sometime thing. As a principle it was repugnant; as a concept it was elusive. Where it was recognizable and effective, as in Greece and Turkey, it was of little consequence as far as European recovery was concerned. And in the more industrialized countries, where all the ambitions of the Marshall Plan would stand or fall, intervention was either unworkable in practice or simply unnecessary.

[37] Bureau of the Budget, *Survey of the ECA*, 1951, pp. 37-39.

14. THEORY AND COERCION IN THE ECA

I

To SAY that the ECA was not running the economies of the Marshall Plan nations was not to say, however, that the agency had no important influence on the internal decisions of the ERP countries. The manipulation of aid that could represent some 3 to 5 percent of a national budget would inevitably have some bearing on the choices available to the national governments. But the "intervention" in this case had a remote quality that was far more characteristic of the ECA. It inhered a continuous pressure on the Marshall Plan countries for basic investment (as opposed to consumption), and this pressure in turn emanated from the antibureaucratic features of the ECA—more specifically, from the basic commitment of the ECA to cut back its program with each successive year.

What we have called the "debureaucratization" features of the ECA referred to the preferences for a decentralized agency that would complete its temporary assignment on schedule and leave no bureaucratic vestiges behind. There was an attendant theory here, also, which suggested that the prospect of a permanent foreign assistance program might undermine the ends of the Marshall Plan. Principally, it was feared that the Europeans would have less incentive to make hard domestic decisions if they thought American aid would always be available as a crutch. As the program wore on, this theory acquired a force of its own, and the debureaucratization theme assumed the weight of a primary commitment or an independent policy value.

When rumors arose in 1949 that the United States might continue the Marshall Plan after 1952, Hoffman declared: "I can think of nothing that will interfere more with achieving the aims of this act than to have the impression get out that this act will be extended. I think this particular activity must end on June 30,

1952." Senator Connally thought the "virility" would be taken out of the program, and Hoffman agreed that "the immediate effect would be to damp the efforts of the people who are really trying to make a success of it. They might slow up."[1] To a surprising degree, this question arose repeatedly in the Congressional hearings, as though Congressmen had to be assured again and again. The ECA reiterated the theme in its official reports, and the executives in the agency continued to affirm the theory.[2]

But what were the *operational* commitments of debureaucratization, and on what basis could we say that this feature achieved the status of an independent or primary value in the program? Here it is possible to identify at least two important empirical standards for the debureaucratization theme: (1) the basing of aid on 1938 consumption levels, and (2) the presumption in favor of standard annual reductions in the country programs of 15 to 25 percent.

Hoffman told the Senate Appropriations Committee in 1950 that the ECA had an "informal" understanding with the Marshall Plan countries that the United States would not underwrite programs that allowed *per capita* consumption to rise above the figures of 1938.[3] For the precise implications of that decision one has to go back a bit further, to the ECA's first annual report, *Recovery Progress and United States Aid.* To arrive at some consistent standard for the allocation of aid, the ECA needed a reliable forecast of investment and consumption in each country. The policy was to finance only that very basic capital investment that a country could not finance for itself, either with its own export production or with diversions from present consumption. But these tests, it was admitted, "could not be applied with precision," and so the ECA was faced with one of those "two-handed" matters of judgment. On the one hand, if standards of living rose above 1938 levels, American financing might simply be used to support more consumption. On the other hand, if consumption were repressed and goods were di-

[1] Senate Foreign Relations Committee, *Hearings on Extension of ERP,* 1949, p. 78.

[2] See, for example, Howard Bruce in *ibid.,* p. 332; Hoffman in Senate Foreign Relations Committee, *Hearings on Extension of ERP,* 1950, p. 23 (and in almost every hearing at which he testified before the foreign relations committees), and Richard Bissell in Senate Committees on Foreign Relations and Armed Services, *Hearings on Mutual Security Act of 1951* (1951), p. 157.

[3] Senate Committee on Appropriations, *Hearings on Foreign Aid Appropriations for 1951* (1950), pp. 172, 241.

verted from the home market into the export trade, there was the danger of a domestic inflation that could wipe out the previous gains and ultimately raise the cost of those export goods themselves. Thus, either alternative had its pitfalls. What the ECA was forced to do was adopt some stable preference in the form of a working rule of thumb:

> There is no easy criterion by which to judge the adequacy of living standards or rates of investment. Nevertheless, wherever there was an indication of an excessive use of resources, actual or proposed, in one of these major categories, the inference was drawn that fewer were needed, that the country could export more or import less, and that the requested volume of ECA aid was larger than necessary.[4]

That is, if living standards rose to such a level that the country seemed able to support more investment, it was *presumed* that it could indeed finance that investment, and that American aid could be diminished. Now, in taking the 1938 figures as the standard, Hoffman had a more precise test. By gearing American aid to the prewar levels of consumption, the ECA hoped to reduce the possibility that Marshall aid would be used to finance the importation of such goods as automobiles, furs, oranges, and bubble gum.

With production rising in the ERP countries, the 1938 standard provided some reasonably intelligible grounds for the future reductions in aid. But in 1949 Hoffman and ECA took an even more drastic step, and here they added a second empirical commitment to their pledge of debureaucratization. It was decided to give the British a 25 percent cut in aid, and lower the allocations to all the other ERP countries by 15 percent. Thomas Finletter, the head of the ECA mission in Britain, thought that "the British themselves took the initiative in whittling down the figure," and so he told the Senate Foreign Relations Committee. But he was apparently misinformed, and Hoffman stepped in to correct the record.

> MR. HOFFMAN. . . . I think I can add a little light on this. In July, when I first met Mr. Stafford Cripps [the British Chancellor of the Exchequer], we were talking about the second year's program. I told him I thought it should be understood that the Americans were very insistent that the second year's

[4] ECA, *Recovery Progress and United States Aid*, 1949, p. 61.

303

program be less than the first year's program, and he asked what amount of cut I had in mind.

"Well," I said, "I think that as it is to be a 4-year program, it would be a good thing to aim at a 25-percent cut."

What figure he had in mind up to that time I do not know. He came out with a 24-percent cut.

SENATOR TYDINGS. What did he say in response to your suggestions?

MR. HOFFMAN. He said "That is a very drastic downward revision."

I said, "Nothing less than a marked revision will convince the Americans that the Europeans are really serious."[5]

The decision was not based on an analysis of projects or a calculation of dollar balances. It flowed exclusively from the presumption in favor of debureaucratization, and it was now the chief operational expression of that commitment. In the next year the British formula was applied across the board, and as Hoffman reported, "instead of asking each country to submit a program for the coming fiscal year based upon its needs for dollars, we asked each country to submit a program based on the assumption of a 25 percent reduction from the aid it will have received in fiscal 1950...."[6]

If Hoffman was able to afford frankness in 1950, it was because the steps had already been taken that subordinated the balance of payments and the dollar theories. When the ECA introduced conditional aid (with "drawing rights") what it did, in effect, was replace the balance of payments as a guideline for aid. From that time forward the amount of assistance that any country would receive would not depend on its overall balance of payments deficit, but on its deficit with the dollar area; and in the latter part of 1949, the ECA freed itself from the dollar theory as well. It was felt that the system, as it stood, provided little incentive for the ERP nations to correct their deficits, for the larger the deficit, the greater was the claim, supposedly, for American aid. Therefore the arrangement posed a fundamental dilemma. If Marshall aid rose or fell in response to fluctuations in the balance of payments, then it

[5] Senate Foreign Relations Committee, *Hearings on Extension of ERP*, 1949, pp. 498 (Finletter) and 499 (Hoffman).

[6] Senate Appropriations Committee, *Hearings on Foreign Aid Appropriations for 1951* (1950), p. 172.

might grow larger in succeeding years rather than smaller, and there could be no assurance at all that it would end by 1952. Yet, if the dollar theory was abandoned, what would one use for standards?

What the ECA finally did was to take the 1949 allocations as a base. From that point it would progressively reduce the allocations with each succeeding year as it moved toward 1952. Henceforth, as Howard Ellis commented, "the incurring of a larger deficit would not establish a presumption in favor of increased aid."[7] The state of the balance of payments or dollar reserves, then, would not be allowed to determine the life or magnitude of the Marshall Plan. Instead, it was the duration of the ECA that would determine the size of the program. Debureaucratization had now achieved the dominance of an independent policy commitment; it was Marshall aid itself that was thrust into a dependent position as a function of the administrative schedule.

As if to firm up that relation as unalterable, the commitment to debureaucratization began to shape now the kind of social science the ECA would use. Conventionally, our discussion of theory in the social sciences follows the categories of prescriptive and descriptive, ethical and empirical. But it is possible that there is variant between the two that might be called a "contingent" theory. That is to say, we may find ourselves in a situation where either one of two descriptive theories, or two sets of empirical assumptions may be equally valid, and yet there may be no means of deciding between them on empirical grounds. There is of course the old question, for example, whether the glass is half full or half empty, or whether the dominant pattern in society is one of conflict or cooperation.

For certain refined purposes of theory-building we might conditionally adopt one assumption rather than another. We might assume, for instance, that conflict is the dominant characteristic of social life, and we might go on from there to draw out some propositions about the management of conflict or the transformation of conflict in an industrial society. The kind of theory I have in mind here would be something like that, but it would also have certain slight differences. It would begin by recognizing that any one of

[7] Howard S. Ellis, *The Economics of Freedom* (New York: Harper and Brothers, 1950), pp. 530-31.

several descriptive theories may be equally accurate or inaccurate, and we would forswear at the outset any effort to decide the issue on empirical terms. Instead, we would choose an "appropriate" descriptive theory on the basis of some intervening value judgment or consideration of policy.

Strange as it might appear on the surface, something of this nature seemed to be at work in the ECA. As we noted earlier, the ECA was faced with some staggering problems in managing its own empirical subject matter. To estimate the balance of payments for the OEEC countries, the economists in the ECA had to forecast the precise direction and volume of trade in various commodities, and the approximate proportions of investment in all the member countries. The result, as they realized, was highly problematic. But even so, there was always something else coming along to throw off the estimates—like the maneuvering that took place before the British devalued in the fall of 1949, or the inventory buildups and the rush for raw materials that followed the outbreak of the Korean war. And yet, admitting all these difficulties, the ECA still had to distribute aid, and it had to find some minimally rational standards by which to do it.

The strategy finally adopted was to construct models based on the most favorable assumptions. Before putting all the estimates together and proceeding "from the diagnosis to an estimate of aid . . . it was necessary *first* to assume that the country in question would achieve self-support status as rapidly as could reasonably be expected, and *then* to forecast what its balance of payments would be."[8] In the early period there seemed to be nothing rigid in this posture. No one's model was better than anyone else's, so it was as reasonable to use an optimistic model as a conservative one. Besides, the ECA seemed to imply that the model was largely hypothetical anyway, and the specific model chosen was far less important than the fact that some model—any model—was used. But it became evident after a while that the commitment to the model was much harder than anyone might have supposed—that it was a reflection, in fact, of the basic commitment to end the program by 1952. Thus, when a sharp difference arose between the ECA and the OEEC in estimating the Europeans' deficit on current account, and it was suggested that the figures of the ECA might have been unrealistic, the ECA tended to dismiss the criticism, not for being

[8] ECA, *Recovery Progress and United States Aid*, p. 62. Emphasis added.

wrong so much as irrelevant. The justification of the ECA surely must have been one of the oddest statements that the people at the OEEC had ever encountered. As the Marshall Plan agency "explained,"

> The ECA has throughout adopted favorable assumptions on economic trends in the participating countries. It believes that the reduction in the over-all deficit on current account in 1948/49 from the level of about $6.04 billion forecast by OEEC to a level of about $5.07 billion, or a reduction by one-sixth, is possible of attainment while maintaining, though not improving, living standards. *It is very important that the over-all deficit be steadily reduced for this is the measure of the ability of the participants to move progressively toward self-support.*[9]

To translate, the OEEC figures suggested that the ECA might be wrong in its empirical estimates. The ECA replied that it could not be wrong, because these were the only estimates that were consistent with its premises: The figures simply had to be correct if the ECA was to reduce the program progressively. Since there was no question that the ECA was going out of business by 1952, there could be no question about the estimates either. If one happened to believe, in addition, that the Europeans would act decisively only if the Marshall Plan was certain to end by 1952, then the lower allocations could also present a self-fulfilling prophecy. If the Europeans believed it, they would have to become more active on their own behalf, and they might even achieve those projected improvements in the balance of payments. If the choice of the more ambitious estimates would actually succeed in prodding the Europeans and bringing about the desired end, then who was to say that these estimates were not, in the final analysis, the most accurate of all?

And happily enough, the dollar deficit of the OEEC nations did decline, dropping from $8.5 billion in 1947 to $1 billion in 1950. In 1951 Richard Bissell could tell a joint Senate committee that the problem of the European dollar deficit with the United States "has largely ceased to exist."[10] By that time, of course, Korea had superseded the questions of debureaucratization and the dollar deficit.

[9] *Ibid.*, p. 70. Emphasis added.
[10] Senate Committee on Foreign Relations and Armed Forces, *Hearings of Mutual Security Act of 1951*, p. 180.

307

Military production was on the rise, and American soldiers were coming to Europe with dollars. The Marshall Plan would be put in the service of the rearmament program, and the ECA itself would end on December 31, 1951, instead of June 30, 1952. The foreign aid program would be continued but with a different emphasis, as reflected in the title of the successor organization, the Mutual Security Agency. But in 1949 and early 1950 it was the commitment to debureaucratization that was still dominant. Hoffman could still tell Senator Fulbright—with no trace of apology—that the program would end by 1952, even though several of the ERP countries could not hope to be fully self-supporting by that time.[11] The ECA could go steadily on its way, then, making annual reductions of 25 percent. In 1950, however, Senator McCarran and the watchdog committee began to catch on to what was happening. They recognized that the ECA was using only a rule of thumb in making its reductions, and that the allocations had lost much of their foundation in economic fact. McCarran's reaction was in part a lecture to the ECA, but in part, also, an exercise in his own expanding recognition of what should have been evident to him for some time:

> When people were near starvation you could calculate requirements for calories, translate them into dollars, and feel some confidence that you had the answer. When factories were idle you could make an estimate of the quantities of copper, coal, and machinery to get them into operation, and you were proved correct if the result was that the factories got into operation. . . . [But] today those objectives have been reached and . . . the problem of determining how much money it is necessary for us to supply . . . is much more difficult.[12]

If the estimates lost their relation to precise standards, McCarran could be forgiven for wondering why Europe needed 25 percent less aid, rather than 50 or 40 or 15 percent.[13] The ECA could respond only by reciting the old slogan of a "cure rather than a palliative," but by this date it failed to convince anyone. The fact was

[11] Senate Foreign Relations Committee, *Hearings on Extension of ERP*, 1949, p. 61.

[12] See Senate Committee on Appropriations, *Hearings on Foreign Aid Appropriation for Fiscal 1951*, pp. 266-67.

[13] *Ibid.*, p. 267.

that the ECA was now disarmed; it had no defense beyond the bare logic of its promise to end the program by 1952. If that seemed to make little sense as a basis for allocating aid to Europe, what sense did it make, after all, as a rule governing the size and resources of the agency itself? The ECA was pressed to show consistent decreases in administrative expenses and personnel; and yet the functions of the agency were not decreasing, but enlarging. Congress had been adding programs rather than deleting them, and in 1950, when the ECA was planning sharp cuts in administrative expenses, it was scheduled to increase its efforts in technical assistance, information, and end-use checking. Also, conditions had changed since that early period when the ECA was shipping large bulk commodities such as wheat. At that time the average ECA voucher was for $143,000. But now that it was shipping items like machine tools, which came in smaller packages, its average transaction was only $12,000 to $13,000. The overall value of American assistance had declined, but the volume of transactions had actually multiplied.[14] In short, the ECA had more to do, not less. Neither the reduction in the ECA nor the drop in the assignments of aid had any relation, then, to the substantive needs of European recovery. They had their origin in another value, and a prior commitment.

This was a logic that might have baffled Alice and the White Queen, but it had its uses. Hoffman was determined to convert the squeeze on resources into a form of pressure on the ERP countries. And in some respects it was a rather apt method for an agency like the ECA that disclaimed any intention of interfering in the decisions of the ERP countries, and which lacked the leverage for major interventions anyway. Thus Hoffman could say, with sincerity, that questions of nationalization were matters exclusively for the local government. Nor did he think it proper, for example, that the United States should refuse textile machinery to Britain for fear of competition.[15] But the concern for economic rationality could also give him the basis for some fine distinctions:

> I have had this [matter of nationalization] out with the British. I have said, so far as we are concerned what they do with their economy is their business, and what we do with our dollars is our

[14] See William Foster's testimony in House Subcommittee on Appropriations, *Hearings on Foreign Aid for Fiscal 1951* (1950), pp. 416-17.

[15] Senate Foreign Relations Committee, *Hearings on Extension of ERP*, 1949, pp. 48, 59-61, 430.

business and if they start playing ducks and drakes with their economy to such a point that they cannot recover and our investment is not worth while, we are going to hold up the investment. . . .[16]

How the British happened to regulate the butchers and the bankers, Hoffman insisted, was no concern of the ECA. However, "they should not use our dollars to engage in social experimentation . . . [but] only for essential imports needed for recovery, and that has been the test." With that line of reasoning he could feel perfectly justified in cutting British aid if he suspected them of social experimentation, while at the same time he could find nothing inconsistent with his professions of noninterference. When more cotton goods began to appear on the consumer market in Britain, Hoffman found it appropriate to cut the British cotton imports by $60 million. Was the government entering the field of housing construction? Then $25 million might be shaved off the Marshall Plan exports of lumber.[17] And this was all compatible with the presumption in favor of basic investment. If the local government could divert funds to consumption, then Marshall aid could be eliminated proportionately. It was not surprising, therefore, that the British Labour Government found some difficulty in maintaining the pace of its social welfare programs. After the first year of the Labour Government, government consumption took 26.2 percent of the resources available for domestic use. By 1948 that figure had been reduced to 18.2 percent. With cuts in the programs for housing, health, and education, that figure was being pushed steadily downward. Projecting the trend, the proportion was expected to decline to 16.8 percent by 1952;[18] and as a result, in part, of these restrictions on welfare and consumption, the British managed to keep investment close to the ECA's target figure of 20 percent of the gross national product.

Still, if influence was to be exerted, it *was* more fitting for an agency with a pluralist orientation that its interventions remain more subtle and indirect. If it had to interfere at all, it was more appropriate for the ECA to do that by arranging incentives rather

[16] *Ibid.*, p. 61.

[17] Senate Foreign Relations Committee, *Hearings on Extension of ERP*, 1949, pp. 502, 507.

[18] See the testimony of Thomas Finletter and the accompanying charts in *ibid.*, pp. 160-61.

than dictating policies. Perhaps the ECA staff expressed it best in its first annual report:

> We are not seeking to impose on other countries any specific economic pattern. The degree to which other governments find it necessary and desirable to exercise direct controls over economic processes is a matter for them to decide. The United States is simply following a common-sense policy which will, if it is successful, reduce the insistent economic pressures that compel governments to ration, to control, and to regulate. . . .[19]

Thus, even where there were conscious goals for directing the Europeans, the ECA was still wedded to a liberal position, and even the irony of its intervention was characteristic: The most effective tool of coercion it had—the pressure of a continuing cutback in program funds—was a product of its own weakness as an agency.

II

We speculated earlier that several themes in the intellectual origins of the Marshall Plan might have converged to create an operating presumption in favor of deemphasizing political considerations. That is, the ECA was to concentrate on economic criteria; it would not (according to our hypothesis) attribute political motives where some other construction was possible, and it would not bring disagreements immediately to the level of overt political contest. Among the various themes these decision rules might have summarized were the following:

—that the ECA would represent a peculiar expertise for dealing with operations of a "business-like" nature, that it possessed a distinct legitimacy based on the perspectives of business management and economic rationality;

—that the preference for "a cure rather than a palliative" in Europe prescribed a full rein for the criteria of economic rationality;

—that nothing more had been decided on the national interest in Europe than the approval of an *economic* aid program—and by implication, if there were any larger political decisions to be made, they were to be reserved for another time and settled on their own terms, rather than simply precipitated by the decisions of the ECA;

[19] ECA, *Recovery Progress and United States Aid*, p. 2.

311

—that the United States should confine its intrusions overseas by concentrating on the problem of reconstruction and avoiding, as much as possible, any involvement in domestic political decisions; and it should observe these limitations because, for one thing, it was more proper, but also because interventions would tend to confirm the propaganda of the Communists.

Unquestionably, the decisions of the ECA in cutting aid allotments could seriously restrict the policy choices open to the Europeans, and Paul Hoffman was one of the first to acknowledge that. Yet, as the passages above make equally clear, he saw nothing in the record that might have contradicted his own frequent insistence that the ECA would avoid any meddling in the internal decisions of the ERP countries. What removed the contradiction for him, apparently, was the belief that the ECA was doing something fundamentally different from political work. The agency was concentrating on economic decisions, and it would dispute the Europeans only on matters relating to the use of American aid. The British could nationalize industry or do anything else with their economy, and it was their business alone. However, if the British succeeded only in damaging their economy as a result of these adventures, they would threaten the usefulness of American aid, and it was at least legitimate at that point to consider the case for reducing American grants. Implicitly, it would not be an issue of intervention anymore, but something closer to a salvage operation for American resources.

But did Hoffman and his colleagues really believe in this distinction, and did they act upon it? It so happened that the annual Senate hearings furnished one of the most precise and thorough tests on this point, thanks in large measure to the persistence of Senator Fulbright. When the legislation was first considered in 1948, Fulbright maintained that the goal of economic integration was insufficient; political integration was the key to peace and the prerequisite to an integrated economic market. Fulbright continued to believe, for that reason, that the Marshall Plan would fail in its objectives so long as the ECA refused to push for political federation in Europe. Moreover, his challenge did not end in 1948 with the passage of the legislation. He used the hearings in the succeeding years to pick away at the performance of the ECA as a method of advancing his thesis. An important part of that argument over the years was to point out to Hoffman and his assistants that their

312

decisions carried important political implications. If the top executives in the ECA could have been made to admit that they were involved in politics after all, then they might have been convinced to go all the way and seek a political solution. But interestingly enough, as doggedly as Fulbright would press the point, the ECA people would continue to resist; and they consistently failed to be persuaded.

When Fulbright asked Hoffman in 1949 why the ECA did not promote political integration instead of merely encouraging the movement of goods, Hoffman replied, "I am an ECA administrator, sir."

> SENATOR FULBRIGHT. Do you feel that because there was nothing in the authorization of the ERP regarding political matters that therefore your jurisdiction is limited to economics? That it would not be within the contemplation of the law that you have anything to do at all with the political pattern in Europe?
>
> MR. HOFFMAN. I think the Congress was very wise in limiting ECA to the economic field. I think that the State Department has an agency set up to deal with the political field. I think that we can do our job with the economic field, because we are an independent agency, perhaps better than could be done as part of a regular Government department. . . . I am certain we do not belong in the political field.[20]

Fulbright found the same resistance as he confronted one after another of the prominent officials in the ECA. At the time of the hearings there were reports in the press about the efforts to form a Council of Europe as a step toward the building of common political institutions. Fulbright was astonished then when Averell Harriman, as the Special Ambassador in Europe, professed to know nothing more about the development than what he read in the press. "I am not involved in the political aspect," Harriman explained, "I am very much involved in the development of cooperation in OEEC."[21]

As Deputy Chief of the ECA mission in Germany, N. H. Collison once withheld American aid until the directors of the German national railways agreed to balance their budget. But since that was obviously an "economic" problem, he too had little reason to sup-

---

[20] Senate Foreign Relations Committee, *Hearings on Extension of ERP*, 1949, pp. 85-86.

[21] *Ibid.*, p. 147; and see also, pp. 139-40.

313

pose that he ever involved himself in politics. "My contacts," he told the Senate committee, "have been on economic matters rather than political matters. I do not recognize that I have any mandate or any responsibility politically under that law. I do have economic responsibility."[22]

On one revealing occasion in the hearings, Fulbright's hammering at the ECA finally moved Chairman Connally to step in:

> May I intervene right there? I want to suggest that under this bill, *which deals only with economics*, I would feel disposed to take disciplinary action against anybody in the ECA who exceeded his authority and began to meddle with the political situation in Europe. It is not the purpose of this bill to deal with the politics of Europe, either for a union or against a union or halfway between them.[23]

Coming as it did from one of the key Senate leaders who guided the original bill through Congress, this support for the peculiar approach of the ECA seemed particularly authoritative.

Was it fair to say, then, that the ECA people denied the presence of political overtones in their decisions, or that in some naïve way they were determined to make economics out of politics? The record would show, on the contrary, that they were not so simpleminded. It would demonstrate, rather, that their understanding followed the sense of our hypothetical operating rules. Hoffman never contended that there was a complete separation between politics and economics. He warned the Senate committee once that "life cannot be neatly divided into economic, political, social, and military compartments. Europe's problem cannot be attacked simply in terms of economics nor solved by our handing over a carefully computed number of dollars. . . ."[24] And after he had time for further reflection, he was able to respond to Fulbright in language that conveyed the essence of our operating rule:

> I do not think I have ever felt there is any real difference between yourself and myself on what should transpire in Europe. We have both agreed, I think, that there must be a greater unity among the free nations of western Europe. *The whole difference*

[22] *Ibid.*, p. 310.

[23] Senate Foreign Relations Committee, *Hearings on Extension of ERP*, 1949, p. 198, and see also p. 309. Emphasis added.

[24] *Ibid.*, p. 13.

314

is a question of method, and I felt quite certain that *as far as ECA was concerned, the Congress intended us to deal on the economic front* and intended us also *to so restrict our efforts* with the clear understanding that you cannot operate in an airtight compartment. What we do has political repercussions and vice versa.[25]

What made this distinction practicable was that the idiom of economics was entirely sufficient to the needs of the ECA. Political judgments were so naturally entangled with the economic, that there was enough to do simply in arguing about these so-called "economic" decisions. The ECA might believe, for example, that British competitiveness was undermined by labor practices that raised costs and retarded modernization. It could feel that the Labour Government was taking too soft a view toward labor, that its acceptance of overly full employment was inhibiting the reforms that were needed for a thorough recovery. But at the very least the British deserved to have that critique documented, for even some of the more articulate critics of the government could not subscribe to that thesis. The government could argue, in return, that the British problems were rooted in the structural changes brought about in the international economy by the war. It could point to the liabilities involved in managing sterling, and it could cite a pattern of neglect for capital investment that started early in the twentieth century. Surely there was enough to argue about in all these issues without flying to the conclusion that the British and American governments were divided on fundamental grounds of principle.

There was actually a coincidence of interests here. Both a decent respect for the British government and a concern for making the wise substantive decision would have suggested the propriety of exploring the factual matter at greater length before the disagreement was brought to the political level. At times, the mere challenging of a decision was enough, because it faced the recipient government with the burden of making a more coherent justification. If the government in question could cite some reasonable economic grounds for the decision, then that was as much as the ECA could legitimately expect, and as far as the Marshall Plan agency was concerned, that was enough in itself to make the decision considerably better. If there was still room for the play of political criteria, then that was the business of the local government; the ECA had

[25] *Ibid.*, p. 525. Emphasis added.

done all it could on behalf of its own criteria. Was there something suspect in the location of two steel plants in France that were built with ECA funds? Then that was the concern of the French government, and it was better not to inquire too deeply into certain things. For was the steel not being produced, and was the production not contributing to the overall plan that measured European recovery?

By following these rules on the use of political criteria, the administrators not only made their own actions more consistent with the pluralist ethic conveyed by Marshall in his address at Harvard; they also contributed something that would last far beyond the life of their own agency: They prevented their own intrusions, which were occasioned by crisis conditions, from achieving the level of principle. The nonintervention doctrine would emerge from the Marshall Plan substantially intact. And thus, Donald Stone, who served throughout the program as the ECA Director of Administration, would consistently refer to the American operation in Greece as a "special case." Few people were as intimately involved in the administration of the Marshall Plan as Stone was, and yet he never saw intervention as the typical form of ECA practice. It was always a matter of some importance to him to maintain the consciousness of the Greek venture as a noticeable exception to a general pattern of conduct.

If the operating presumptions in favor of economic criteria had not been held sincerely, it would be hard to account for the process by which the Marshall Plan was generalized from a limited European assistance effort to a permanent foreign aid program with universal application. In 1951 the Marshall Plan had been converted into an economic support program for the European rearmament effort. For many in the ECA the change was not merely one of emphasis, but an alteration that destroyed the very meaning of the Marshall Plan. Two months before the ECA was scheduled to close itself out, Donald Stone entered his own dissent in an almost emotional memorandum (he admitted in the preface that he was "all steamed up" when he wrote it). Stone objected to the new concept of aid, which subordinated economic assistance to military production. He still believed in the organizational decision of 1948—that the Marshall Plan was an autonomous program, with its own distinctive ends. Those ends, he declared, were in making a better life for the citizens of the recipient countries, to show them that democracy was an effective and worthwhile alterna-

316

tive to communism. It was a humanitarian program that demonstrated to the people of Europe that the United States was concerned with them as individuals and wanted to see them improve their lives. But this new program, according to Stone, would hold up a different meaning to the world. It would tell the Asians, for example, that the United States was "not really interested in improving conditions of life, that we are interested only in *their help* for *our defense* against communism." (Stone's emphasis.) What the new program was doing was throwing overboard what Stone saw as the theory of postwar foreign policy since 1947, "that security, peace, and in fact victory in our contest with communism, must be built upon sound economic foundations. . . ." There was a connection in Stone's mind between the goal of world peace and the commitment to economic welfare programs. Peace would come "only when enough government leaders and other important people . . . reflect in their personal lives those moral values which produce stable and democratic institutions." In turn, those values were acquired "when a sense of individual and national responsibility begins to be felt for human misery wherever it may be found. . . ."[26]

That same year, Paul Hoffman (now retired as Administrator of the ECA) published his own book, *Peace Can Be Won*. In it, Hoffman had the chance to give an account of his own work in the Marshall Plan and express his own understanding of the foreign aid program. Characteristically, he fell back on the old liberal cliché of commerce as a great healer. The Marshall Plan raised production, diffused prosperity, and in this way helped to prevent totalitarian revolutions in Europe.[27] In one of those strange conversions that occurs in public life, the practical man of affairs had become very much a man of theory. For the difference between a practical and a theoretical man must surely lie in a certain sensitivity to the detail and texture of particular cases, and to the circumstances that make some situations truly separate. And yet what practical man of affairs, having administered the Marshall Plan, would write as Hoffman did in 1951, that "We have learned in Europe what to do in Asia"? For where, after all, were the similarities, and what had Hoffman learned?

[26] Donald Stone to F. J. Lawton, "Implications of Mutual Security Act and Requirements for Action," October 6, 1951, Bureau of the Budget, Series 39.27.

[27] Paul G. Hoffman, *Peace Can Be Won* (Garden City, New York: Doubleday and Company, Inc., 1951), p. 20.

> While in Europe we concentrated on turbines and tractors, in Asia we are primarily concerned with vaccines and fertilizers. But the political principle remains the same. Only the deeds of democracy can enable the peoples still undecided between the lures of despotism and the life of freedom to make an honest choice.[28]

The principle, apparently, was that democracy got the goods to the people in time. When the minimal needs of the people were taken care of, when desperation was removed, then the people were able to sit back and make a rational choice among the competing political systems. This was the voice of Hoffman, the former used car salesman; it was all, in the final analysis, a matter of consumer's choice.

Yet, what was there in the program these two men administered that led them to such an understanding of the Marshall Plan? To say that the program improved the lives of the people by raising production or serving the "general good" is surely too broad and vague. If these characterizations by Stone and Hoffman meant anything, they had to mean something very close to the picture drawn by Hoffman of an active competition for the favor of the populace. That is, the Marshall Plan would have demonstrated the effectiveness of democracy by bringing dramatic improvement to the standard of living for the vast majority of Europeans. It would have been a form of Tory socialism that lured the workers away from the appeals of radical ideologies, and it would have done it by bribing the people, as it were, with a more egalitarian distribution of material goods. But it would require a wide stretching of the facts to make the record of the Marshall Plan fit this theory. As we have already seen, one of the most basic operating tests used by the ECA was to keep per capita consumption approximately at 1938 levels. The object was to allow additions to consumption only where that was necessary to check a potential inflation. Otherwise resources were to be directed toward investment, and manufactured goods were to be diverted from the domestic economy into the export market.

Hoffman himself admitted in 1950 that the ECA had taken no interest in promoting wage increases or a better standard of living for workers. At this same time he expressed his hope that the policy of transferring resources from consumption to investment "will, *after we have pulled out*, enable them to increase their standard of

[28] *Ibid.*, pp. 130-31.

living considerably."[29] Improvements in the standard of living were to be deferred until *after* the Marshall Plan.

Real wages did in fact rise during this period. But that was not due to any increased assertiveness on the part of labor in demanding a larger share of the national wealth. The general pattern in wages was one of restraint. With the exception of the Netherlands, there was no direct control on wages, but there were some very successful programs of voluntary restraint, which held up until the wage-pull pressures of the post-Korean period, when there was a scarcity of labor. Labor governments were in an especially advantageous position to cajole the unions into restraint, and they backed up their own part of the bargain by a vigorous policy of taxing excess profits. At one point in the Netherlands the unions even accepted a cut in real wages as a contribution to a deflationary policy.[30] Here, as elsewhere in Europe, unions gave their support to austerity programs. As in Italy, workers came to appreciate the fact that their future consumption might depend on a stiff deflationary policy, which could make saving meaningful again. But the benefits in these cases were all in the long run; labor was not bribed into support for the political system with immediate payoffs. In fact, labor acceptance of these arrangements made sense only because the union members were already integrated into their political communities. If the situation was as Hoffman described it, with the population waiting to be sold on entering the political system, it might well have been irrational for the workers to have accepted these sacrifices. Deferring short-term advantages for long-term gains would have made far less sense if the working classes were still without leverage in their respective political systems; for they would have had far less assurance in that case that benefits were really being deferred, and that their governments would indeed make good on their promises later. What made this renunciation of self-interest possible was the fact that the workers were not outside their political communities, but thoroughly committed. One could not account for the behavior of European labor in this period, then, in the familiar terms of a consumers' politics. Instead, the analysis would require some rather traditional and unrevolutionary concepts like party loyalty, enlightened self-interest, or even civic obligation.

[29] Senate Committee on Appropriations, *Hearings on Foreign Aid Appropriation for Fiscal 1951* (1950), p. 241. Emphasis added.
[30] See UN, *Economic Survey of Europe Since the War*, p. 72.

319

Finally, the ECA was bound to a conceptual apparatus that blocked it off from an active interventionist policy. The balance of payments analysis was a rather gross analytical tool, but for an agency that was equipped to do little more than pump goods into Europe, it was good enough. It was sufficient for dealing with advanced industrial nations, when the ECA had to do little more than authorize the procurement of goods. There was practically no need to provide facilities for unloading the materials or distributing them inside the country. It was unnecessary to teach the recipients what to do with the raw materials or how to market them when they were turned into finished goods. Thus, there was really no need for the ECA to inject itself in the production decisions of specific industries, even if it had the capacity to become involved. For this particular program, then, and for this particular set of nations, the balance of payments offered a fairly comfortable analysis. Moreover, the balance of payments had relevance for some of the more sophisticated problems facing these nations in the form of trade imbalances; and besides that, it seemed to do no special harm.

But the limits of the theory became evident in 1951, when an effort was made to mesh the operations of the ECA with the military aid program. In developing estimates for Fiscal 1952, it was found that the ECA was still using a modified balance of payments analysis. What the military required, however, was a very detailed model covering the entire production system. It was essential to have specific information on the total resources available in the participating countries for meeting targets of military production.[31] However, as long as the ECA was operating with the balance of payments analysis, it was incapable of dealing with specific production issues. It was virtually predictable, then, that when a new foreign aid agency moved into the underdeveloped areas and took up the responsibility for an assistance program in Southeast Asia, the balance of payments theory would have to be abandoned. Almost all of these countries had surpluses in dollars or other hard currencies as a result of selling raw materials to the West. Here, instead of providing a rough but useful index of a real economic problem, the theory worked to obscure a fundamental need for development.[32]

Nothing seems more fanciful, therefore, than the notion that an

[31] See Bureau of the Budget, *Survey of the ECA*, September 1951, p. 63. Series 39.32.

[32] See *ibid.*, pp. 35-36.

agency like the ECA, operating from afar with the bluntest of tools, could possibly regulate the distribution policies of the ERP countries and direct them toward egalitarian ends. The ECA did nothing to credit some of the early fears among conservatives that the Marshall Plan would project the New Deal abroad. If, in retrospect, Hoffman and Stone tried to generalize the Marshall Plan as a program of welfare economics, they were misleading themselves.[33] But these were intelligent men, who were in the center of operations. There must have been something in the Marshall Plan that gave even that erroneous explanation some grounding in fact. And what that basis seemed to be was the sense of distinctiveness for the Marshall Plan as an autonomous program with a concentration on economic policy. Stone had difficulty in articulating the philosophy of the Marshall Plan, but there was no doubt in his mind that it was fundamentally different from the military program. From that persuasion it was a shorter step to the view that the Marshall Plan also had its own distinctive ends, which had to be related to the autonomy of its peculiar criteria. But was that not the essential content of Vandenberg's thinking in 1948, when he moved to separate the ECA from the State Department? Yes, but it was dependent also on several other strands of thought in the Marshall Plan, which combined in support of some concrete working rules. It was not simply that the people at ECA *perceived* themselves as separated from the State Department, but that the character of their agency actually made them different in their day-to-day work. Thus, to know how the Marshall Plan came to be generalized after 1951 one would have to account for that unshakable assurance with which Hoffman seemed to understand the exact character and place of his agency—how he could admit so blithely that the decisions of ECA were surrounded with political implications, and yet maintain through it all that in "ERP, however, our attention is focused on economic problems."

[33] For some reason there is a tendency to overlook the fact that the ECA subordinated the principle of "need" in 1949 when it decided to take the existing allocations as a base and make proportionate cuts with each successive year. The matter turned in part on the question of incentives. If aid was reduced when a country's deficit contracted, it would have penalized improvement. Instead, the ECA determined to shift its incentives to reward success, even if it meant that aid might not go where it was most vitally needed. If there was any allocating principle more removed from the premises of a welfare orientation, it would have been hard to imagine. See Ellis, *op.cit.*, pp. 531-32.

15. THE REGIME AND THE NATIONAL INTEREST

LOOKING BACK on the Marshall Plan, one is struck by the sense of an almost transparent rationality in the main outline of the legislative decisions. Of course the program could not be tailored to the partisan fancies of everyone who participated in the Executive and Congressional discussions. But there was a total complex of considerations here that was constructed in part by previous decisions in foreign aid, and that made some alternatives less clearly defensible than others. As a result, it would be hard for anyone but the most unreserved isolationist to deny the essential reasonableness of what was done in 1948. Stop-gap measures like relief aid had failed to prevent a serious worsening in the European economy. Even a large loan venture, like the $3.75 billion British credit, had melted away, leaving little more behind than a further charge on the British balance of payments. By the time Marshall came to speak at Cambridge, then, the principal alternatives had already been played out. Against this background, the declaration for a "cure rather than a mere palliative" contained nothing that was radical or extravagant. It was the choice of a prudent and cautious man, who knew that if there was going to be a next step, it had to involve massive injections of aid, and on a grant rather than a loan basis.

The center of the immediate crisis was in the breakdown of European trade and production. Admittedly, the raw material shortages were temporary, and such complicating factors as the bad winter of 1946-47 were simply "freak" occurrences. But the disintegration of the European system was not a transitory phenomenon; it had been in the making since the beginning of the twentieth century, and it was accelerated with the movement toward policies of economic autarchy. However much we may value the fruits of the welfare state, it is still necessary to recognize that the commitment to full employment, along with the attendant controls on for-

322

eign trade and the movement of capital, promised only to complicate this breakdown of integration. In these circumstances, there were good reasons to conclude, with Marshall and the State Department, that the United States should put the weight of its policy in the opposite direction and press for a closer coordination of resources in Europe. If it made sense for the United States to place its weight in this way against the tendencies toward national autarchy, it made equally good sense to have some basic American enforcement in the program, including some minimal supervision overseas. If, in turn, there was to be meaningful enforcement, the granting of aid could not be removed from the hands of the United States and distributed in some automatic or unconditional fashion. If the commitment was not open-ended, it was wise to make that clear to the Europeans by inserting a definite date of termination. And if the United States was genuinely determined to exert a continuing pressure on the Europeans for cooperation and reform, it would certainly have been inconsistent to disarm the ECA in advance by providing no means of terminating aid before the end of four years.

But if one accepted all these propositions, there were certain alternatives for organization that were clearly more appropriate than others. If the Marshall Plan was irrevocably limited to a four-year term and could even end sooner, then the burden of argument rested more properly with those who advocated centralization. For the sake of a temporary program, it hardly seemed justifiable to strip functions away from established agencies. It was arguable, of course, that the purposes of the Marshall Plan *were* superior, but in view of the temporary status of the program, the presumption surely had to lie with the agencies that had already exercised these functions for several years. On the same grounds, it was less justifiable, also, to use the Marshall Plan as the occasion for reorganizing the committee structure in Congress. Nor did it seem appropriate to create a huge government apparatus that could supersede private channels of trade and direct all procurement transactions between American exporters and the recipient countries.

If the commitment was short-term, and if it could end at any time before the four years were up, then the logic of administering through a corporation was considerably weaker. If one added a preference for Congressional control, the traditional corporate autonomy was misplaced. If one preferred an agency that would limit its operations and allow Congress more time to reflect on the precise content of the American interest in Europe, then there was little room in that vision for an agency with the flexible powers of corporate ownership.

Nothing in this chain of reasoning depended on the application of radical premises. If one did nothing more than accept an American interest in a foreign aid program (and it was harder to deny that interest after so much had already been invested) all these considerations would have been persuasive. And if one assented to them, however grudgingly, one would have had to accept the decisions that gave the program its essential character.

Part of our argument has been that it was indeed possible to identify the essential character of the program. We have suggested, further, that the separate decisions could be related more coherently to one another if we cast them in terms of operating presumptions. The object has been to show that in the relation between any two parts of the legislation, the presumptions were placed in favor of one and, correlatively, against the other. On that basis we could declare that one value had been subordinated to another, or that the significance of one policy value depended on the variations in another. In that way, we could pull the disparate parts of the legislation together in an integrated structure in which it was possible to distinguish the independent from the dependent values or the primary from the secondary commitments.[1]

---

[1] To treat a legislative text in this way carries a considerable risk of implying that the intentions of the legislators were characterized by a comparable degree of integration. That is a view, however, that we have never urged. The assumptions behind this approach have been rather more modest. We have assumed, first, that it is generally better to be clearer on the precise meaning of any policy, even at the risk of imposing a coherence on the legislation that might not have been evident to the legislators themselves. If nothing else, the effort to reconcile the various parts of the legislation may be quite valuable in demonstrating that coherence is lacking.

Moreover, even if the legislation does represent a patchwork of compromises, the actual administration of the program creates pressures toward some minimal consistency. It is not so easy for administrators to insulate themselves from the consequences of discordant politics, for what they do under one clause of the legislation will often affect their performance in other areas as well. Thus, if the ECA had not resisted the demands for a more intensive effort in the Small Business program, it might not have been able to add as many people to the Controller's office in the later phases of the Marshall Plan. Similarly, it was only natural that the ECA would have been far more sensitive than Congress to the added dollar costs of the ship-

After identifying the dominant values in the program, it was possible to extend the analysis and say something further about the relations among the independent values as well. Thus the evidence strongly suggests that the most important effects of debureaucratization and economic pattern maintenance were to enforce the values of pluralism. Debureaucratization reduced the administrative capacities of the ECA that would have been necessary for any sustained program of intervention. A good case in point occurred when the ECA found it impracticable to continue its anti-cartel efforts. In view of its own limited resources, the agency decided to take a less ambitious route and treat the problem merely as one of raising production. Thereafter it would be satisfied with a modest technical assistance program. In explaining its decision, the agency staff made an explicit connection between the strands of debureaucratization and pluralism:

> Given the deep roots and wide extent of restrictive business practices in Europe, the problem of just what ECA can do in this field is very difficult. *ECA is an organization with a short life.* It is committed in principle and by the obvious dictates of practical policy to *refrain from interference in the internal political affairs of the participating countries.* In this situation the limitations on direct ECA action are obvious.[2]

By supporting a preference for private facilities and private channels of trade, pattern maintenance contributed to this weakness of the ECA. But it also enforced the pluralist orientation in another and more direct way. Goods traveled through the normal channels of trade, so they were procured, for the most part, in ordinary commercial transactions. Leaving aside the financing arrangement for the dollars, it was the European importer who was ordering and paying for these goods. What that did was relieve the ECA of the very complicated and delicate task of defining an alternative principle for distribution. If commercial sale had not been the basis of allocation, the ECA would have had to enter the recipient country, examine the various importers and industries, and decide who was to receive the goods in each specific case. In using commercial

---

ping provision and the extent to which that subsidy collided with other policies that were more basic to the program.

[2] ECA, *Eighth Report* (Quarter ending March 31, 1950), p. 11. Emphasis added.

channels, however, the ECA could stand aloof from the whole process, which meant also that it could look the other way when the local governments made their own adjustments in distribution. Thus the procurement process would not circumvent the state trading organizations in Britain and France, and there were instances, as in Italy and Greece, where the national government had its own favorites among the importers. Fortunately, the ECA was spared the necessity of concerning itself too deeply in these matters, and this must surely stand as one of the paradoxes of the Marshall Plan, particularly for the Communist argument. Instead of projecting American capitalism abroad as an instrument for dominating the Europeans, the pattern maintenance values enforced the tendency to be more allowing and liberal.

As these examples have already suggested, the most striking characteristic to emerge from this analysis of the program was the ascendance of the pluralist values. The benefit of the doubt was placed solidly on the side of the ERP country and in favor of keeping the program going. The threat to cut off assistance was abandoned very early as a practical weapon.[3] The primacy of national interests and the reluctance of the participating countries to move toward integration were accepted as facts of life. The ECA hoped to build a multilateral structure for the European economy, but its aspirations were finally focused on the European Payments Union. In place of the continuous testing of the ERP countries for cooperative behavior, the ECA put all its hopes in the long run and was content to accept formal commitments to supranational institutions.

When it was decided to base further allocations on the 1949 figures and separate the allocation of aid from the balance of payments deficit, that was but another step away from the continuous testing of the Marshall Plan countries. Although it was a decisive step, it was part of an overall pattern that might have been detected as early as the first year. It was determined almost at the outset of the program that the ECA would presume in favor of the figures provided by the OEEC, and in support of that presumption it

[3] After the Dutch intervention in Indonesia, the ECA temporarily suspended aid, but that was done also to forestall a Congressional amendment. In preventing Congressional action, the ECA was in a better position to maintain the status of the suspension as a temporary measure. By freeing itself from the complications of legislation, it was able to reinstate aid to the Netherlands fairly quickly.

would not make immediate adjustments, either upward or downward, in response to changes in the balance of payments. As the ECA explained in its final annual report,

> It is the stated policy of the ECA to make [changes in the OEEC allocations] *only where they are clearly justified.* It is of very great importance to the success of the ERP that, once a specified amount of aid has been allotted to a country, the amount should remain fixed for at least a year *unless the most compelling circumstances* justify a change.[4]

The device of counterpart funds symbolized the cardinal preference for shared authority. The United States did not circumvent the local government to deal directly with the population or private industry. There was some mention of working through private business when the ECA gave up its attack on restrictive practices and decided to concentrate on the technical assistance program; but under the procedures finally adopted, contracts had to be approved by the national government, and the projects themselves were frequently organized under government auspices. Whatever sharing of authority was implied in the use of counterpart funds was tilted to the benefit of the ERP nations. The approval of counterpart releases could give the United States some residue of bargaining power, but it offered no real leverage for effective intervention. That was especially true because of the priorities followed by the ECA in counterpart releases. The ECA leaned toward anti-inflation programs and debt retirement, and to the extent those preferences were followed, the ECA was that much less involved in determining the allocation of productive investment.

The United States did not impose its own assumptions of bipolarity upon the Europeans. Despite the virtual cessation of American trade with the Soviet bloc, the ERP countries were allowed—and even encouraged—to continue their traditional trade with Eastern Europe. The ECA was inclined to be permissive, also, in enforcing the export restrictions on strategic materials that threatened to find their way from the ERP countries into the Soviet zone. It was only after the start of the Korean war, and some rather forceful nudging on the part of Congress, that the ECA began to tighten up on its enforcement.

[4] ECA, *Recovery Progress and United States Aid*, 1949, p. 67. Emphasis added.

Under the "cure rather than a palliative" doctrine, the ECA could narrow the scope permitted to the more self-regarding interests of American groups. Empirically, this line of policy was linked to the dollar theory. If more goods and services could be purchased in Europe rather than the United States, the ECA could move toward recovery on several fronts. First, and most obviously, it could pump more resources into the European economy. Second, it could reduce the dollar charges on the United States and lessen the exaggerated dependence of the Europeans on the dollar area. Third, in taking this approach, the ECA could cultivate some nondollar sources of supply for the Europeans (e.g., the manufacture of machine tools in Britain) and possibly enlarge their capacity to earn dollars—as surely would have been the case if Congress had agreed to lend vessels to the Europeans and share the shipping business in the Marshall Plan. Faced with the choice of either subsidizing American business or buying in Europe (where it could also save on dollar costs), the ECA presumed in favor of buying abroad.[5] The coal and machine tool industries felt the pinch of this operating presumption very keenly, and in a time of recession. Only Congressional reaction saved the merchant marine from losing its special provisions in the program, and when that same Congressional support failed to materialize, the milling industry found its own little subsidy whittled away.

As registered in the legislation, the major surplus agricultural commodities were served with the priority of an independent policy value. Agricultural goods could not be purchased overseas for use in the program so long as there were surpluses available in the United States. But as soon as one passed the most important products, such as wheat, cotton, corn, tobacco, and wool, the other commodities found themselves on the wrong side of the operating presumptions. The burden was thrown upon Congress to take up the cause of specific commodities in an ad hoc manner. When concessions were granted, they were for a particular commodity at a particular time; no general rules were created, no general pattern of patronage was sustained.

[5] As Hoffman told the Senate Foreign Relations Committee, Congress would have to give the ECA "very specific and direct instructions, because if you do not give us those instructions we are going to buy where we can buy at the lowest price. If that is not the way you want the program run, we want to be told that." Senate Foreign Relations Committee, *Hearings on Extension of ERP*, 1949, p. 54.

When Congress added an amendment for the benefit of small business, the ECA shifted the presumptions again, this time placing the burdens on the very people who were the supposed beneficiaries. The small businessmen themselves had to take the initiative for acquiring information, not only about the program, but also about the intricate legal and commercial problems involved in entering the export trade. On the issue of acquiring strategic materials from the ERP countries, the ECA again turned the presumptions around, but in a more subtle way. The presumptions in the fact-finding process were set in favor of accumulating more and more information, as though the agency was seeking an almost perfect certitude before it would even begin to negotiate contracts. It was the action of an agency that honored its nominal commitment under the law, but sought to evade its intent by administering the policy with a strong bias in favor of its clientele countries. At the same time, the burden of detecting this critical turnabout of presumptions fell upon Congress. It required an uncommonly articulate opinion, in this instance on the part of the watchdog committee, before the policy could be reversed.

Despite the enthusiasms in Congress for the "business-like" approach, the dollar theory provided a justification that made the decline of the loan program acceptable. Instead of putting a further charge on the Europeans' balance of payments through the use of large-scale loans, the presumptions were placed clearly in favor of grant aid. But if the business approach was downgraded, that was a disparagement only of some of the more familiar techniques of the business world. On a far more consequential level, though, in the basic assumptions of the program about institutions and processes, the commitment to business as a system was more than adequately preserved: an economy in which property and exchange were organized almost entirely under private auspices continued to be one of the central suppositions of the Marshall Plan.

Thus, in surveying the experience of the ECA, what stood out as the independent policy values were the ones we identified under the labels of pluralism, economic pattern maintenance, debureaucratization, and a "cure rather than a palliative." Within the collection of independent values the combined weight of the presumptions centered on pluralism as the peak value in the program. But to outline this ranking of values is to recapitulate, in essence, the same hierarchy of interests we discovered in the original legislative decisions. That is not to minimize the serious changes in policy that

329

occurred; nor is it to pretend that there were no serious disputes between Congress and the ECA over the meaning of the program itself. It is to recognize, instead, that the legislation provided a code, rather than a rigid collection of imperatives. The administrators worked within an established structure of values, which offered some guidance in making choices and furnished a frame of reference, in addition, for any disputes that happened to arise. Thus, despite the alterations that took place, one would have to conclude that the program was administered in a remarkably principled way; it remained faithful in practice to that peculiar ordering of values that defined the Marshall Plan.

One intent of this project was to show that those values represented valid "interests," and that they were as relevant to the definition of the American national interest in the Marshall Plan as considerations of geography or military capabilities. In fact, it was these interests that were dominant in the consideration of the program. The Marshall Plan was subjected to an exhaustive series of analyses in committees drawn from Congress, the Executive, and private groups, and extending over a period of nine months. Yet, as we have already shown, it would be hard to maintain that it proceeded from any clear or explicit sense of what the strategic interest might have been in Western Europe, either politically or militarily. That might prove nothing, of course, except the absence of statesmanship, and a pitiless verdict of that sort could be fair enough were it not for the opaque and conditional nature of the problem itself.

The question of military interest, which was supposedly so firm in its outlines, was hedged in on every side with uncertainties. They were uncertainties, mainly, about the intentions of the Soviet Union and the real portents of the coup in Czechoslovakia. There were basic doubts, too, as to what the United States might have been able to do in the case of Czechoslovakia and, indeed, what it might be able to accomplish elsewhere with the reach of military power. Beyond that, there was no clarity on the military requirements of the situation, and even if there had been, there was no consensus on what the United States was prepared to do or the price it was willing to pay.

Senator McClellan warned, with the voice of realism, that the Marshall Plan would create an American stake in Europe, and it might become necessary at some future date to protect that investment. Unless they were prepared, as he was, to defend that commitment with military action, he urged his colleagues to think twice before taking that critical first step. But there was no agreement in Congress on that ultimate question, particularly in the Republican majority, and so, rather than thrusting the question to its ultimate political level, the Congressional leaders decided to separate the issues. What they endorsed now was an economic program, and they made it clear that the question of a political commitment was something they were deferring until later. Thus, the decision for the Marshall Plan could be made without some final and definitive judgment on the nature of the strategic interest in Europe.

Moreover, as long as the issue remained on the level of strategic interests, as long as it was enveloped in abstract questions of "power" and "security," it was bound to remain hopelessly speculative. Although the words bear connotations of hardness, "power" and "security" are essentially neutral concepts, which lack any substantive content in themselves. "Power" is usually defined as the capacity to realize one's will—i.e., to achieve a given set of ends. "Security," too, implies the "securing" of something, the protection of some central core of values. Either one, then, assumes that there are ends to be served, and they both acquire their meaning only in relation to their substantive ends. Without some understanding of what the ends of American policy were in Europe, it was virtually meaningless to ponder what the interests of "power" prescribed. Nor did it advance the question to say that there was an American interest in Europe—*some* kind of interest—although it could not be defined just yet. That did nothing to explain the extent of the American interest in Europe or to clarify the precise interests that were engaged. The deeper problem here was not that the criteria of power were simply too flaccid to resolve the substantive issue, but that they were incapable of generating the kinds of policy cues that could move the inquiry along. Thus, as we have argued, it was not until the decision-makers could turn to the practical task of administering the program that the question of national interest could finally be approached with some degree of concreteness. It was not until then that the alternatives would become visible and the question of costs could be posed in a meaningful way.

The problem of administration spoke in the language of counterpart funds, export controls, private channels of trade, annual authorizations, and the jurisdictions of other agencies. They were prosaic terms, to be sure, but in a remarkably concrete manner they summarized the most important substantive questions that had to be raised in the program. It was in these terms, largely, that the decision-makers would fix the relation of the United States with the Marshall Plan countries, the relative ranking of the ECA in the Administration, and the relation of government to the private sector of the economy.

Facing the question of authority under the program was a means of establishing the relative priority of the Marshall Plan interest, and inevitably, also, it merged with the older question of duties and rights. Did the massive outlay of resources entitle the United States to a position of predominant authority in the program? Would the American relation to the Europeans be one of hierarchical direction or shared authority—and to that extent, would the United States use its leverage to compress the possibilities for European socialism, or would it take a more lenient and deferential course? Would the United States be warranted in using the program as a device for subsidizing certain hard-pressed industries, or were the American people obliged to show a greater measure of discipline? Were they expected to display a sense of detachment when goods were siphoned off the domestic market in a time of inflation? Were they willing to return to a system of rationing in some commodities; were they willing to accept a restoration of controls for the sake of spending what was truly necessary in Europe? Was the Marshall Plan charged with such overwhelming social import that it deserved to override the authority of the established agencies in their own spheres and take precedence over the groups whose interests had been invested in those agencies? These and many more were the questions raised by the problem of administration, and they illuminated the full range of interests that were implicated in this program.

In deciding on the relative precedence of the Marshall Plan interest, the decision-makers were compelled to affirm once again their overall sense on the ordering of public policy; for either implicitly or explicitly the Marshall Plan had to be set against the complex of institutional interests. Thus, Alan Kline of the Farm Bureau Federation argued that the American interest in the Marshall Plan would end as soon as the program became so large, and the drain on the American economy so extensive, that the government would have to reinstate controls. Enforcing economic controls in peacetime was a precedent for Kline that revised the American system in a fundamental way. In this fashion the question of administration removed the "national interest" from the speculative criteria of power and brought the discussion back to the basic stand-ard for any definition of interest: the character of the society itself or, more accurately, the character of the political regime.

It is common to refer to the "national interest" as though one were using a wholly descriptive term, whose meaning remained fixed over time. But as they function in our language, terms like "na-tional interest" or "national security" have the import of moral words. That is, they move beyond mere statements of personal taste or subjective preference, and they claim to say something about the standards for what is generally or universally good—which is to say, good for others as well as oneself. In the case of "public interest" or "national interest," the "others" refers to the whole society, and those who use these words use them with an awareness of the po-litical act as a means of creating commitments: Political decisions are decisions that are potentially binding on all members of the so-ciety, and anyone who seeks in this way to commit others besides himself will usually acknowledge his responsibility to cite some-thing more than his personal tastes. As long as he would commit no one but himself, expressions such as "I like this" are fully ade-quate. But once he moves beyond that level and seeks to commit others, he is forced to accept an entirely new set of obligations. He can be obligated now to give reasons—to cite evidence, point to standards and considerations that are not merely subjective or idio-syncratic, but capable of being understood by the people he is obliged to convince.

In this sense, there is something in the very logic of moral dis-course that compels anyone who engages in it to elaborate the factual content of his values; and to the extent that that occurs, the separation between facts and values is partially bridged. In the process, values become something more than arbitrary expressions of wants. They acquire an empirical dimension, which opens the possibilities for rational discourse, and in some cases that alone could make the difference between arbitrary policy and one that has some legitimate claim to bind.[6]

[6] A much fuller development of this analysis has already been provided by Richard Flathman in his excellent book, *The Public Interest* (New York: John Wiley and Sons, 1966). See also R. M. Hare, *Freedom and Reason* (New York: Oxford University Press, 1963), *The Language of Morals* (New York: Oxford University Press, 1952), part II; Stephen E. Toulmin, *An Examination of the Place of Reason in Ethics* (Cambridge: Cambridge

It is one thing, though, to observe that moral terms have an empirical content; it is quite another to insist that their meaning is entirely descriptive. If the "national interest" was a purely descriptive term, it might, indeed, refer to some fixed empirical standard that endured over time. But a situation of that kind is simply foreign to the nature of ethics, which must remain, as Aristotle said, a matter of practice: Any action implies some understanding of good and bad, better and worse; and as long as men continue to act, their actions will continue to raise questions about standards. Unless we can assume that moral rules will never come into conflict, or that new circumstances may never arise to defy the old rules, we would have to conclude, as Aristotle did, that decisions will still have to be made, and that questions will continue to be raised about the standards for deciding.[7]

It is in the nature of ethics, then, that it cannot simply come to an end. It is a continuing process of inquiry into the standards for what is "good," and for that very reason it must allow the possibility that values may change over time. If the standards of "good" theater, for example, were codified in ancient Rome, they might have included in their list of essential requirements the slaughtering of a martyr or the staging of a live crucifixion. Conceivably, those early patrons of the "living theater" might have gone on in this way, filling in the descriptive content of "good" theater in a very precise and exhaustive manner. And if "good theater" was nothing more than a descriptive term, those empirical standards would have been frozen into the meaning of the words. Henceforth, we would not have been justified in labeling any dramatic performance as "good theater" unless it contained the slaughtering of a martyr and the enactment of a live crucifixion. Nor could we have called a play anything but "good" if it included these features.

But obviously, moral terms cannot be restricted in that way. They must have the capacity to disengage themselves from the current standards of what is good and call those very standards into question. That is to say, moral terms must have an empirical or substantive content, and part of their function is to describe, but this descriptive function can never exhaust their meaning. They must have, in addition, a prescriptive or commendatory function,

University Press, 1950); and Paul Edwards, *The Logic of Moral Discourse* (Glencoe: The Free Press, 1958).
   [7] See Aristotle, *Ethics*, Book II, ch. 1; also Book X, ch. 9.

334

which allows them to commend what current fashions have not yet accepted (or to condemn what current practice has sanctioned). Even in the face of a very impressive effort to clarify the empirical meaning of "good," we would still claim the freedom to hold ourselves back and say, "Yes, you've defined all the ingredients of what you regard as 'good' theater, but still we can't bring ourselves to agree that the kind of theater you describe is something we could call 'good.' There are certain considerations you've overlooked, certain perverse points in your reasoning, which prevent us from agreeing now that this is a form of drama that even you should have found acceptable."

The use of the term "national interest" is analogous: It does convey a substantive meaning, but it would violate the logic of the term to suggest that it refers to some hard empirical standard that eludes the play of time and circumstance. In the nineteenth century the "national interest" of Britain could be equated with fragile and shifting alliances, and the maintenance of a balance of power in Europe. It would be foolish to assert, though, that the British have the same interest in the balance of power today, in the sense that "balance of power" was understood in the nineteenth century. Clearly, the standards of national interest had to change, and not merely as a response to changes in the technology of warfare. More critical were the changes that occurred in the character and goals of the major powers. It was not simply the techniques that altered, but the ideological basis of the interstate system; and when that change came about, the fairly modest standards that guided diplomacy in the nineteenth century became virtually irrelevant. The requirements of an "adequate" defense in the nineteenth century had far less sufficiency when the actors were moved by opposing ideologies and the ends of power had been drastically reshaped.

The term "national interest" is being misued, then, when it is treated as a purely descriptive term, and when it is placed in the context of serious policy disputes, the results may be quite misleading. It is common to hear it said today that "The defense of South Vietnam is in no way related to the national interest of the United States"—as though one were simply applying an empirical yardstick. A very persuasive argument could, in fact, be made to show the Vietnam war is not in the real interests of the United States; but like the argument that could be made for the other side, it would have its own problematic qualities, including several weak spots of conjecture that could reasonably admit further exploration.

335

The critical point is that a proposition of this sort about the national interest cannot be a definitive, terminal statement, but the prelude to a substantive argument and the presentation of evidence.

One could object at this point that we court the same fallacy in the use of "national interest" when we do what I have urged and start from the base of the political regime in defining the national interest. If the essential features of the regime can be specified with some exactness, we would have a firm empirical standard, and once again we would seem to foreclose the possibility of change. We would seem to imply that we are taking the regime as a "given," and cutting ourselves off from the privilege of questioning the social order. Conversely, if the character of the regime is open to question, how can we look to it for the standards of national interest in foreign policy?

The problem is a familiar one in ethical theory, and the best answer is that moral rules are *defeasible*:[8] We may be committed to a very precise set of rules, but we may also be willing to test the rules continuously in specific cases. We may be able to suspend the rules in certain exceptional cases without disturbing the validity of the rules themselves; but at the same time, if enough "special cases" begin to accumulate, we may eventually find reason to modify the rules.

Similarly, it is possible to ascribe a definite character to a political system, even though the system may be open to revision in its various parts. In the American regime, for example, the right to counsel was enlarged considerably in the twenty-one years between *Betts* v. *Brady* and *Gideon* v. *Wainwright*, until it reached a position of far greater centrality as a constitutional feature. Did that make it any less meaningful to speak of the American "constitution" in 1942 or impute a definite character to the American regime? In fact, what is the discipline of constitutional law itself if not an ongoing process for articulating the values that may be implicit in the regime?

To insist, then, that the national interest in foreign policy should take its primary reference to the character of the political regime is not to plead for something alien to our understanding. It asks nothing more of statesmen than we ordinarily ask of judges, but it asks the highest thing we could demand of anyone: to make deci-

[8] On this point see H.L.A. Hart's essay, "The Ascription of Responsibility and Rights," in Anthony Flew (ed.), *Logic and Language*, First Series (Oxford: Basil Blackwell, 1951).

sions for this society that are reasoned, self-conscious, and above all, *good* decisions—decisions that are faithful to the character of this political community, but unfaithful, if need be, if it is a bad community.

It may be fashionable in the current flirtation with systems theory to devalue the question of regimes as a second-order problem. Its concerns seem to pale before the more grandiose question of how political systems in general manage to persist over time. In the view of general systems theory, the Cuba of Batista and the Cuba of Castro are moments in the history of the same system. They represent merely different forms in which the same system has been able to survive.

This brand of theory may beguile the academics, but for most people, who respond with some natural sense of politics, the most significant questions continue to be those that are bound up with the state of the regime—the priority, for example, of Negro rights, the welfare claims of the poor, or the demands for revolutionary change. To the natural understanding, the differences between Nazi Germany and Weimar are, in fact, the most weighty differences in politics. To treat these two regimes as merely phases in the maintenance of the same system would betray a certain naïve scientism, not to say an obliviousness to the kinds of data that give politics its moral consequence.

One can hardly exaggerate the centrality of the regime in political life, and on sober reflection it does not claim too much to contend, as Leo Strauss has, that "when the classics were chiefly concerned with the different regimes, and especially with the best regime, they implied that the paramount social phenomenon, or that social phenomenon than which only the natural phenomena are more fundamental, is the regime."[9] And if one begins with this kind of clarity on the central problem of politics, the problem of foreign policy falls more easily into its proper place. The foreign environment is a source of grave and disruptive pressures that threaten to disorder the community in a fundamental way. The need to cope with external dangers may place such an enormous burden on the system that it seriously distorts the use of moral and material resources. It threatens to distract the community in its efforts to order its internal life according to its own evolving sense of purpose, and in line with its own established understandings on the proper means of exercising authority. Even in those extreme cases where the dan-

[9] *Ibid.*, p. 137.

ger of annihilation is present, the danger arises from the fact that the community is threatened with "alien" rule—i.e., the instruments of power may fall into the hands of men who feel no sense of moral identity with the population they are ruling and no moral compunctions, therefore, in their use of force.

But the prospect of exterminating an entire subject population is very rare. What is more likely to occur, at the worst, is the absorption of the populace into some larger empire, the imposition of an occupation regime, or the creation of a puppet government. In any event, what is at stake in most cases is not the physical existence of the populace, but the existence of a community that defines its identity as a community through its own political institutions.

In the metaphors of "national security," though, a fictive image is sustained in which the danger seems to focus on the biological survival of the nation, rather than the maintenance of a certain regime. From there it is a far shorter step to equate the "national integrity" with the maintenance of a geographic frontier or the simple preservation of sovereignty. In reality, the national interest may well be served at times by the contraction of national boundaries; and who would contend, for example, that the United States would lose its identity as a nation if *any* part of its territory was detached? The paramount question must remain, as ever, "What is the best regime?," and by that standard the national interest might not only be served by a reduction in territory, but it may be advanced as well through an actual defeat in war and the temporary loss of sovereignty. Does it merely impose morals across cultures, or could we claim with some truth that no one served the interests of Germans better in 1945 than the Allied armies that penetrated from the west and dislodged a vicious, depraved regime?

But to say, as we have, that the national interest must begin with the understanding of a good regime rather than the metaphors of physical security does not mean, as some people have inferred, that there must be an immediate and overwhelming military threat before the regime could be said to be endangered. To argue in that way is to fall once again into the fallacy of defining the national interest by the standards of physical security. Once we free ourselves from that convention, we would have to recognize the possibility that the regime may be threatened even without the existence of an imminent military danger. In this respect, the test of an immediate physical threat is quite as insufficient as a guide

338

to decision as the cognate formula of a "clear and present danger" in our constitutional law; and the comparison is worth considering for a moment.

The clear and present danger test may be a very useful limiting device in a certain class of cases, but it can never begin to comprehend the full universe of things that the law must cope with in speech cases. We can cite many instances in which the authorities would not be bound to wait for an overt act or for the actual inflicting of harm before they would be justified in stepping in and restricting forms of expression.[10] But the point might be made well enough if we considered only the problem of libel: Even if we restricted libel to the narrowest test—a palpable injury to one's "trade" or business—it might be impossible to demonstrate any connection between the utterance of certain defamatory words and a dropoff in business. Even if a man's business happens to fall off at the time the libel occurred, could we prove that it was the libel that caused customers to withdraw their accounts? Would we have to call in the customers and take testimony from them, and try to probe their hidden reasons for taking their business elsewhere? And what about the new customers who might have come forward, but who held back as a result of the libel? How could we ever find them and prove the effect of the defamation? Could it be then that the plausibility of libel rests largely on our understanding of the way in which certain words naturally function in our language and the consequences we can normally expect them to have? To have

[10] One need only consider a case of this kind: All night long a crowd stands outside the home of the first Negro family to move into the neighborhood. The crowd does not resort to violence; no bottles or rocks are thrown. It merely stands there all night chanting in a low tone, and at times it makes no sound at all. It simply stands there in silence, intimidating by its very presence. Despite the fact that the crowd is engaged in "peaceful" assembly and protest, and even though it is engaged in an act of an authentic "political" nature, we would have no scruples about calling the police and having the crowd dispersed. On the willingness of the court to restrict the crowd "outside the house"—even in the case of a public official—see Justice Black's opinion in *Gregory* v. *Chicago*, 394 U.S. 111 (1969), especially 125-26. We have been able to avoid the implications of this problem in the past by insisting that it is "conduct" we are restricting in these cases rather than "speech." But that is a dodge that should fool no one any longer, and it is an escape that is no longer even available: Under the press of libertarian argument, it has now been accepted in our law that forms of conduct like the burning of a draft card or the wearing of arm bands in school may be protected as forms of "symbolic speech."

it said of a car dealer, for example, that he is "thoroughly dishon-est" is something we could only expect would injure his business. We may not know how widely it has spread, but we know it is an expression whose tendency can only be to harm.

And what can be said in this vein for the problem of libeling individuals can be said with even greater consequence in the mat-ter of group libel, a concept that for the moment seems to have been cast aside in our law. Here, too, the complaint has centered on the problem of proving injury: A libel so broad that it covers a whole group may strike at no one in particular. It would be fool-ish, in this view, if someone made general anti-Negro remarks on national television and we permitted individual blacks to flock into courts across the country seeking damages. A pamphlet that at-tacked Negroes for being inclined as a group to filth, immorality, and crime, could not be said then to reflect on all blacks, or to in-jure anyone directly. And yet, the cumulative effect of group libels may be highly destructive, even if we cannot show immediate and visible injuries. A libel so broad may effectively taint all members of the group. It becomes that much harder for any one individual to resist the sweep of the libel, and it creates the possibility that men may in fact be libeled through the group.[11] The fact that words of this kind may injure is something we may tend to resist when the problem is phrased as a "speech" issue; but when phrased in an-other way, it is something we have come to accept as a matter of course: For who would deny today, in the current climate of opinion —and after knowing what we do—that certain minority groups in this country have in fact suffered serious material injuries as a re-sult of racist stereotypes that have been perpetuated in the public mind? But to recognize in this way the common sense of the matter is to recognize the old truth that words and ideas have con-sequences. A doctrine that holds that "mere" words are untouch-able either does not have much respect for the power of ideas, or it supports a libertarian ethic on the bases of "truths" that are merely conventional or convenient.

---

[11] That is particularly true if we are dealing with a racial or religious group, rather than a more voluntary association from which it would be easier to withdraw. For a good statement of the arguments on either side of the group libel question, see the opinions of Justices Frankfurter and Black in *Beauharnais* v. *Illinois*, 343 U.S. 250 (1952), and compare David Riesman's classic article, "Democracy and Defamation," 42 *Columbia Law Review*, 727 (1942).

340

Lincoln understood this all very well when he observed that if slavery were morally right, "all words, acts, laws, and constitutions against it, are themselves wrong, and should be silenced, and swept away."[12] And in the same way, he understood the influence of the republican idea in the United States on the state of opinion elsewhere in the world; in a very realistic sense, he recognized the challenge it presented to the permanence of authoritarian regimes. (One recalls his complaint that the Kansas–Nebraska Act, with its promise of extending slavery, "deprives our republican example of its just influence in the world.")[13] At a time when democratic revolutions had been aborted and the political drift in Europe was to the right, the fate of the republican experiment in the United States could have a profound effect on the course of political change elsewhere: For men who were at present indecisive, it could confirm the view that democracies were inherently unstable, that they were fundamentally inadequate to the tasks of government.[14]

For the same reason, it seemed to follow that the destruction of democratic regimes abroad could have a serious effect on opinion in the United States. In a period of great division and instability, the trends at work in the rest of the world could weaken the support for popular government and a system of constitutional restraints. A democracy that could enslave blacks could start restricting once again the franchise of whites; and as the authorities began to take the steps that were necessary to preserve the new arrangements of power, the coercive aspects of the system could become more pronounced, while the "popular" features of the regime would begin to recede. The spread of authoritarian governments abroad had to be considered then as an event that threatened the support for republican government in the United States. If America held back from a course of intervention overseas, it could not have been on grounds of principle, therefore, but prudence. There was

[12] *The Collected Works of Abraham Lincoln*, ed. Roy P. Basler (New Brunswick, N.J.: Rutgers University Press, 1953), Vol. III, p. 549 (Cooper Union Speech).

[13] Quoted in Harry V. Jaffa, *Crisis of the House Divided* (Garden City: Doubleday and Co., Inc., 1959), pp. 85-86.

[14] Exactly how "problematic" the American experiment could appear at the time—and therefore how fully serious Lincoln was when he spoke of preserving republican government for a world in which it was disappearing —was brought out very well by David Potter in his review of the historical setting. See his *The South and the Sectional Conflict* (Baton Rouge: Louisiana State University Press, 1968), ch. XI, pp. 287-99.

a serious question of whether it was within the means of the United States to reach abroad with its military power and create the conditions for republican government. It was not that the case for republican government was any less valid in principle for an alien people; it was a question, rather, of the moral condition of the people, and the practical possibilities that existed for the support of republican institutions. And if one tended to be pessimistic in these assessments, then the natural preference of the conservative was to avoid the path of intervention. Rather than spreading republican institutions through the world with the force of arms, America would act upon the outside world through the power of its own example. Against the varieties of authoritarian regimes that existed in the rest of the world, the United States would hold up the standard of a democratic system that could not only endure, but one that would be fully adequate to the ends of government.[15]

Still, that left certain questions unanswered. What did one do, for example, when the threat was not scattered, but centered in an aggressive and expansive nation with a massive military potential (as in the case of Nazi Germany)? What did one do in the case that Mill allowed, where a democratic government was in danger of being overthrown, not because of the balance of support in the country, but the momentary balance of arms?[16] And in the meantime, what if the resources available to the United States were not quite as limited as one previously supposed, particularly in the middle of the nineteenth century?

These questions all begin to raise dark intimations, including the prospect, so widely out of favor today, that one power may take it upon itself to act as a kind of "policeman of the world." But the problem, as I would hope one could see by now, is that there are no *principled* grounds on which one could reject that course out of hand in every case. It would clearly be untenable to argue, for example, that events within a country—like the change of regime that occurred in Germany after 1933—may never have consequences that extend beyond the national borders and seriously affect the lives of people elsewhere. Therefore, it could never strictly be true

[15] The disagreement, in this respect, between Lincoln and Douglas is treated by Harry Jaffa in *Crisis of the House Divided* (Garden City: Doubleday and Co., Inc., 1959), ch. IV.

[16] John Stuart Mill, "A Few Words on Non-Intervention," in *Essays on Politics and Culture*, ed. Gertrude Himmelfarb (Garden City: Doubleday and Co., Inc., 1962), p. 410.

that the "internal" affairs of any country are none of the business of other nations, or even a legitimate cause, at times, for intervention. One could always take the line of an ethical relativist and argue that one nation cannot possibly have the standards to judge events in another country, much less prescribe the kind of political regime that might be better or worse, because there are no moral standards that remain valid across cultures. But apart from everything else we are likely to find unacceptable in that position, it could be shown that an argument of that kind would strike at the very premises of a constitutional order and cut the ground out from under the case for democratic government itself.[17]

As in so many other problems of ethics, the question of intervention can be addressed only on a case-by-case basis. There are times when it may be the only decent course to play the "policeman of the world" and intervene in a civil war; and there are times when that alternative would not only be futile, but would probably prolong a bitter war and enlarge the total measure of human suffering.

Now of course we have all been alerted to the possibility that the extension of our commitments abroad may strain the quality of our domestic life. Even before the disruptions over Vietnam there was a concern that an aggressive posture in the Cold War would only distend the power of the military and create a "garrison state" at home. And the possibility of that kind of connection between our commitments in foreign policy and the state of the domestic regime is one we would surely have to credit. But in principle one would have to admit, too, that the regime may be threatened by the growth of an antidemocratic current abroad, or by the spread of anticonstitutional ideologies that suddenly acquire a certain dynamism in the world, until they begin to appear plausible, or even fashionable, among sections of one's own population. To ask how important that can really be is to ask what difference it makes for a democratic politics when the support for a system of legal restraint and constitutional process has vanished from a portion of the population. To gauge the question more precisely we would have to consult the experience of countries with party systems more fragmented than our own, where antidemocratic factions have been drawn more directly into the power balance. As they become ac-

---

[17] On this point see Harry Jaffa's analysis in *Equality and Liberty* (New York: Oxford University Press, 1965), pp. 175-78.

ceptable allies for one purpose or another, these parties cease to look all that different from the run of other groups that fill in the landscape. On the one hand, they break down the sensibilities of their political allies, who come to believe that an antidemocratic party may be just as "usable" as any other ally they could pick up on the street. On the other hand, they corrupt the judgment of citizens, who are encouraged to believe now that in a democracy no idea is so base that it cannot be regarded as respectable.

It is probably fortunate that as far as remedies go we are usually restrained in these matters by a sense of prudence and a sober calculation of costs. But if the truth could be faced, the protection of the national interest would legitimately encompass things that we have been wise in the past to have left unexplored, and that for our own good, perhaps, we have rarely had the nerve to consider.

344

16. BUREAUCRACY, REGIME, AND THE MARSHALL PLAN

THE DEFINITION of the Marshall Plan did not start from a concept of interest defined in terms of power. But that did not mean that the program lost its grounding in concrete and definable interests, or that it became attached to vague moralisms. Instead, the concepts were much more specific and intelligible. The legislation referred to "private channels of trade," the facilities of government agencies, counterpart funds, and personnel ceilings. Nor did this degree of specificity fragment the bill into petty details that could obscure the larger pattern of values. The link between provision and premise was clearer; if anything, the relation to general principles was more firmly established. Thus, to speak of connecting foreign policy to basic values was not to speak in hopeless abstractions, and to concentrate on interests defined as power was by no means to deal with unambiguous realities.

If the program remained faithful in practice to its legislative definition, it was because the legislation did considerably more than order something to be done. What the Administration and Congress did was to create a structure for the program and a hierarchy among policy values. That was accomplished largely by dealing with the issues of administration, and here Congress was particularly effective. For the Congressional leaders, shaping administration was something they had now learned to do as a matter of course. With an artful switch of language—perhaps from "when the Administrator believes" to "when the Administrator determines"—they could alter a fact-finding procedure, regulate the channels of access by affecting appeal rights, or simply make it easier for some things to be done more quickly. If someone had raised this point to Senators Vandenberg or George, they would have found nothing unusual. Creating administrative agencies, structuring and restructuring them, was all a matter of routine. The strange part was that their practice in this area belied their theory.

345

If these men had followed their own administrative theories, they would not have designed the ECA in the way they did, and they might have been prevented from dealing with the administrative issue as well.

Despite all their practical experience with administration (and the traditional clichés about American pragmatism), the Congressional leaders were very much theoretical men of their age. They shared all the ideologies and the standard slogans of administrative theory that were then in vogue. They were impressed with the doctrine of "unity of command," not merely as a rule of thumb, but as something close to a natural law of administration. The politics–administration dichotomy was so much a part of their thoughts that it shaped their perception of problems even beyond the scope of administration as ordinarily conceived.[1] It became a standing refrain in the Congressional hearings, both among the Congressmen and the witnesses, to assert that forms of administration did not really matter—that in the long run the success of the program would depend on getting good men as administrators. But if it was merely a matter of defining the policy, or of getting good men and giving them all "authority commensurate with their responsibility," then it was either futile or irresponsible to treat the issues of administration in any greater detail. It would have been senseless, apparently, to make any effort toward defining priorities or fixing the relations between agencies.

It was quite common in the hearings to advocate positions based entirely on abstract theories of administrative efficiency, without any reference to the ends of the program. For the sake of efficiency Raymond Baldwin had urged a large, centralized agency with supreme authority over export controls. To minimize waste, Bernard Baruch would have had the ECA coordinate all purchasing in the program, even for the foreign governments. Former Secretary of War Robert Patterson opposed administration by a board on the grounds that boards tended to prevent rather than encourage ac-

---

[1] Marshall had a taste of this in the House hearings. Congressman Judd tried to illuminate the distinction between "policy" and "operations" by citing Marshall's own wartime experience. "Once the foreign policy has been determined—say, war with Germany, the Secretary of State could not determine what you, as Chief of Staff, do in achieving that foreign policy objective. You ran the Army. . . . We need exactly the same sort of a set-up for this job." Marshall dismissed the analysis courteously as an "overstatement." House Committee on Foreign Affairs, *ERP Hearings*, 1948, p. 85.

tion. Like many others, he regarded it as an axiom of administration that an agency headed by a single administrator would show greater energy and decisiveness. But there was no explanation as to why the ECA should have been more energetic, or why it deserved to have its own policies enacted so quickly. For Patterson, one gathers, vigor was simply the most naturally desirable quality for any agency, much in the way that a healthy horse seemed naturally better than a sick one.

There were occasions, too, when people were led by their administrative theories into conclusions that seemed patently at odds with their own policy preferences. Christian Herter, for example, was a Congressman with strong internationalist credentials. His work on the Select Congressional Committee on Foreign Aid had contributed significantly toward building support in Congress for the Marshall Plan, and yet Herter found himself opposing the fundamental decision to use counterpart funds. The counterpart device was essential to the pluralist values of the program, but for Herter it happened to be incompatible with the corporate form of organization he was proposing. He saw no escape from the logic of corporate autonomy, which had to mean exclusive rather than shared control over program funds. The consequence of this theoretical scrupulousness, however, was to place him in the same camp with Henry Hazlitt and the interventionists.

The Brookings report had clearly marked the turning point in the issue of State Department control over the ECA. It armed Vandenberg with the support of an outside agency, which he used to great effect on the Senate floor. A close reading of the report, though, would show that its premises were not at all in harmony with the dominant Republican position. The Brookings report started from the assumption that nothing could avoid the ultimate need for Presidential coordination. For that reason it recommended an agency with cabinet status, so that the lines of responsibility would be clearer and the appeal to the President could be relatively unencumbered with legal obstacles. However, as the comments of Wherry, Taft, and Mundt indicated, the preference of the Congressional Republicans was to reduce the traditional dominance of the President in foreign policy. The object was to make the ECA more responsive to Congress, and as Karl Mundt explained, that was the rationale for annual authorizations and appropriations. As long as the Brookings report justified the separation of the ECA from the State Department, that seemed to be good enough for its purposes, and Vandenberg could still consider it the great charter for what he had done in 1948.

But there was a real question as to whether Vandenberg had understood the Brookings report. A few days after he had released it to the press, and after the interests of other agencies had cropped up in the hearings, Vandenberg wrote to Harold Moulton, the president of Brookings, to sound him out on a possible "refinement." The Brookings plan accepted an advisory board, though it was one that "would not be vested with administrative responsibility." Vandenberg wondered if Moulton and his staff would give their support to a board that might contain all the consultative machinery. It would represent State, Agriculture, Commerce, and Treasury in addition to "eminent citizens." But then the twist came:

> Then suppose that the decisions of the Administrator are final unless some one of the four Cabinet Secretaries is unable to agree with the Administrator . . . and under such circumstances the Administrator's decision is suspended pending final decision by the President.[2]

That is, one dissent would have stopped all action. It is hard to believe Vandenberg could not have been alert to the significance of the change—that it promised to do something more than expand consultation. Nevertheless, Moulton and the Brookings staff did understand the potential consequences, and they refused to lend their approval. Moulton wrote back to Vandenberg that "a proposal along the lines you suggest would, it seems to us, go a long way toward placing responsibility for administration in a board rather than in an individual administrator with Cabinet status."[3] What was more surprising, the arrangement would have given the State Department the kind of capacity to interfere in the operations of the ECA that Vandenberg had been opposing all along.

If Vandenberg and his colleagues had followed their administrative theories, they would never have been able to deal with the structure of the ECA as effectively as they did, or with the same consciousness of value questions. In fact, they might not have dealt with the question of administration at all. Something inherent in

[2] Vandenberg to Moulton, January 26, 1948, The Brookings Institution (Files of the Institution). Quoted with the permission of the Brookings Institution.

[3] Moulton to Vandenberg, January 27, 1948, The Brookings Institution (Files of the Institution). Quoted with the permission of the Institution.

the legislative process forced them to break away from the hindrance of their own thought, and go on to do a creditably rational and responsible job. The explanation, I would argue, would again have to start with the American regime. In this particular case, it would be found in rational-legality and the separation of powers.

"Rational-legal," of course, is a term that comes to us from Max Weber, and although the concept was important for large sections of his writings on law and sociology, it is probably best remembered in connection with his classic analysis of bureaucracy. The problem, though, is that the fuller meaning of rationality has become obscured in the literature on bureaucracy as distortions have accumulated, and the analysis has drifted farther from Weber's original understanding. What has happened, as a result, is that the fundamental meaning of bureaucracy as a carrier of rational-legal norms has been lost.[4]

Now it is true that Weber frequently dwelt on the domination theme, and he did return quite often to the features of hierarchy or monocratic authority. But unless we rip the discussion out of its context, it would be hard to claim that hierarchy was given an ascendant place in the model of bureaucracy. Besides, as a conservative, and one who had little patience for utopian dreams, Weber made an early peace with the domination theme. That some people in the society would always have more power than others was something he could accept without anguish.

What continued to trouble him, though, was the steady expansion of the bureaucratic sphere, which threatened to engulf the area of private law and erode the political arena. Bureaucracy promised to spread its routinizing, "disenchanting" effects through the rest of the society, until all the vital areas of political controversy were sucked into the orbit of bureaucratic management. And for some-

---

[4] To take just one example, Stanley Udy has written that "One of Weber's main points, *in effect*, is that rational characteristics do not invariably tend to be associated with bureaucracy." Stanley H. Udy, Jr., " 'Bureaucracy' and 'Rationality' in Weber's Organization Theory: An Empirical Study," *American Sociological Review*, XXIV (1959), pp. 792-95. Emphasis added. Udy, however, offers no textual support for this assertion, and yet, citing nothing more than Udy's remark, Robert Presthus could state rather emphatically that "Weber himself noted that bureaucratic structure was not always associated with rationality." Robert V. Presthus, "Weberian v. Welfare Bureaucracy in Traditional Society," *Administrative Science Quarterly*, V, No. 1 (June 1960), pp. 2-3.

one who viewed the progress of bureaucracy in this rather more refined light, it was not the feature of hierarchy that was decisive.

Bureaucracy had a very exact place in Weber's sociology; it was tied to the foundations of a rational-legal polity, and it is important for the concerns of this work that the terms of that linkage be fixed. It would say something more definite, first, about the kind of political regime reflected in the model of bureaucracy; but with that, too, it would direct us to other sources in the behavior of the ECA, including the part held by Congress in the process of administration.

I

The discussion of bureaucracy occurs late in the *Theory of Social and Economic Organization*, long after Weber established his conceptual framework. Starting with modes of social action, he went on to their manifestations in group action, and from there to the typology of groups. But as a social scientist, whose concerns were naturally directed to regularities, Weber was led past the phenomenon of the group as a numerical fact to the concept of "order" within the group. To paraphrase Weber, he focused on that significantly regular behavior that arose from the probability that action would be oriented to certain established rules.[5]

It was the phenomenon of order in this special sense that raised the problem of authority, and as Weber moved toward the treatment of authority, his modes of social action were converted into patterns of legitimacy. By the time he arrived at the "pure types of legitimate authority," these strands of legitimacy had been reduced to the three clear ideal types that have now become familiar: charismatic, traditional, and rational-legal. As it was reflected in the scheme of his presentation, the design of the theory was quite striking. At the foundation were beliefs in legitimacy. Each set of beliefs gave rise to its own characteristic form of authority, and each form of authority evolved its own structures of social action. "According to the kind of legitimacy which is claimed," wrote Weber, "the type of obedience, the kind of administrative staff developed to guarantee it, and the mode of exercising authority, will

[5] *Max Weber: The Theory of Social and Economic Organization*, ed. Talcott Parsons (Glencoe: The Free Press, 1947), pp. 124-26. Cited hereafter as *Theory*.

350

all differ fundamentally."[6] Bureaucracy was the peculiar form of administration that attached to rational-legal authority. It was specifically "rational," said Weber, in its exercise of control based on knowledge—in its "rationally delimited" spheres, its emphasis on functional recruitment and specialization, and its reliance on written records and precedents.[7] It was also the "purest type of exercise of legal authority,"[8] a system of administration "bound by rules," using stable and precise jurisdictions, applying abstract rules to specific cases in a general, impartial way.

Other systems of authority could have administrative staffs, but they were not bureaucratic. Administrative staffs were employed in the old Germanic and Mongolian empires, but rather than having full-time specialists with permanent tenure, the administrators were drawn from court servants and table companions. In some places, too, it was common to use slaves or conscripts. There was no separation, in these instances, between official activity and private life. The control over subordinates was diffuse and exhaustive, rather than partial and delimited. Instead of an impartial administration of the laws, the arrangements were consciously tailored to a system of arbitrary personal power on the part of the rulers.[9]

But the sharpest opposition to bureaucracy arose from charismatic authority. In place of that reliance on standing rules created in a formal way, legitimacy rested on the "specific and exceptional sanctity, heroism, or exemplary character of an individual person, and of the normative patterns or order revealed or ordained by him."[10] The legitimacy of the charismatic leader was intrinsically, irreducibly personal; it could not be transferred or communicated, much less codified in the form of written regulations. "Charismatic authority," declared Weber, "is outside the realm of everyday routine and the profane sphere," and in contrast to bureaucratic authority, it was "specifically irrational in the sense of being foreign to all rules."[11]

Thus, as Weber himself came to recognize, the polar opposites in his scheme were really charismatic and rational-legal authority.

[6] *Ibid.*, p. 325.

[7] See *ibid.*, pp. 329-36, 339, and generally, *From Max Weber: Essays in Sociology*, trans. and ed. H. H. Gerth and C. Wright Mills (New York: Oxford University Press, 1946), pp. 196-204. Cited hereafter as *Essays*.

[8] *Theory*, p. 333.   [9] See *Essays*, pp. 196-97; *Theory*, p. 347.

[10] *Theory*, p. 328.   [11] *Ibid.*, p. 361.

The critical line of division ran between charismatic authority and the other ideal types:

> Both rational and traditional authority are specifically forms of everyday routine control of action; while the charismatic type is the direct antithesis of this. Bureaucratic authority is specifically rational in the sense of being bound to intellectually analysable rules. . . . Traditional authority is bound to the precedents handed down from the past and to this extent is also oriented to rules. Within the sphere of its claims, charismatic authority repudiates the past, and is in this sense a specifically revolutionary force. . . .[12]

Against the claims of the standing law to produce a result that is *formally rational* in the sense of being legal or fair, the charismatic leader brings the insight of personal revelation. The claim he presents is the claim to *substantive rationality*, i.e., to a decision that is not merely legal, but in some objective sense, just.

The hazards, however, are fairly obvious. Revelation may at times be the best source of truth, but it is beyond any controls we could devise. Empirical evidence is the only kind of evidence that lends itself to intersubjective controls, and it is only through an emphasis on procedure and empirical evidence that we could hope to escape the play of arbitrariness in the law.

The contribution of formalism to the law lay precisely in this emphasis on the "external characteristics of the facts," as Weber put it, and by that he meant perceptible sense data—the doing of a deed, the utterance of words, the execution of a signature. Formalism in the law depended on the extent to which "only unambiguous, general characteristics of the facts of the case are taken into account."[13] Yet, as Weber noted, it was possible for the law to be formal and at the same time irrational. Ancient methods of adjudication by means of oracles and ordeals could take on a rigorously formal character through the use of elaborate procedures. A trial could focus on specific empirical issues, employ intricate procedures, and still there might be no logical connection between data, ritual, and decision. Without the binding element of logical

[12] *Ibid.*, pp. 361-62.

[13] *Max Weber on Law in Economic and Society*, ed. Max Rheinstein; trans. Edward Shils (Cambridge: Harvard University Press, 1954), p. 63. Cited hereafter as *Law*.

352

method—without the presence, in short, of rationality as well as formalism—the process could still be wholly arbitrary.

Rationality brought the discipline of logical method in interpreting the facts of the case and extracting the legally relevant data; but beyond that, it brought the use of logical generalization. The law could advance then from isolated judgments, handed down in individual cases, to the formation of "fixed legal concepts in the form of highly abstract rules,"[14] and that, too, was an added source of constraint.

In substantive law, on the other hand—the law represented by the charismatic leader—the decision was influenced by "norms different from those obtained through logical generalization of abstract interpretations of meaning." As a practical necessity, there was some use of logical reasoning, but the law-finder stepped away from the body of fixed legal concepts and acted upon "ethical imperatives, utilitarian and other expediential rules and political maxims."[15] Still, one may ask, what practical difference does it make? The charismatic leader may well define a system of rampant arbitrariness, but how can a system of that sort be institutionalized? As Weber himself suggested, the charismatic regime was inherently fragile. It threatened to lose its revolutionary dynamism, along with its capacity for arbitrary action, as soon as it settled down to the daily tasks of administering the state.[16] How could a regime of that kind maintain its character when saddled with the responsibilities for routine administration? How could it offer a practical alternative to bureaucracy as a means of administering the modern state?

Fortunately, Weber brought the issue to a practical level for us when he turned to forms of adjudication, or the practical means of administering the laws. There, the system of Kadi justice was the clear analogue of charismatic authority, and Weber's descriptions of Kadi law run parallel to his accounts of the charismatic leader. Decisions were reached through informal judgments on a case-by-case basis, and they could "advance to a prophetic break with all tradition." The Kadi judge worked on a clean slate; he could pick out any aspect of the case before him, choose any criterion he pleased, and appeal ultimately to revelation.[17] There was no prior constraint on his discretion, no definition of legally relevant data

---

[14] *Ibid.*, cf. also pp. 1-li, 59.   [15] *Ibid.*, pp. 63-64.

[16] See, in this respect, Weber's chapters on the "routinization of charisma," *Theory*, pp. 363-92.

[17] *Essays*, pp. 216, 220-21.

that could bind him in advance. It was not incumbent upon him to show any logical connection between the evidence and the judgment. He was not compelled to justify the decision in terms of the governing criteria, and neither was he obliged, therefore, to explain what the governing criteria were. What issued was the decision and nothing more. Like the charismatic leader, Kadi justice knew "no reasoned judgment whatever."

The alternatives to Kadi law were "rational" and "empirical" justice. Rational justice proceeded "on the basis of strictly formal conceptions." Like the code law of the Continent, it worked in a deductive way by starting from an internally consistent system of abstract concepts and applying the rules to specific cases. In contrast, empirical justice resembled the common law. It worked from case to case through the use of analogy and precedent. Whatever doctrines emerged in the form of general rules developed gradually, through an accumulation of cases.

But despite their apparent differences, rational and empirical justice shared one vital feature that set them radically apart from Kadi law: They were both disciplined in their exercise of discretion by the constraint of general rules. It was not that rules were simply available as a guide to decisions, but that the decisions themselves would have to be justified in reference to a standing body of law. As Weber indicated, both rational and empirical justice acknowledged the authority of precedent,[18] and the significance of precedent goes beyond the advantages of consistency in the law. It casts a new set of presumptions and alters the basic structure of decision-making. The logic of precedent implies that the rule created in the present case will be presumptively binding *on all similar cases* in the future. Under these conditions, the burden of proof would be thrust upon the administrator who would seek to avoid the implications of his previous decision. It is his burden now to distinguish the present case from the preceding one, to show why the facts are different, and why the standing rule should not be applied.

---

[18] To recall his words once again, "Both rational and traditional authority are specifically forms of everyday routine control of action . . . . [By "rational" and "traditional" read: rational and empirical justice, their counterparts in methods of adjudication.] Bureaucratic authority is specifically rational in the sense of being bound to intellectually analysable rules . . . . Traditional authority is bound to precedents handed down from the past and to this extent is also oriented to rules." *Theory*, pp. 361-62.

Thus, the principal indictment against Kadi law is not that it works in a case-by-case manner, or that it appeals at times to ethical considerations outside the formal law. The Supreme Court of the United States works through the format of adversary cases, and like any agency of adjudication it is forced to break away at times from the positive law and appeal to the "higher law" of the Constitution or the reason of natural law. The difference, though, is that the Court is compelled to offer reasons, and once a new rule is created, it will take its place in the standing law. The Court may want to depart from that ruling in the future, but once again it will have to accept the burden of argument.

When Ernst Fraenkel condemned the Nazi system for using a case-by-case approach, he was not really objecting, then, to the practice of deciding cases singly. He was reacting, rather, to situations in which the rules were suspended and the cases were thrown open to the reception of more and more data, until something could be found to trigger the prejudices of the decision-makers. They were cases in which an applicant might suddenly be denied a driver's license because he had been in a concentration camp, or a woman might be denied a license for midwifery because something in the record called her loyalty into question.[19] The Nazi administrators were not bound in advance to established categories that could define the limits of what was legally relevant. And there was no guarantee, of course, that the criteria invoked in the present case would be applied to the next one. Lacking this central discipline, freed from the responsibility to justify decisions, the connection between data and decision, between action and crime, became tenuous.

The result was a revolutionary change in the character of law as an instrument of social control. The experience is one we have partially known ourselves through the problem of vague statutes: When the law loses its explicitness, the line between the permissible and the punishable becomes indistinct. The presumptions in the law are turned about, and it becomes the burden of the citizen now to establish his innocence. Faced with a hazardous situation in which the difference between guilt and innocence may no longer be calculable, the citizen will have to be especially cautious. Very likely, he will respond by steering a wider course from the area of

[19] See Ernst Fraenkel, *The Dual State*, trans. Edward A. Shils (New York: Oxford University Press, 1941), pp. 41, 43-44, 53-54, 102-103.

potential offense. If he is a teacher in a state that is free to dismiss teachers without reason, merely by failing to send out a new contract, and the state suddenly becomes interested in the associations of its teachers, he may well be induced to join fewer organizations and reduce the circle of his acquaintances. In that way, the combination of legal power and ill-defined rules may have a wider deterrent effect on the behavior of individuals. It may discourage forms of conduct that are thoroughly innocent, and which the authorities themselves might be powerless to forbid if they were forced to work their will through an explicit statute.[20]

If incidents of this kind can crop up occasionally in our own law, where they appear as aberrations, why could they not, in fact, be institutionalized in other systems, where the political leadership holds a monopoly of power and is subject to fewer constraints? There are unique intimidations that arise in a truly totalitarian system, where the controls of the regime penetrate every corner of the society: People who lose in politics do not retire to the practice of law or go on to a dazzling success in the social world; nor can the resisting bureaucrat simply leave the government and take refuge in private industry. For some reason, the prospect has been hard for social scientists to conceive, and yet a regime of this sort can reverse the presumptions in the law even as a matter of routine operation. It can place an extraordinary burden on subjects and bureaucrats alike to demonstrate their loyalty or withdraw their opposition, even when the coercive apparatus of the state is not bearing directly upon them.

The definition of rational law marked the distinction, then, between two radically different kinds of regimes. The character of these two systems was reflected in their peculiar modes of administration, and bureaucracy, with its precision and predictability, its rational use of knowledge and reliance on stable procedure, provided the "purest type of . . . legal authority." For Weber, bureaucratic administration was not indispensable to a legal order, but where it existed it represented the perfection of legal administration, and it could occur only in a system of rational-legality. Bureaucracy, therefore, was the symbol *par excellence* of a rational-

[20] A good case in point, from which the example of the teacher is drawn, is *Shelton* v. *Tucker*, 360 U.S. 479 (1960). Cf. Justice Harlan's comments on the Shelton case in *Konigsberg* v. *State Bar* 366 U.S. at 53 (1961), and Justice Brennan's analysis in *Bantam Books* v. *Sullivan*, 372 U.S., especially 69-70 (1963).

legal regime. And it is this, I believe, along with an understanding of the role played by precedent and presumption in the analysis, that brings us back to the Marshall Plan.

II

Bureaucracy showed its concern for clear jurisdictions and predictable rules because it was a part of what we would call a constitutional order. If it displayed in its internal processes the features of rational-legality, it was because those characteristics had come to be identified more widely in the society with the way in which decisions ought to be made if they are to be regarded as authoritative. The bureaucracy, like other legal institutions, reflected some of the understandings that were current in the society about the arrangements of justice and the conditions of legitimacy. Naturally, according to their separate functions, the different branches of the government will show important discrepancies in their patterns of operation. The Pentagon is not apt to be mistaken for the Supreme Court. Congress has incomparably more discretion in making law than the courts have, and theoretically it is even justified in making wholesale and sudden revisions. Yet even with these differences, there are certain constraints that touch almost all institutions in a rational-legal order and make them closer to one another than to any institutions in a totalitarian regime that were supposedly comparable in function. The Soviet legislature may indeed find a useful role to play as an adjunct to the bureaucracy; still, the members of the Supreme Soviet are not likely to behave like American administrators, or even like Congressmen doing case work. Despite those highly touted "bureaucratizing" effects that are supposed to come along with industrial maturity, the Soviet government is not likely to lose cases it cares about merely because of things like vague statutes, or because it happened to be lax in observing certain rules of evidence. Government regulation of business in the United States will probably never achieve its potential for social change, because we do not seem willing even here to resort to Kadi-like forms of control. Under the discipline of politics in a republican government, Congress will always look more like the Supreme Court, and politicians will always resemble judges more than Kadis.

What presses Congress closer to this judicial character is the mechanics of legality itself. Like the courts, the legislature is faced with a standing body of laws. New legislation has to be attached to that structure, and because of this requirement alone, inconsistencies with the previous laws are often made more visible. Very often the legislator will have to introduce his measure as an amendment to an existing set of laws, but when he does that he activates a complicated system of signals. He stirs the groups who have joined their interests to different sections of the present statutes. He may rekindle an old debate or threaten an earlier political settlement that everyone had thought secure. In addition to the various groups, he may have to confront the purposes that were expressed in the earlier legislation, and it will probably fall to him to carry the burden of argument in showing why conditions have changed, or why the earlier values have lost their validity. The fact that a politics of group interests is endemic in a democracy may help to explain, then, why legislative decisions are usually as incremental as they are, and why they often resemble the more empirical pattern of judicial decisions.[21]

If we look only at that title of the 1948 foreign aid legislation that dealt with the European Recovery Program, we would find that the legislation was interspersed with references to sixteen separate statutes. To give the ECA more flexibility in personnel, Congress had to amend the Federal Employees Classification Act of 1946, the Classification Act of 1923, and the Foreign Reserve Act of 1946. The operations of the ECA had to be adjusted to the standing regulations on government procurement, disposal, contracts, claims, capital stock, and surpluses. To bring the Export-Import Bank into the picture, Congress had to amend the Bretton Woods Act. In assigning responsibilities to the Administrator in the field of export controls, it had to deal rather carefully with the Na-

---

[21] Legislative histories of this kind are all about us. For the Marshall Plan in particular, the long chain of legislation culminating in the Government Corporation Control Act of 1945 is especially relevant. In this regard, also, an interesting comparison could be drawn between Jerold Israel's argument on the way the Supreme Court should have overruled the Betts decision in *Gideon* v. *Wainwright* and Irving Brant's description of the way in which the Virginia legislature came to revise the old entail and escheat laws. The Virginia legislature would have come far closer than the Supreme Court in meeting Israel's standards of jurisprudence. Cf. Jerold H. Israel, "Gideon v. Wainwright: The 'Art' of Overruling," *The Supreme Court Review*, ed. Philip B. Kurland (Chicago: University of Chicago Press, 1964), pp. 211-72; and Irving Brant, *James Madison: The Virginia Revolutionist* (Indianapolis: The Bobbs-Merrill Company, 1941), pp. 300-301.

tional Defense Act of 1940, which contained the original delegation of authority to the President. If Congress had decided to use
that amendment as an opportunity to take export controls away
from the Department of Agriculture, it would have opened up a
politically charged issue of reorganization within the Executive.

Now one could argue, of course, that legislators can often share
the faults, as well as the virtues, of judges. They, too, can be
sloppy and inarticulate in their work. They are quite capable of
adding a new piece of legislation that undermines one of their
previous decisions without explicitly overruling it. And in that way,
they could avoid the need to face the contradictions in their own
work or open themselves to reasoned argument. But in the American system the situation may be ameliorated somewhat by an added inhibition in the separation of powers. Legislation may be
passed, but it must be enforced by an Executive agency, which
means that a decision has to be made in Congress: Either the function will be added to the duties of an existing unit, or an entirely
new agency will have to be created. In either case the task falls to
Congress to spell out the administrative arrangements.[22]

But once that responsibility is taken up, Congress finds itself im-
mersed in the substantive issues. As it sought to incorporate the
ECA into the Executive establishment, for example, it was forced
to weigh the relative interests and purposes of the other departments. The most telling illustration here came from Raymond
Baldwin, who appeared before the House Foreign Affairs Committee as an expert on administration. True to form, Baldwin
grounded his argument in theories of administration. He started
from the premise that the ECA should have all the authority it
would need in preserving the program against the attrition of
bureaucratic conflict. His recommendation then was for a mammoth, centralized ECA. But to someone like Congressman Vorys,
who had to manage the bill in the House, this was all rather abstract. He therefore asked Baldwin to try his hand at a specific
problem and bring in a recommendation for the distribution of
export controls. In making his study Baldwin had to review the
relevant statutes on export controls, and as a result, when he finally
submitted his memorandum to the committee a significant change
had occurred: He recognized now that other agencies had legiti-

[22] The major exception would be a wartime emergency in which Congress
might authorize the President to carry out certain reorganizations on his
own order.

mate interests in the field. While he still insisted on the efficiency of centralizing export controls, he was willing to settle for an arrangement in which the controls would be allocated by a committee including the major interested departments, as well as the ECA.[23] It seemed momentous, of course, that Baldwin would recognize the legitimate interests of other agencies, but it was a result that was virtually foretold once he approached the question as Congress had to approach it.

Similarly, as the Congressional leaders worked over the issues that emanated from the questions of organization, they were forced to articulate their own understanding of the program. To the extent that they were interested in influencing the performance of the ECA, their motives led them to act on the structure of the organization in more than the superficial manner of naming the agency. They defined the relations among the departments, they suggested priorities among policies, and they stamped the program with a set of operating presumptions.

Moreover, these rationalizing effects were reinforced as Congress continued its involvement in administration through the practice of legislative oversight. With annual authorizations and appropriations, the ECA seemed to spend an inordinate amount of time in preparing for legislative hearings or in adjusting to new legislation. Thus, for a relatively small agency, the ECA possessed an unusually large legal staff. Thirty-two men were kept busy in the Office of the General Counsel, either preparing legislation or drafting the regulations needed to enforce the annual amendments added by Congress. If one characterized an agency by its prominent operations, then the ECA might have earned the reputation of a "legal" agency. A very large share of its activities was devoted to the careful scrutiny of its own legislation, and to the task of assuring that everyone in the organization was aware of his precise statutory responsibilities.

In addition, the annual hearings in Congress imparted a special coherence to the programming process itself. Programming was nearly continuous in the ECA, but in the weeks preceding the Congressional presentations the organization would hold intensive "brokerage sessions" lasting well into the night, for six or seven days a week. The various perspectives on the estimates would be brought together; area specialists would confront experts in com-

[23] See House Foreign Affairs Committee, *ERP Hearings*, 1948, p. 1670.

modities and trade; the review would go country by country, then commodity by commodity, with the experts picking at one another's assumptions, until at the end the estimates would be reconciled in a coherent program. As the head of the Industry Division later admitted to an interviewer, it was really the Congressional presentation that gave focus to the whole planning operation.[24]

But what was equally important, the effects were relayed back to act upon Congress. When the ECA composed a coherent program, it became that much more difficult to strike at any single part of the package without casting up value questions. When Hoffman was impolite enough to ask the Senate Foreign Relations Committee whether it believed in "a cure rather than a palliative" or whether it preferred to subsidize the shipping industry, he was facing the Committee with the same policy dilemmas that the ECA had to wrestle with. As the price of power, the Congressional leaders were forced to take their own part in the problems of principled action. As novel issues were posed to them, they had to decide again what they valued and how they chose to define the program.

Thus, legislative oversight was not simply a means by which Congress sought to keep the administration of the Marshall Plan responsive to an original Congressional intent. It was a means, rather, of cultivating that intent. For the Congressmen who participated in the committee hearings, it was a means toward their own understanding, and since legislation was a continuing affair, it is true to say that it was a fundamental part of their deliberation.

To restate the argument, then, the separation of powers gave Congress a practically unavoidable constitutional responsibility to construct the agency. It compelled the Congressional managers to treat the detailed matters of administrative structure, and it was this task that led them to deal with the kinds of issues that were most essential to the definition of the national interest in the Marshall Plan. That responsibility to design the agency activated the "rational" features implicit in the legal order, in the sense that Congress now had to attach the agency to a standing body of laws and administrative jurisdictions. It had to confront once again the purposes that were embodied in the earlier laws and the previous assignments of authority; and as it brought the ECA into being, it had to make direct, explicit connections to the very framework of

[24] Bureau of the Budget, *Interviews in Survey of the ECA*, 1951. Interview with Bernard Rothman, June 12, 1951, Series 39.32.

the regime. Thus, there was something in the system itself that diverted the Congressional leaders from their own administrative theories and forced them into that chain of inquiry that began with the questions of administration, but led back to the nature of the regime itself.

Because of the separation of powers, Congress remained deaf to the old advice that legislative bodies should not interfere in questions of administration. Yet it was only because they involved themselves in administration that the Congressional leaders were able to test the consequences of their policy preferences. In the last analysis it is only the fanatic who is unconcerned with the test of concrete cases and who is unwilling to consider the consequences that result from acting out his values. We may raise the question, then, as to whether the responsible man may properly act in any other way; and what is true of the responsible individual must be even truer of the men whose decisions will touch every member of the society as binding law. We may question whether Congress can really legislate in any meaningful sense without testing the consequences of its decisions. And we might conclude on that basis that it is largely through its responsibilities in administration that Congress fulfills its highest deliberative function as a legislature. "The House of Commons," said Gladstone, "is a great and noble school," and when he made that observation he was looking back on his apprenticeship in the days when the British legislature was much more heavily involved in administration than it is today—and for that reason, perhaps, was much more of a legislature. "It is a school," he continued, "for all the qualities of force, suppleness, and versatility of intellect. . . . It is a school of temper. It is also a school of patience. It is a school of honour, and it is a school of justice."

APPENDIX A

April 3, 1948 to April 3, 1951 (in thousands of dollars)

Industrial commodities	$ 5,032,119
Food and agriculture	4,884,627
Ocean freight	725,829
Technical services	47,344
European Payments Union	350,000
ECA prepaid account	56,000
	$11,095,919

By country:

Britain	$ 2,703,049
France (and territories)	2,223,880
Italy	1,213,059
Germany	1,188,757
Netherlands	949,779
Belgium–Luxembourg	529,765
Austria	513,978
Greece	432,516
Denmark	239,270
Norway	218,659
Ireland	146,200
Turkey	117,262
Sweden	116,334
Portugal	45,745
Trieste	33,247
Iceland	18,419
	$10,689,919[a]

[a] Excludes charges for freight and the European Payments Union.
SOURCE: ECA, Press Release No. 2145.

363

APPENDIX B

First Quarter, 1949

Commodity	Total Exports (in millions of dollars)	Percent Taken by ERP
Corn	74.0	82.8
Wheat (grain)	235.5	72.5
Peanuts	26.4	70.5
Cotton	249.1	63.9
Tobacco and mfrs.	65.4	50.9
Wheat flour	68.7	47.6
Coal	69.8	47.4
Lard	22.6	45.1
Dairy products	45.7	40.1
Misc. foodstuffs	173.9	39.8
Petroleum and products	155.8	36.6
Chemicals	206.9	26.7
Steel mill products	191.5	19.1
Machinery and vehicles	922.9	18.8
Other commodities	715.8	25.2
	3,224.0	34.5[a]

[a] Weighted average.
SOURCE: ECA, *Fourth Report* (Quarter ending March 31, 1949).

364

APPENDIX C

3. *Economic Pattern Maintenance*

ASSOCIATED STATEMENTS:

Treasury's insistence in the interdepartmental discussions on emphasizing private channels of trade, a view that was eventually inserted in the legislation. Supported by Marshall in his testimony on Interim Aid

Wayne Taylor's urging that the program should not sanction property rights for the American government overseas

Alan Kline's statement that the American interest in the Marshall Plan ended as soon as the diversion of goods from the domestic market became large enough to strain the economy and threaten the return of controls

Concern of Hazlitt and Gwinn that the ECA might legitimize European socialism or encourage planning and controls

Labor's interest in the free labor movement abroad

Congressional rejection of a corporation that would own assets abroad

Senator George's opposition to the creation of a large government procurement bureaucracy

Insistence by Vandenberg, Wherry, and Brooks that the new aid program would have a different character, and that the critical change would be in the accent on business-like methods

The most important formal statement here appeared in the form of an operating rule, followed by specific supporting arrangements.

AUTHORITATIVE STATEMENTS AND DECISIONS:

". . . [F]acilitate and maximize the use of private channels of trade" (Section 111 (b)) (Operating presumption), and to that end allow the following methods of payment:

365

> By letters of commitment issued in accordance with supply programs approved by the Administrator; or
>
> Withdrawals made by participating countries or their agents or other persons "upon presentation of contracts, invoices or other documentation specified by the Administrator" (Section 111 (b)(1)(i-ii))

To encourage private investment with guarantees

> For projects approved by the Administrator, including those involved in informational media (Section 111 (b)(3))
>
> But for convertibility only—i.e., the "transfer into United States dollars of other currencies, or credits . . . received by such persons as income from the approved investment, as repayment or return thereof . . . or as compensation for the sale or disposition of all or any part thereof. . ." (Section 111 (b)(3)(i))
>
> Not exceeding the dollar value of the project (*ibid.*)

Loans

> ECA Administrator determines the use of credits and the terms after consultation with National Advisory Council on International Monetary and Financial Problems (Section 111 (c)(1)). But administration is given over to the Export-Import Bank (Section 111 (c)(2))

Financing

> Not immediately by appropriated funds
>
>> The Administrator is authorized to issue notes "from time to time" to be purchased by the Treasury up to a limit of $1 billion.
>>
>> The funds received from the sale of these notes will be given to the Export-Import Bank to finance the loans.
>>
>> Preferences for source of funds: In allocating funds to the Export-Import Bank the Administrator "shall first utilize such funds realized from the sale of notes . . . and when such funds are exhausted, or after the end of one year . . . whichever is earlier, he shall utilize any funds appropriated under this title." (Section 111 (c)(2)) (Operating presumption)

4. *". . . a cure rather than a mere palliative"*

ASSOCIATED STATEMENTS:

Marshall's Harvard speech: ". . . [A]ssistance . . . must not be on a piecemeal basis as various crises develop. Any assistance that this Government may render in the future should provide a cure rather than a mere palliative. . . . [T]here must be some agreement among the countries of Europe as to the requirements of the situation and the part those countries themselves will take. . . . The program should be a joint one. . . ."

Vandenberg's argument for a four-year authorization as the difference between relief and reconstruction

Vandenberg's rejection of the Taft amendment to reduce the size of the first authorization—for the same reason

AUTHORITATIVE STATEMENTS AND DECISIONS:

Expectation of a four-year program ending June 30, 1952 (Section 122 (a))

Goal of achieving an economic recovery so thorough that at the end of the program Europe may be "independent of extraordinary outside assistance." (Section 102 (a) and (b); Section 115 (b)(1))

Special Representative in Europe as commitment to regional integration (Section 108)

Continuous multilateral cooperation as the condition of American aid (Section 102 (a))

Membership depends on adherence to multilateral pledges. (Section 115 (b))

The continuance of aid is contingent upon "continuous effort of the participating countries to accomplish a joint recovery program through multilateral undertakings. . . ." (Section 114 (d))

The desire to cooperate is manifested in part by participation in a "continuing organization" or institution which seeks to produce those "sustained common efforts" to accomplish a joint recovery program. (Section 115 (b))

Continuous efforts toward cooperative goals

Integration

Progressive reduction of trade barriers (Section 102 (a), (b) (3); Section 115 (b) (3))

Recommend relevance of the American model as "a large domestic market" with no internal barriers (Section 102 (a))

Helping one another in raising production, stabilizing currency, and balancing budgets (Section 115 (b)(1)(2)(3))

Coordinating the use of resources, for greater efficiency and rationality (Section 115 (b)(4))

Use of the International Refugee Organization as an instrument in seeking "the largest practicable utilization of manpower available" (Section 115 (e))

ON ORGANIZATION:

Aid conditioned on continuous activity in a common European organization (Section 115 (b))

Aid may be extended to countries that have not yet signed bilateral or multilateral agreements but which intend to sign the appropriate agreements, and which seem to subscribe to the cooperative purposes of the program.

For the first three months of the program, aid may be furnished to countries that participated in the CEEC conference, but which apparently were not about to sign an agreement. But this would involve only immediate relief goods, such as food, fertilizer, medical supplies, and fuel. It would be given in order to prevent "serious economic retrogression" in the general course of European recovery. (Section 115 (d))

5. *ECA Autonomy*

ASSOCIATED STATEMENTS:

Vandenberg preference for a business-like program with administrators having credentials unrelated to diplomacy

Brookings recommendation of an independent agency responsible directly to the President

Mundt statement that the ECA Administrator will be an "independent agent so far as the administration is concerned"

Senator Taft's remark that the bill was "infinitely more acceptable" as a result of separating the ECA from the State Department

AUTHORITATIVE STATEMENTS AND DECISIONS:

ECA Administrator appointed by President

Cabinet status: "shall have a status in the executive branch comparable to that of the head of an executive department" and shall function "under the control of the President" (Section 104 (a))

ECA as a distinct organizational entity

Separate membership for the ECA on the National Advisory Council (rather than being represented through the State Department) (Section 106)

Provision to prevent the President from avoiding the appointment of an ECA Administrator and thus allow the State Department to carry on the program (Section 104 (c))

General powers in the substantive field

Procuring goods (and having access to government stock); processing, storing, transporting, repairing; providing technical information and assistance; transferring commodities and services; allocating funds to specific projects (Section 111)

But, all these functions, particularly those under Section 111 (a), to be performed with a view to the Congressional imperative to "utilize private channels of trade" to the maximum extent possible

Authority vis-à-vis the OEEC countries

Review and appraisal of country requirements (Section 105 (a))

Authority under counterpart procedure to share in decisions on the use of proceeds from American aid (Section 115 (b)(6))

Enforce basic bilateral conditions

Evaluate continuity of cooperation in pursuit of common goals (e.g., reductions of trade barriers, currency stabilization) (Section 115 (b))

Getting repayment in scarce materials, access to resources for American industry, and promoting development projects for the production of scarce materials (Section 115 (b) (9); 117 (a))

Authority to admit countries to membership (Section 115 (b)(6)), and to terminate assistance (Section 118)

(Subject, however, to presumptions favoring the Europeans, as mentioned earlier)

Organizational flexibility

Administrator may appoint other advisory boards in addition to the Public Advisory Board provided in the statute (Section 107 (b))

May create a corporation for special purposes (Section 194 (d)(1))

with approval of President

subject to the Government Corporation Control Act of 1945 (i.e., the severely restricted corporation) (Section 104 (d)(2)(iv))

> Operating Presumption: None of these corporations will last beyond the life of the ECA without explicit approval of Congress (Section 104 (d)(2)(iii))

Permission to use consultants (Section 104 (e))

Exemption from various personnel regulations, including pay and classification (Section 104 (e)), capacity to appoint to Foreign Service status (Section 110), and restrictions on the use of consultants (Section 120)

Powers to dispose of commodities

> Not however by exclusive ECA authority, but by transferring goods for that purpose to another agency of the government
>
> And by the ECA itself, only when it is necessary because of possible spoilage (Section 113 (b)) (Operating Presumption)

Internal Organization

> The chief of the local ECA mission in a participating country "shall be appointed by the Administrator, shall receive his instructions from the Administrator, and shall report to the Administrator" (Section 109 (a))
>
> In a reversal of the Administration bill, the ECA mission was obligated only to keep the diplomatic mission head "fully and currently informed"
>
> > And if the latter disagreed with any policy, he could do no more than communicate that disagreement to the Special Representative in Paris and the head of the local ECA mission, who in turn would refer the matter to Washington.

Special Representative in Paris

receives his instructions from the Administrator

and coordinates the local missions (Section 108)

Relation to the State Department

> Instead of "direction and control" by Secretary of State, Administrator keeps him "fully and currently informed"
>
> When the Secretary "believes" that any action, proposed action or failure to act on the part of the ECA is inconsistent with United States foreign policy "he shall consult with the Administrator" and the matter may be referred to the President if "differences of view are not adjusted." (Section 105 (b)(2))

Appeal open also to the Administrator against any action of the State Department which seems inconsistent with the objectives of the Marshall Plan (Section 105 (b)(3))

6. *Decentralization*

ASSOCIATED STATEMENTS:

Marshall testimony at Interim Aid hearings—that the program could be administered by a fairly simple agency, since the operations consisted, in most cases, of "activities now being performed by a number of government agencies in cooperation with business, agricultural, and labor groups."

View of the Budget Bureau Staff Memorandum of November 4 —that the program could be put into operation more quickly if maximum reliance was placed on existing facilities

Opposition of Secretaries Harriman and Anderson to the proposal to centralize export controls in a new corporation, and thus take them away from the Departments of Commerce and Agriculture

Arguments by John Foster Dulles and William Batt—that coordination would be improved by the interdependence of the agencies

AUTHORITATIVE STATEMENTS AND DECISIONS:

The ECA may use the "services and facilities of any department, agency, or establishment of the Government" as the President may direct, or,

with the consent of the head of the department or agency (Section 111 (b) (2))

Provisions for reimbursing an agency for its administrative costs in connection with activities undertaken for the ECA (Section 113 (a))

Export controls

When the Administrator "believes" that any action of any department or officer administering export controls is inconsistent with the purposes of the Marshall Plan, "he shall consult" with the department or officer, and if the differences are not adjusted, the matter will be referred to the President. (Section 105 (c))

Reliance on other agencies

Clear the decisions on loans and grants with the NAC (Section 111 (c)(1))

371

Have the loans administered by the Export-Import Bank

Acquire funds for loans by selling notes to the Treasury at interest rates determined by the Treasury (Section 111 (c) (2))

The Secretary of Agriculture determines what agricultural goods are in surplus in the United States, and may therefore be purchased only in the United States for use in the Marshall Plan. (Section 112 (d) and (d) (1))

Depend on the State Department to

Negotiate the necessary bilateral agreements with each country which are prerequisite to membership in the program (Section 115 (a))

Provide office space, facilities, and general administrative services for the Special Representative and his staff, and for the special mission in each country (Section 109 (c))

Press for agreement among the interested countries by which capital equipment scheduled to be removed from Germany as reparations may be retained "if such retention will most effectively serve the purposes" of the European recovery program (Section 115 (f))

Accounts may be established on the books of other agencies to facilitate procurement

or in banking institutions—on terms approved by the Secretary of the Treasury

and expenditures under these accounts shall be subject to standard government documentation (and subject to the audit of the Comptroller General) (Section 111 (b) (1))

Disposal of commodities

principally by transferring them to other government agencies (Section 113 (b))

7. *Debureaucratization*

ASSOCIATED STATEMENTS:

Marshall testimony for Interim Aid: Because the ERP nations had the skills necessary to run the program, only a simple administrative unit was necessary on the American side.

"The establishment of a U.S. Government corporation to procure, deliver and manage is not only unnecessary but would constitute a threat to private enterprise in this country and to sovereign governments in Europe."

"The operations . . . can be carried out almost entirely through private channels and existing governmental agencies."

View shared by State Department and Budget Bureau that a smaller agency would be easier to liquidate

Hazlitt: Bureaucracy as domination

> Better not to add to the federal bureaucracy by creating a new unit
>
> > Provide only a relief program and administer it through international agencies

Fritsche: Use specialized economic agencies such as the Export-Import Bank

> Prevent the introduction of political criteria, which would disrupt economic rationality

Belief held by Senator Revercomb that "business-like" organizations would not be "imperialistic" in their relations with other agencies

Senator George's opposition to a possible TVA in the foreign aid field

Preference for private channels of trade

AUTHORITATIVE STATEMENTS AND DECISIONS:

> Goal of making the Europeans "independent of extraordinary outside assistance"—i.e., that the program would be temporary only
>
> ". . . [F]acilitate and maximize the use of private channels of trade. . ."
>
> "Using the services and facilities of any department, agency or establishment of the Government. . . ."
>
> Program is to terminate on June 30, 1952
>
> > or *sooner*, if there is a joint Congressional resolution to that effect (Section 122 (a))
>
> Access to government stocks and reliance on the facilities of other agencies (See section on "Decentralization")
>
> Limitations on number of executives by restrictions on the number of personnel receiving salaries above $10,000 (Section 104 (e))
>
> Personnel ceilings in appropriation bill
>
> Permit use of consultants (Section 104 (e))
>
> Repayments on loans returned to the Treasury, rather than to the ECA (Section 111 (c)(2))

Provisions for reimbursing agencies out of ECA funds for their contribution of services or facilities (Section 113 (a))

8. *Congressional Authority in Foreign Policy*

ASSOCIATED STATEMENTS:

Karl Mundt's remark that the ECA Administrator will be more responsive to Congress because of the requirement of annual authorizations and appropriations

Vandenberg's remark, after the 1943 dispute with Hull and Roosevelt, that henceforth Congress would have a more important part in making foreign policy

Herter's argument that foreign aid brought a larger constitutional role for the House of Representatives in foreign affairs, because of the need for large appropriations

Argument advanced by Kenneth Keating to reinterpret the Curtiss-Wright decision

AUTHORITATIVE STATEMENTS AND DECISIONS:

Requirement of annual authorizations and appropriations (Section 114 (c)) and quarterly reports (Section 115 (b)(7))

Option of terminating the program before June 30, 1952, by a joint Congressional resolution (Section 122 (a))

Apply restrictions of the Government Corporation Control Act to the privilege of using a corporation

The survival of any corporation beyond the life of the ECA would require the explicit approval of Congress (Section 104 (d)(2)(iii))

Procurement shall be documented under regulations promulgated by the Administrator with the approval of the Comptroller General (Section 111 (a))

Creation of Joint Congressional Committee "to make a continuous study of the programs of United States economic assistance to foreign countries, and to review the progress achieved in the execution and administration of such programs." (Section 124 (b))

9. *Bipolarity and Universalism*

AUTHORITATIVE STATEMENTS AND DECISIONS:

In case of scarcities at home

"No export shall be authorized" to *nonparticipating* countries if it is determined by the department administering export controls that the supply of the commodities in the United States would be insufficient to meet the needs of the European Recovery Program as determined by the ECA Administrator (Operating Presumption)

> However, such export may be allowed if the department administering export controls determines that it is "otherwise in the national interest of the United States" (Section 112 (g))

Restricting exports to ERP countries on behalf of national security goals

> ECA Administrator may refuse delivery to participating countries of commodities that may go into the production of other commodities for eventual delivery to *nonparticipating* European countries, which commodities would be refused export licenses in the interests of national security if they were scheduled for direct shipment to the nonparticipating countries (Section 117 (d))

Restricting exports to non-ERP countries on behalf of ERP goals

> ECA Administrator may oppose the grant of an export license for export of commodities to nonparticipating countries whenever he "believes" that issuing the export license would be inconsistent with the purposes of the Marshall Plan

> He shall so "advise" the administering department, and the matter may be referred to the President if the differences are not adjusted (Section 117 (d)) (Operating Presumption)

Transferring functions to the United Nations

> The President may request the cooperation of the United Nations and the use of its facilities, and may make reimbursements for these services out of the funds appropriated for the Marshall Plan (Section 121 (a))

BIBLIOGRAPHY

PUBLIC DOCUMENTS

Committee on European Economic Cooperation. *General Report.* Washington: Department of State Publication, September, 1947.

Organization for European Economic Cooperation. *Annual Reports.* London: 1948–51.

Sparrow, John C. *History of Personnel Demobilization in the United States Army.* Washington: Office of the Chief of Military History, Department of the Army, 1951.

United Nations Relief and Rehabilitation Administration. *Reports to Congress on United States Participation in Operations of the UNRRA.* 12 Reports. Washington: Government Printing Office, 1944–48.

U. S. Congress, Joint Committee on Foreign Affairs, *Hearings on Interim Aid for Europe.* 80th Cong., 1st Sess., 1947.

U. S. Congress, Committees on Foreign Affairs and Foreign Relations. *The European Recovery Program: Basic Documents and Background Information.* 80th Cong., 1st Sess., 1947.

U. S. Congress, Joint Committee on Foreign Economic Cooperation. *Report, ECA and Strategic Materials.* 81st Cong., 1st Sess., Senate Report No. 140, March, 1949.

U. S. *Congressional Record.* Vol. XCIV.

U. S. Department of State. *United States Economic Policy Toward Germany.* Washington: Government Printing Office, n.d.

―――. *United States and Italy 1936–46: Documentary Record.* Washington: Government Printing Office, 1946.

―――. *Germany, 1947–49: The Story in Documents.* Washington: Government Printing Office, 1950.

―――. *Foreign Relations: Conference of Berlin (Potsdam).* 3 Vols. Washington: Government Printing Office, 1960.

U. S. Economic Cooperation Administration. *Quarterly Reports to Congress.* 13 Reports. Washington: Government Printing Office, 1948–51.

U. S. Economic Cooperation Administration. *Recovery Progress and United States Aid.* Washington: Government Printing Office, February, 1949.

————. *A Checklist of Operations.* Washington: 1950.

————. *Country Data Books.* Washington: 1950 and 1951.

————. *Commodity Imports and Exports of Participating Countries.* Washington: 1951.

————. Pamphlets and Miscellaneous Publications.

————. Press Releases.

U. S. House of Representatives. Select Committee on Foreign Aid. *Final Report on Foreign Aid.* Report No. 1845. 80th Cong., 2nd Sess., 1948.

U. S. House of Representatives. Committee on Foreign Affairs. *Hearings on European Recovery Program.* 80th Cong., 1st Sess., 1948.

————. *Hearings on Extension of European Recovery.* 81st Cong., 1st Sess., 1949.

————. *Hearings on Extension of European Recovery.* 81st Cong., 2nd Sess., 1950.

U. S. House of Representatives. Subcommittee on Appropriations. *Hearings on Foreign Aid Appropriations for 1951.* 81st Cong., 2nd Sess., 1950.

U. S. President (Truman). President's Committee on Foreign Aid. *Report. European Recovery and American Aid.* Washington: Government Printing Office, November, 1947.

U. S. Senate. Committee on Foreign Relations. *Hearings on European Recovery Program.* 80th Cong., 2nd Sess., 1948.

————. *Hearings on Extension of European Recovery.* 81st Cong., 1st Sess., 1949.

————. *Report. Extension of European Recovery Program.* Report No. 100. 81st Cong., 1st Sess., 1949.

————. *Hearings on Extension of European Recovery.* 81st Cong., 2nd Sess., 1950.

U. S. Senate. Committees on Foreign Relations and Armed Services. *Hearings on Mutual Security Act.* 82nd Cong., 1st Sess., 1951.

U. S. Senate. Committee on Appropriations. *Hearings on Appropriations for European Recovery Program.* 80th Cong., 2nd Sess., 1948.

————. *Hearings on Foreign Aid Appropriations for 1951.* 81st Cong., 2nd Sess., 1950.

378

————. *Hearings on Mutual Security Program Appropriations for 1952*. 82nd Cong., 1st Sess., 1951.

————. *Report. Foreign-Aid Program in Europe*. 83rd Cong., 1st Sess., 1953.

U. S. *Statutes at Large*. LXII, Part 1.

BOOKS

Acheson, Dean. *Sketches From Life*. New York: Harper and Brothers, 1959.

————. *Present at the Creation*. New York: Norton, 1969.

Alperovitz, Gar. *Atomic Diplomacy: Hiroshima and Potsdam*. New York: Simon and Schuster, 1965.

Armstrong, Ann. *Unconditional Surrender*. New Brunswick, N. J.: Rutgers University Press, 1961.

Balfour, Michael. *Four-Power Control in Germany, 1945–46*. London: Oxford University Press, 1956.

Beugel, Ernst Hans van der. *From Marshall Aid to Atlantic Partnership: European Integration as a Concern of American Foreign Policy*. Amsterdam and New York: Elsevier Publishing Co., 1966.

Blalock, Hubert M., Jr. *Social Statistics*. New York: McGraw-Hill, 1960.

Bloom, Sol. *The Treaty-Making Power*. Washington: 1944.

Borkenau, Franz. *European Communism*. London: Faber, 1953.

Brown, William Adams, Jr., and Opie, Redvers. *American Foreign Assistance*. Washington: The Brookings Institution, 1953.

Brzezinski, Zbigniew. *The Soviet Bloc, Unity and Conflict*. Cambridge: Harvard University Press, 1960.

————. *Alternative to Partition*. New York: McGraw-Hill, 1965.

Bundy, McGeorge. *The Pattern of Responsibility*. Boston: Houghton Mifflin, 1952.

Byrnes, James F. *Speaking Frankly*. New York: Harper, 1947.

Churchill, Winston S. *Triumph and Tragedy*, Vol. VI: *The Second World War*, Boston: Houghton Mifflin, 1953.

Claude, Inis L., Jr. *Swords Into Plowshares*. New York: Random House, 1956.

Clay, Lucius D. *Decision in Germany*. Garden City: Doubleday, 1950.

Committee on Records of War Administration, U. S. Bureau of the Budget, *The United States at War*. Washington: Government Printing Office, 1946.

Bibliography

Dalton, Hugh. *High Tide and After*. London: Frederick Muller, 1962.

Davenport, Nicholas. *The Split Society*. London: Gollancz, 1964.

Dedijer, Vladimir. *Tito*. New York: Simon and Schuster, 1953.

De Gaulle, Charles. *Memoirs*, Vol. III: *Salvation, 1944-46*. New York: Simon and Schuster, 1960.

Dewhurst, J. Frederic, Coppock, John O., Yates, P. Lamartine, and Associates. *Europe's Needs and Resources*. New York: Twentieth Century Fund, 1961.

Diebold, William, Jr. *Trade and Payments in Western Europe*. New York: Harper, 1952.

Djilas, Milovan. *Conversations with Stalin*. New York: Harcourt, Brace, and World, 1962.

Easton, David. *The Political System*. New York: Alfred A. Knopf, 1953.

————. *A Systems Analysis of Political Life*. New York: John Wiley and Sons, 1965.

Eisenhower, Dwight D. *Crusade in Europe*. Garden City: Doubleday, 1948.

Ellis, Howard S. *The Economics of Freedom: The Progress and Future of Aid to Europe*. New York: Harper, 1950.

Fleming, D. F. *The Cold War and Its Origins*, Vol. I, Garden City: Doubleday, 1961.

Furniss, Edgar S. *France, Troubled Ally*. New York: Council on Foreign Relations, 1960.

Galbraith, John K. *Recovery in Europe*. Washington: National Planning Association, 1946.

Geiger, Theodore, and Cleveland, H. van B. *Making Western Europe Defensible*. Washington: National Planning Association, 1951.

Graubard, Stephen R. (ed.). *A New Europe?* Boston: Houghton Mifflin, 1964.

Halle, Louis J. *Civilization and Foreign Policy*. New York: Harper, 1955.

————. *The Cold War as History*. New York: Harper and Row, 1967.

Hare, R. M. *Freedom and Reason*. London: Oxford University Press, 1963.

Harris, Seymour E. *The European Recovery Program*. Cambridge: Harvard University Press, 1948.

Heiser, Hans J. *British Policy with regard to the unification efforts on the European continent.* Leyden: A. W. Sythoff, 1959.

Hirschman, Albert O. *National Power and the Structure of Foreign Trade.* Berkeley and Los Angeles: University of California Press, 1945.

Hoffman, Paul G. *Peace Can Be Won.* Garden City: Doubleday, 1951.

Horowitz, David. *The Free World Colossus.* New York: Hill and Wang, 1965.

———— (ed.). *Containment and Change.* Boston: Beacon Press, 1967.

Hull, Cordell. *Memoirs*, 2 vols. New York: The Macmillan Co., 1948.

Jaffa, Harry V. *Crisis of the House Divided.* Garden City: Doubleday, 1959.

Jones, Joseph M. *The Fifteen Weeks.* New York: The Viking Press, 1955.

Kaplan, Morton A. *System and Process in International Politics.* New York: John Wiley and Sons, 1957.

Kennan, George F. *American Diplomacy 1900–1950.* New York: Mentor Books, 1952.

————. *Memoirs, 1925–50.* Boston: Little, Brown, and Company, 1967.

Kitzinger, U. W. *The Politics and Economics of European Integration.* New York: Praeger, 1963.

Korbel, Joseph. *The Communist Subversion of Czechoslovakia.* Princeton: Princeton University Press, 1957.

Lane, A. B. *I Saw Poland Betrayed.* Indianapolis: Bobbs-Merrill, 1948.

Lansing, Robert. *The Peace Negotiations.* Boston: Houghton Mifflin, 1921.

Lawrence, Samuel A. *United States Merchant Shipping Policies and Politics.* Washington: The Brookings Institution, 1966.

Leahy, William D. *I Was There.* New York: McGraw-Hill, 1950.

Lefever, Ernest. *Ethics and United States Foreign Policy.* New York: Meridian Books, 1957.

Lichtheim, George. *The New Europe.* New York: Praeger, 1955.

Lincoln, Abraham. *Collected Works.* Vols. II and III. Edited by Roy P. Basler. New Brunswick, N. J.: Rutgers University Press, 1953.

Bibliography

Litchfield, Edward H. *Governing Post-War Germany*. Ithaca: Cornell University Press, 1953.

McNeill, William H. *America, Britain, and Russia: Their Cooperation and Conflict, 1941–46*. London: Oxford University Press, 1953.

————. *Greece: American Aid in Action*. New York: The Twentieth Century Fund, 1957.

Marx, Fritz Morstein (ed.). *Elements of Public Administration*. Englewood Cliffs, N. J.: Prentice-Hall, 1946.

Matusow, Allen J. *Farm Policies and Politics in the Truman Years*. Cambridge: Harvard University Press, 1967.

Meade, James Edward. *The Balance of Payments*. London: Oxford University Press, 1951.

Menderhausen, Horst. *Dollar Shortage and Oil Surplus in 1949–50*. Princeton: Princeton University Press, 1950.

Mill, John Stuart. *Essays on Politics and Culture*. Edited by Gertrude Himmelfarb. Garden City: Doubleday, 1962.

Millis, Walter (ed.). *The Forrestal Diaries*. New York: The Viking Press, 1951.

Morgenthau, Hans J. *In Defense of the National Interest*. New York: Alfred A. Knopf, 1952.

————. *Politics Among Nations*. 3rd ed. revised. New York: Alfred A. Knopf, 1960.

Nettl, J. P. *The Eastern Zone and Soviet Policy in Germany, 1945–50*. London: Oxford University Press, 1951.

Neustadt, Richard E. *Presidential Power*. New York: Signet Books, 1964.

Osgood, Robert E. *Ideals and Self-Interest in America's Foreign Relations*. Chicago: University of Chicago Press, 1953.

Patterson, Gardner, and Behrman, Jack N. *Survey of U. S. International Finance, 1950*. Princeton: Princeton University Press, 1951.

Pogue, Forrest C., and Harrison, Gordon. *George C. Marshall: Education of a General*. New York: Viking Press, 1963.

Potter, David. *The South and the Sectional Conflict*. Baton Rouge: Louisiana State University Press, 1968.

Price, Don K. (ed.) *The Secretary of State*. American Assembly Series. Englewood Cliffs, N. J.: Prentice-Hall, 1960.

Price, Harry E. *The Marshall Plan and Its Meaning*. Ithaca: Cornell University Press, 1955.

382

Pritchett, C. Herman. *The American Constitution*. New York: McGraw-Hill, 1959.

Ratchford, B. U., and Ross, William D. *Berlin Reparations Assignment*. Chapel Hill: University of North Carolina Press, 1947.

Reitzel, William, Kaplan, Morton A., and Coblenz, Constance G. *United States Foreign Policy, 1945–55*. Washington: The Brookings Institution, 1956.

Rogers, Lindsay. *Constitutional Aspects of Foreign Affairs*. Williamsburg, Va.: 1944.

Rubinstein, Alvin Z. (ed.). *The Foreign Policy of the Soviet Union*. New York: Random House, 1960.

Sherwood, Robert E. *Roosevelt and Hopkins*, Vol II. New York: Bantam Books, 1950.

Shonfield, Andrew. *British Economic Policy Since the War*. Hamondsworth, Middlesex: Penguin Books, 1958.

Shulman, Marshall D. *Stalin's Foreign Policy Reappraised*. Cambridge: Harvard University Press, 1963.

Simon, Herbert A., Smithburg, Donald W., and Thompson, Victor A. *Public Administration*. New York: Alfred A. Knopf, 1950.

Smith, Walter Bedell. *My Three Years in Moscow*. Philadelphia: J. P. Lippincott Company, 1950.

Stettinius, Edward R., Jr. *Lend-Lease: Weapon for Victory*. New York: The Macmillan Co., 1944.

Stimson, Henry L., and Bundy, McGeorge. *On Active Service in Peace and War*. New York: Harper, 1947.

Strauss, Leo. *Natural Right and History*. Chicago: University of Chicago Press, 1953.

Thompson, Victor A. *Modern Organization*. New York: Alfred A. Knopf, 1961.

———. *The Regulatory Process in OPA Rationing*. New York: King's Crown Press, 1950.

Truman, Harry S. *Public Papers, 1948*. Washington: Government Printing Office, 1964.

———. *Memoirs*. 2 Vols. Garden City: Doubleday, 1955 and 1956.

Tsou, Tang. *America's Failure in China, 1941–50*. Chicago: University of Chicago Press, 1963.

United Nations, Department of Economic Affairs. *Economic Surveys of Europe Since the War*. Geneva: 1948–53.

Vandenberg, Arthur, Jr. (ed.). *The Private Papers of Senator Vandenberg.* Boston: Houghton Mifflin, 1952.

Warburg, James P. *Put Yourself in Marshall's Place.* New York: Simon and Schuster, 1948.

Ward, Barbara. *The West at Bay.* New York: W. W. Norton, 1951.

————. *Policy for the West.* New York: W. W. Norton, 1951.

Max Weber: The Theory of Social and Economic Organization. ed. Talcott Parsons. Glencoe: The Free Press; paperback edition, 1964.

From Max Weber: Essays in Sociology. Trans. and ed. H. H. Gerth and C. Wright Mills. New York: Oxford University Press; Galaxy paperback edition, 1958.

Max Weber on Law in Economy and Society. ed. Max Rheinstein, trans. Edward Shils. Cambridge: Harvard University Press, 1954.

White, Leonard D. *Introduction to the Study of Public Administration.* Rev. edition. New York: The Macmillan Co., 1955.

White, Theodore H. *Fire in the Ashes: Europe in Mid-Century.* New York: William Sloane Associates, 1953.

Williams, Phillip. *Politics in Post-War France.* London: Longmans Green, 1954.

Woodbridge, George. *UNRRA: The History of the United Nations Relief and Rehabilitation Administration.* 3 Vols. New York: Columbia University Press, 1950.

Worswick, G.D.N., and Ady, P. H. (eds.). *The British Economy, 1945–50.* Oxford: Clarendon Press, 1952.

Young, Roland (ed.). *Approaches to the Study of Politics.* Evanston, Ill.: Northwestern University Press, 1958.

Zetterberg, Hans L. *On Theory and Verification in Sociology.* Stockholm: Almqvist and Wiksell, 1954.

ARTICLES AND PERIODICALS

American Federationist. Vols. LV–LVI.

Burns, Arthur F. "The Defense Sector: An Evaluation of Its Economic and Social Impact," *Congressional Record,* CXV (March 10, 1969), S2523–27.

Churchill, Winston S. "Alliance of English-Speaking People," *Vital Speeches of the Day,* XII (March 15, 1946), 329–32.

Eisenstadt, S. N. "Bureaucracy, Bureaucratization, and De-bureaucratization," *Administrative Science Quarterly*, IV (December 1959), 302–20.

————, and Katz, Elihu. "Some Sociological Observations on the Response of Israeli Organization to New Immigrants," *Administrative Science Quarterly*, V (June 1960), 113–33.

Foreign Affairs. Vols. XXV–XXX.

Hart, H.L.A. "The Ascription of Responsibility and Rights," in *Logic and Language*, First Series. Edited by Anthony Flew. Oxford: Basil Blackwell, 1951, 151–74.

International Labor Review. Vols. LV–LXVI.

International Monetary Fund. *Staff Papers*. Vols. I–II.

Joseph, J. J. "European Recovery and United States Aid," *Science and Society*, XII (Summer 1948), 293–383.

Lindblom, Charles E. "The Science of 'Muddling Through,'" *Public Administration Review*, XIX (Spring 1959), 79–88.

London Economist. Vols. CLII–CLXIII.

Mosely, Philip E. "The Occupation of Germany: New Light on How the Zones Were Drawn," *Foreign Affairs*, XXVIII (July 1950), 580–604.

New York Times. 1948–51.

Presthus, Robert V. "Weberian v. Welfare Bureaucracy in Traditional Society," *Administrative Science Quarterly*, VI (June 1961), 1–24.

Pritchett, C. Herman. "The Paradox of the Government Corporation," *Public Administration Review*, XL (June 1946), 495–509.

————. "The Government Corporation Control Act of 1945," *American Political Science Review*, I, No. 4 (Summer 1941), 381–89.

Riesman, David. "Democracy and Defamation: Control of Group Libel," *Columbia Law Review*, XLII (May 1942), 727–80.

Selznick, Philip. "An Approach to a Theory of Bureaucracy," *American Sociological Review, VIII* (February 1943), 47–54.

Simon, Herbert A. "Birth of an Organization: The Economic Cooperation Administration," *Public Administration Review*, XIII (Autumn 1953), 227–36.

Udy, Stanley H., Jr. "'Bureaucracy' and 'Rationality' in Weber's Organization Theory: An Empirical Study," *American Sociological Review*, XXIV (1949), 792–95.

385

Bibliography

U. S. Department of State. *Bulletin.* Vols. XVI–XVII.

Wallace, Henry A. "The Way to Peace," *Vital Speeches of the Day,* XII (October 1946), 738–41.

Williams, John H. "The British Crisis: A Problem in Economic Statesmanship," *Foreign Affairs,* XXVIII (October 1949), 1–17.

UNPUBLISHED MATERIAL

The Brookings Institution. Vandenberg-Moulton Correspondence. Files of the Institution.

————. Working papers on the Brookings Recommendation for the Administration of the European Recovery Program. Files of the Institution.

Rice, Stuart A. "Europe and the Recovery Program: Traveler's Notes, April–May, 1949," Bureau of the Budget, Series 39.32.

U. S. Bureau of the Budget. *Records on Foreign Assistance Programs.* Series 39.18, 39.27, and 39.32.

————. *Survey of the Economic Cooperation Administration.* Series 39.32, September, 1951.

————. *Interviews in Survey of the ECA.* Series 39.32.

INDEX

Acheson, Dean, 48-51, 52-53, 92-93, 95, 100, 120, 133-34, 183-84, 194n
administrative theory, as ideology, 346-49
agriculture, 165-66, 208-9, 236, 240-41, 259-62, 328
Agriculture, U.S. Department of, 60, 61-63, 68, 82, 87, 103, 107, 120, 121, 122, 123, 128, 208-9, 228, 230, 231, 246, 247, 348, 359, 371, 372
Air Force, U.S., 164
Allied Control Council, 22, 30, 31n, 39n, 41n
Alsop, Joseph, 74, 75n, 86, 90
American Farm Bureau Federation, 103, 121, 158, 332
American Federation of Labor (AFL), 103
Americans for Democratic Action, 145
Anderson, Clinton, 62-63, 371
Anglo-American Council of Productivity, 299
anti-cartel efforts, 325
anti-Federalists, 162
Appropriations Committee, U.S. Senate, 250, 302
Arends, Leslie, 108
Argentina, 274
Aristotle, 7-8, 334
Army, U.S., 58, 78n, 87
"associated statements," 201
Atomic Energy Act, 105
Austria, 55n, 238, 285, 286, 293
"authoritative statements," 201

balance of payments, 20, 49-50, 186, 196, 206, 222, 225-26, 242, 251-52, 259, 267, 304, 306, 307, 320, 326, 329

Baldwin, Raymond, 116, 118-20, 123, 346, 359-60
Balfour, Michael, 32n, 35n
Ball, Joseph H., 110, 217
Bank of International Settlements, 190
Bantam Books v. *Sullivan,* 356n
Barkley, Alben, 136, 170
Barrows, Leland, 296
Baruch, Bernard, 116-18, 119, 346
Batt, William, 122-23, 371
Beauharnais v. *Illinois,* 340n
Belgium, 55n, 188-89, 243, 256, 262, 275, 294, 296
Benelux, 135
Betts v. *Brady,* 336
Bevin, Ernest, 30-31, 41, 97, 135, 140, 147, 154
Bidault, Georges, 135
Big Three Conference (June 1947), 55, 135
bilateral agreements: in Marshall Plan, 147, 163, 207-8, 224, 369, 372; in post-UNRRA aid, 46
bilateral payments agreements, 187. *See also* European payments agreements
bilateral structure of trade and payments, 186-90, 195, 197-98
bipolarity and universalism, 216-18, 222, 327, 374-75
Bissell, Richard, 235n, 253-54, 302n, 307
Black, Hugo, 340n
Blaisdell, Thomas, 63, 79
Blalock, Hubert M., 202n
Bland, Schuyler Otis, 168, 269
Bloom, Sol, 95, 126
Bonesteel, Charles, 78
Bradley, Omar, 184
Brennan, William, 356n
Bretton Woods Act, 358

387

Index

Bretton Woods Agreement, 48, 92, 106
Bridges, Styles, 109, 280
Britain, 19-21, 30-31, 35-36, 44, 46, 47-48, 55, 135, 136, 147-48, 157, 165, 166, 167, 169, 186-87, 188-89, 239, 242, 251, 253, 256n, 258, 262, 266, 274, 275, 278, 281n, 286, 292, 293, 294, 296, 299, 303-4, 306, 309-10, 315, 323, 326, 328, 335
Brookings Institution, 84-90, 104-5, 347-48, 368
Brooks, C. Wayland, 140
Brooks, William, 103n, 121-22
Brown, Harvey, 121, 207
Brown, William Adams, Jr., 138n, 157n, 273n, 285, 288
Bruce, David, 143, 257
Bruce, Howard, 142, 229n, 235n, 247n, 281-82, 302n
Brussels Pact, 112, 256
Buckley, Daniel, 264
bureaucracy: foundations in "rational-legal" authority, 12, 349-55. *See also* Max Weber
Bureau of Federal Supply, 63, 72
Bureau of the Budget, U.S., 62, 66, 69, 70, 71, 74ff, 82, 108n, 142, 143n, 167, 193, 229, 231-32, 234, 248, 252, 271, 284, 299, 371, 373
Burke, Edmund, 179
Burton, Ralph, 171, 233n
"business-like" practices and operations, 99-102, 112, 113, 154-55, 160-61, 205, 206, 211, 220, 221, 237, 250-51, 254-55, 311, 329, 365, 368
Byrnes, James F., 22, 28-33, 35-39, 45, 48, 97, 98n, 118n

Canada, 262
centralization, decisions on, 115ff
Chamber of Commerce, U.S., 122
Cheseldine, Raymond M., 79, 80
Chiang Kai-shek, 91
China, 91n, 96, 129n, 182-83
Churchill, Winston S., 19, 29n, 43
Civil Service Commission, 73-74, 125
Clay, Lucius, 19, 21-22, 26-28, 35-37, 41-42, 148n
Clayton, Will, 100

coal, 167, 169, 264-65, 328
Coal Exporters' Association, 264
Cold War, 19, 23-24, 216-17, 343
Collison, N.H., 313-14
Combined Raw Materials Board, U.S. (First World War), 122-23
Comecon, 23
Cominform, 23, 135, 137
Commerce, U.S. Department of, 60ff, 68, 87, 93, 103, 107-8, 120, 121, 123, 128, 130, 228, 229, 230, 233, 252, 271, 348, 371
Committee for European Economic Cooperation (CEEC), 55-56, 59, 141, 187, 368. *See also* Organization for European Economic Cooperation
Commodity Credit Corporation, 63, 209, 236-37
Communist parties, European, 40, 137
Comptroller General, 117, 125, 126, 127-28, 213, 217, 372, 374
"conditional aid" (dollar aid furnished by the ECA to Marshall Plan countries in proportion to the credits they made available to other ERP nations with whom they were expected to show a surplus in the balance of payments), 189, 304
Congress, U.S. (and Congressional authority), 12, 14, 73, 75-76, 79, 82-83, 89n, 94-96, 102, 104, 108, 109, 111, 116, 123, 124, 126-27, 128, 129-31, 134, 162, 168, 170-71, 180, 186, 197, 205-6, 207, 209, 212-13, 215-16, 217-18, 220, 221, 222, 225, 231, 233, 254-55, 259-62, 264, 268-69, 273, 275-76, 280-84, 309, 315, 322-23, 327, 328, 329, 330, 345-50, 357-62, 365, 370, 373, 374
Congress of Industrial Organizations (CIO), 103
Connally, Tom, 95, 169, 302, 314
convertibility guarantee, 250-51, 366
Cooper, John Sherman, 179n
corn, 170, 262, 328
corporate ECA, proposals for, 125-28

388